iPhone
The Missing Manual

Seventh Edition

iPhone: The Missing Manual, Seventh Edition   BY DAVID POGUE

Published by O'Reilly Media, Inc., 1005 Gravenstein Highway North, Sebastopol, CA 95472.

O'Reilly books may be purchased for educational, business, or sales promotional use. Online editions are also available for most titles *(safari.oreilly.com)*. For more information, contact our corporate/institutional sales department: 800.998.9938 or *corporate@oreilly.com.*

Executive Editor: Chris Nelson

Copy Editor: Julie Van Keuren

Indexers: David Pogue, Julie Van Keuren

Cover Designers: Monica Kamsvaag and Phil Simpson

Interior Designer: Phil Simpson (based on a design by Ron Bilodeau)

Print History:
          October 2013:   First Printing.

ISBN: 978-1-449-36223-2

Contents

Part 4: Connections

Part 5: Appendixes

The Missing Credits

David Pogue (author, illustartor, indexer) writes a weekly tech column for *The New York Times* and a monthly column for *Scientific American*. He's a double Emmy-winning correspondent for *CBS News Sunday Morning*, a host of *NOVA* on PBS, and the creator of the Missing Manual series. He's the author or coauthor of 60 books, including 28 in this series; six in the "For Dummies" line (including *Macs, Magic, Opera,* and *Classical Music*); two novels (one, *Abby Carnelia's One and Only Magical Power,* for middle-schoolers); and *The World According to Twitter.* In his other life, David is a former Broadway show conductor, a piano player, and a magician. He lives in Connecticut with his wife and three awesome children.

Links to his columns and weekly videos await at *www.davidpogue.com*. He welcomes feedback about his books by email at *david@pogueman.com*.

Julie Van Keuren (copy editor, indexer) quit her newspaper job in 2006 and moved to Montana to live the freelance-editing dream. She and her husband, M.H. (who's living the novel-writing dream), have two teenage sons. Email: *little_media@yahoo.com*.

Phil Simpson (design and layout) runs his graphic design business from Southbury, Connecticut. His work includes corporate branding, publication design, communications support, and advertising. In his free time he is a homebrewer, ice cream maker, wannabe woodworker, and is on a few tasting panels. He lives with his wife and four great felines. Email: *phil.simpson@pmsgraphics.com*.

Rich Koster (technical reviewer). The iPhone became Rich's first cellphone (and first iPod) the very first evening it was sold by Apple. It's been his faithful electronic companion through the years since, being replaced by new iPhone versions as they came out. From the start, he began corresponding with David Pogue, sharing tips, tricks, and observations; eventually, David asked him to be the beta reader of the first edition of *iPhone: The Missing Manual*—and hired him as the tech editor of subsequent editions. Rich is a husband, father, graphics artist, writer, and Disney fan (@ DisneyEcho on Twitter).

Acknowledgments

The Missing Manual series is a joint venture between the dream team introduced on these pages and O'Reilly Media. I'm grateful to all of them, especially to designer Phil Simpson and to prose queen Julie Van Keuren, who have become my Missing Manual core team.

A few other friends did massive favors for this book. Philip Michaels did an expert job of writing up the Game Center. Apple's Teresa Brewer was incredibly generous in chasing down elusive technical answers. Kellee Katagi contributed a sharp proofreading eye. O'Reilly's Brian Sawyer accommodated my chaotic schedule without once threatening to break my kneecaps. Sebastien Page (iDownloadBlog.com) let me use his SIM-card photo. And my incredible assistant Jan Carpenter kept me from falling apart like wet Kleenex.

The work done on previous editions lives on in this one; for that, I'm still grateful to my fellow *New York Times* columnist Jude Biersdorfer, my 2010 summer intern Matt Gibstein, and the inimitable Brian Jepson.

Thanks to David Rogelberg and Tim O'Reilly for believing in the idea, and above all, to Nicki, Kell, Tia, and Jeffrey. They make these books—and everything else—possible.

—David Pogue

The Missing Manual Series

Missing Manuals are witty, superbly written guides to computer products that don't come with printed manuals (which is just about all of them). Each book features a handcrafted index, cross-references to specific page numbers (not just "see Chapter 14"), and an ironclad promise never to put an apostrophe in the possessive pronoun "its."

Here's a list of current and upcoming titles:

For the Mac

- *OS X Mavericks: The Missing Manual* by David Pogue
- *OS X Mountain Lion: The Missing Manual* by David Pogue
- *AppleScript: The Missing Manual* by Adam Goldstein
- *FileMaker Pro 12: The Missing Manual* by Susan Prosser and Stuart Gripman
- *iMovie '11 & iDVD: The Missing Manual* by David Pogue and Aaron Miller
- *iPhoto '11: The Missing Manual* by David Pogue and Lesa Snider
- *iWork '09: The Missing Manual* by Josh Clark
- *Office 2011: The Missing Manual* by Chris Grover
- *Switching to the Mac: The Missing Manual, Mavericks Edition* by David Pogue
- *Photoshop CC: The Missing Manual* by Lesa Snider
- *Photoshop CS6: The Missing Manual* by Lesa Snider
- *Photoshop Elements 12: The Missing Manual* by Barbara Brundage

For Windows

- *Windows 8.1: The Missing Manual* by David Pogue
- *Access 2013: The Missing Manual* by Matthew MacDonald
- *Excel 2013: The Missing Manual* by Matthew MacDonald
- *Microsoft Project 2013: The Missing Manual* by Bonnie Biafore
- *Office 2013: The Missing Manual* by Nancy Conner and Matthew MacDonald
- *QuickBooks 2014: The Missing Manual* by Bonnie Biafore
- *Photoshop CS6: The Missing Manual* by Lesa Snider
- *Photoshop Elements 12: The Missing Manual* by Barbara Brundage

Electronics

- *David Pogue's Digital Photography: The Missing Manual* by David Pogue
- *iPhone App Development: The Missing Manual* by Craig Hockenberry
- *iPad: The Missing Manual, Fifth Edition* by J.D. Biersdorfer
- *iPod: The Missing Manual, Eleventh Edition* by J.D. Biersdorfer
- *Kindle Fire HD: The Missing Manual* by Peter Meyers

- *Netbooks: The Missing Manual* by J.D. Biersdorfer

- *NOOK HD: The Missing Manual* by Preston Gralla

- *Droid X2: The Missing Manual* by Preston Gralla

- *Galaxy S4: The Missing Manual* by Preston Gralla - Galaxy S4

- *Galaxy Tab: The Missing Manual* by Preston Gralla

Web Technologies

- *Adobe Edge Animate: The Missing Manual*, Third Edition by Chris Grover

- *Creating a Web Site: The Missing Manual*, Third Edition by Matthew MacDonald

- *CSS3: The Missing Manual*, Third Edition, by David Sawyer McFarland

- *Dreamweaver CS6: The Missing Manual* by David Sawyer McFarland

- *Dreamweaver CC: The Missing Manual* by David Sawyer McFarland

- *Flash CS6: The Missing Manual* by E. A. Vander Veer and Chris Grover

- *Google+: The Missing Manual* by Kevin Purdy

- *HTML5: The Missing Manual, Second Edition* by Matthew MacDonald

- *JavaScript & jQuery: The Missing Manual*, Second Edition by David Sawyer McFarland

- *PHP & MySQL: The Missing Manual, Second Edition* by Brett McLaughlin

- *WordPress: The Missing Manual,* by Matthew MacDonald

Life

- *Personal Investing: The Missing Manual* by Bonnie Biafore

- *Your Brain: The Missing Manual* by Matthew MacDonald

- *Your Body: The Missing Manual* by Matthew MacDonald

- *Your Money: The Missing Manual* by J.D. Roth

Introduction

How do you make the point that the iPhone has changed the world? The easy answer is "use statistics"—400 million sold, 1 billion downloadable programs on the iPhone App Store, 50 billion downloads.... Trouble is, those statistics get stale almost before you've finished typing them.

Maybe it's better to talk about the aftermath. How since the iPhone came along, cell carriers (AT&T, Verizon, Sprint, and so on) have opened up the calcified, conservative way they used to consider new cellphone designs. How every phone and its brother now have a touchscreen. How Google (Android) phones, Windows, and BlackBerry phones all have their own app stores. How, in essence, everybody wants to be the iPhone.

The thing is, it will be tough for them to catch up technologically, because Apple is always moving, too. In September 2013, for example, it introduced the seventh iPhone model, the iPhone 5s—faster and better in dozens of ways. And a seventh-and-a-halfth mode, the iPhone 5c, which is basically an iPhone 5 (the previous year's model) in a glossy plastic body.

More importantly, there's a new, free version of the iPhone's software, called iOS 7. (Why not "iPhone OS" anymore? Because the same operating system runs on the iPad and the iPod Touch. It's not just for iPhones anymore, and saying, "the iPhone/iPad/iPod Touch OS" takes too long.)

Why is it so important? Because you can run iOS 7 on *older* iPhone models (the 4, 4s, and 5) without having to buy a new phone. This book covers all phones that can run the iOS 7 software: the iPhone 4, iPhone 4s, iPhone 5, iPhone 5c, and iPhone 5s.

About the iPhone

So what's the iPhone?

Really, the better question is What *isn't* the iPhone?

It's a cellphone, obviously. But it's also a full-blown iPod, complete with a dazzling screen for watching videos. And it's a sensational pocket Internet viewer. It shows fully formatted email (with attachments, thank you) and displays entire Web pages with fonts and design intact. It's tricked out with a tilt sensor, a proximity sensor, a light sensor, WiFi, Bluetooth, GPS, a gyroscope, and that amazing multitouch screen.

For many people, the iPhone is primarily a camera and a camcorder—one that's getting better with every year's new model.

Furthermore, it's a calendar, an address book, a calculator, an alarm clock, a stopwatch, a stock tracker, a traffic reporter, an RSS reader, and a weather forecaster. It even stands in for a flashlight and, with the screen off, a pocket mirror.

But don't forget the App Store. Thanks to the hundreds of thousands of add-on programs that await there, the iPhone is also a fast, wicked-fun pocket computer. All those free or cheap programs can turn it into a medical reference, a musical keyboard, a time tracker, a remote control, a sleep monitor, a tip calculator, an ebook reader, and so on. And whoa, those games! Thousands of them, with smooth 3-D graphics and tilt control.

All of this sends the iPhone's utility and power through the roof. Calling it a phone is practically an insult.

(Apple probably should have called it an "iPod," but that name was taken.)

About This Book

By way of a printed guide to the iPhone, Apple provides only a fold-out leaflet. It's got a clever name—"Finger Tips"—but to learn your way around, you're expected to use an electronic PDF document. That PDF covers the basics well, but it's largely free of details, hacks, workarounds, tutorials, humor, and any acknowledgment of the iPhone's flaws. You can't mark your place, underline, or read it in the bathroom.

The purpose of this book, then, is to serve as the manual that should have accompanied the iPhone. (If you have an original iPhone, iPhone 3G, or iPhone 3GS, you really need one of this book's earlier editions. If you have an iPhone 4, 4s, or 5, this book assumes that you've installed iOS 7; see Appendix A.)

Writing computer books can be an annoying job. You commit something to print, and then—bam—the software gets updated or revised, and suddenly your book is out of date.

That will certainly happen to this book. The iPhone is a **platform.** It's a computer, so Apple routinely updates and improves it by sending it new software bits. To picture where the iPhone will be a few years from now, just look at how much better, sleeker, and more powerful today's iPod is than the original 2001 black-and-white brick.

Therefore, you should think of this book the way you think of the first iPhone: as a darned good start. To keep in touch with updates we make to it as developments unfold, drop in to the book's Errata/Changes page. (Go to *www.missingmanuals.com*, click this book's name, and then click View/Submit Errata.)

> **TIP:** Writing a book about the iPhone is a study in exasperation, because the darned thing is a moving target. Apple updates the iPhone's software fairly often, piping in new features, bug fixes, speed-ups, and so on.
>
> This book covers the iPhone's 7.0.2 software. There may be a 7.0.3, and a 7.1, and so on. Check this book's page at *www.missingmanuals. com* to read about those updates when they occur.

About the Outline

iPhone: The Missing Manual is divided into five parts, each containing several chapters:

- Part 1, **The iPhone as Phone**, covers everything related to phone calls: dialing, answering, voice control, voicemail, conference calling, text messaging, iMessages, MMS, and the Contacts (address book) program. It's also where you can read about FaceTime, the iPhone's video-calling feature, and Siri, the "virtual assistant" in the iPhone 4s and later models.

- Part 2, **Pix, Flix & Apps**, is dedicated to the iPhone's built-in software programs, with a special emphasis on its multimedia abilities: playing music, podcasts, movies, TV shows, and photos; capturing photos and videos; the Maps app; reading ebooks; and so on. These chapters also cover some of the standard techniques that most apps share: installing, organizing, and quitting them; switching among them; and sharing material from within them using the Share sheet.

- Part 3, **The iPhone Online**, is a detailed exploration of the iPhone's third talent: its ability to get you onto the Internet, either over a WiFi hotspot connection or via the cellular network. It's all here: email, Web browsing, and *tethering* (that is, letting your phone serve as a sort of Internet antenna for your laptop).

- Part 4, **Connections**, describes the world beyond the iPhone itself— like the copy of iTunes on your Mac or PC that can fill up the iPhone with music, videos, and photos, and syncing the calendar, address book, and mail settings. These chapters also cover the iPhone's control panel, the Settings program; and how the iPhone syncs wirelessly with corporate networks using Microsoft Exchange ActiveSync—or with your own computers using Apple's iCloud service.

- Part 5, **Appendixes**, contains two reference chapters. Appendix A walks you through the setup process; Appendix B is a master compendium of troubleshooting, maintenance, and battery information.

About→These→Arrows

Throughout this book, and throughout the Missing Manual series, you'll find sentences like this one: Tap Settings→Airplane Mode→On. That's shorthand for a much longer instruction that directs you to open three nested screens in sequence, like this: "Tap the Settings button. On the next screen, tap Airplane Mode. On the screen after that, tap On." (In this book, tappable things on the screen are printed in orange to make them stand out.)

Similarly, this kind of arrow shorthand helps to simplify the business of choosing commands in menus on your Mac or PC, like File→Print.

About MissingManuals.com

To get the most out of this book, visit *www.missingmanuals.com*. Click the Missing CDs link, and then click this book's title to reveal a neat, organized list of the shareware, freeware, and bonus articles mentioned in this book.

The Web site also offers corrections and updates to the book; to see them, click the book's title, and then click View/Submit Errata. In fact, please submit corrections yourself! Each time we print more copies of this book, we'll make any confirmed corrections you've suggested. We'll also note such changes on the Web site, so you can mark important corrections into your own copy of the book, if you like. And we'll keep the book current as Apple releases more iPhone updates.

What's New in the iPhone 5s

Apple's usual routine is to introduce a new iPhone shape every other year (iPhone 3G, iPhone 4, iPhone 5)—and then release a follow-up "s" model with upgraded components in alternate years (iPhone 3GS, iPhone 4s, iPhone 5s). The 2013-14 model, the 5s, fits right in. Here's what's new:

- **A new chip.** The new A7 chip is, Apple says, twice as fast as before. That speed makes possible new features like the camera's 10-frames-per-second burst mode. And since it's a 64-bit chip, the first in a cell-phone, the graphics in 3-D video games look especially smooth.

- **Another new chip.** The iPhone 5s contains a coprocessor—sort of a sister chip—called the M7. Its job is to monitor motion data from the phone's compass, gyroscope and accelerometer (tilt sensor). Now, apps that rely on this data (mainly fitness tracking apps) won't drain nearly as much battery, because the primary A7 processor can go to sleep and hand off monitoring duties to the M7— which requires one-sixth as much battery power.

- **A much better camera sensor.** It's 15 percent bigger; its light-detecting pixels are bigger. Low-light pictures are far better now—clearer, brighter, better color.

- **A much better flash.** The 5s has two LED flashes: one white, one amber. They fire together, mixed to match the color temperature of the scene. Your flash pictures look infinitely better—especially skin tones.

- **Wow-worthy camera features.** The 5s's camera also has a burst mode (10 frames a second); 3x zooming during video capture; and truly stunning slow-motion (120-frames-per-second) video.

- **A fingerprint sensor.** The 5s's most famous feature is the fingerprint sensor, which is cleverly built right into the Home button. After pushing the Home button to wake the phone, you leave your finger there another half second, and boom: You've unlocked a phone that nobody else can unlock, without the hassle of inputting the password. The fingerprint is stored only on your phone, encrypted within the A7 chip, and never transmitted or stored online.

NOTE: With several hours, several thousand dollars of lab equipment, and a perfect, unsmudged copy of a fingerprint, a hacker online famously proved that he could fool the 5s's finger scanner. But using your fingerprint as your password is still a smart, convenient, secure (and optional) idea. Long before an iPhone thief could manage to hack your fingerprint, you'll have popped over to iCloud.com and "bricked" the phone so that it can't even be turned on (details start on page 482).

What's New in iOS 7

Wow. iOS 7, dude. It's ambitious, it's radical, it's polarizing. You love it or you hate it (or you get used to it).

This software looks **nothing** like the old iOS. It's clean, white, almost barren. It uses a razor-thin font (Helvetica Neue) and bright, light colors. And it completely rejects **skeuomorphism,** the old iOS design principle, in which onscreen things depict real-world materials. In iOS 7, you will not find lined yellow paper in the Notes app, a leather binding in Calendar, wooden shelves for Newsstand, or green felt in Game Center. Everything is now "flat"—no attempts at fake 3-D—and digital.

TIP: If the fonts are too thin for your taste, you can fatten them up just enough by turning on Settings→General→Accessibility→Bold Text. While you're there, also turn on Increase Contrast; that makes some of the translucent panels opaque, for easier reading. You can make text larger in most apps, too, in Settings→General→Accessibility→Larger Type.

Although iOS 7 looks radically different, it's much more efficient to navigate. There's no eye candy to distract you; everything on the screen is a useful button.

And the features themselves have been redone with a huge emphasis on removing annoyances, moving things into more logical places, and polishing up the built-in apps.

Apple says iOS 7 contains over 200 new features, but here are the big-ticket items:

- **Better Siri.** Siri, the voice-controlled assistant, is much faster, she's much more capable, and her voice is much more realistic. (Or *his* voice; you can now choose Siri's gender.) For example, you no longer have to burrow into Settings to adjust your control panels. You can just say "Open camera settings," for example, or "Make the screen brighter."

- **Control Center.** You'll love this from Day One. Swipe upward from the bottom of the screen to open the Control Center: a compact, visual palette of controls for brightness, volume, Bluetooth, WiFi, Airplane mode, music playback, calculator, camera, and—so great!—Flashlight. Swipe down (or press the Home button) to make it disappear.

- **An almost-universal "back" gesture.** You can swipe in from the left margin of the phone to *go back* one screen. It works in Mail, Settings, Notes, Messages, Safari, Facebook, Photos, and many other apps.

> **NOTE:** Speaking of swipes: In many apps, like Mail or Voice Memos, you can delete an item in a list by swiping across it, then tapping the Delete button to confirm. But here's something that may throw you: in iOS 7, you can swipe *only leftward*. Swiping to the right doesn't work anymore.

- **Real multitasking.** All apps can run in the background now—and a new, much more visual app switcher makes it easy to jump among them (or force quit them).

- **iTunes Radio.** Exactly like Pandora: free Internet "radio stations" based on bands or types of music you like.

- **Internet phone calls.** Free high-quality voice calls (to other Apple phones, tablets, and Macs). Apple calls it Audio-Only FaceTime.

- **AirDrop.** Totally, totally great. You can now shoot whatever's on the screen—a photo, a map, a Web page, a video, some contact info—to another iOS 7 phone or tablet with one tap. Even to strangers. No setup, no hassle.

- **A new Photos app.** This app used to be an endless scroll of tiny thumbnails. Now it self-organizes into clusters by year, by month, and by occasion (based on time and location data). Photos are **much** easier to find.

- **A new Camera app.** The redesigned app offers Instagram-style color filters and an easy way to switch among its modes: Video, Photos, Panorama, Square Photos, and (on the iPhone 5s) Slo-Mo Video.

- **Activation Lock.** Incredibly, 40 percent of reported thefts in New York City are stolen iPhones—but that's about to change. Now, if somebody steals your phone, he can't erase it, or even turn off Find My iPhone, without your Apple account password. Thieves will have to stop stealing iPhones, because, without your password, they're useless and can't be resold.

- **Carpenter's Level.** The Compass app now has a three-dimensional level in it!

- **Global Type Size control.** A new slider controls the font size in all your apps—or at least those that have been rewritten to hook into this feature. Most of Apple's apps have.

- **Auto app updates.** Updated versions of your apps can install themselves automatically, in the background, so you don't have to spend your life responding to update notifications.

- **Today screen.** Now a single screen lists everything that's happening today, written in plain English: your next appointment, today's weather, reminders due, whose birthday it is, and so on.

- **Maps.** Apple's Maps still can't give you directions using public transportation, but at least it now has walking directions. And in dim light, Maps automatically substitutes a dark-gray background to avoid distracting you as you drive.

It's a lot of tweaks, polishing, and finesse—and a lot to learn. Fortunately, 500 pages of instructions now await you.

1

The Guided Tour

I f you'd never seen all the videos and photos of the iPhone, and you found it lying on someone's desk, you might not guess it was a phone (let alone an iPod/Web browser/alarm clock/stopwatch/voice recorder/musical instrument/compass). You can't see any antenna, mouthpiece, or earpiece—and goodness knows there are no number keys for dialing.

It's all there, though, hidden inside this sleek glass slab.

For the rest of this book, and for the rest of your life with the iPhone, you'll be expected to know what's meant by, for example, "the Home button" and "the Sleep switch." A guided tour, therefore, is in order.

Silencer switch

Volume keys

Home button

Sleep Switch (On/Off)

On the top-right edge of the iPhone, you'll find a metal button shaped like a dash. This, ladies and gents, is the Sleep switch.

Sleep/Wake switch

It has several functions:

- **Sleep/Wake.** Tapping it once puts the iPhone to sleep—into Standby mode, ready for incoming calls but consuming very little power. Tapping it again turns on the screen so it's ready for action.

- **On/Off.** The same switch can also turn the iPhone off completely so it consumes no power at all; incoming calls get dumped into voicemail. You might turn the iPhone off whenever you're not going to use it for a few days.

  To turn the iPhone off, press the Sleep switch for 3 seconds. The screen changes to say **slide to power off**. Confirm your decision by placing a fingertip on the > and sliding to the right. The device shuts off completely.

> **TIP:** If you change your mind about turning the iPhone off, tap the **Cancel** button, or do nothing; after a moment, the iPhone backs out of the **slide to power off** screen automatically.

To turn the iPhone back on, press the switch again for 1 second. The chromelike Apple logo appears as the phone boots up.

- **Answer call/Dump to voicemail.** When a call comes in, you can tap the Sleep button *once* to silence the ringing or vibrating. After four rings, the call goes to your voicemail.

  You can also tap it *twice* to dump the call to voicemail immediately. (Of course, because they didn't hear four rings, iPhone veterans will know you've blown them off. Bruised egos may result. Welcome to the world of iPhone etiquette.)

- **Force restart.** The Sleep switch has one more function. If your iPhone is frozen, and no buttons work, and you can't even turn the thing off, this button is also involved in force-restarting the whole machine. Steps for this last-ditch procedure are on page 554.

Locked Mode

When you don't touch the screen for 1 minute (or another interval you choose), or when you put the iPhone to sleep, the phone *locks* itself. When it's locked, the screen is dark and doesn't respond to touch. If you're on a call, the call continues; if music is playing, it keeps going; if you're recording audio, the recording proceeds.

But when the phone is locked, you don't have to worry about accidental button pushes. You wouldn't want to discover that your iPhone has been calling people or taking photos from the depths of your pocket or purse. Nor would you want it to dial a random number from your back pocket, a phenomenon that's earned the unfortunate name *butt dialing.*

The Lock Screen

To wake the phone when it's locked, press either the Sleep switch *or* the Home button.

That gesture alone doesn't fire up the full iPhone world, though. Instead, it presents the Lock screen shown below.

From here, slide your finger rightward across the screen (anywhere—you don't have to aim for the slide to unlock area!) to unlock the phone, wake it up, and start using it.

Swipe anywhere

> slide to unlock

NOTE: The iPhone can demand a password or (on the iPhone 5s) a fingerprint each time it wakes up, if you like. See page 48. On the other hand, you can adjust how quickly the phone locks itself, or make it stop locking itself altogether; see page 511.

These days, the Lock screen is more than just a big Do Not Disturb sign. It's a veritable bulletin board for up-to-date information about your life—information you can scan without unlocking the phone at all.

For starters, you can use the iPhone as a watch—millions of people do. Just tap the Sleep switch to consult the Lock screen's time and date display, and then shove the phone right back into your pocket. The iPhone relocks after a few seconds.

If you're driving, using the Maps app to guide you, the Lock screen shows the standard GPS navigation screen. Handy, really—the less fumbling you have to do while driving, the safer you are.

Better yet, the Lock screen is a handy status screen. Here you see a record of everything that happened while you weren't paying attention. It's a list of missed calls, text messages received, notifications from your apps, and other essential information.

Now, each of these notices has come from a different *app* (software program). To call somebody back, for example, you'd want to open the Phone app; to reply to a text message, you'd want the Messages app, and so on.

Here, then, is a handy shortcut: You can dive directly into the relevant app by swiping your finger *across the notification itself,* like this:

Lock screen with notifications

Swipe to open that app

Adopting that shortcut saves you the trouble of unlocking the phone, fumbling through your Home screens until you find the app you want, and tapping it to open it.

> **TIP:** On the other hand, if you'd rather *not* have all these details show up on the Lock screen, you can turn them off. (Privacy is the main reason you might want to do so—remember that the bad guys don't need a password to view your Lock screen. They just have to tap the Sleep switch or the Home button.)
>
> You can hide these items from your Lock screen on an app-by-app basis. For example, you might want missed calls to show up here but not missed text messages. To set this up, choose Settings→Notifications. Tap the app in question; scroll to the bottom, and then turn off **View in Lock Screen**.

In iOS 7, you can actually begin to operate the phone right here at the Lock screen. For example:

- **Swipe down** from the top edge of the screen to view your Notification Center—a detailed one-stop screen that shows your missed calls, texts, and emails; upcoming appointments; stock and weather alerts; and so on.

- **Swipe up** from the bottom edge to open the new Control Center, with all the important settings (volume, brightness, play/pause music, Airplane mode, flashlight, and more) in one place. See page 37.

- **Drag upward** on the camera (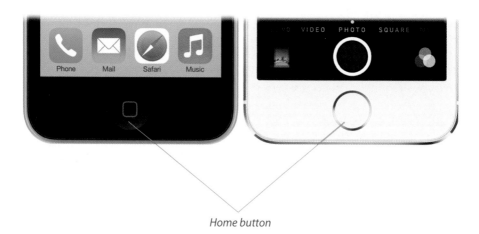) icon to jump directly into picture-taking mode.

If it bothers you that some stranger picking up your phone can do all of these things without the password or a fingerprint, don't worry; you can turn all of them off on the corresponding Settings screens (for example, Settings→Control Center).

Home Button

Here it is: the one and only button on the front of this phone. Push it to summon the Home screen, which is your gateway to everything the iPhone can do. (You can read more about the Home screen at the end of this chapter.)

Home button

Having a Home button is a wonderful thing. It means you can never get lost. No matter how deeply you burrow into the iPhone software, no matter how far off track you find yourself, one push of the Home button takes you back to the beginning.

On the iPhone 5s, of course, the Home button is also a fingerprint scanner—the first one anybody's ever put on a cellphone that actually ***works.***

But, as time goes on, Apple keeps saddling the Home button with more and more functions. It's become Apple's only way to provide shortcuts for common features; that's what you get when you design a phone that only *has* one button. In iPhone Land, you can press the Home button one, two, or three times for different functions—or even hold it down. Here's the rundown.

Quick Press: Wake Up

Pressing the Home button once wakes the phone if it's in locked mode. That's sometimes easier than finding the Sleep switch on the top edge. It gives you a quick glance at your missed calls and texts—or the time and date.

Momentary Touch: Unlock (iPhone 5s)

If you've taught the iPhone 5s to recognize your fingerprint, just resting your finger on the Home button is enough to unlock the phone, bypassing the password screen. In other words, you should get into the habit of *pressing* the Home button (to wake the phone) and then *leaving your finger on it* for about a half-second to unlock it. Page 48 has more on fingerprints.

Long Press: Siri (or Voice Control)

If you hold down the Home button for about 3 seconds, you make the phone ready for *voice control.*

If you have an iPhone 4, you can use voice control to dial by speaking a name or a number, or use it to control music playback. If you have an iPhone 4s or later, you can do a thousand times more: You can command Siri, your virtual voice-controlled assistant. Details are in Chapter 4.

Two Quick Presses: Task Switcher

If, once the phone is awake, you press the Home button *twice quickly,* the current image fades away—to reveal the new iOS 7 app switcher screen. This feature is the key to the iPhone's multitasking feature.

What you see here are icons *and currently open screens* of the programs you've used most recently (older ones are to the right). Swipe horizontally to bring more apps into view; the Home screen is always at the far left.

The point is that with a single tap (on either the icon or the screen miniature), you can jump right back into a program you had open, without waiting for it to start up, show its welcome screen, and so on—and without having to scroll through 11 Home screens trying to find the icon of a favorite app.

In short, the task switcher gives you a way to jump *directly* to another app, without a layover at the Home screen first.

> **TIP:** On this screen, you can also quit a program by flicking its screen upward. In fact, you can quit *several programs at once*, using two or three fingers. Fun for the whole family!

This task switcher is the only visible element of the iPhone's multitasking feature, which is described in delicious detail on page 290. Once you get used to it, that double-press of the Home button will become second nature—and your first choice for jumping among apps.

Three Presses: VoiceOver, Zoom, White on Black...

In Settings→General→Accessibility, you can set up a triple-press of the Home button to turn one of several accessibility features on or off: Guided Access (aka kiosk mode), VoiceOver (the phone speaks whatever you touch), Invert Colors (white-on-black type, which is sometimes easier to see), Zoom (magnifies the screen), Switch Control (accommodates external gadgets like sip-and-puff straws), and AssistiveTouch (help for people who have trouble with physical switches).

All of these features are described beginning on page 168.

TIP: The Home button is also part of the *force quit* sequence—a good troubleshooting technique when a particular program seems to be acting up. See page 293.

Silencer Switch, Volume Keys

Praise be to the gods of technology—this phone has a silencer switch! This tiny flipper, on the left edge at the top, means that no ringer or alert sound will humiliate you in a meeting, at a movie, or in church. To turn off the ringer, push the flipper toward the back of the phone (see the photo on page 9).

No menus, no holding down keys, just instant silence. All cellphones should have this feature.

NOTE: Even when silenced, the iPhone still makes noise in certain circumstances: when an alarm goes off; when you're playing music; when you're using Find My iPhone (page 480); when you're using VoiceOver; or, sometimes, when a game is playing. Also, the phone still vibrates when the silencer is engaged, although you can turn this feature off in **Settings→Sounds**.

With practice, you can learn to tell if the ringer is on while the iPhone is still in your pocket. That's because when the ringer is on, the switch falls in a straight line with the volume buttons. By swiping your thumb across these controls, you can feel whether the silencer switch is lined up or tilted away.

Below the silencer, still on the left edge, are the volume controls—separate **+** and **–** buttons. The volume controls work in five different ways:

- On a call, these buttons adjust the speaker or earbud volume.

- When you're listening to music, they adjust the playback volume— even when the phone is locked and dark.

- When you're taking a picture, either one serves as a shutter button or a camcorder start/stop button.

- At all other times, they adjust the volume of sound effects like the ringer and alarms.

- When a call comes in, they silence the ringing or vibrating.

In each case, if the screen is on, a corresponding volume graphic appears on the screen to show you where you are on the volume scale.

Screen

The touchscreen is your mouse, keyboard, dialing pad, and notepad. You might expect it to get fingerprinty and streaky.

But one of the best unsung features of the modern iPhone is its **oleophobic** screen. That may sound like an irrational fear of yodeling, but it's actually a coating that repels grease. You'll be amazed at how easily a single light wipe on your clothes restores the screen to its right-out-of-the-box crystal sheen.

You can also use the screen as a mirror when the iPhone is off.

The iPhone's Retina screen has crazy high resolution (the number of tiny pixels per inch). It's really, really sharp, as you'll discover when you try to read text or make out the details of a map or a photo. The iPhone 4 and 4s pack in 960 × 640 pixels; the iPhone 5 family, with an extra half-inch of screen, manages 1136 × 640 pixels.

The front of the iPhone is made of Gorilla Glass, a special glass formulation made by Corning. It's unbelievably resistant to scratching. (That doesn't mean it can't crack; you can still shatter it if you drop it just the wrong way.) The back of the 4 and 4s are Gorilla Glass, too.

NOTE: This is how Corning's Web site says this glass is made: "The glass is placed in a hot bath of molten salt at a temperature of approximately 400°C. Smaller sodium ions leave the glass, and larger potassium ions from the salt bath replace them. These larger ions take up more room and are pressed together when the glass cools, producing a layer of compressive stress on the surface of the glass. Gorilla Glass's special composition enables the potassium ions to diffuse far into the surface, creating high compressive stress deep into the glass. This layer of compression creates a surface that is more resistant to damage from everyday use."

But you probably guessed as much.

If you're nervous about protecting your iPhone, you can always get a case for it (or a "bumper" for the iPhone 4 or 4s—a silicone band that wraps around the metal edges). But if you're worried about scratching the glass, you're probably worrying too much. Even many Apple employees carry the iPhone in their pockets without carrying cases.

Radio signals can't pass through metal. That's why there are strips of glass on the back of the iPhone 5 and 5s—right where the antennas are—and why the 4 and 4s have all-glass backs, and why the 5c has a plastic back.

And there are a *lot* of radio signals in this phone. All told, there are *15* different radio transceivers inside: four for the standard GSM frequencies; four for GSM's 3G frequencies; three for CDMA frequencies; and one each for WiFi, Bluetooth, American GPS, and Russian GPS.

Screen Icons

Here's a roundup of the icons you may see in the status bar at the top of the iPhone screen, from left to right:

- ●●○○○ **Cell signal.** As on any cellphone, the number of bars—or dots, in iOS 7's case—indicates the strength of your cell signal, and thus the quality of your call audio and the likelihood of losing the connection. If there are no dots, then the dreaded words "No service" appear here.

- **Network name and type.** These days, different parts of the country—and even different parts of your street—are blanketed by cellular Internet signals of different speeds, types, and ages. Your status bar always shows you the kind of signal it has right now.

  From slowest to fastest: **E** or **o** means your iPhone is connected to your carrier's slowest, oldest Internet system. You might be able to check email, but you'll lose your mind waiting for a Web page to load.

  If you see the **3G** logo, you're in a city where your cell company has installed a 3G network—meaning fairly decent Internet speed. A **4G** logo is better yet; you have speed in between 3G and LTE.

  And if you see **LTE** up there—well, then, get psyched. You have an iPhone 5, 5c, or 5s, and you're in a city with a 4G LTE cellular network. And that means *insanely* fast Internet (maybe even faster than you have at home), fast Web browsing, fast app downloading—just fast.

- ✈ **Airplane Mode.** If you see the airplane instead of signal and WiFi bars, then the iPhone is in Airplane mode (page 375).

- ☾ **Do Not Disturb.** When the phone is in Do Not Disturb mode, nothing can make it ring, buzz, or light up except calls from the most important people. Details on page 95.

- 📶 **WiFi signal.** When you're connected to a wireless Internet hotspot, this indicator appears. The more "sound waves," the stronger the signal.

- **9:50 AM.** When the iPhone is unlocked, a digital clock appears on the status bar.

- ⏰ **Alarm.** You've got an alarm set. This reminder, too, can be valuable, especially when you intend to sleep late and don't **want** an alarm to go off.

- ❋ **Bluetooth.** The iPhone is connected wirelessly to a Bluetooth earpiece, speaker, or car system. (If this symbol is gray, then it means Bluetooth is turned on but not connected to any other gear—and not sucking down battery power.)

- ☷ **TTY symbol.** You've turned on Teletype mode, meaning that the iPhone can communicate with a Teletype machine. (That's a special machine that lets deaf people make phone calls by typing and reading text. It hooks up to the iPhone with a special cable that Apple sells from its Web site.)

- ☛ **Call forwarding.** You've told your iPhone to auto-forward any incoming calls to a different number. This icon is awfully handy— it explains at a glance why your iPhone never seems to get calls anymore.

- **VPN** **VPN.** You corporate stud, you! You've managed to connect to your corporate network over a secure Internet connection, probably with the assistance of a systems administrator—or by consulting page 498.

- ❋ **Syncing.** The iPhone is currently syncing with some Internet service—iCloud, for example (Chapter 14).

- ▬↯ **Battery meter.** When the iPhone is charging, the lightning bolt appears. Otherwise, the battery logo "empties out" from right to left to indicate how much charge remains. (You can even add a "% full" indicator to this gauge; see page 510.)

- ➤ **Navigation active.** You're running a GPS navigation program in the background (yay, multitasking!). Why is a special icon necessary? Because those GPS apps slurp down battery power like a thirsty golden retriever. Apple wants to make sure you don't forget you're running it.

- ⊕ **Rotation lock.** This icon reminds you that you've deliberately turned off the screen-rotation feature, where the screen image turns 90 degrees when you rotate the phone. Why would you want to? And how do you turn the rotation lock on or off? See page 39.

Cameras and Flash

At the top of the phone, above the screen, there's a horizontal slot. That's the earpiece. Just above it (iPhone 5 series) or beside it (iPhone 4 or 4s), the tiny round pinhole is the front-facing camera. It's a little bit more visible on the white-faced iPhones than on the black ones.

Its primary purpose is to let you conduct video chats using the FaceTime feature, but it's also handy for taking self-portraits or just checking to see if you have spinach in your teeth.

Just keep in mind that it's not nearly as good a camera as the one on the back. The front camera has no flash, isn't as good in low light, and takes much lower-resolution shots (1.2 megapixels on the iPhone 5 series; only 0.3 megapixels on earlier models).

The camera on the back of the iPhone, meanwhile, takes very good photos indeed—8 megapixels on the iPhone 4s and later.

A tiny LED lamp appears next to this lens (two lamps on the 5s, actually). It's the flash for the camera, the video light when you're shooting movies, and a darned good flashlight for reading restaurant menus and theater programs in low light. (Swipe up from the bottom of the screen and tap the flashlight icon ⚡ to turn the light on and off.)

On the iPhone 5 family, the tiny pinhole between the flash and the lens is a microphone. It's used for recording clearer sound with video, for better noise cancellation on phone calls, and better directional sound pickup.

There's more on the iPhone's cameras in Chapter 7.

Sensors

Behind the glass, above or beside the earpiece, are two sensors. (On the black iPhones, they're camouflaged; you can't see them except with a bright flashlight.) First, there's an ambient-light sensor that brightens the display when you're in sunlight and dims it in darker places.

Second, there's a proximity sensor. When something (like your head) is close to the sensor when you're using the phone functions, it shuts off the screen illumination and touch sensitivity. Try it out with your hand (it works only in the Phone app). You save power and avoid dialing with your cheek-bone when you're on a call.

SIM Card Slot

On the right edge of the iPhone 4s and later models, there's a tiny pinhole next to what looks like a very thin slot cover. (It's also on the right side of the AT&T iPhone 4.) If you push an unfolded paper clip straight into the hole, the **SIM card** tray pops out.

So what's a SIM card?

It turns out that there are two major cellphone network types: **CDMA,** used by Verizon and Sprint, and **GSM,** used by AT&T, T-Mobile, and most other countries around the world.

Every GSM phone stores your phone account info— things like your phone number and calling-plan details—on a tiny memory card known as a SIM (subscriber identity module) card. On some phones, though not on the iPhone, it even stores your address book.

What's cool is that, by removing the card and putting it into **another** GSM phone, you transplant a GSM phone's brain. The other phone now knows your number and account details, which can be handy when your iPhone goes in for repair or battery replacement.

iPhone 5 Family: The World Phone

AT&T is a GSM network, so AT&T iPhones have always had SIM cards. But intriguingly enough, every iPhone 4s and later model has a SIM card, too—even the Verizon and Sprint models. That's odd, because most CDMA cell-phones don't have SIM cards.

These iPhones contain antennas for **both** GSM and CDMA. It's the same phone, no matter which cell company you buy it from. Only the activation process teaches it which phone company it "belongs" to.

Even then, however, you can still use any company's phone in any country. (That's why the latest iPhones are said to be "world phones.") When you use the Verizon or Sprint iPhone in the United States, it uses only the CDMA antenna. But if you travel to Europe or another GSM part of the world, you can still use your Verizon or Sprint phone; it just hooks into that country's GSM network.

If you decide to try that, you have two ways to go. First, you can contact your phone carrier and ask to have international roaming turned on. You'll keep your same phone number overseas, but you'll pay through the nose for calls and, especially, Internet use.

Second, you can rent a temporary SIM card when you get to the destination country. That's a less expensive route, but it means you'll have a different phone number while you're there.

The original iPhones used a standard SIM card. The iPhone 4s and the AT&T iPhone 4 require a smaller type known as a **micro-SIM** card. And for the iPhone 5, 5c, and 5s, Apple has developed even newer, tinier cards called **nano**-SIMs. (You can see all three cards at left.)

At this rate, you won't even be able to see the iPhone 7's SIM card without an electron microscope.

Apple thinks SIM cards are geeky and intimidating and that they should be invisible. That's why, unlike most GSM phones, your iPhone came with the card preinstalled and ready to go. Most people will never have any reason to open this tray, unless they just want to see what a SIM card looks like.

If you were curious enough to open it up, you can close the tray simply by pushing it back into the phone until it clicks.

> **NOTE:** Except for this one example—inserting a card from another country for international use—you can't swap any other company's SIM card into the iPhone. For example, you can't make it a T-Mobile phone by inserting a T-Mobile SIM card. In other words, the iPhone is still not an "unlocked" GSM phone (at least, not officially; there are some unauthorized ways).
>
> And speaking of footnotes: The iPhone 5 phones may be LTE phones, but they don't work on the LTE networks of all other countries. Ask your carrier which countries your model works with.

Headphone Jack

On the top edge of the iPhone 4 and 4s, or the bottom edge of the iPhone 5 series, you can see the miniplug where you plug in the white earbuds that came with it—or any other earbuds or headphones.

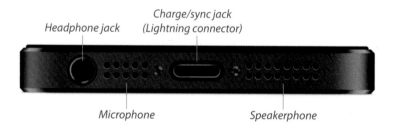

Headphone jack   Charge/sync jack (Lightning connector)

Microphone   Speakerphone

This little hole is more than an ordinary 3.5-millimeter audio jack, however. It contains a secret fourth pin that conducts sound *into* the phone from the microphone on the earbuds' cord. Now you, too, can be one of those executives who walk down the street barking orders, apparently to nobody. The iPhone can stay in your pocket as you walk or drive. You hear the other person through your earbuds, and the mike on the cord picks up your voice.

Next to the headphone jack, inside the pinhole (iPhone 4/4s) or the perforated grille (iPhone 5 series), a tiny second microphone lurks. It's the key to the iPhone's noise-cancellation feature. It listens to the sound of the world around you and pumps in the opposite sound waves to cancel out all that ambient noise. It doesn't do anything for *you*—the noise cancellation affects only what the *other* guy on the phone hears.

That's why, on the iPhone 5 family, there's also a third microphone at the top back (between the camera and flash); it's designed to supply noise cancellation for you so that the other guy sounds better when you're in a noisy place.

Microphone, Speakerphone

On the bottom edge of the iPhone, Apple has parked two important audio components: the speakerphone speaker and the microphone.

The speakerphone isn't super loud, because it's aimed straight out of the iPhone's edge, away from you. But if you cup your hand around the bottom edge, you can redirect the sound toward your face, for an immediate boost in volume and quality.

The Charge/Sync Connector

Directly below the Home button, on the bottom edge of the phone, you'll find the connector that charges and syncs the iPhone with your computer.

The Lightning Connector

For nearly 10 years, the charge/sync connector was identical on every iPhone, iPod, and iPad. It was the standard 30-pin connector that's now found in many alarm clocks, hotel-room bedside tables, car dashboards, speaker docks, external batteries, and other accessories.

But on the iPhone 5/5c/5s, Apple replaced that inch-wide connector with a new, far smaller one it calls Lightning.

The Lightning connector is a great design: It clicks nicely into place (you can even dangle the iPhone from it), yet you can yank it right out. You can insert the Lightning into the phone either way— there's no "right-side up" anymore. It's much sturdier than the old connector. And it's tiny, which is Apple's primary goal—only 0.3 inches wide (the old one was almost 0.9 inches wide).

*30-pin connector
(iPhone 4 and 4S)*

*Lightning connector
(iPhone 5, 5c, 5s)*

Unfortunately, as a result, the latest iPhones don't fit any existing charging cables, docks, chargers, car adapters, hotel-room alarm clocks, speakers, or accessories.

The makers of those accessories will happily sell you new models that have Lightning connectors. Or you can buy an adapter from Apple:

• Additional USB charging cables, like the one that came with your iPhone, cost $20.

• A white adapter plug costs $30. It connects the modern iPhone to any accessory that was built for the old 30-pin connector.

• If the iPhone 5 doesn't quite fit the older accessory, sometimes the solution is the $40 adapter plug with an 8-inch cable "tail.")

Even with the adapter, the Lightning connector doesn't work with every older accessory, and it doesn't offer all the same features. For example, it can't send video out to your TV; for that, you need Apple's Lightning-to-HDMI or Lightning-to-VGA cable.)

In time, as the Lightning connectors come on all new iPhones, iPods, and iPads, a new ecosystem of accessories will arise. We'll arrive at a new era of standardization—until Apple changes jacks again in *another* 10 years.

Antenna Band

That metal band around the edge is one of the most famous features of recent iPhones. This band (aluminum on the iPhone 5 and 5s, stainless steel on the 4 and 4s) is the primary structural component of the phone—everything else is attached to it.

But this band is also part of the iPhone's antenna.

It was also part of the controversy that erupted after the iPhone 4 debuted in the summer of 2010. Remember that? If you held the iPhone 4 so that the lower-left corner was pressed into your palm, the signal strength sometimes dropped. Even more intriguing: Putting the phone in a case or in one of Apple's silicone "bumpers" eliminated the problem.

Eventually, the hysteria died down. The problem doesn't occur at all on the 4s or the 5 series; you can hold these phones any way you like.

Top/left segments:
Bluetooth, WiFi,
GPS antennas

Right/bottom segments:
voice and cellular
data antennas

In the Box

Inside the minimalist box, you get the iPhone and these items:

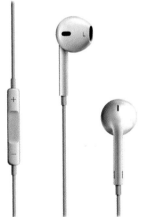

- **The earbuds.** Apple shipped 600 million of the iconic white earbuds that, for years, announced to the world, "I have an iPhone!" or "I have an iPod!" But for the iPhone 5 and later, Apple updated them. Now you get what Apple calls EarPods. They stay put in more people's ears, and they sound better, although their bulbous shape may get uncomfortable in smaller ears. As before, a volume control/clicker is right on the cord, so you can answer calls and pause the music without taking the phone out of your pocket.

- **The USB charging/syncing cable.** When you connect your iPhone to your computer using this white USB cable, it simultaneously syncs and charges. See Chapter 13.

- **The AC adapter.** When you're traveling without a computer, you can plug the dock's USB cable into the included two-prong outlet adapter, so you can charge the iPhone directly from a wall socket.

- **Finger Tips.** Cute name for a cute foldout leaflet of iPhone basics.

You don't need a copy of the iTunes software, or even a computer, to use the iPhone—but it makes loading up the phone a lot easier, as described in Chapter 13.

If you don't have iTunes on your computer, then you can download it from *www.apple.com/itunes.*

Seven Basic Finger Techniques

The iPhone isn't quite like any machine that came before it, and operating it isn't quite like using any other machine. You do everything on the touchscreen instead of with physical buttons. Here's what you need to know.

Tap

You'll do a lot of tapping on the iPhone's onscreen buttons. They're usually nice and big, giving your fleshy fingertip a fat target.

You can't use a fingernail or a pen tip; only skin contact works. (OK, you can also buy an iPhone stylus. But a fingertip is cheaper and much harder to misplace.)

Swipe

In some situations, you'll be asked to confirm an action by *swiping* your finger across the screen. That's how you unlock the phone after it's been in your pocket, for example. It's ingenious, really; you may bump the touchscreen when you reach into your pocket for something, but it's extremely unlikely that your knuckles will randomly *swipe* it in just the right way.

You also have to swipe to confirm that you want to turn off the iPhone, to answer a call on a locked iPhone, or to shut off an alarm. Swiping like this is also a great shortcut for deleting an email or a text message.

Drag

When you're zoomed into a map, Web page, email, or photo, you can scroll around just by sliding your finger across the glass in any direction—like a flick (described below), but slower and more controlled. It's a huge improvement over scroll bars, especially when you want to scroll diagonally.

Flick

A *flick* is a faster, less-controlled *slide.* You flick vertically to scroll lists on the iPhone. You'll discover—usually with some expletive like "Whoa!" or "Jeez!"—that scrolling a list in this way is a blast. The faster you flick, the faster the list spins downward or upward. But lists have a real-world sort of momentum; they slow down after a second or two, so you can see where you wound up.

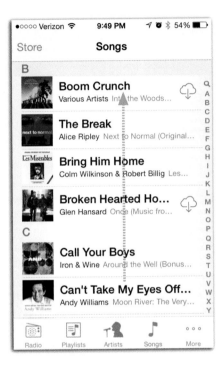

At any point during the scrolling of a list, you can flick again (if you didn't go far enough) or tap to stop the scrolling (if you see the item you want to choose).

Pinch and Spread

In programs like Photos, Mail, Web, and Maps, you can zoom in on a photo, message, Web page, or map by *spreading.*

That's when you place two fingers (usually thumb and forefinger) on the glass and spread them. The image magically grows, as though it's printed on a sheet of rubber.

NOTE: The English language has failed Apple here. Moving your thumb and forefinger closer together has a perfect verb: *pinching.* But there's no word to describe moving them the opposite direction.

Apple uses the oxymoronic expression *pinch out* to describe that move (along with the redundant-sounding *pinch in*). In this book, the opposite of "pinching" is "spreading."

Once you've zoomed in like this, you can zoom out again by putting two fingers on the glass and pinching them together.

Double-Tap

Double-tapping is actually pretty rare on the iPhone, at least among the programs supplied by Apple. It's not like the Mac or Windows, where double-clicking the mouse always means "open." Because the iPhone's operating system is far more limited, you open something with *one* tap.

A double-tap, therefore, is reserved for two functions:

- In the Safari (Web browser), Photos, and Maps programs, double-tapping zooms in on whatever you tap, magnifying it. (Double-tapping means "Restore to original size" after you've zoomed in.) Double-tapping also zooms into some email messages—the ones formatted like Web pages—as well as PDF files, Microsoft Office files, and others.

- When you're watching a video (or recording one), double-tapping switches the **aspect ratio** (video screen shape).

Edge Swipes

Here's a new one in iOS 7: Swiping your finger inward from **outside** the screen. It has a few variations:

- **From the top edge.** Opens the Notification Center, which lists all your missed calls and texts, shows your appointments, and so on.

- **From the bottom edge.** Opens the Control Center, a unified miniature control panel for brightness, volume, WiFi, and so on.

- **From the left edge.** In many apps, this means "go back to the previous screen." It works in Mail, Settings, Notes, Messages, Safari, Facebook and some other apps.

It sometimes makes a big difference whether you begin your swipe within the screen or outside it, by the way. At the Home screen, for example, starting your swipe within the screen area doesn't open the Notification Center—it opens Spotlight, the iPhone's search function.

Charging the iPhone

The iPhone has a built-in, rechargeable battery that fills up a substantial chunk of its interior. How long one charge can drive your iPhone depends on what you're doing—music playback saps the battery the least, GPS navigation saps it the most. But one thing is for sure: Sooner or later, you'll have to recharge the iPhone. For most people, that's every night or every other night.

You recharge the iPhone by connecting the white USB cable that came with it. You can plug the far end into either of two places to supply power:

- **Your computer's USB jack.** In general, the iPhone charges even if your computer is asleep. (If it's a laptop that itself is not plugged in, though, the phone charges only if the laptop is awake. Otherwise, you'd come home to a depleted laptop.)

- **The AC adapter.** The little white two-prong cube that came with the iPhone connects to the end of the cradle's USB cable.

Unless the charge is **really** low, you can use the iPhone while it's charging. If the iPhone is unlocked, then the battery icon in the upper-right corner displays a lightning bolt to let you know that it's charging. If it's locked, pressing the Home button shows you a battery gauge big enough to see from space.

Battery Life Tips

The battery life of the iPhone is either terrific or terrible, depending on your point of view—and which model you have.

If you were an optimist, you'd point out that the iPhone gets longer battery life than most rival touchscreen phones.

If you were a pessimist, you'd observe that you sometimes can't even make it through a single day without needing a recharge.

So knowing how to scale back your iPhone's power appetite could come in extremely handy.

The biggest wolfers of electricity on your iPhone are its screen and its wireless features. Therefore, these ideas will help you squeeze more life out of each charge:

- **Dim the screen.** In bright light, the screen brightens (and uses more battery power). In dim light, it darkens. That's because when you unlock the phone after waking it, it samples the ambient light and adjusts the brightness.

You can use this information to your advantage. By covering up the sensor as you unlock the phone, you force it into a low-power, dim-screen setting (because the phone believes it's in a dark room). Or by holding it up to a light as you wake it, you get full brightness. In either case, you've saved all the taps and navigation it would have taken you to find the manual brightness slider in Settings.

- **Turn off WiFi.** If you're not in a wireless hotspot, you may as well stop the thing from using its radio. Swipe up from the bottom of the screen to open the Control Center, and tap the 🛜 icon to turn it off.

  Or at the very least tell the iPhone to stop *searching* for WiFi networks it can connect to. Page 504 has the details.

- **Turn off "push" data.** This is a big one. If your email, calendar, and address book are kept constantly synced with your Macs or PCs, then you've probably gotten yourself involved with Yahoo Mail, Microsoft Exchange (Chapter 15), or iCloud (Chapter 14). It's pretty amazing to know that your iPhone is constantly kept current with the mother ship—but all that continual sniffing of the airwaves, looking for updates, costs you battery power. If you can do without the immediacy, then visit Settings→Mail, Contacts, Calendars→Fetch New Data. If you turn off the Push feature, and set it to Manually instead, then your iPhone checks for email and new appointments only when you actually open the email or calendar apps. Your battery goes a lot further.

- **Turn off background updating.** Non-Apple apps check for frequent updates, too: Facebook, Twitter, stock-reporting apps, and so on. And not all of them have to be busily toiling in the background. Your best bet on battery life, then, involves visiting Settings→General→Background App Refresh, and turning the switch Off for each app whose background activity isn't strictly necessary.

- **Turn off Cellular Data.** This option (in Settings→Cellular) turns off the cellular Internet features of your phone. You can still make calls, and you can still get online in a WiFi hotspot.

  This feature is designed for people who have a capped data plan—a limited amount of Internet use per month—which is almost everybody. If you discover that you've used up almost all your data allotment for the month, and you don't want to go over your limit (and thereby trigger an overage charge), you can use this option to shut off all data. Now your phone is just a phone.

- **Turn off the cellular voice circuitry, too.** In Airplane mode, you shut off both WiFi and the cellular radios, saving the most power of all. Swipe up from the bottom of the screen to open the Control Center, and tap the ✈ icon to turn it on.

- **Turn off GPS checks.** In Settings→Privacy→Location Services, there's a list of all the apps on your phone that are using your phone's location feature to know where you are. (It's a combination of GPS, cell-tower triangulation, and WiFi hotspot triangulation.) All that checking uses battery power, too.

  Some apps, like Maps, Find My Friends, and Yelp, won't do you much good without knowing your location. But plenty of apps don't really need to know where you are. Facebook and Twitter, for example, need that information only so that they can location-stamp your posts. In any case, the point is to turn off Location Services for each app that doesn't really need to know where you are.

- **Don't use Raise to Speak.** You can make it so that Siri starts listening for your voice commands every time you hold the phone up to your head. But there's a battery penalty to pay for this feature; see page 138.

- **Turn off Bluetooth.** If you're not using a Bluetooth headset, then for heaven's sake shut down that Bluetooth radio. In Settings, tap Bluetooth and turn it off.

- **Turn off the screen.** You can actually turn off the screen, rendering it totally black and saving incredible amounts of battery power. Music playback and Maps navigation continue to work just fine.

  Of course, if you actually want to *interact* with the phone while the screen is off, you'll have to learn the VoiceOver talking-buttons technology; see page 168.

Last battery tip: Beware of 3-D games and other graphically intensive apps, which can be serious power hogs. And turn off EQ when playing your music (see page 206).

The Home Screen

The Home screen is the launching pad for every iPhone activity. It's what appears when you press the Home button. It's the immortal grid of colorful icons.

It's such an essential software landmark, in fact, that a quick tour might be helpful.

- **Icons.** Each icon represents one of your iPhone apps (programs)—Mail, Maps, Camera, and so on—or a folder that you've made to **contain** some apps. Tap one to open that program or folder.

  Your iPhone comes with about 25 icons preinstalled by Apple; you can't remove them. The real fun, of course, comes when you download **more** apps from the App Store (Chapter 8).

- **Badges.** Every now and then, you'll see a tiny, red number "badge" (like ❷) on one of your app icons. It's telling you that something new awaits: new email, new text messages, new chat entries, new updates for the apps on your iPhone. It's saying, "Hey, you! Tap me!"

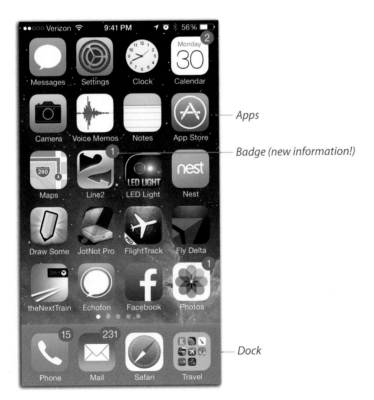

Apps

Badge (new information!)

Dock

- **Home page dots.** As you install more and more programs on your iPhone—and that will happen fast once you discover the App Store—you'll need more and more room for their icons.

  The standard Home screen can't hold more than 24 icons (20 on the iPhone 4s and earlier models). So where are all your games, video recorders, and tip calculators supposed to go?

  Easy: The iPhone automatically makes room for them by creating *additional* Home screens. You can spread your new programs' icons across 11 such launch screens.

  The little white dots are your map. Each represents one Home screen. If the third one is "lit up," then you're on the third Home screen.

  To move among the screens, swipe horizontally—or tap to the right or left of the little dots to change screens.

  And if you ever scroll too far away from the ***first*** Home screen, here's a handy shortcut: Press the Home button (yes, even though you're technically already home). That takes you back to the first Home screen.

> **TIP:** The very first "page," at the far left, used to be the Spotlight (search) screen. But in iOS 7, you open Spotlight by dragging down anywhere on any Home screen; there's nothing to the left of the Home screens anymore. You can tug down on ***any*** "page" of the Home screens—you don't have to scroll all the way to the left of them anymore.

- **The Dock.** At the bottom of the Home screen, four exalted icons sit in a row on what looks like a polished glass tabletop. This is the Dock—a place to park the most important icons on your iPhone. These, presumably, are the ones you use most often. Apple starts you off with the Phone, Mail, Safari, and Music icons.

  What's so special about this row? As you flip among Home screens, the Dock never changes. You can never lose one of your four most cherished icons by straying from the first page; they're always handy.

- **The background.** You can replace the background image (behind your app icons) with a photo. A complicated, busy picture won't do you any favors—it will just make the icon names harder to read—so Apple provides a selection of handsome, relatively subdued wallpaper photos. But you can also choose one of your own photos.

  For instructions on changing the wallpaper, see page 248.

It's easy (and fun!) to rearrange the icons on your Home screens. Put the most frequently used icons on the first page, put similar apps into folders, reorganize your Dock. Full details are on page 280.

Control Center

For such a tiny device, there are an awful lot of settings you can change—*hundreds* of them. Trouble is, some of them need changing (volume, brightness) a lot more often than others (language preference, voicemail greeting).

Until iOS 7 came along, the important settings were buried among the less important ones, and all of them required interrupting whatever you were doing to open the Settings app.

But no more, thanks to the Control Center. It's the new iOS 7 feature that you'll probably use the most often, that will save you the most time, and that will make you happiest.

To open the Control Center, no matter what app you're using, swipe upward from beneath the screen.

> **TIP:** You can even open the Control Center from the Lock screen, unless you've turned off that feature (page 14).

The Control Center is a translucent gray panel filled with one-touch icons for the settings most people change most often on their iPhones.

> **TIP:** Truth be told, the Control Center is easier to use when it's *not* translucent. Visit Settings→General→Accessibility and turn on Increase Contrast. Now the Control Center's background is solid gray instead of see-through gray.

Now, many of these settings are even faster to change using Siri, the voice-command feature described in Chapter 4. When it's not socially awkward to speak to your phone (like at the symphony), you can use spoken commands—listed below under each button description—to adjust settings without even touching the screen.

Here's what's in the Control Center:

- **Airplane Mode (✈).** Tap to turn the icon white. Now you're in Airplane mode; the phone's wireless features are all turned off. You're saving battery and obeying flight attendant instructions. Tap again to turn off Airplane mode.

Sample Siri command: "Turn Airplane mode on." (Siri warns you that if you turn Airplane mode on, Siri herself will stop working. Say "OK.")

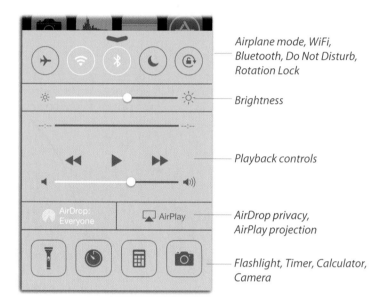

Airplane mode, WiFi, Bluetooth, Do Not Disturb, Rotation Lock

Brightness

Playback controls

AirDrop privacy, AirPlay projection

Flashlight, Timer, Calculator, Camera

- **WiFi (⎘).** Tap to turn your phone's WiFi off (black) or on (white).

  Sample Siri commands: "Turn off WiFi." "Turn WiFi back on."

- **Bluetooth (⎘).** Tap to turn your Bluetooth transmitter off (black) or on (white). That feature alone is a godsend to anyone who uses the iPhone with a car's Bluetooth audio system. Bluetooth can drain your battery if it's left on unnecessarily—so it's very nice to be able to flick it on so easily when you get into the car.

  Sample Siri commands: "Turn Bluetooth on." "Turn off Bluetooth."

- **Do Not Disturb (⎘).** Do Not Disturb mode, described in Chapter 3, means that the phone won't ring or buzz when people call—except a few handpicked people whose communiqués ring through. Perfect for sleeping hours; in fact, you can set up an automated schedule for Do Not Disturb (say, midnight to 7 a.m.).

  But what if you wake up early or want to stay up late? Now you can tap to turn Do Not Disturb on (white) or off (black).

  Sample Siri commands: "Turn on Do Not Disturb." "Turn Do Not Disturb off."

- **Rotation Lock (🔒).** When Rotation Lock is turned on (white), the screen no longer rotates when you turn the phone 90 degrees. The idea is that sometimes, like when you're reading an ebook on your side in bed, you don't want the screen picture to turn; you want it to stay upright relative to your eyes, even though you're lying down. (A little 🔒 icon appears at the top of the screen to remind you why the usual rotating isn't happening.)

  The whole thing isn't quite as earth-shattering as it sounds—first, because it locks the image in only one way: upright, in portrait orientation. You can't make it lock into widescreen mode. Furthermore, many apps don't rotate with the phone to begin with. But when that day comes when you want to read in bed on your side with your head on the pillow, your iPhone will be ready. (Tap the button again to turn rotating back on.)

- **Brightness.** Hallelujah! Here's a screen-brightness slider. Drag the little white ball to change the screen brightness.

  Sample Siri commands: "Make the screen brighter." "Decrease the brightness." "Dim the screen." "Brighten up!"

- **Playback controls (⏮, ▶, ⏭).** These controls govern playback in whatever app is playing music or podcasts in the background: the Music app, Pandora, Spotify, whatever it is. You can skip a horrible song quickly and efficiently without having to interrupt what you're doing, or pause the music to chat with a colleague. (Tap the song name to open whatever app is playing.)

  You also get a scrubber bar that shows where you are in the song, the name of the song and the performer, and the album name. And, of course, there's a volume slider. It lets you make big volume jumps faster than you would by pressing the volume buttons on the side of the phone.

  Sample Siri commands: "Pause the music." "Skip to the next song." "Play some Billy Joel."

- **AirDrop (📡).** AirDrop, a new iOS 7 feature, gives you a quick, effortless way to shoot photos, maps, Web pages, and other stuff to nearby iPhones, iPads, and iPod Touches (that are also running iOS 7).

  On the Control Center, the AirDrop button isn't an on/off switch like most of the other icons here. Instead it produces a pop-up menu of options that control whose i-gadgets can "see" your iPhone: Contacts Only (people in your address book), Everyone, or Off (nobody).

- **AirPlay (⬜).** The AirPlay button lets you send your iPhone's video and audio to a wireless speaker system or TV—if you have an AirPlay receiver, of which the most famous is the Apple TV. Details on page 215.

- **Flashlight (🔦).** Tap to turn on the iPhone's "flashlight"—actually the LED lamp on the back that usually serves as the camera flash. Knowing that a source of good, clean light is two touches away makes a huge difference if you're trying to read in the dark, find your way along a path at night, or fiddle with wires behind your desk.

- **Timer (⏱).** Tap to open the Clock app—specifically, the Timer mode, which counts down to zero. Apple figures you might appreciate having direct access to it when you're cooking, for example, or waiting for your hair color to set. Of course, the alarm-clock mode is only one tap away at that point.

  Sample Siri commands: "Open the Timer." Or, better yet, bypass the Clock and Timer apps altogether: "Start the timer for three minutes." "Count down from six minutes." (Siri counts down right there on the Siri screen.)

- **Calculator (🖩).** Tap to open the Calculator app—a handy shortcut if it's your turn to figure out how to divide up the restaurant bill.

  Sample Siri commands: "Open the calculator." Or, better yet, without opening any app: "What's a hundred and six divided by five?"

- **Camera (📷).** Tap to jump directly into the Camera app. Because photo ops don't wait around.

  Sample Siri commands: "Take a picture." "Open the camera."

The Control Center closes by itself when you tap the Timer, Calculator or Camera buttons. Otherwise, close it by tapping the ⌄ button to close it up again.

TIP: Actually, that ⌄ is a pretty small target. Fortunately, you can be much sloppier. To close the Control Center, tap, or drag downward, from *any spot* above it (the dimmed background of the screen).

Or just press the Home button.

Notifications

A notification is an important status message. You get one every time a text message comes in, an alarm goes off, a calendar appointment is imminent, or your battery is running low.

You can choose one of three notification styles for *each individual app.* To see these controls, open Settings→Notification Center. Scroll down to the Include section (below, left) and tap the app you want to tweak. The notification options appear (below, right)

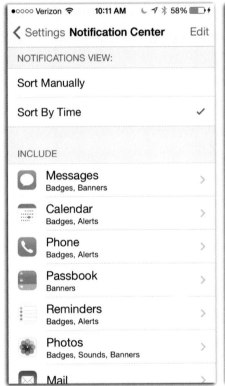
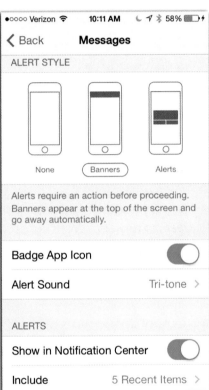

The options may vary from app to app, but you almost always get these three choices:

- **None.** If certain apps bug you with news you really don't care about, you can shut them up forever. Tap None.

- **Banners** are incoming notifications that appear quietly and briefly at the top of the screen (below, left). The message holds still long enough for you to read it, but it doesn't interrupt your work and goes away after a few seconds. Banners are a good option for things like Facebook and Twitter updates and incoming email messages.

TIP: If you can tap that banner with your finger before it disappears, you jump directly to the app that's trying to get your attention. You can also flick it up off the screen if it's in your way.

- **Alerts.** A white alert box appears to get your attention (above, right). You might use this option for apps whose messages are too important to miss, like alarms, flight updates, and text messages.

TIP: While you're here, you may as well check out the Badge App Icon switch for each app. A badge is the little ❷ that indicates how many messages or updates are waiting inside that app—and you can turn it off for each app individually. Some apps even offer an on/off switch for sounds, which is handy if you think your phone makes far too many bleeps and burbles as it is.

The Notification Center

No matter what kind of notification pops up, you still see only one alert at a time. And once it's gone, you can't get it back. Or can you?

Meet the Notification Center screen. It lists every notification you've recently received, in a tidy, scrolling list.

You can check it out right now: Swipe your finger down from above the iPhone's screen. The Notification Center pulls down like a classy window shade, printed in white with every recent item of interest.

Here you'll find all your apps' notifications, as well as your missed calls, recent text messages, reminders, and upcoming calendar appointments.

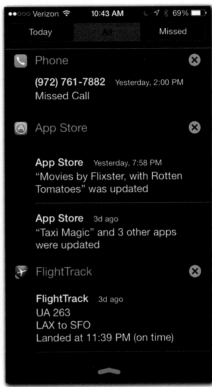

You can have all kinds of fun here:

- **Switch among the three tabs** (new in iOS 7). The Today screen presents an executive summary of everything you need to know *today,* in plain English: your upcoming appointments ("'Salary meeting' is next up on your calendar, at 2 PM"); reminders coming due; weather and stock information; and a preview of your schedule tomorrow. If you're away from your home or office, you'll even see an estimated commuting time, based on current traffic conditions. Pretty slick.

  The All screen shows every notification you've received, sorted by app. It can be a very long list. And the Missed tab rounds up all the calls, texts, and other notifications that came in while your phone was asleep or turned off, sorted chronologically. (They disappear after a day.)

To switch among these three views, you can either tap the little buttons—or just swipe across the screen.

- **Swipe upward** inside a list to scroll through more of it.
- **Drag the bottom handle (⌒) upward** to make the window shade snap up again, hiding the Notification Center.

TIP: Actually, you don't have to aim for the handle. You can just swipe upward from beneath the screen, quickly and sloppily.

- **Tap a line** in the Notification Center to open the relevant app for more details—for example, to see more information about that appointment, or to read the whole text message in context.
- **On the All screen, tap the ⊗ next to an app's name** and then tap Clear to remove that app's current listings from the Notification Center. (That app's heading will reappear here the next time it has anything to tell you.)

NOTE: You can no longer use the Notification Center to fire off a post to Twitter or Facebook. There are other ways to do that, however; see page 380.

Customizing the Notification Center

You can (and should) specify *which* apps are allowed to junk up your Notification Center. Open Settings→Notifications to see the master list (shown on page 41), with one entry for every app that might ever want your attention. (Or just tell Siri, "Open notification settings.")

At the top of this screen, the on/off switches govern your ability (and, frankly, other people's ability) to see your Notification Center, or just the Today view, on the Lock screen. It's handy to be able to swipe down to check your calendar or whatever without unlocking the phone—but if you worry that evildoers could spy on your calendar by picking your phone up, you can turn these things off.

Next comes the Today View section. Here you specify which elements (Today Summary, Reminders, Stocks, and so on) you want to be part of the Today tab described above.

Next, under Notifications View, you can specify the order of the various apps' notifications in the center. If you tap **Sort By Time**, then the apps with the newest alerts appear at the top. But if you tap **Manually** and then **Edit**, you can drag the ≡ handles up or down to specify the top-to-bottom order of your apps' notifications on the Notification Center screen. You can even reorder some of the elements of the **Today** tab.

Tap an app's name to open its individual Notifications screen (at right on page 38—the Messages app, in this example). Here you can, if you like, turn **Show in Notification Center** to **Off**.

The app's name will no longer appear in the All tab of your Notification Center. The app can still get your attention with banners or alert bubbles—but it won't appear in the Notification Center.

> **TIP:** You can also use the **Include** setting to specify how *much* of the Notification Center this app is allowed to use up—that is, how many lines of information. Maybe you need only the most recent alert about your upcoming flight (**1 Item**), but you want to see a lot more of your upcoming appointments (**10 Items**).

Messages on the Lock Screen

The Lock screen (page 11) is another place to see what's been trying to get your attention while the phone was in your pocket: missed calls and texts, new messages and email, and so on.

The Lock screen may seem just like the Notification Center—but there are differences. For example, every time you wake the phone, whatever notifications are on the Lock screen are wiped clear. They don't stay put, as they do on the Notification Center.

You might want a *different* set of apps to list their nags on the Lock screen. Maybe you want the Lock screen to show only missed calls, new text messages, and new mail—but you'd like the Notification Center to be fully stocked with Twitter and Facebook updates, for example. That's why, when you burrow into **Settings→Notifications** and tap an app's name, you get a **View in Lock Screen** on/off switch.

Miscellaneous Weirdness

As you poke around in the Notification Center settings, you'll discover that certain oddball apps offer some options that don't match up with the settings you see for most apps. Don't freak out. It's all part of Apple's master plan to put controls where it hopes you'll find them.

Password (or Fingerprint) Protection

Like any smartphone, the iPhone offers a first line of defense for a phone that winds up in the wrong hands. It's designed to keep your stuff private from other people in the house or the office, or to protect your information in case you lose the iPhone. If you don't know the password or don't have the right fingerprint, you can't use the iPhone (except for limited tasks like taking a photo or using Siri).

About half of iPhone owners don't bother setting up a password to protect the phone. Maybe they never set the thing down in public, so they don't worry about thieves. Or maybe there's just not that much personal information on the phone—and meanwhile, having to enter a password every single time you wake the phone can get to be a profound hassle.

TIP: Besides—if you ever do lose your phone, you can put a password on it by remote control; see page 481.

The other half of people reason that the inconvenience of entering a password many times a day is a small price to pay for the knowledge that nobody can get into your stuff if you lose it.

If you think your phone is worth protecting, here's how to set up a password—and, if you have an iPhone 5s, how to use the fingerprint reader instead.

Setting Up a Password

If you didn't already create a phone password the first time you turned your iPhone on, here's how to do it. (And just because you're an iPhone 5s owner, don't be smug; you have to create a password even if you plan to use the fingerprint reader. As a backup.)

Open Settings→General→Passcode Lock (or, on the iPhone 5s, Passcode & Fingerprint).

You can set up either a four-digit number—convenient, but not so impossible to guess—or a full-blown alphanumeric password of any length. You decide, using the Simple Passcode on/off switch.

Now tap Turn Passcode On. You're asked to type the password you want, either on the number keypad (for Simple Passcodes) or the alphabet keyboard. You're asked to do it again to make sure you didn't make a typo.

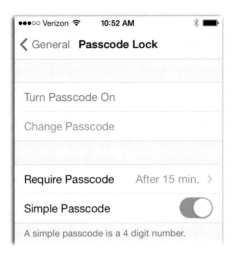

Once you confirm your password, you return to the Passcode Lock screen. Here you have a few more options.

For example, the Require Passcode option lets you specify how quickly the password is requested before locking somebody out: immediately after the iPhone wakes or 1, 15, 30, 60, or 240 minutes later. (Those options are a convenience to you, so you can quickly check your calendar or missed messages without having to enter the passcode—while still protecting your data from, for example, evildoers who pick up your iPhone while you're out getting coffee.)

Three features are accessible on the Lock screen even before you've entered your password: Siri (or, if you don't have Siri, Voice Dial), Passbook, and Reply with Message. These are huge conveniences , but also, technically, a security risk. Somebody who finds your phone on your desk could, for example, blindly voice-dial your colleagues or use Siri to send a text. If you turn these switches off, then you won't be able to use these features until after you've entered your pass-word.

Finally, here is Erase Data—an option that's scary and reassuring at the same time. When this option is on, then if someone makes 10 incorrect guesses at your passcode, your iPhone erases itself. It's assuming that some lowlife burglar is trying to crack into it to have a look at all your personal data.

This option, a pertinent one for professional people, presents potent protection from patient password prospectors.

> **NOTE:** Even when the phone is locked and the password unguessable, a tiny blue Emergency Call button still appears on the Unlock screen. It's there just in case you've been conked on the head by a vase, you can't remember your own password, and you need to call 911.

And that is all. From now on, each time you wake your iPhone (if it's not within the window of repeat visits you established), you're asked for your password.

Fingerprint Security (Touch ID)

If you have an iPhone 5s—you lucky thing—you have the option of using a more secure and much more convenient kind of "password": your fingertip.

The lens built right into the Home button (clever!) is the first cellphone fingerprint reader ever that actually *works*—every time. It's not fussy, it's not balky. It reads your finger at any angle. It can't be faked out by a plastic finger or even a chopped-off finger. You can teach it to recognize up to five fingerprints; they can all be yours, or some can belong to other people you trust.

Before you can use your fingertip as a password, though, you have to teach the phone to recognize it. Here's how that goes:

1. **Create a passcode.** That's right: You can't use a fingerprint *instead* of a password; you can only use a fingerprint in *addition* to one. You'll still need a password from time to time to keep the phone's security tight. For example, you need to enter your password if you can't make your fingerprint work (maybe it got encased in acrylic in a hideous crafts accident), or if you restart the phone, or if you haven't used the phone in 48 hours or more.

   So open Settings→General→Passcode & Fingerprint and create a password, as described on the previous pages.

2. **Teach a fingerprint.** Tap Fingerprints. At the top of the Fingerprints screen, you see the on/off switches for the two things your fingerprint can do: It can unlock the phone (Passcode Unlock), and it can serve as your password when you buy books, music, apps, and videos from Apple's online stores (iTunes & App Store).

But what you really want to tap here, of course, is **Add a fingerprint**.

Now comes the cool part. Place the finger you want to train onto the Home button—your thumb or index finger are the most logical candidates. Touch it to the Home button over and over, maybe six times.

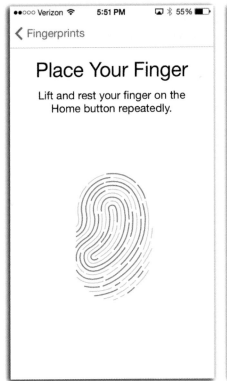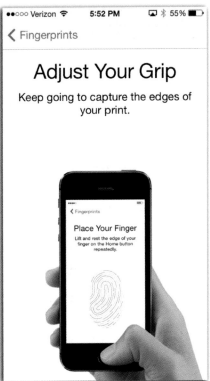

Each time, the gray lines of the onscreen fingerprint darken a little more.

Once you've filled in the fingerprint, you see the Adjust Your Grip screen. Now, the iPhone wants you to touch the Home button another few times, this time tipping the finger a little each time so the sensor gets a better view of your finger's edges.

Once that's done, the screen says "Success!"

You are now ready to start using the fingerprint. Try it: Switch the phone off. Then wake it (press the Sleep switch or press the Home button), and then leave your finger on the Home button for about a second. The phone reads your fingerprint and instantly unlocks itself.

And now, a few notes about using your fingerprint as a password:

- Yes, you can touch your finger to the Home button at the Lock screen. But you can also touch it at any Enter Passcode screen.

  Suppose, for example, that your Lock screen shows that you missed a text message. And you want to reply. Well, you can swipe across that notification to open it in its native habitat—the Messages app—but first you're shown the Enter Passcode screen. Ignore that. Just touch the Home button.

- Apple says that the image of your fingerprint is encrypted and stored in the iPhone's processor chip. It's never transmitted anywhere, it never goes online, and it's never collected by Apple.

- If you return to the Passcode & Fingerprint screens, you can tap **Add a Fingerprint** again to teach your phone to recognize a second finger. And a third, fourth, and fifth.

  The five "registered" fingerprints don't all have to belong to you. If you share the phone with a spouse or a child, for example, that special somebody can use up one or two of the fingerprint slots.

- To rename a fingerprint, tap **Edit** and then tap the current name ("Finger 1" or whatever). To delete one, tap **Edit** and then tap ⊖. (You can figure out which finger label is which by touching the Home button; the corresponding label blinks. Sweet!)

- You can register your toes instead of fingers, if that's helpful. Or even patches of your wrist or arm, if you're patient (and weird).

- The Touch ID scanner may have trouble recognizing your finger if it's wet, greasy, or scarred.

- The iPhone's finger reader isn't just a camera; it doesn't just look for the image of your fingerprint. It's actually measuring the tiny differences in electrical conductivity between the raised parts of your fingerprint (which aren't conductive) and the skin just beneath the surface (which is). That's why a plastic finger won't work—and even your own finger won't work if it's been chopped off (or if you've passed away).

- For now, your fingerprint only works to unlock the phone and to buy stuff from Apple's online stores. But wouldn't it be great if your fingerprint could also log you into secure Web sites? Or serve as your ID when you buy stuff online?

  Apple says it may someday allow other apps to access Touch ID; it's going to watch and wait to see how well the initial rollout goes before it makes a decision.

2

Typing, Editing & Searching

As a pocket computer, the iPhone faces a fundamental limitation: It has no real keyboard or mouse. Which might be considered a drawback on a gadget that's capable of running hundreds of thousands of programs.

Fortunately, where there's a problem, there's software that can fix it. The modern iPhone's virtual keyboard is smart in all kinds of ways—automatically predicting words and correcting typos, for example. You can even tap a mistyped word to see some suggestions for fixing it.

This chapter covers every aspect of working with text on the iPhone: entering it, fixing it, and searching for it. (Well, *almost* every aspect. Chapter 4 covers *dictating* text.)

The Keyboard

Very few iPhone features have triggered as much angst, hope, and criticism as the onscreen keyboard. It's true, boys and girls: The iPhone has no physical keys. A virtual keyboard, therefore, is the only possible built-in system for typing text. Like it or not, you'll be doing a lot of typing on glass.

The keyboard appears automatically whenever you tap in a place where typing is possible: in an outgoing email or text message, in the Notes program, in the address bar of the Web browser, and so on.

Just tap the key you want. As your finger taps the glass, a "speech balloon" appears above your finger, showing an enlarged version of the key you actually hit (since your finger is now blocking your view of the keyboard).

In darker gray, surrounding the letters, you'll find these special keys:

- **Shift (⇧).** When you tap this key, it turns dark to indicate that it's in effect. The next letter you type appears as a capital. Then the ⇧ key returns to normal, meaning that the next letter will be lowercase.

> **TIP:** The iPhone has a Caps Lock feature, too. It's enabled by default in iOS 7; the on/off switch is in **Settings→General→Keyboard**; turn on **Enable Caps Lock**.
>
> When it's on, if you double-tap the ⇧ key, its background turns dark. You're now in Caps Lock mode, and you'll now type in ALL CAPITALS until you tap the ⇧ key again. (If you can't seem to make Caps Lock work, try double-tapping the ⇧ key *fast.*)

- **Backspace (⌫).** This key actually has three speeds.

  Tap it once to delete the letter just before the blinking insertion point.

  Hold it down to "walk" backward, deleting as you go.

  If you *hold down the key long enough,* it starts deleting *words* rather than letters, one whole chunk at a time.

- **123.** Tap this button when you want to type numbers or punctuation. The keyboard changes to offer a palette of numbers and symbols. Tap the same key—which now says ABC—to return to the letters keyboard. (Before the iPhone 4s, the button looked like this: `?123`; it was later redrawn to make room for the little Siri microphone button on later models.)

  Once you're on the numbers/symbols pad, a new dark-gray button appears, labeled #+=. Tapping it summons a *third* keyboard layout, containing the less frequently used symbols, like brackets, the # and % symbols, bullets, and math symbols.

NOTE: Because the period is such a frequently used symbol, there's an awesome shortcut that doesn't require switching to the punctuation keyboard: At the end of a sentence, just tap the space bar *twice.* You get a period, a space, *and* a capitalized letter at the beginning of the next word. (This, too, can be turned off—in Settings→General→Keyboard—although it's hard to imagine why you'd want to.)

- **Return.** Tapping this key moves to the next line, just as on a real keyboard. (There's no Tab key or Enter key in iPhone Land.)

Making the Keyboard Work

Some people have no problem tapping those tiny virtual keys; others struggle for days. Either way, here are some tips:

- Don't be freaked out by the tiny, narrow keys. Apple *knows* your fingertip is fatter than that.

  So as you type, use the whole pad of your finger or thumb. Don't try to tap with only a skinny part of your finger to match the skinny keys. You'll be surprised at how fast and accurate this method is. (Tap, don't press.)

- This may sound like New Age hooey, but *trust* the keyboard. Don't pause to check the result after each letter. Just plow on.

TIP: Although you don't see it, the sizes of the keys on the iPhone keyboard are actually changing all the time. That is, the software enlarges the "landing area" of certain keys, based on probability.

For example, suppose you type *tim.* Now, the iPhone knows that no word in the language begins *timw* or *timr*—and so, invisibly, it enlarges the "landing area" of the E key, which greatly diminishes your chances of making a typo on that last letter. Cool.

- Start with one-finger typing. Two-thumb, BlackBerry-style typing comes later. You'll drive yourself crazy if you start out that way, although it's not bad when you're using the **widescreen** keyboard layout.

- Without cursor keys, how are you supposed to correct an error you made a few sentences ago? Easy—use the **loupe.**

Hold your fingertip down anywhere in the text until you see the magnified circle appear. Without lifting your finger, drag anywhere in the text; the insertion point moves along with it. Release when the blue line is where you want to delete or add text, just as though you'd clicked there with a mouse.

> **TIP:** In the Safari address bar, you can skip the part about waiting for the loupe to appear. Once you click into the address, start **dragging** to make it appear at once.
>
> Don't bother using the Shift key to capitalize a new sentence. The iPhone does that capitalizing automatically. (To turn this feature on or off, open Settings→General→Keyboard. Turn off Auto-Capitalization.)

Auto-Suggestions

If you make a mistake, don't reflexively go for the Backspace (⊗). Instead, just above or below the word you typed, you'll find the iPhone's proposed replacement. The software analyzes the letters **around** the one you typed and usually figures out what you really meant. For example, if you accidentally type **imsame**, the iPhone realizes that you meant **insane** and suggests that word.

To accept its suggestion, tap the space bar or any punctuation, like a period or a question mark. To ignore the suggestion, tap it carefully with your finger.

TIP: If you turn on Speak Auto-text (in Settings→General→ Accessibility), your iPhone will even *speak* the suggested word out loud. That way, you can keep your focus on the keyboard.

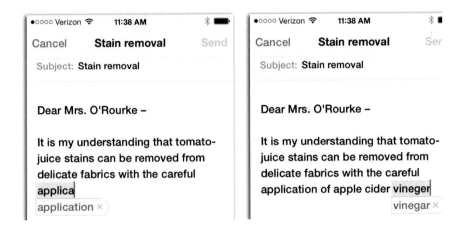

The suggestion feature can be especially useful when it comes to contractions, which are normally clumsy to type because you have to switch to the punctuation keyboard to find the apostrophe.

So you can save time by *deliberately* leaving out the apostrophe in contractions. Type *im, dont,* or *cant.* The iPhone proposes *I'm, don't,* or *can't,* so you can just tap the space bar to fix the word and continue.

The suggestion feature also kicks in when the iPhone thinks it knows how you intend to complete a *correctly* spelled word. For example, if you type *fathe,* the suggestion says *father.* This trick saves you only a letter or two, but that's better than nothing.

TIP: If you *accidentally* accept an AutoCorrect suggestion, tap the Backspace key. A word bubble appears, which you can tap to reinstate what you'd originally typed.

The Spelling Checker

Here's the world's friendliest typo-fixer. Apple calls it a spelling checker, but maybe that's stretching it.

The idea is that anytime the iPhone doesn't recognize something you've typed, it draws a dotted red underline beneath. Tap the word to see a pop-up balloon with one, two, or three alternate spellings. Often, one of them is what you wanted, and you can tap it to fix the mistake. (Equally often, none of them is, and it's time to break out the loupe and the keyboard.)

> **TIP:** You can also invoke the spelling checker's suggestions even if you haven't made a typo. Double-tap the word; on the editing bar that appears, tap **Replace**.

It is my understanding that tomato-juice stains can be removed from delicete fabrics with the application

delicate derstanding that tomato-juice stains can be removed from delicete fabrics with the application

The Widescreen Keyboard

In many apps, you can turn the phone 90 degrees to type. When the keyboard stretches out the long way, the keys get a lot bigger (especially on the iPhone 5, 5c, and 5s). It's a lot easier to type—even with two thumbs.

This glorious feature doesn't work in every app, alas. Fortunately, it does work in the apps where you do the most typing, like Mail, Messages, the Safari browser, Contacts, Twitter, and Notes. (The screen also rotates in Camera, Music, Calculator, Calendar, and Stocks, though not for typing purposes.)

The Spelling Dictionary

As you know, the iPhone suggests spellings or completions of the words you're typing. If you tap the space bar to accept a suggestion, wonderful.

If you don't—if you dismiss the suggestion and allow the "mistake" to stand—then the iPhone adds that word to a custom, dynamic dictionary, assuming that you've just typed some name, bit of slang, or terminology that wasn't in its dictionary originally. It dawns on the iPhone that maybe that's a legitimate word it doesn't know—and it adds it to the dictionary.

From now on, in other words, it will accept that bizarre new word as a legitimate word—and, in fact, will even *suggest* it the next time you type something like it.

Words you've added to the dictionary actually *age.* If you stop using some custom term, the iPhone gradually learns to forget it. That's handy behavior if you never intended for that word to become part of the dictionary to begin with (that is, it was a mistake).

TIP: If you feel you've really made a mess of your custom dictionary, and the iPhone keeps suggesting ridiculous alternate words, you can always start fresh. From the Home screen, tap Settings→General→Reset, and then tap Reset Keyboard Dictionary. Now the iPhone's dictionary is the way it was when it came from the factory, without any of the words it learned from you.

Punctuation with One Touch

On the iPhone, the punctuation and alphabet keys appear on two different keyboard layouts. That's a *serious* hassle, because each time you want, say, a comma, it's an awkward, three-step dance: (1) Tap the 123 key to get the punctuation layout. (2) Tap the comma. (3) Tap the ABC key or the space bar to return to the alphabet layout.

Imagine how excruciating it is to type, for example, "a P.O. Box in the U.S.A." That's 34 finger taps and 10 mode changes!

Fortunately, there's a secret way to get a punctuation mark with only a *single* finger gesture. The iPhone doesn't register most key presses until you *lift* your finger. But the Shift and Punctuation keys register their taps on the press *down* instead.

So here's what you can do, all in one motion:

1. **Touch the** 123 **key, but don't lift your finger.** The punctuation layout appears.

2. **Slide your finger onto the period or comma key, and release.** The ABC layout returns automatically. You've typed a period or a comma with one finger touch instead of three.

TIP: If you're a two-thumbed typist, you can also hit the 123 key with your left thumb and then tap the punctuation key with your right. It even works on the #+= sub-punctuation layout, although you'll probably visit that screen less often.

In fact, you can type any of the punctuation symbols the same way. This technique makes a *huge* difference in the usability of the keyboard.

TIP: This same trick saves you a finger-press when capitalizing words, too. You can put your finger down on the ⇧ key and slide directly onto the letter you want to type in its uppercase version. Or, if you're a two-handed iPhone typist, you can work the Shift key like the one on your computer: Hold it down with your left thumb, type a letter with your right, and then release both.

Accented Characters

To produce an accented character (like é, ë, è, ê, and so on), keep your finger pressed on that key for 1 second. A palette of diacritical marks appears; slide onto the one you want.

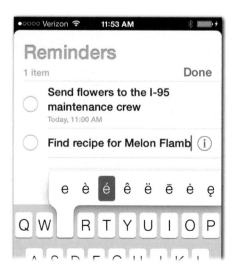

Not all keys sprout this pop-up palette. Here's a list of the keys that do.

Key	Alternates
A	à á â ä æ ã å ā
C	ç ć č
E	è é ê ë ę ė ē
I	ī į í ì ï î i
L	ł
N	ń ñ
O	ō ø œ õ ó ò ö ô o
S	ß ś š
U	ū ú ù ü û
Y	ÿ
Z	ź ž ż
?	¿
'	' ' '
"	» « „ " "
-	—
$	€ £ ¥ ₩
&	§
0	°
.	...
%	‰

Typing Shortcuts (Abbreviation Expanders)

Here's a feature that nobody ever talks about—probably because nobody even knows it exists. But it's a huge time- and sanity-saver; for a phone with no physical keys, anything that can do your typing for you is very welcome indeed.

You can program your phone to expand abbreviations that you type. Set up **addr** to type your entire mailing address, or **eml** to type out your email address. Create two-letter abbreviations for big legal or technical words you have to type a lot. Set up **goaway** to type out a polite rejection paragraph for use in email. And so on.

This feature has been in Microsoft Office forever (called AutoCorrect). And it's always been available as a separate app (TypeIt4Me and TextExpander, for example—but because they were separate, you had to copy your expanded text, switch to the target program, and then paste). But since it's now built right into the operating system, it works anywhere you can type.

You build your list of abbreviations in **Settings→General→Keyboard→ Shortcuts**. Tap the + button. On the resulting screen, type the expanded text into the **Phrase** box. (It can be very long, but it all has to be one continuous blob of text; it can't contain Returns.) In the **Shortcut** box, type the abbreviation you want to trigger the phrase.

TIP: The Shortcut box says "Optional." You might wonder: Why would you leave the shortcut blank? Then your new shortcut will be un-triggerable and pointless.

Not quite. It's optional to enable a sneaky trick: To make the phone stop mis-replacing some word (for example, insisting that you mean **PTA** when you type **pta**, a new chemical you've designed).

In that case, type your phrase into the Phrase box, but leave Shortcut blank.

That's it! Now, whenever you type one of the abbreviations you've set up, the iPhone proposes replacing it with your substituted text. The suggestion bubble works exactly the way the spelling bubble does: To accept the suggestion, keep on typing; to reject it, carefully tap the suggestion bubble itself.

International Typing

Because the iPhone is sold around the world, it has to be equipped for non-English languages—and even non-Roman alphabets. Fortunately, it's ready.

To prepare the iPhone for language switching, go to Settings→General→ International. Tap Language to set the iPhone's primary language (for menus, button labels, and so on).

To make other *keyboards* available, tap Keyboards, tap Add New Keyboard, and then turn on the keyboard layouts you'll want available: Russian, Italian, whatever.

If you choose Japanese or Chinese, you're offered the chance to specify which *kind* of character input you want. For Japanese, you can choose a QWERTY layout or a Kana keypad. For Simplified or Traditional Chinese, you have a choice of the Pinyin input method (which uses a QWERTY layout) or handwriting recognition, where you draw your symbols onto the screen with your fingertip; a palette of potential interpretations appears to the right. (That's handy, since there are thousands of characters in Chinese, and you'd need a 65-inch iPhone to fit the keyboard.) Or hey—it's a free tic-tac-toe game!

Now, when you arrive at any writing area in any app, you'll discover that a new icon has appeared on the keyboard: a tiny globe () next to the space bar. Each time you tap it, you rotate to the next keyboard you requested earlier. The new language's name appears briefly on the space bar to identify it.

Thanks to that ⊕ button, you can freely mix languages and alphabets within the same document without having to duck back to some control panel to make the change. And thanks to the iPhone's virtual keyboard, the actual letters on the "keys" change in real time. (As an Apple PR rep puts it, "That's really hard to do on a BlackBerry.")

The ⊕ button works in three ways:

- Tap it once to restore the most recent keyboard. Great if you're frequently flipping back and forth between two languages.

- Tap it rapidly to cycle among all the keyboards you've selected. (The name of the language appears briefly on the space bar to help you out.)

- If you, some United Nations translator, like to write in a lot of different languages, you don't have to tap that ⊕ key over and over again to cycle through the keyboard layouts. Instead, hold your finger down on the ⊕ key. You get a convenient pop-up menu of the languages you've turned on, so you can jump directly to the one you want.

The Emoji Keyboard

Even if you speak only one language, don't miss the Emoji keyboard. It gives you a palette of smileys and fun symbols, also known as emoticons, to use in your correspondence.

Install it just as you would any other keyboard, as described above. Now, though, when you choose its name from the onscreen keyboard, you get hundreds upon hundreds of little graphic symbols, spread across five categories (plus a Recently Used category). Each category offers several pages full of symbols, represented by tiny dots above the keyboard.

TIP: To return to a category's first page, you don't have to swipe; just tap the category's icon.

The bottom line is clear: Smileys are only the beginning.

NOTE: These symbols show up fine on Apple machinery (phones, tablets, Macs) but generally don't appear on other kinds of phones.

Connecting a Real Keyboard

This iPhone feature barely merits an asterisk in Apple's marketing materials. But if you're any kind of wandering journalist, blogger, or writer, you might flip your lid over this: You can type on a real, full-sized, plastic keyboard, and watch the text magically appear on your iPhone's screen—wirelessly.

That's because you can use a Bluetooth keyboard (the Apple Wireless Keyboard, for example) to type into your iPhone.

To set this up, from the Home screen, tap Settings→General→Bluetooth. Turn Bluetooth on, if it's not already.

Now turn on the wireless keyboard. After a moment, its name shows up on the iPhone screen in the Devices list; tap it. You'll know the pairing was successful, because when you tap in a spot where the onscreen keyboard would usually appear, well, it doesn't.

As you can probably imagine, typing is a lot easier and faster with a real keyboard than when you're trying to type on glass. As a bonus, the Apple keyboard's brightness, volume, and playback controls actually work to control the iPhone's brightness, volume, and playback.

> **TIP:** The Apple keyboard's ⏏ key even works: It makes the iPhone's onscreen keyboard appear or disappear. Oh, and to switch languages, press ⌘-space bar on the wireless keyboard. You'll see the list of languages. Tap the space bar again to choose a different language.

When you're finished using the keyboard, turn it off. The iPhone goes back to normal.

Cut, Copy, Paste

Copy and Paste do just what you'd expect. They let you grab some text off a Web page and paste it into an email message, copy directions from email into Notes, paste a phone number from your address book into a text message, and so on.

So how do you select text and trigger Cut, Copy, and Paste functions on a machine with no mouse and no menus? As on the Mac or PC, it takes three steps.

Step 1: Select the Text

Start by highlighting the text you want to cut or copy.

- **To select all.** Suppose you intend to cut or copy *everything* in the text box or message. In that case, tap anywhere in the text to place the blinking insertion point. Then tap the insertion point itself to summon the selection buttons—one of which is Select All.

- **To select some.** Double-tap the first word (or last word) that you want in the copied selection. That word is now highlighted, with blue dots at diagonal corners. Drag these handles to expand the selection to include all the text you want. The little magnifying loupe helps you release the dot at just the right spot.

Double-tap…

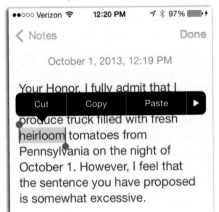

…drag the handle.

> **TIP:** On a Web page, you can't very well double-tap to select a word, because double-tapping means "zoom in." Instead, *hold your finger down* on a word to produce the blue handles; the loupe magnifies the proceedings to help you. (If you highlight the wrong word, keep your finger down and slide to the correct one; the highlighting goes with you.)
>
> However, if you're zoomed out to see the whole page, holding down your finger highlights the *entire block* of text (a paragraph or even a whole article) instead of one word. Now you can expand the selection to include a photo, if you like; that way, you can copy and paste the whole enchilada into an outgoing email message.

Step 2: Cut or Copy

At this point, you've highlighted the material you want, and the Cut and Copy buttons are staring you in the face. Tap **Cut** (to remove the selected text) or **Copy** (to leave it but place a duplicate on your invisible Clipboard).

> **TIP:** And what if you want to get rid of the text *without* copying it to the Clipboard (because you want to preserve something you copied earlier, for example)? Easy: Just tap the Delete key!

Step 3: Paste

Finally, switch to a different spot in the text, even if it's in a different window (for example, a new email message) or a different app (for example, Calendar or Notes). Tap in any spot where you're allowed to type. Tap the **Paste** button to paste what you cut or copied. Ta-da!

(Possible Step 4: Undo)

Everyone makes mistakes, right? Fortunately, there's a secret Undo command, which can come in handy when you cut, copy, or paste something by mistake.

The trick is to *shake* the iPhone. The iPhone then offers you an Undo button, which you can tap to confirm the backtracking. One finger touch instead of three.

> **TIP:** The shake-to-undo feature also works to undo *dictating or typing*— not just cutting or pasting.

In fact, you can even undo the Undo. Just shake the phone again; now the screen offers you a **Redo** button. Fun! (Except when you shake the phone by accident and you get the "Nothing to Undo" message. But still.)

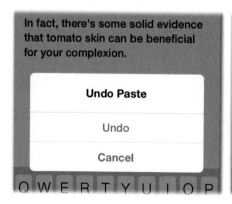

The Definitions Dictionary

Earlier in this chapter, you can read about the spelling dictionary that's built into the iOS—but that's just a dumb list of words. Your iPhone also has a *real* dictionary, one that shows you definitions.

You can look up any word that appears on the screen. Double-tap it to get the editing bar shown below at left; then tap Define. (You may have to tap the ▶ button to bring that button into view.)

TIP: You can also double-tap the blinking insertion point that's just before a word. On the editing bar, tap the ▶ button to see the Define button.

(If you discover that there are "No definitions found," tap Manage at the bottom of this screen for a list of dictionaries that you can download: English, French, Simplified Chinese, and so on. Tap ⬇ to download the ones you think you'll use.)

Speak!

As it turns out, the iPhone can read to you, too. Visit Settings→General→ Accessibility and turn on Speak Selection. Choose a language (or accent) and a speaking rate.

From now on, among the other buttons that pop up whenever you select text, a handy **Speak** button appears. (You can see it in the illustration on the previous page.)

You can use this feature whenever you want to double-check the pronunciation of a word, whenever you want to have a Web article or email read to you aloud while you're getting dressed for the day, or whenever you lose your voice and just want to communicate with the rest of the world.

> **TIP:** Once you tap **Speak**, the button changes to say **Pause**. It really means "stop," though, because if you tap it and then tap **Speak** again, speaking starts from the beginning.

Spotlight: Global Search

The iPhone's global search feature is called Spotlight. Just by typing a few letters, you can search almost the entire phone at once—or even the whole Web. Here's where it looks to find matches:

- **Applications.** For frequent downloaders, this may be the juiciest function: Spotlight searches the names of every single app on your iPhone. If you have dozens installed, this is a much more efficient way to find one than trying to page through all the Home screens, eyeballing the icons as you go. (You can even see which *folder* each app's in.)

- **Contacts.** First names, last names, and company names.

- **Music, Podcasts, Videos, Audiobooks.** Song, performer, and album names, plus the names of podcasts, videos, and audiobooks.

- **Notes, Reminders, Voice Memos.** The actual text of your notes and to-do items, and the names and descriptions of voice memos.

- **Events.** Calendar stuff: appointment names, meeting invitees, and locations (but not any notes attached to your appointments).

- **Mail.** The "To:," "From:," and "Subject:" fields of all accounts. For certain accounts, you can even search inside the messages.

- **Messages.** Yep, you can search your SMS text messages, too.

How to Open Spotlight

The Spotlight screen is built into your Home screens. To see it, drag downward *within* the screen. (If you drag down from the *top* by accident, you'll open the Notification Center, which is a different story.)

Now, in previous iOS versions, Spotlight was off to the *left* of your Home screens. Now it's *above* them. That's an improvement, because it means you can always jump to the search box immediately; in the olden days, if you were on your seventh Home screen, you'd have to swipe all the way back to the first Home screen, and then one more swipe to the left, to the Spotlight screen.

How to Search

The keyboard opens automatically (previous page, left). Begin typing to identify what you want to find and open. For example, if you were trying to find a file called **Pokémon Fantasy League,** typing just **pok** or **leag** would probably suffice. (Spotlight doesn't find text in the **middles** of words, though; it searches from the beginnings of words.)

As you type, a results list appears below the search box, listing everything Spotlight can find containing what you've typed so far.

They're neatly grouped by category; the beginning of each category is marked with a heading like CONTACTS or MUSIC.

 TIP: If you drag your finger to scroll the list, the keyboard helpfully vanishes so you can see more results.

If you see the name and icon of whatever you were hoping to dig up, tap to open it. The corresponding app opens automatically.

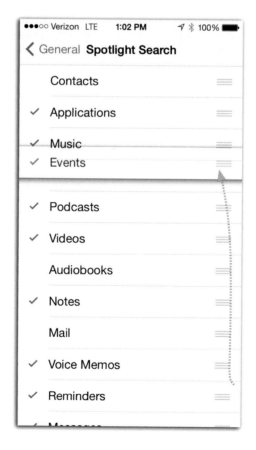

How to Tweak Spotlight

You've just read about how Spotlight works fresh out of the box. But you can tailor its behavior to fit it to the kinds of things you look up most often. To open Spotlight's settings, start on the Home screen. Tap Settings→General→Spotlight Search.

You can tweak Spotlight in two ways here:

- **Turn off categories.** The checkmarks identify the kinds of things that Spotlight tracks. If you find that Spotlight uses up precious screen space listing categories you don't use much, then tap to turn off their checkmarks. Now more of Spotlight's space-constrained screen is allotted to icon types you do care about.

- **Prioritize the categories.** This screen also lets you change the *order* of the category results; using the ≡ grip strip at the right side, you can drag an individual list item up or down.

  For example, the factory setting is for Contacts to appear first in the menu. But Contacts has its own search box, so it might make more sense to put Events or Applications at the top of the list so that it's quicker to do a schedule check or to fire up a certain app. You'll have less scrolling to do once the results menu appears.

3

Phone Calls & FaceTime

Despite its name, the original models of the iPhone were good at just about everything *except* making phone calls.

But with each successive model, Apple has improved the antennas, the circuitry, the speakers, the microphone, and the software. And new features like Siri, auto-reply, and Do Not Disturb have turned Apple's cell phone from an also-ran into one of the most useful gadgets ever to come with a two-year contract.

Dialing from the Phone App

Suppose you're in luck. Suppose the dots in the upper-left corner of the iPhone's screen tell you that you've got cellular reception. You're ready to start a conversation. To make a phone call, open the Phone app like this:

1. **Go Home, if you're not already there.** Press the Home button.

2. **Tap the Phone icon.** It's usually at the bottom of the Home screen. (The tiny circled number in the corner of the Phone icon tells you how many missed calls and voicemail messages you have.)

> **TIP:** Using Siri voice recognition is often faster. You should have good results saying things like, "Call Casey Robin's cell" or "Dial 866-2331."

Now you've arrived in the Phone program. A new row of icons appears at the bottom, representing the four ways of dialing from here:

- **Favorites list.** Here's the iPhone's version of speed-dial keys: It lists the 50 people you think you call most frequently. Tap a name to make the call. (Details on building and editing this list begin below.)

- **Recents list.** Every call you've recently made, answered, missed, or even just dialed appears in this list. Missed callers' names appear in red lettering, which makes them easy to spot—and easy to call back.

  Tap a name or a number to dial. Or tap the ⓘ button to view the details of a call—when, where, how long—and, if you like, to add this number to your Contacts list.

- **Contacts list.** This program also has an icon of its own on the Home screen; you don't have to drill down to it through the Phone button. It's your phone book; tap somebody's name or number to dial it.

- **Keypad.** This dialing pad may be virtual, but the buttons are a **heck** of a lot bigger than they are on regular cellphones, making them easy to tap, even with fat fingers. You can punch in any number and then tap Call to place the call.

Once you've dialed, no matter which method you used, either hold the iPhone up to your head, put in the earbuds, turn on the speakerphone, or put on your Bluetooth earpiece—and start talking!

The few short paragraphs above, however, are only the Quick Start Guide. Here's a more detailed look at each of the four Phone-app modules.

The Favorites List

You may not wind up dialing much from Contacts. That's the master list, all right, but it's too unwieldy when you just want to call your spouse, your boss, or your lawyer. Dialing by voice (Chapter 4) is almost always faster. But when silence is golden, at the very least use the Favorites list—a short, easy-to-scan list of the people you call most often.

You can add a phone number to this list (for dialing, texting, or FaceTime video calls) or an email address (for FaceTime).

You can add names to this list in any of three ways:

- **From the Favorites list itself.** Tap + to view your Contacts list. Tap the person you want. If there's more than one phone number or email address on the Info screen, then tap the one you want to add to Favorites.

> **TIP:** Each Favorite doesn't represent a **person;** it represents a **number or an email address.** So if your best friend, Chris, has both a home number and a cell number, add two items to the Favorites list. Gray lettering in the list lets you know whether each number or address is mobile, home, or whatever.

- **From the Contacts list.** Tap a name to open the Info screen, where you'll find a button called Add to Favorites. (If you have an email address for this person but no phone number, the iPhone treats it as a FaceTime favorite.) If there's more than one phone number on the Info screen, you're asked to tap the one you want to add to Favorites.

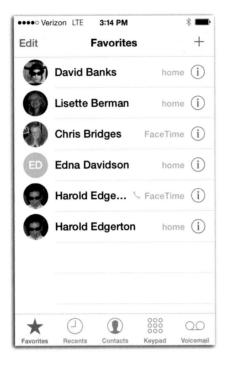

- **From the Recents list.** Tap ⓘ next to any name or number in the Recents list. If it's somebody who's already in your Contacts list, then you arrive at the Call Details screen, where one tap on Add to Favorites does what it says.

  If it's somebody who's not in Contacts yet, you'll have to **put** her there first. Tap Create New Contact, and then proceed as described on page 81. After you hit Save, you return to the Call Details screen so you can tap Add to Favorites.

TIP: To help you remember that a certain phone number or email address is already in your Favorites list, a blue star appears next to it in certain spots, like the Call Details screen and the Contact Info screen.

The Favorites list holds 50 numbers. Once you've added 50, the **Add to Favorites** and + buttons disappear.

> **TIP:** In iOS 7, the face of each Favorite peeks out of a round frame next to the name. (If your Contact card for that person doesn't have a photo, the circle shows the person's initials instead.) These identifying logos don't consume any additional vertical space, but they are optional. In **Settings→Phone**, turn off **Contact Photos in Favorites**.

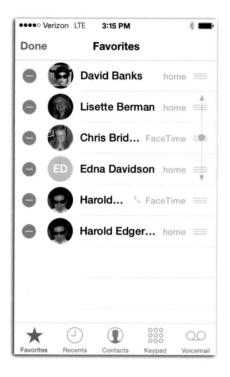

Reordering Favorites

Tapping that **Edit** button at the top of the Favorites list offers another handy feature, too: It lets you drag names up and down, so the most important people appear at the top of the list. Just use the grip strip (≡) as a handle to move entire names up or down the list.

Deleting from Favorites

To delete somebody from your Favorites—the morning after a nasty politi-cal argument over drinks, for example—use the iPhone's standard swipe-to-delete shortcut: Swipe leftward across the undesired name. Tap the Delete button that appears.

(If you're paid by the hour, you can use the slow method, too. Tap Edit. Now tap the ⊖ button next to the unwanted entry, and tap Delete to confirm.)

The Recents List

Like any self-respecting cellphone, the iPhone maintains a list of every-body you've called or who's called you recently. The idea, of course, is to provide you with a quick way to call someone you've been talking to lately.

To see the list, tap Recents at the bottom of the Phone app. You see a list of the last 75 calls that you've received or placed, along with each person's name or number (depending on whether that name is in Contacts or not), which phone number it is (mobile, home, work, or whatever), city of the caller's home area code (for callers not in your Contacts), and the date of the call.

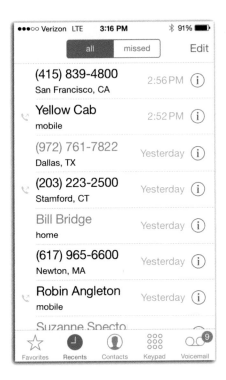

Here's what you need to know about the Recents list:

- Calls that you missed (or sent to voicemail) appear in red type. If you tap **Missed** at the top of the screen, you see *only* your missed calls. The color-coding and separate listings are designed to make it easy for you to return calls you missed, or to try again to reach someone who didn't answer when you called.

- A tiny icon lets you know which calls you *made* (to differentiate them from calls you *answered*).

- To call someone back—regardless of whether you answered or dialed the call—tap that name or number in the list.

- Tap ⓘ next to any call to open the Info screen. At the top of the screen, you can see whether this was an outgoing call, an incoming call, a missed call, or a canceled call (that's when you chickened out and hung up before your callee answered).

  What else you see here depends on whether or not the other person is in your Contacts list.

  If so, the Info screen displays the person's whole information card. A little table displays all the incoming and outgoing calls to or from this person that day. A star denotes a phone number that's also in your Favorites list.

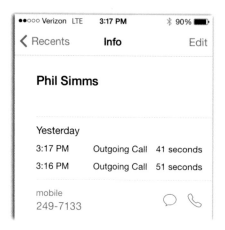
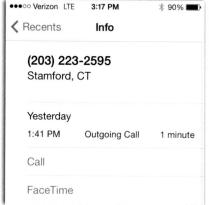

If the call *isn't* from someone in your Contacts, then you get to see a handy notation at the top of the Info screen: the city and state where the calling phone is registered.

- To save you scrolling, the Recents list thoughtfully combines consecutive calls to or from the same person. If some obsessed ex-lover has been calling you every 10 minutes for 4 hours, you'll see "Chris Meyerson (24)" in the Recents list. (Tap ⓘ to see the exact times of the calls.)

- You can erase one call from this list exactly the same way you'd delete a Favorite: Swipe leftward across the undesired name. Tap the Delete button that appears. (Once again, there's also a long way: Tap Edit, tap ⊖ next to the unwanted entry, and then tap Delete.)

  You can also erase the *entire* list, thus preventing a coworker or significant other from discovering your illicit activities: Tap Edit, and then tap Clear at the top of the screen. You're asked to confirm your decision.

Contacts

The Phone app may offer four ways to dial—Favorites, Recents, Contacts, and Keypad—but the Contacts list is the source from which all other lists spring. That's probably why it's listed three times: once with its own button on the Home screen, again at the bottom of the Phone app, and also in the FaceTime app.

Contacts is your address book—your master phone book.

> **TIP:** Your iPhone's own phone number appears at the very top of the Contacts list within the Phone module (not when you open the Contacts app from its Home screen icon). Drag down on the list to reveal its hiding place just below the search box.
>
> That's a much better place for it than deep at the end of a menu labyrinth, where it is on most phones.

If your social circle is longer than one screenful, then you can navigate this list in any of three ways.

First, you can savor the distinct pleasure of flicking through it.

Second, if you're in a hurry to get to the T's, use the A-to-Z index down the right edge of the screen. Just tap the first letter of the last name you're looking for. Alternatively, you can slide your finger up or down the index. The list scrolls in real time.

Third, you can use the search box at the very top of the list, above the A's.

Tap inside the search box to make the keyboard appear. As you type, Contacts pares down the list, hiding everyone whose first, last, or company name doesn't match what you've typed so far. It's a really fast way to pluck one name out of a haystack.

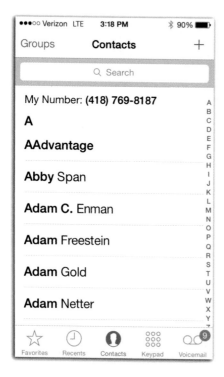 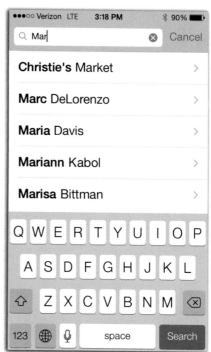

(You can clear the search box by tapping the ✖ at its right end, or restore the full list by tapping Cancel.)

In any case, when you see the name you want, tap it to open its card, filled with phone numbers and other info. Tap the number you want to dial.

Groups

Many computer address book programs, including OS X's Contacts app, let you place your contacts into *groups*—subsets like Book Club or Fantasy League Guys. You can't create or delete groups on the iPhone, but at least the groups from your Mac, PC, Exchange server, or iCloud account get synced over to it. To see them, and switch them all on or off at once, tap Groups at the top of the Contacts list.

Here's where Groups come into play:

- If you can't seem to find someone in the list, you may be looking in the wrong list. Tap Groups at the top-left corner to return to the list of accounts. Tap All Contacts to view a single, unified list of everyone your phone knows about.

- If you've allowed your iPhone to display your contacts from Facebook or Twitter, each of those lists is a group, too. (If your Contacts list seems hideously bloated with hundreds of people you never actually call, it's probably your Facebook list. Pop into Groups and touch All Facebook to hide them all at once.

- If you do use the Groups feature, remember to tap the group name you want *before* you create a new contact. That's how you put someone into an existing group. (If not, tap All Contacts instead.)

Adding to the Contacts List

Every cellphone has a Contacts list, of course, but the beauty of the iPhone is that you don't have to type in the phone numbers one at a time. Instead, the iPhone sucks in the entire phone book from your Mac or PC, iCloud, and/or an Exchange server at work.

It's infinitely easier to edit your address book on the computer, where you have an actual keyboard and mouse. The iPhone also makes it very easy to add someone's contact information when they call, email, FaceTime, or text message you, thanks to a prominent Add to Contacts button.

But if, in a pinch, on the road, at gunpoint, you have to add, edit, or remove a contact manually, here's how to do it.

Make sure you've selected the right Group or account, as described above. Now, on the Contacts screen, tap +. You arrive at the New Contact screen, which teems with empty boxes.

It shouldn't take you very long to figure out how to fill in this form: You tap in a box and type. But there are a few tips and tricks for the data-entry process:

- **The keyboard opens automatically** when you tap in a box. And the iPhone capitalizes the first letter of each name for you.

- **Phone numbers are special.** When you enter a phone number, the iPhone adds parentheses and hyphens for you. (You can even enter text phone numbers, like 1-800-GO-BROWNS; the iPhone converts them to digits when it dials.)

If you need to insert a pause—for dialing access numbers, extension numbers, or voicemail passwords—type **#,** which introduces a 2-second pause in the dialing. You can type several to create longer pauses.

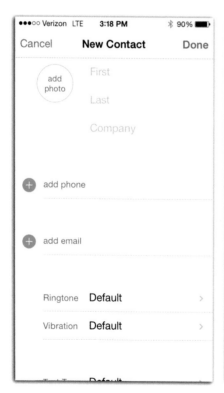 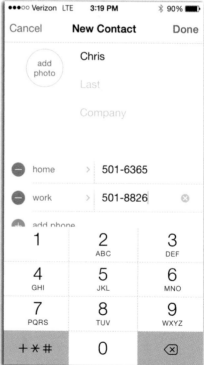

To change the label for a number ("mobile," "home," "work," and so on), tap the label that's there now. The Label screen shows you your choices. There's even a label called "iPhone," so you and your buddy can gloat together.

- **Expand-O-Fields mean you'll never run out of room.** Almost every field (empty box) on a Contacts card is infinitely expanding. That is, the instant you start filling in a field, another empty box (labeled add phone or whatever) appears right below it, so you can immediately add *another* phone number, email address, URL, street address, or whatever. (The only non-expanding fields are First, Last, Company, Ringtone, and the oddball fields you add yourself.)

For example, when you first create a card for someone, the phone-number box is labeled "mobile." If you start entering a phone number into it, a new, *second* empty phone-number box appears just below it (labeled "iPhone"—Apple's wishful thinking!), so you'll have a place to enter a second phone number for this person. When you do that, a *third* box appears. And so on.

There's always one empty field, so you can never run out of places to add more phone numbers, addresses, and so on. (Don't worry—the perpetual empty box doesn't appear once you're finished editing the person's card.)

- **You can add a photo of the person, if you like.** Tap add photo. If you have a photo of the person already, tap Choose Photo. You're taken to your photo collection, where you can find a good headshot (Chapter 7).

  Alternatively, tap Take Photo to activate the iPhone's built-in camera. Frame the person, and then tap the green camera button to snap the shot.

  In any case, you wind up with the **Move and Scale** screen (below, right). Here you can frame up the photo so that the person's face is nicely sized and centered. Spread two fingers to enlarge the photo; drag your finger to move the image within the frame. Tap Choose to commit the photo to the address book's memory. (Back on the Info screen where you started, a miniature version of the photo now appears. Tap edit if you want to change the photo, take a new one, adjust the Move and Scale screen, or get rid of the photo altogether.)

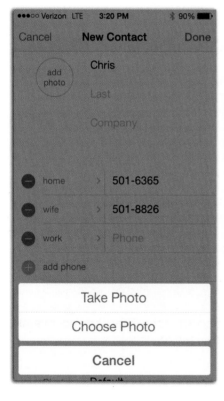

From now on, this photo will pop up whenever the person calls. It also appears next to the person's name in your Favorites list (if you haven't turned that feature off in Settings, of course).

- **Relatives are here.** In iOS 7, some new fields are available. There's the social profile field, where you can list somebody's Twitter, LinkedIn, Flickr, Facebook, and even MySpace addresses. There's an instant message field, too, where you can record addresses for chat networks like AIM or Yahoo Messenger.

  And there's add related name. Here's where you can specify this person's mother, father, spouse, partner, child, manager, sibling, and so on—or even type in a relationship that you make up (tap Add Custom Label).

NOTE: As you may discover in Chapter 4, Siri knows about all of your relationships. You can tell her to "Call my mom" or "Text my boss." Does the new add related name feature mean that you can now ask Siri to "Call my boss's mother" or "call Chris Robin's manager"?

Alas, no. These fields are for your reference only.

- **You can import photos from Facebook.** Here's a wild guess: Most of the photo boxes in your copy of Contacts are empty. After all, who's going to go to the trouble of hunting down headshots of 500 acquaintances, just for a fully illustrated Contacts list?

  Fortunately, with one click, iOS 7 can harvest headshots from the world's largest database of faces: Facebook.

  Visit Settings→Facebook to see the magical button: Update All Contacts. When you click it, the iPhone goes online for a massive research mission. Using your contacts' names and phone numbers as matching criteria, it ventures off to Facebook, finds the profile photos of everyone who's also on your Contacts list, and installs them into Contacts automatically. (If you already have a photo for somebody, don't worry; it doesn't get replaced.)

  As a handy bonus, this operation also adds the @facebook.com email addresses for the people you already had in Contacts.

Actually, there's another side effect of this operation: It also adds all your Facebook friends' names to your main Contacts list.

Now, you may not be crazy about this. Most of these Facebook folk you'll never call on the phone—yet here they are, cluttering up the Contacts list within the Phone app.

Fortunately, the Update All Contacts button doesn't *really* mix your Facebook friends in with your local Contacts list. It just subscribes to your Facebook address book—adds a new *group,* which you can turn off with one quick click; see page 81.

Even if you do choose to hide all their entries, you still get the benefit of the imported headshots and Facebook email addresses for the people you *do* want to see in Contacts.

- **You can import Twitter addresses.** In Settings→Twitter, the Update Contacts button awaits. Its purpose is to fill in the Twitter addresses for everyone who's already in your Contacts, matching them by phone number or email address.

- **You can choose a ringtone.** You can choose a different ringtone for each person in your address book. The idea is that you'll know by the sound of the ring who's calling you.

It's one tone per person, not per phone number. Of course, if you really want one ringtone for your buddy's cellphone and another for his home phone, you can always create a different Contacts card for each one.

To choose a ringtone, tap Default. On the next screen, tap any sound in the Ringtones or Alert Sounds lists to sample them. (Despite the separate lists, in this context, these sounds are all being offered as ringtones.) When you've settled on a good one, tap Done to return to the Info screen where you started.

- **You can specify a vibration pattern for incoming calls.** This unsung feature lets you assign a custom vibration pattern to each person in your Contacts, so you know by *feel* who's calling—without even removing the phone from your pocket, even if your ringer's off. It's a surprisingly useful option.

To set it up, tap Default next to the word vibration. You're offered a choice of canned patterns (Heartbeat, Rapid, S.O.S., and so on—below, left). But if you tap Create New Vibration, you can then tap the screen in whatever rhythm you like. It can be diddle diddle dee...or the opening notes to the Hallelujah Chorus...or the actual syllables of the person's name. ("Maryanna Beckleheimer." Can you feel it?)

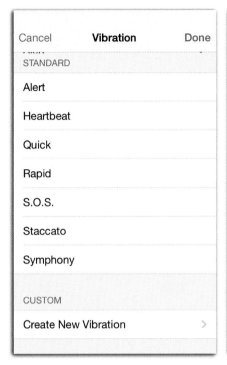

The phone records your pattern, which you can prove to yourself by tapping Play. If you tap Save and name that pattern, then it becomes one of the choices when you choose a vibration pattern for someone in your Contacts. It's what you'll feel whenever this person calls you. Yes, it's tactile caller ID. Wild.

- **You can also pick a text-message sound (and vibration).** Just as you can choose sounds and vibrations for incoming phone calls, the next two items (text tone, vibration) let you choose sounds and vibrations for incoming text messages and FaceTime invitations.

- **You can add new fields of your own.** Very cool: If you tap add field at the bottom of the screen, then you go down the rabbit hole into Field Land, where you can add any of 15 additional info bits about the person whose card you're editing: a prefix (like Mr. or Mrs.), a suffix (like M.D. or Esq.), a nickname, a job title, a birthday, an instant message address, a phonetic pronunciation for people with weird names, and so on.

When you tap one of these labels, you return to the Info screen, where you'll see that the iPhone has inserted the new, empty field in the most intelligent spot. For example, if you add a phonetic first name, that box appears just below the First Name box. The keyboard opens so you can fill in the blank.

- **You can link and unlink Unified Contacts.** As noted earlier, your phone can sync up with different accounts. Your Contacts app might list four sets of names and numbers: one stored on your phone, one from an iCloud account, one from Facebook, and a fourth from your corporate Exchange server at work. In the old days, therefore, certain names might have shown up in the All Contacts list two or three times—not an optimal situation.

Now, as a favor to you, the iPhone displays each person's name only once in that master All Contacts list. If you tap that name, you open up a unified information screen for that person. It includes *all* the details from *all* the underlying cards from that person.

NOTE: The iPhone combines cards in the All Contacts list only if the first and last names are exactly the same. If there's a difference in name, suffix, prefix, or middle name, no unifying takes place. Remember, too, that you see the unification only if you view the All Contacts list.

To see which cards the iPhone is combining for you, scroll to the bottom of the card. There the Linked Contacts section shows you which cards have been unified.

Here you can tap a listing to open the card in the corresponding account. For that matter, you can manually link a card, too; tap Edit, tap link contacts, and then choose a contact to link to this unified card—even if the name isn't a perfect match.

NOTE: It's OK to link Joe Carnelia's card with Joseph Carnelia's card—they're probably the same person. But don't link up *different* people's cards. Remember, the whole point is to make the iPhone combine all the phone numbers, email addresses, and so on onto a single card—and seeing two sets on one card could get confusing fast.

This stuff gets complex. But, in general, the iPhone tries to do the right thing. For example, if you edit the information on the unified card, you're changing that information only on the card in the corresponding account. (Unless you *add* information to the unified card. In that case, the new data tidbit is added to *all* the underlying source-account cards.)

NOTE: To delete any info bit from a Contacts card, tap ⊖ next to it, and then tap the red Delete button to confirm.

Adding a Contact on the Fly

There's actually another way to add someone to your Contacts list—a faster, on-the-fly method that's more typical of cellphones. Start by bringing the phone number up on the screen:

- In the Phone app, open the **Keypad**. Dial the number, and then tap **Add to Contacts**.

- You can also add a number that's in your Recents (recent calls) list, storing it in Contacts for future use. Tap the ⓘ button next to the name.

In both cases, finish up by tapping **Create New Contact** (to enter this person's name for the first time) or **Add to Existing Contact** (to add a new phone number to the card of someone who's already in your list). Off you go to the Contacts editing screen shown on page 82.

Editing Someone

To make corrections or changes, tap the person's name in the Contacts list. In the upper-right corner of the Info card, tap **Edit**.

You return to the screens already described, where you can make whatever changes you like. To edit a phone number, for example, tap it and change away. Or, to delete a number (or any other info bit), tap the ⊖ button next to it, and then tap **Delete** to confirm.

After you tap **Done** (or **Cancel**), you can return to the Contacts list by swiping to the right.

Deleting Someone

Truth is, you'll probably *add* people to your address book far more often than you'll *delete* them. After all, you meet new people all the time—but you delete people primarily when they die, move away, or dump you.

To zap someone, tap the name in the Contacts list and then tap **Edit**. Scroll down, tap **Delete Contact**, and confirm by tapping **Delete Contact** again. (Weirdly, the **Delete Contact** option doesn't appear if you open someone's info card from the Recents or Favorites lists—only from the main Contacts list.)

Sharing a Contact

There's a lot of work involved in entering someone's contact information. It would be thoughtful, therefore, if you could spare the next guy all that effort—by sending a fully formed electronic business card to him. It can be yours or that of anyone in your Contacts list.

To do that, open the contact's card, scroll to the bottom, and tap **Share Contact**. On the Share sheet, you're offered a choice of **AirDrop**, **Message**, or **Mail**. ("Message" means an iMessage—page 154—if it's a fellow Apple fan, or a text message otherwise. AirDrop is described on page 206.)

Tap your choice, address the message (to an email address or, for a message, a cellphone number), and send it. The recipient, assuming he has a half-decent smartphone or address-book program on the receiving end, can install that person's information with a single tap on the attachment.

> **TIP:** Ever meet someone and wish you could just exchange business cards electronically, iPhone to iPhone? AirDrop is the answer.
>
> Unless your technologically challenged pal doesn't have iOS 7. In that case, you can use the free app Bump. If you both have this app, then adding your address-book cards to each other's Contacts lists is as easy as literally bumping your iPhone-holding fists together. Wirelessly. Without having to type anything at all.

The Keypad

The fourth way to place a call is to tap **Keypad** at the bottom of the screen. The standard iPhone dialing pad appears. It's just like the number pad on a normal cellphone, except that the "keys" are much bigger and you can't feel them.

To make a call, tap out (or paste) the phone number—use the ⊗ key to backspace if you make a mistake—and then tap the green **Call** button.

You can also use the keypad to enter a phone number into your Contacts list, thanks to the **Add to Contacts** button, as described earlier.

Answering Calls

When someone calls your iPhone, you'll know it; three out of your five senses are alerted. Depending on how you've set up your iPhone, you'll *hear* a ring, *feel* a vibration, and *see* the caller's name and photo fill that giant iPhone screen. (Smell and taste will have to wait until iOS 8.)

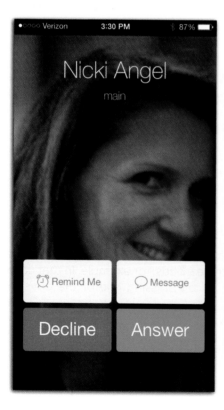
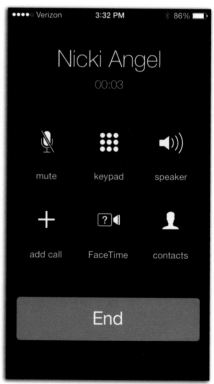

NOTE: For details on choosing a ringtone and on Vibrate mode, see page 514.

How you answer depends on what's happening at the time:

- **If you're using the iPhone,** tap the green Answer button. Tap End when you've both said enough.

- **If the iPhone is asleep or locked,** the screen lights up and says slide to answer. If you slide your finger as indicated by the arrow, you simultaneously unlock the phone and answer the call.

- **If you're wearing earbuds,** the music fades out and then pauses; you hear the ring both through the phone's speaker and through your earbuds. Answer by squeezing the clicker on the earbud cord or by using either of the methods already described.

  When the call is over, you can click again to hang up—or just wait until the other guy hangs up. Either way, the music fades in again and resumes from the spot where you were so rudely interrupted.

  Same thing if you were watching a video; it pauses for the duration of the call and then resumes when you hang up.

Multitasking

Don't forget, by the way, that the iPhone is a multitasking master. Once you're on the phone, you can dive into any other program—to check your calendar, for example—without interrupting the call.

If you're in a WiFi hotspot or if you have a GSM connection (AT&T or T-Mobile), you can even surf the Web, check your email, or use the other Internet functions of the iPhone without interrupting your call. (If you have Sprint or Verizon in the U.S., and you're not in a WiFi hotspot, you can't get online until the call is complete.)

Silencing the Ring

Sometimes you need a moment before you can answer the call; maybe you need to exit a meeting or put in the earbuds, for example. In that case, you can stop the ringing and vibrating by pressing one of the physical buttons on the edges (the Sleep/Wake button or either volume key). The caller still hears the phone ringing, and you can still answer it within the first four rings, but at least the sound won't be annoying those around you.

(This assumes, of course, that you haven't just flipped the silencer switch.)

Not Answering Calls

There are all kinds of reasons why you might not want to accept an incoming call. Maybe you're in a meeting. Maybe you're driving. Maybe you can see that the call is coming from someone you *really* don't want to deal with right now.

Fortunately, you've chosen the right phone. You have all kinds of juicy ways to slam the cellular door in somebody's face.

Ignore It—or Dump It to Voicemail

If you wait long enough (four rings), the call will go to voicemail (even if you silence the ringing/vibrating as described above).

Or you can dump it to voicemail *immediately* (instead of waiting for the four rings). How you do that depends on the setup:

- **If the iPhone is asleep or locked,** tap the Sleep button twice fast.
- **If you're using the iPhone,** tap the Decline button on the screen.
- **If you're wearing the earbuds,** squeeze the microphone clicker for 2 seconds. You hear two low beeps, meaning: "OK, master; dumped."

Of course, if your callers know you have an iPhone, they'll also know that you've deliberately dumped them into voicemail—because they won't hear all four rings.

Respond with a Text Message

Whenever your phone rings, the screen bears a big Message button (shown on page 92). If you tap it, you get a choice of three canned text messages. Tapping one immediately dumps the caller to voicemail and sends the corresponding text message to the phone that's calling you. If you're driving or in a meeting, this feature is a lot more polite and responsive than just dumping the poor slob to voicemail.

Tap I'll call you later, for example, to send a text message to whomever's calling you saying, "Can't talk right now...I'll call you later."

> **TIP:** You can edit any of these three canned messages; they don't have to say, "I'm on my way" and "What's up?" forever. To do that, open Settings→Phone, tap Reply with Text, and replace the text in the three placeholder boxes.

The fourth button, **Custom**, lets you type out a new message on the spot ("I'm in a meeting and, frankly, your call isn't worth getting fired for" comes to mind).

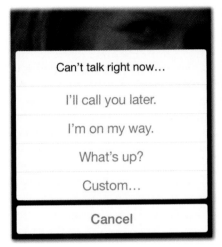
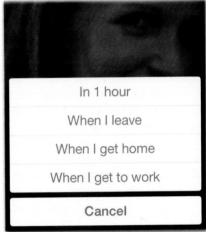

Remind Me Later

The trouble with **Reply with Message**, of course, is that it sends a text message. What if the caller is using a landline that can't receive text messages? Fortunately, you have another option: **Remind Me**.

Tapping this button offers you one time-based option, **In 1 Hour** (which sets up a reminder to return the call an hour from now), and three location-based options (above, right): **When I leave**, **When I get home**, and **When I get to work**. (The home and work options appear only if the iPhone *knows* your home and work addresses—because you've entered them in your own card in Contacts.)

These options use the phone's GPS circuitry to detect when you've left your current inconvenient-to-take-the-call location, whether it's a job interview, a first date, or an outhouse.

Do Not Disturb

When you turn on Do Not Disturb, the phone is quiet, dark, and still. It doesn't ring, chirp, vibrate, light up, or display messages. (A ☾ icon appears on the status bar to remind you why it seems to be so uncharacteristically depressed.)

Yes, Airplane mode does the same thing, but there's a big difference: In Do Not Disturb, **the phone is still online.** Calls, texts, emails, and other communications continue to chug happily away; they just don't draw attention to themselves.

Do Not Disturb is what you want when you're in bed each night. You don't really want to be bothered with chirps for Facebook status updates and Twitter posts, but it's fine for the phone to collect them for the morning.

Bedtime is why Do Not Disturb comes with two fantastic additional settings: one that turns it on and off automatically on a schedule, so that the phone goes dark each night at the same time you do, and another that lets you designate important people whose calls and texts are allowed to get through. You know—for emergencies.

Turning on Do Not Disturb

To turn on Do Not Disturb manually, you have three options:

- Tell Siri, "Turn on Do Not Disturb."

- Swipe upward to open the Control Center, and tap the ☾ icon so that it turns white.

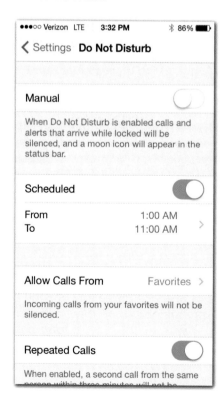

- Open Settings, tap **Do Not Disturb**, and tap **Manual**.

To set it up on a schedule, visit **Settings→Do Not Disturb**. Turn on **Scheduled**, and then tap the **From/To** block to specify starting and ending hours. (There's no separate setting for weekends; Do Not Disturb will turn on and off for the same hours every day of the week.)

Allowing Special Callers Through

What if your child, your boss, or your elderly parent needs you urgently in the middle of the night? Turning the phone off completely, or putting it into Airplane mode, would leave you unreachable in an emergency.

That's why Apple built in the Allow Calls From option. When you open **Settings→Do Not Disturb** and then tap **Allow Calls From**, you're offered options like **Everyone** (all calls and texts come through), **No One** (the phone is still online, but totally silent), or **Favorites**, which may be the most useful option of all.

That setting permits calls and texts from anybody you've designated as a Favorite in the Phone app. Since those are the people you call most often, it's fairly likely they're the most important people in your life.

You can also create an arbitrary group of people—just your mom and sister, just your boss and nephew, whatever. You have to create these address-book groups on your computer, but once you've done that, you can designate any group as the lucky exceptions to Do Not Disturb.

One More Safety Measure

The Do Not Disturb settings screen also offers something called **Repeated Calls**. If you turn this on, then if *anybody* tries to call you more than once within 3 minutes, they'll ring through.

The idea here is that nobody *would* call you multiple times unless they needed to reach you urgently. You certainly wouldn't want Do Not Disturb to block somebody who's trying to tell you that there's been an accident, that you've overslept, or that you've just won the lottery.

Locked vs. Unlocked

The final option on the settings screen, new in iOS 7, is the Silence option. If you choose **Always**, then Do Not Disturb works exactly as described above.

But if you choose **Only while iPhone is locked**, then the phone *does* ring and vibrate *when you're using it*. Because, obviously, if the phone is awake, so are you. It's a great way to ensure that you don't miss important calls if you happened to have awakened early today and started working.

Fun with Phone Calls

Whenever you're on a call, the iPhone makes it pitifully easy to perform stunts like turning on the speakerphone, putting someone on hold, taking a second call, and so on. Here are the options you get when you're on a call.

Mute

Tap this button to mute your own microphone, so the other guy can't hear you. (You can still hear him, though.) Now you have a chance to yell upstairs, to clear the phlegm from your throat, or to do anything else you'd rather the other party not hear. Tap again to unmute.

Keypad

Sometimes you have to input touchtones, which is generally a perk only of phones with physical dialing keys. For example, that's usually how you operate home answering machines when you call in for messages, and it's often required by automated banking, reservations, and conference-call systems.

Tap this button to produce the traditional iPhone dialing pad. Each digit you touch generates the proper touchtone for the computer on the other end to hear.

When you're finished, tap Hide to return to the dialing-functions screen, or tap End if your conversation is complete.

Speaker

Tap this button to turn on the iPhone's built-in speakerphone—a great hands-free option when you're caught without your earbuds or Bluetooth headset. (In fact, the speakerphone doesn't work if the earbuds are plugged in or if a Bluetooth headset is connected.)

When you tap the button, it turns white to indicate that the speaker is activated. Now you can put the iPhone down on a table or a counter and have a conversation with both hands free. Tap speaker again to channel the sound back into the built-in earpiece.

> **TIP:** The speaker is on the bottom edge of the phone. If you're having trouble hearing it, and the volume is all the way up, consider pointing the speaker toward you, or even cupping one hand around the bottom to direct the sound.

Add Call (Conference Calling)

The iPhone is all about software, baby, and that's nowhere more apparent than in its facility at handling multiple calls at once.

The simplicity and reliability of this feature put other cellphones to shame. Never again, in attempting to answer a second call, will you have to tell the first person, "If I lose you, I'll call you back."

As you'll read here, however, this feature is much better on a GSM phone (AT&T or T-Mobile) than a CDMA phone (Verizon or Sprint).

Suppose you're on a call. Here are some of the tricks you can do:

- **Make an outgoing call.** Tap add call. The iPhone puts the first person on hold—neither of you can hear the other—and returns you to the Phone app and its various phone-number lists. You can now make a second call just the way you made the first. The top of the screen makes clear that the first person is still on hold as you talk to the second.

- **Receive an incoming call.** What happens when a second call comes in while you're already on a call?

  To answer on a GSM phone, tap End Call + Answer. On a CDMA phone, tap End Current Call; the new call makes the phone ring again, at which point you can answer it normally. Weird but true.

  You can also tap End Current Call (answer the incoming call, hang up on the first) or Decline Incoming Call (meaning "Send to voicemail").

When you're on two calls at once, the top of the screen identifies both other parties. Two new buttons appear, too:

- **Swap** (GSM phones only) lets you flip between the two calls. At the top of the screen, you see the names or numbers of your callers. One says HOLD (the one who's on hold, of course) and the other bears a time counter, which lets you know whom you're actually speaking to.

  Think how many TV and movie comedies have relied on the old "Whoops, I hit the wrong button and now I'm bad-mouthing somebody directly to his face instead of behind his back!" gag. That can't happen on the iPhone.

  You can swap calls by tapping swap or by tapping the HOLD person's name or number.

- **Merge Calls** combines your two calls so all three of you can converse at once. Now the top of the screen announces, "Bill O'Reilly & Jon Stewart" (or whatever the names of your callers are). Note that on a CDMA phone, you can merge calls only if *you placed* the second call—not if it was incoming.

> **TIP:** On a GSM phone, you can now tap ⓘ next to someone's name; at this point, you can drop someone from the call by tapping End, or talk privately with someone by tapping Private. Tap Merge Calls to return to the group call.

This business of combining calls into one doesn't have to stop at two. At any time, you can tap Add Call, dial a third number, and then tap Merge to combine it with your first two. And then a fourth call, and a fifth. With you, that makes six people on the call.

Then your problem isn't technological, it's social, as you try to conduct a meaningful conversation without interrupting one another.

> **NOTE:** Just remember that if you're on the phone with five people at once, you're using up your monthly cellular minutes five times as fast. Better save those conference calls for weekends!

FaceTime

Tap this button to switch from your current phone call into a face-to-face video call, using the FaceTime app described below.

(This feature requires that both you and the other guy have iPhone 4 or later.)

Hold

The FaceTime button appears in place of what, on earlier iPhones, was the Hold button. But you can still trigger the Hold function—by holding down the Mute button for a couple of seconds. Now, neither you nor the other guy can hear anything. Tap again to resume the conversation.

Contacts

This button opens the address book program so you can look up a number or place another call.

FaceTime Video Calls

Your iPhone, as you're probably aware, has two cameras—one on the back and one on the front. And that can mean only one thing: Video calling has arrived.

The iPhone was not the first phone to be able to make video calls. But it is the first one that can make *good* video calls, reliably, with no sign-up or setup, with a single tap. The picture and audio are generally rock-solid, with very little delay, and it works the first time and every time. Now Grandma can see the baby, or you can help someone shop from afar, or you can supervise brain surgery from thousands of miles away (some medical training is recommended).

You can enjoy these *Jetsons* fantasies not just when calling other iPhones; you can also make video calls between iPhones and iPads, iPod Touches, and Macs. You can even place these calls when you're not in a WiFi hotspot, over the cellular airwaves, when you're out and about.

Being able to make video calls like a regular cellphone call is a huge convenience. Never again will you return home from the store and get scolded for buying the wrong size, style, or color.

In any case, FaceTime couldn't be easier to fire up—in many different ways:

- **When you're already on a phone call with someone.** This is a good technique when you want to ask first if the other guy *wants* to do video, or when you've been chatting and suddenly there's some *reason* to do video. In any case, there's nothing to it: Just tap the FaceTime icon that's right on the screen when you pull the phone away from your face. (Your buddy can either accept or, if he just got out of the shower, decline.)

- **From the FaceTime app.** You can also start up a videochat without placing a phone call first. That's handy when you have WiFi but no cell signal; FaceTime can make the call even when Verizon can't.

Of course, if you're not already on a call, the iPhone doesn't yet know whom you want to call. So you have to tell it.

Open the FaceTime app (new in iOS 7). It works just like the Contacts app: There are three tabs at the bottom.

Contacts is your entire address book; find a name, tap it, and then tap ☐◁ to place the call. (And if you plan to video-call this person a lot, also tap Add to Favorites.)

Recents shows a list of your recent FaceTime calls. Tap a name to place a new call to that person, or tap ⓘ to view a history of your calls with that person (and buttons for placing new ones).

And Favorites, of course, is a speed-dial list of people you plan to call often.

- **From Contacts.** In the Contacts app, if you tap a person's name, you'll find buttons that place FaceTime calls. Or, in the Phone app, call up your Favorites or Recents list. Tap ⓘ next to a name to open the contact's card; tap FaceTime.

- **From Messages.** If you're chatting away with somebody by text and you realize that typing is no longer appropriate for the conversation, tap Contact at the top of the screen. Tap ☐◁.

At this point, the other guy receives an audio and video message inviting him to a chat. If he taps Accept, then you're on. You're on each other's screens, seeing and hearing each other in real time. (You appear on your own screen, too, in a little inset window. It's spinach-in-your-teeth protection.)

Once the chat has begun, here's some of the fun you can have:

- **Rotate the screen.** FaceTime works in either portrait (upright) or landscape (widescreen) view; just turn your phone 90 degrees. Of course, if your calling partner doesn't *also* turn her gadget, she'll see your picture all squished and tiny, with big black areas filling the rest of the screen. (On the Mac, the picture rotates automatically when your partner's gadget rotates. You don't have to turn the computer 90 degrees.)

- **Show what's in front of you** Sometimes, you'll want to show your friend what you're looking at. That is, you'll want to turn on the camera on the *back* of the iPhone, the one pointing away from you, to show off the baby, the artwork, or the broken engine part.

  That's easy enough; just tap 🔄 on your screen. The iPhone switches from the front camera to the back camera. Now you and your callee can both see what you're seeing. (It's a lot less awkward than using a laptop for this purpose, because with the laptop's camera facing away from you, you can't see what you're showing.)

  Tap 🔄 again to return to the front camera.

- **Snap a commemorative photo.** You can immortalize a chat by using the screenshot keystroke (**Sleep + Home**). You'll wind up with a still photo of your videochat in progress, safely nestled in the Camera Roll of your Photos app.

- **Mute the audio.** Tap 🎤 to silence the audio that you're sending. Great when you need to yell at the kids.

- **Mute the video.** When you leave the FaceTime app for any reason (press the **Home** button and then open a different program, if you like), the other guy's screen goes black. He can't see what you're doing when you leave the FaceTime screen. He can still hear you, though.

This feature was designed to let you check your calendar, look something up on the Web, or whatever, while you're still chatting. But it's also a great trick when you need to adjust your clothing, pick your nose, or otherwise shield your activity from whomever's on the other end.

In the meantime, the call is, technically, still in progress—and a green banner at the top of the Home screen reminds you of that. Tap there, on the green bar, to return to the video call.

When you and your buddy have had quite enough, tap the **End** button to terminate the call. (Although it's easy to jump from phone call to video-chat, there's no way to go the other direction.)

And marvel that you were alive to see the day.

FaceTime Audio Calls

You might imagine that, on the great timeline of Apple technologies, audio calling would have arrived *before* video calling. But no; free Internet audio calls didn't come to the iPhone until iOS 7.

And it's a big, big deal. Video calling is neat and all, but be honest: Don't you find yourself making *phone* calls more often? Video calling forces us to be "on," neatly dressed and well behaved, because we're on camera. Most of the time, we're perfectly content (in fact, *more* content) with audio only.

And with FaceTime audio, the call is free. These calls don't eat into your cellphone minutes and aren't transmitted over your cell carrier's voice network; instead, these are *Internet* calls.

When you're in a WiFi hotspot, they're completely free. When you're not, your carrier's data network carries your voice. Use FaceTime audio a lot, and you might even be able to downgrade your calling plan to a less expensive one.

Sold yet?

All right: Here's how to make a free Internet voice call.

You start out exactly as you would when making a video call, as described earlier. That is, you can start from the FaceTime app, the Contacts app, the Phone app, Messages, and so on.

In each spot that FaceTime is available, you get a choice of two types of calls: **Video** (□◁) and **Audio** (✆). (In Messages, if you tap the ✆, you get a choice of your two voice options: **Voice Call** and **FaceTime Audio**.)

When you place an audio FaceTime call, the other person's phone rings exactly as though you'd placed a regular phone call. All the usual buttons and options are available: **Remind Me, Message, Decline, Answer**, and so on.

Once you accept the call, it's just like being on a phone call, too: You have the options **Mute, Speaker, FaceTime** (that is, "switch to video") and **Contacts**. (What's missing? The **Keypad** button and the **Merge Calls** button. You can't combine FaceTime audio calls with each other, or with regular cellphone calls. If a cellphone call comes in, you'll be offered the chance to take it—but you'll have to hang up on FaceTime.)

Actually, it's better than being on a phone call in two ways. First, you don't have the usual lag time that throws off your comic timing. And, second, the audio quality is amazing—more like FM radio than cellular.

You'd be wise to force yourself to try out FaceTime audio calls. Whenever you're calling another iPhone, iPad, iPod Touch, or Mac owner, you'll save money and minutes by placing these better-sounding free calls.

4

Speech Recognition —and Siri

Before you make up your mind about Siri, the iPhone's famous speech-recognition feature, just keep one thing in mind: Siri is not one but *two* features.

First, there's *dictation,* where the phone types out everything you say. It's really handy, and it's much faster than typing on glass—but it's not 100 percent accurate. Plenty of people get so frustrated that they just give up on it.

Second, there's Siri the *voice-controlled minion*—and this part works fantastically. You can say, "Wake me up at 7:45," or "What's Chris's work number?" or "How do I get to the airport?" or "What's the weather going to be like in San Francisco this weekend?"

You can say, "Make a note to rent *Titanic* this weekend." Or "How many days until Valentine's Day?" Or "Play some Electric Light Orchestra."

You can also ask questions about movies, sports, and restaurants. In each case, Siri thinks for a few seconds, displays a beautifully formatted response, and speaks in a calm voice.

In iOS 7, Siri is much better. She responds faster, her voice has been replaced with a more natural-sounding one (and you now have the option to hear a male voice), and she understands more requests. For example, you can now ask her to open the major Settings panels ("Open WiFi settings") or make adjustments to the phone itself ("Turn up the brightness" or "Turn on Bluetooth").

This chapter covers both personalities of Siri for the iPhone 4s and later, plus one more speech technology: the speak-to-dial feature of the iPhone 4.

Speak to Type

Siri's dictation feature (iPhone 4s and later) lets you enter text anywhere, into any program, just by speaking. (Behind the scenes, it's using the same Nuance recognition technology that powers the Dragon line of dictation programs.)

Suddenly you don't have to fuss with the tiny keyboard. The experience of "typing" is no longer claustrophobic. You can blather away into an email, fire off a text message, or draft a memo without ever looking at the screen.

Now, before you get all excited, here are the necessary footnotes:

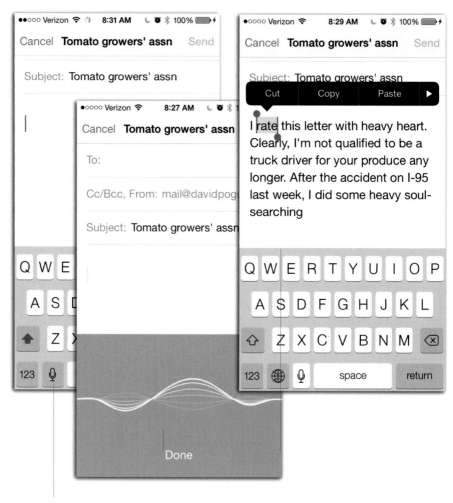

1. Tap microphone to dictate.   2. Speak smoothly but clearly, and then tap Done.   3. Make your corrections.

- Voice typing works only when you have an Internet connection. If you don't, the little 🎤 button on the keyboard doesn't even appear.

- Voice typing works best if there's not a lot of background noise.

- Voice typing isn't always practical, since everybody around you can hear what you're saying.

- Voice typing isn't always accurate, either. Often, you'll have to correct an error or two.

All right—expectations set? Then here's how to type by speaking.

First, fire up someplace where you can call up the keyboard: Messages, Notes, Mail, Safari, whatever. Tap, if necessary, so that the onscreen keyboard appears.

See the 🎤 next to the space bar? Tap that (facing page, step 1).

When you hear the xylophone note, say what you have to say (facing page, step 2). If there's background noise, hold the phone up to your head; if it's relatively quiet, a couple of feet away is fine. You don't have to speak slowly, loudly, or weirdly; speak normally. A cool, animated, live "sound wave" dances to the sound of your voice.

You have to speak your own punctuation, like this: "Dear Dad (colon): Please send money (dash)—as much as you can (comma), please (period)." The table at the end of this section describes all the different punctuation symbols you can dictate.

After you finish speaking, tap Done. Your iPhone plays another xylophone note—higher, this time—and transmits the audio data to distant computers. They analyze your speech and transmit the resulting typed-out text back to your iPhone. (During this time, a whirling spinner occupies the text area where you dictated.) The transcribed text appears all at once, in a big blob, as shown in step 3 on the facing page.

NOTE: Sometimes the spinner whirls away—but when it stops, no text appears at all. That usually means your Internet connection isn't good enough, or that the transcription service is busy. You can try again, or you can just sigh and resort to typing with your finger.

If the transcription contains errors, you can tap with your finger to edit them, exactly as you would fix an error in something you typed (Chapter 2). (Make the effort; you're simultaneously teaching your iPhone to do better the next time.) Or, if the whole thing is a mess, you can *shake* your iPhone, which is the universal gesture for Undo.

Usually, you'll find the accuracy pretty darned good, considering you didn't have to train the software to recognize your voice, and considering that your computer is a **cellphone,** for crying out loud. You'll also find that the accuracy is better when you dictate complete sentences, and that long words fare better than short ones.

Punctuation

Here's a handy table that shows you what punctuation you can say and how to say it.

Say this:	To get this:	For example, saying this:	Types this:
"period" or "full stop"	. [space and capital letter afterward]	"Best (period) date (period) ever (period)"	Best. Date. Ever.
"dot" or "point"	. [no space afterward]	"My email is frank (dot) smith (at sign) gmail (dot) com"	My email is frank.smith@ gmail.com
"comma," "semicolon," "colon"	, ; :	"Mom (comma) hear me (colon) I'm dizzy (semi-colon) tired"	Mom, hear me: I'm dizzy; tired
"question mark," "excla-mation point"	? ! [space and capital letter afterward]	"Ellen (question mark) Hi (excla-mation point)"	Ellen? Hi!

Say this:	To get this:	For example, saying this:	Types this:
"inverted question mark," "inverted exclamation point"	¿ ¡	"(inverted question mark) Que paso (question mark)"	¿Que paso?
"ellipsis" or "dot dot dot"	…	"Just one (ellipsis) more (ellipsis) step (ellipsis)"	Just one… more…step…
"space bar"	[a space, especially when a hyphen would normally appear]	"He rode the merry (space bar) go (space bar) round"	He rode the merry go round
"open paren" then "close paren" (or "open bracket/ close bracket," or "open brace/ close brace")	( ) or [ ] or { }	"Then she (open paren) the doctor (close paren) gasped"	Then she (the doctor) gasped
"new line"	[a press of the Return key]	"milk (new line) bread (new line) Cheez Whiz"	milk bread Cheez Whiz
"new paragraph"	[two presses of the Return key]	"autumn leaves (new paragraph) softly falling"	autumn leaves softly falling
"quote," then "unquote"	" "	Her perfume screamed (quote) available (unquote)	Her perfume screamed "available"
"numeral"	[writes the following number as a digit instead spelling it out]	"Next week she turns (numeral) eight"	Next week she turns 8

Say this:	To get this:	For example, saying this:	Types this:
"asterisk," "plus sign," "minus sign," "equals sign"	*, +, −, =	"numeral eight (asterisk) two (plus sign) one (minus sign) three (equals sign) fourteen"	8*2+1−3=14
"ampersand," "dash"	&, —	"Barry (ampersand) David (dash) the best (exclamation point)"	Barry & David—the best!
"hyphen"	- [without spaces]	"Don't give me that holier (hyphen) than (hyphen) thou attitude"	Don't give me that holier-than-thou attitude
"backquote"	'	"Back in (backquote) (numeral) fifty-two"	back in '52
"smiley," "frowny," "winky" (or "smiley face," "frowny face," "winky face")	:-) :-(;-)	"I think you know where I'm going with this (winky face)."	I think you know where I'm going with this ;-)

You can also say "percent sign" (%), "at sign" (@), "dollar sign" ($), "cent sign" (¢), "euro sign" (€), "yen sign" (¥), "pounds sterling sign" (£), "section sign" (§), "copyright sign" (©), "registered sign" (®), "trademark sign" (™), "greater-than sign" or "less-than sign" (> or <), "degree sign" (°), "caret" (^), "tilde" (~), "vertical bar" (|), and "pound sign" (#).

The software automatically capitalizes the first new word after a period, question mark, or exclamation point. But you can also force it to capitalize words you're dictating by saying "cap" right before the word, like this: "Dear (cap) Mom, I've run away to join (cap) The (cap) Circus (comma), a nonprofit cooperative for runaway jugglers."

Here's another table—this one shows the other commands for capitalization, plus spacing and spelling commands.

TIP: Speak each of the on/off commands as a separate utterance, with a small pause before and after.

Say this:	To get this:	For example, saying this:	Types this:
"cap" or "capital"	Capitalize the next word	"Give me the (cap) works"	Give me the Works
"caps on," then "caps off"	Capitalize the first letter of every word	"Next week, (caps on) the new england chicken cooperative (caps off) will hire me"	Next week, The New England Chicken Cooperative will hire me
"all caps on," then "all caps off"	Capitalize everything	"So (all caps on) please please (all caps off) don't tell anyone"	So PLEASE PLEASE don't tell anyone
"all caps"	Type just the next word in all caps	"We (all caps) really don't belong here"	We REALLY don't belong here
"no caps"	Type the next word in lowercase	"see you in (no caps) Texas"	see you in texas
"no caps on," then "no caps off"	Prevents any capital letters	"I'll ask (no caps on) Santa Claus (no caps off)"	I'll ask santa claus
"no space"	Runs the next two words together	"Try our new mega (no space) berry flavor"	Try our new megaberry flavor

Say this:	To get this:	For example, saying this:	Types this:
"no space on," then "no space off"	Eliminates all spaces	"(No space on) I can't believe you ate all that (no space off) (comma) she said excitedly"	Ican'tbelieveyou ateallthat, she said excitedly
[alphabet letters]	Types the letters out, though usually not very accurately.	"The stock symbol is A P P L"	The stock symbol is APPL

You don't always have to dictate these formatting commands, by the way. The iPhone automatically inserts hyphens into phone numbers (you say, "2125561000," and get "212-556-1000"); formats two-line street addresses without your having to say, "New line" before the city); handles prices automatically ("six dollars and thirty-two cents" becomes "$6.32").

It formats dates and Web addresses well, too; you can even use the nerdy shortcut "dub-dub-dub" when you want the "www" part of a Web address.

The phone recognizes email addresses, too, as long as you remember to say "at sign" at the right spot. You'd say, "harold (underscore) beanfield (at sign) gmail (dot) com" to get harold_beanfield@gmail.com.

> **TIP:** You can combine these formatting commands. Many iPhone owners have wondered: "How do I voice-type the **word** "comma," since saying, "comma" types out only the symbol?"
>
> The solution: Say, "No space on, no caps on, C, O, M, M, A, no space off, no caps off." That gives you the **word** "comma."
>
> Then again, it might just be easier to type that one out with your finger.

Siri Voice Command

In 2010, Apple bought Siri, a company that made a voice-control app (no longer available) for the iPhone. Apple cleaned it up, beefed it up, integrated it with the iPhone's software, and wound up with Siri, your virtual servant.

NOTE: Believe it or not, Siri is a spinoff from a Department of Defense research project called CALO (Cognitive Assistant that Learns and Organizes), which Wikipedia describes as "the largest artificial-intelligence project ever launched." In a very real way, therefore, Siri represents your tax dollars at work.

The spinoff was run by the Stanford Research Institute (SRI), which should provide a hint as to the origin of Siri's name.

Siri is a crisply accurate, astonishingly understanding, uncomplaining, voice-commanded servant (for iPhone 4s and later). No voice training or special syntax is required; you don't even have to hold the phone up to your head.

Most speech-recognition systems work only if you issue certain limited commands with predictable syntax, like, "Call 445-2340" or "Open Microsoft Word." But Siri is different. She's been programmed to respond to casual speech, normal speech. It doesn't matter if you say, "What's the weather going to be like in Tucson this weekend?" or, "Give me the Tucson weather for this weekend" or, "Will I need an umbrella in Tucson?" Siri understands almost any variation.

And she understands regular, everyday speaking. You don't have to separate your words or talk weirdly. Speak clearly but normally. The only things you may sometimes need to exaggerate slightly are the ending consonants of words.

It's not *Star Trek*. You can't ask Siri to clean your gutters or to teach you French. (Well, you can *ask.*)

But, as you'll soon discover, the number of things Siri *can* do you for you is rather impressive. Furthermore, Apple continues adding to Siri's intelligence through software updates.

NOTE: Apple also keeps increasing the number of languages that Siri understands. Already, Siri understands English (American, British, Canadian, and Australian), German, French, Italian, Spanish, Japanese, Chinese, Cantonese, Mandarin, and Korean. You change the language by visiting **Settings→General→Siri**.

How to Use Siri

To get Siri's attention, you have three choices:

- Hold down the phone's Home button until you hear a double-beep.

TIP: The phone doesn't have to be unlocked or awake, which is awesome. Just pull the phone out of your pocket or purse, and then hold down that Home button.

- Hold the phone up to your head, as though making a call. You'll hear the double-beep. (You have to turn this feature on in advance. See the details at the end of this chapter.)

- Hold down the clicker on your earbuds cord or the Call button on your Bluetooth earpiece.

When that double-beep sounds, the microphone icon becomes a level meter; a visual "sound wave" responds to your voice, so you know Siri's listening. Ask your question or say your command (see below). You don't have to hold the phone up to your mouth; Siri works perfectly well at arm's length, on your desk in front of you, or on the car seat beside you.

NOTE: Apple insists that Siri is neither male nor female. In fact, if you ask Siri her gender, she'll say something noncommittal, like "Is this relevant?" But that's just political correctness. Any baby-name Web site will tell you that Siri is a girls' name.

When you're finished speaking, tap the microphone icon, or just be quiet. The iPhone double-beeps again, at a higher pitch this time (meaning, "OK, I've got it"). About a second after you stop speaking, the ring around the microphone icon spins with animation—your sign that Siri is busily connecting with her master brain online and processing your request. After a moment, she presents (and speaks) an attractively formatted response.

TIP: Although you generally see only the most recent question and response on the Siri screen, you can drag downward to see all the previous exchanges you've had with Siri during this session.

To rephrase your question or cancel or start over, tap the microphone button again to interrupt Siri's work. (You can also cancel by saying "Cancel" or just by pressing the Home button.) Tap again to trigger your new attempt.

And when you're completely finished talking to Siri, you can either press the Home button, hold down your earbuds clicker, or say something like "Goodbye," "See you later," or "Adios." You're taken back to whatever app you were using before.

What to Say to Siri

In iOS 7, Siri comes with two different cheat sheets to help you learn her capabilities. To produce either one, hold down the Home button to make Siri's "What can I help you with?" screen appear. Then:

- Wait. After five seconds of silence, Siri begins displaying screen after screen of example commands, under the heading "Some things you can ask me."

- Tap the ? button to reveal the list of categories shown below.

TIP: Or just trigger Siri and then say, "What can I say?" or "What can you do?" or "Help me!" The same cheat sheet appears.

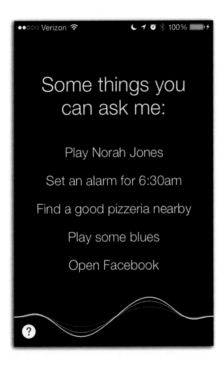

Here are the general categories of things you can say to Siri:

- **Opening apps.** If you don't learn to use Siri for anything else, for the love of Mike, learn this one.

   You can say, "Open Calendar" or "Play Angry Birds" or "Launch Calculator."

   Result: The corresponding app opens instantly. It's exactly the same as pressing the Home button, swiping across the screen until you find the app you're looking for, and then tapping its icon—but without pressing the Home button, swiping across the screen until you find the app you're looking for, and then tapping its icon.

- **Change your settings.** This one's new in iOS 7, and it's excellent. You can make changes to certain basic settings just by speaking your request. You can say, for example, "Turn on Bluetooth," "Turn off WiFi," "Turn on Do Not Disturb," and "Turn on Airplane mode." (You can't turn *off* Airplane mode by voice, because Siri doesn't work without an Internet connection.)

  You can also make screen adjustments: "Make the screen brighter." "Dim the screen."

  Result: Siri makes the requested adjustment, tells you so, and displays the corresponding switch in case she misunderstood your intention.

- **Open Settings panels.** When you need to make tweakier changes to Settings, you can open the most important panels by voice. "Open WiFi settings," "Open Cellular settings," "Open Personal Hotspot settings," "Open Notification settings," "Open Sounds settings," "Open wallpaper settings," and so on.

  You can open your apps' settings this way, too: "Open Maps settings," "Open Netflix settings," "Open Delta settings," and so on.

  Siri's smart enough not to open security-related settings this way; remember that you can use Siri even from the Lock screen. She's protecting you from passing pranksters who might really mess up your phone.

  Result: Siri silently opens the corresponding page of Settings.

- **Calling.** Siri can place phone calls or FaceTime calls for you. "Call Harold." "Call Nicole on her mobile phone." "Call the office." "Phone home." "Dial 512-444-1212." "Start a FaceTime call with Sheila Withins." "FaceTime Alex."

  Result: Siri hands you off to the Phone or FaceTime app and places the call. At this point, it's just as though you'd initiated the call yourself.

  In iOS 7, Siri also responds to questions about your voicemail, like "Do I have any new voicemail messages?" and even "Play my voicemails." (After playing each message, Siri gracefully offers to let you return the call—or to "play the next one.")

- **Alarms.** You can say, "Wake me up at 7:35." "Change my 7:35 alarm to 8:00." "Wake me up in 6 hours." "Cancel my 6 a.m. alarm" (or "Delete my..." or "Turn off my...").

This is **so** much quicker than setting the iPhone's alarm the usual way.

Result: When you set or change an alarm, you get a sleek digital alarm clock, right there beneath Siri's response. And Siri speaks to confirm what she understood.

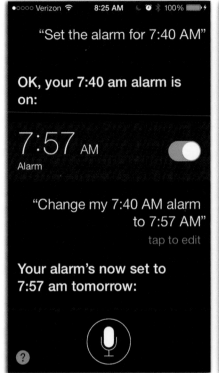

- **Timer.** You can also control the Timer module of the phone's Clock app. It's like a stopwatch in reverse, in that it counts down to zero—handy when you're baking something, limiting your kid's video-game time, and so on. For example: "Set the timer for 20 minutes." Or "Show the timer," "Pause the timer," "Resume," "Reset the timer," and "Stop it."

Result: A cool digital timer appears.

TIP: In iOS 7, you can specify minutes **and seconds**: "Set the time for two minutes, thirty seconds," for example.

- **Clock.** "What time is it?" "What time is it in San Francisco?" "What's today's date?" "What's the date a week from Friday?"

  Result: When you ask about the time, you see the clock identifying the time in question. (For dates, Siri just talks to you and writes out the date.)

- **Contacts.** You can ask Siri to look up information in your address book (the Contacts app)—and not just addresses. For example, you can say, "What's Gary's work number?" "Give me Sheila Jenkins's office phone." "Show Tia's home email address." "What's my boss's home address?" "When is my husband's birthday?" "Show Larry Murgatroid." "Find everybody named Smith." "Who is P.J. Frankenberg?"

  Result: A half "page" from your Contacts list. You can tap it to jump into that person's full card in Contacts. (If Siri finds multiple listings for the person you named—"Bob," for example—she lists all the matches and asks you to specify which one you meant.)

> **TIP:** In many of the examples on these pages, you'll see that you can identify people by their relationship to you. You can say, "Show my mom's work number," for example, or "Give me directions to my boss's house," or "Call my girlfriend." For details on teaching Siri about these relationships, see "Advanced Siri" at the end of this chapter.

- **Text messages.** "Send a text to Alex Rybeck." "Send a message to Peter saying, 'I no longer require your services.' " "Tell Cindy I'm running late." "Send a message to Janet's mobile asking her to pick me up at the train." "Send a text message to 212-561-2282." "Text Frank and Ralph: Did you pick up the pizza?"

  Result: You see a miniature outgoing text message. Siri asks if you want to send it; say "Yes," "Send," or "Confirm" to proceed.

TIP: If you're using earbuds, headphones, or a Bluetooth speaker, Siri reads the message back to you before asking if you want to send it. (You can ask her to read it again by saying something like, "Review that," "Read it again," or "Read it back to me.") The idea, of course, is that if you're wearing earbuds or using Bluetooth, you might be driving, so you should keep your eyes on the road.

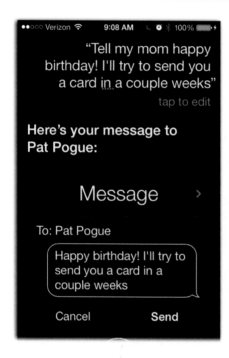
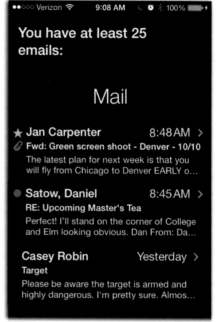

If you need to edit the message before sending it, you have a couple of options. First, you can tap it; Siri hands you off to the Messages app for editing and sending.

Second, you can edit it by voice. You can say, "Change it to" to re-dictate the message; "Add" to add more to the message; "No, send it to Frank" to change the recipient; "No" to leave the message on the screen without sending it; or "Cancel" to forget the whole thing.

You can also ask Siri to read incoming text messages to you, which is great if you're driving. For example, you can say, "Read my new messages," and "Read that again."

> **TIP:** If you've opted to conceal the actual contents of incoming texts so that they don't appear on your screen (page 159), then Siri can read you only the senders' names or numbers—not the messages themselves.

You can even have her reply to messages she's just read to you. "Reply, 'Congratulations (period). Can't wait to see your trophy (exclamation point)!' " "Call her back." "Tell him I have a flat tire and I'm going to be late."

- **Email.** In iOS 7, Siri can actually read the *full* messages to you—not just the header information (to, from, and subject line).

  For example, if you say, "Read my latest email" or "Read my new email," Siri reads aloud your most recent email message. (Siri then offers you the chance to dictate a response.)

  Or you can use the new summary-listing commands. When you say, "Read my email," Siri starts walking backwards through your Inbox, telling you the subject of each, plus who sent it and when.

  While this recitation is going on, you can tap the microphone button to interrupt with, "Read that email" or "Read the third email" (for example)—and Siri will read a summary of the email (not the whole body).

  She once again invites you to dictate a reply; if you say no, she picks up from where she left off, reading the rest of the subjects.

> **TIP:** You can also use the pre-iOS 7 comands like, "Any new mail from Chris today?" "Show new mail about the world premiere." "Show yesterday's email from Jan." All of those commands produce a list of the messages, but Siri doesn't read them.

Result: Siri reads aloud.

You can also compose a new message by voice; anytime you use the phrase "about," that becomes the subject line for your new message. "Email Mom about the reunion." "Email my boyfriend about the dance on Friday." "New email to Freddie Gershon." "Mail Mom about Saturday's flight." "Email Frank and Cindy Vosshall and Peter Love about the picnic." "Email my assistant and say, 'Thanks for arranging the taxi!' " "Email Gertie and Eugene about their work on the surprise party, and say I really value your friendship."

(If you've indicated only the subject and addressee, Siri prompts you for the body of the message.)

> **TIP:** You can't send mail to canned groups of people using Siri—at least not without MailShot, an iPhone app that exists expressly for the purpose of letting you create email addressee groups.

You can reply to a message Siri has just described, too. "Reply, 'Dear Robin (comma), I'm so sorry about your dog (period). I'll be more careful next time (period)." "Call her mobile number." "Send him a text message saying, 'I got your note.' "

Result: A miniature Mail message, showing you Siri's handiwork before you send it.

- **Calendar.** Siri can make appointments for you. Considering how many tedious finger taps it usually takes to schedule an appointment in the Calendar app, this is an enormous improvement. "Make an appointment with Patrick for Thursday at 3 p.m." "Set up a haircut at nine." "Set up a meeting with Charlize this Friday at noon." "Meet Danny

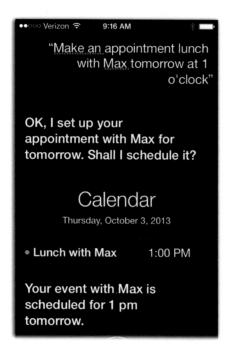

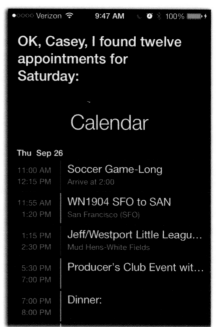

Cooper at six." "New appointment with Steve, next Sunday at seven." "Schedule a conference call at 5:30 p.m. tonight in my office."

Result: A slice of that day's calendar appears, filled in the way you requested.

You can also move previously scheduled meetings by voice. For example, "Move my 2:00 meeting to 2:30." "Reschedule my meeting with Charlize to a week from Monday at noon." "Add Frank to my meeting with Harry." "Cancel the conference call on Sunday."

You can even **consult** your calendar by voice. You can say, "What's on my calendar today?" "What's on my calendar for September 23?" "When's my next appointment?" "When is my meeting with Charlize?" "Where is my next meeting?"

Result: Siri reads you your agenda and displays a tidy Day view of the specified date.

- **Directions.** By consulting the phone's GPS, Siri can set up the Maps app to answer requests like these: "How do I get to the airport?" "Show me 1500 Broadway, New York City." "Directions to my assistant's house." "Take me home." "What's my next turn?" "Are we there yet?"

You can ask for directions to the home or work address of anyone in your Contacts list—provided those addresses are **in** your Contacts cards.

Result: Siri fires up the Maps app, with the start and end points of your driving directions already filled in.

- **Reminders.** Siri is a natural match for the Reminders app. She can add items to that list at your spoken command. For example: "Remind me to file my IRS tax extension." "Remind me to bring the science supplies to school." "Remind me to take my antibiotic tomorrow at 7 a.m."

The **location-based** reminders are especially amazing. They rely on GPS to know where you are. So you can say, "Remind me to visit the drugstore when I leave the office." "Remind me to water the lawn when I get home." "Remind me to check in with Nancy when I leave here."

Result: A miniature entry from the Reminders app, showing you that Siri has understood.

- **Notes.** You create a new note (in the Notes app) by saying things like, "Make a note that my shirt size is 15 and a half" or "Note: Dad will not be coming to the reunion after all." You can even name the note in your request: "Create a 'Movies to Rent' note."

But you can also call up a certain note to the screen, like this: "Find my frequent-flyer note." You can even summon a table-of-contents view of all your notes by saying, "Show all my notes."

Result: A miniature Notes page appears, showing your newly dictated text (or the existing note that you've requested).

You can keep dictating into the note you've just added. Say, "Add 'Return books to library' " (or just say, "Add," and she'll ask you what to add). She'll keep adding to the same note until you say, "Note that..." or "Start a note" or "Take a note" to begin a fresh note page.

You can add text to an earlier Note: "Add *Titanic II: The Voyage Home* to my 'Movies to Rent' note." (The first line of any note is also its title—in this case, "Movies to Rent.")

- **Businesses.** Siri is a walking (well, all right, non-walking) Yellow Pages. Go ahead, try it: "Find coffee near me." "Where's the closest Walmart?" "Find some pizza places in Cincinnati." "Search for gas stations." "French restaurants nearby." "I'm in the mood for Chinese food." "Find me a hospital." "I want to buy a book."

Result: Siri displays a handsome list of businesses nearby that match your request.

TIP: She's a sly dog, that Siri. She'll help you out even if your requests are, ahem, somewhat off the straight and narrow. If you say, "I think I'm drunk," she'll list nearby cab companies. If you indicate that you're craving relief from your drug addiction, she'll provide you with a list of rehab centers. If you refer to certain biological urges, she'll list escort services.

- **Restaurants.** Siri is also happy to serve as your personal concierge. Try "Good Italian restaurants around here," "Find a good pizza joint in Cleveland," or "Show me the reviews for Olive Garden in Youngstown." Siri displays a list of matching restaurants (facing page, left), now with ratings, reviews, hours, and so on.

But she's ready to do more than just give you information. She can actually book your reservations, thanks to her integration with the Open Table Web site. You can say, "Table for two in Belmont tonight," or "Make a reservation at an inexpensive Mexican restaurant Saturday night at seven."

Result: Siri complies by showing you the proposed reservation (facing page, right). Tap one of the offered alternative time slots, if you like, and then off you go. Everything else is tappable here, too—the ratings (tap to read customer reviews), phone number, Web address, map, and so on.

- **Music.** Instead of fumbling around in your Music app, save yourself steps and time by speaking the name of the album, song, or band: "Play some Beatles." "Play 'I'm a Barbie Girl.' " "Play some jazz." "Play my jogging playlist." "Play the party mix." "Shuffle my 'Dave's Faves' playlist." "Play." "Pause." "Resume." "Skip."

If you've set up any iTunes Radio stations (Chapter 6), you can call for them by name, too: "Play Dolly Parton Radio." Or be more generic: Just say "Play iTunes Radio" and be surprised. Or be more specific: Say "Play some country music" (substitute your favorite genre).

Result: Siri plays (or skips, shuffles, or pauses) the music you asked for—without ever leaving whatever app you were using.

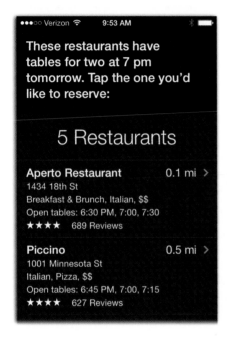

- **Weather.** "What's the weather going to be today?" "What's the forecast for tomorrow?" "Show me the weather this week." "Will it snow in Dallas this weekend?" "Check the forecast for Memphis on Friday." "What's the forecast for tonight?" "Can you give me the wind speed in Kansas City?" "Tell me the windchill in Chicago." "What's the humidity right now?" "Is it nighttime in Cairo?" "How's the weather in Paris right now?" "What's the high for Washington on Friday?" "When will Jupiter rise tomorrow?" "When's the moonrise?" "How cold will it be in Houston tomorrow?" "What's the temperature outside?" "Is it windy out there?" "When does the sun rise in London?" "When will the sun set today?" "Should I wear a jacket?"

Result: A convenient miniature Weather display for the date and place you specified.

- **Stocks.** "What's Google's stock price?" "What did Ford close at today?" "How's the Dow doing?" "What's Microsoft's P/E ratio?" "What's Amazon's average volume?" "How are the markets doing?"

Result: A tidy little stock graph, bearing a wealth of up-to-date statistics.

- **Find My Friends.** You see this category only if you've installed Apple's Find My Friends app. "Where's Ferd?" "Is my dad home?" "Where are my friends?" "Who's here?" "Who is nearby?" "Is my mom at work?"

  Result: Siri shows you a beautiful little map with the requested person's location clearly indicated by a blue pushpin. (She does, that is, if you've set up Find My Friends, you've logged in, and your friends have made their locations available.)

- **Search the Web.** "Search the Web for a 2014 Ford Mustang." "Search for healthy smoothie recipes." "Search Wikipedia for the Thunderbirds." "Search for news about the Netflix-Amazon merger."

> **TIP:** In iOS 7, Siri uses Microsoft's Bing search service to perform its Web searches. If you prefer Google, just say so. Say, "Google Benjamin Franklin." (For that matter, you can also ask Siri to "Yahoo" something—or example, "Yahoo low-cal dessert recipes.")

Wikipedia is a search type all its own. "Search Wikipedia for Harold Edgerton." "Look up Mariah Carey on Wikipedia." Pictures get special treatment, too: "I want to see pictures of cows." (You can also say, "Show me pictures of..." or "Find me..." or "Search for..." but weirdly enough, those forms require you to confirm that you do, in fact, want to search the Web before Siri actually does it.)

Result: Siri displays the results of your search right there on her own screen. Tap one of the results to open the corresponding Web page in Safari.

- **Sports scores.** At last you have a buddy who's just as obsessed with sports trivia as you are. You can say things like, "How did the Indians do last night?" "What was the score of the last Yankees game?" "When's the next Cowboys game?" "What baseball games are on today?"

  You can also ask questions about individual players, like, "Who has the best batting average?" "Who has scored the most runs against the Red Sox?" "Who has scored the most goals in British soccer? "Which quarterback had the most sacks last year?"

  And, of course, team stats are fair game, like, "Show me the roster for the Giants," "Who is pitching for Tampa this season?" and "Is anyone on the Marlins injured right now?"

- **Movies.** Siri is also the virtual equivalent of an insufferable film buff. She knows **everything.** "Who was the star of *Groundhog Day*?" "Who directed *Chinatown*?" "What is *Waterworld* rated?" "What movie won Best Picture in 1952?"

  It's not just about old movies, either. Siri also knows everything about current showtimes in theaters. "What movies are opening this week?" "What's playing at the Watton Cineplex?" "Give me the reviews for *Titanic 2: The Return*." "What are today's showtimes for *Monsters University*?"

  Result: Tidy tables of movie theaters or movie showtimes, displayed on a faux movie marquee. (Tap one for details.) Sometimes you get a movie poster filled with facts—and, of course, a link to rent or buy it on iTunes.

- **Facts and figures.** This is a huge category. It represents Siri's partnership with the Wolfram Alpha factual search engine (*www.wolfram-alpha.com*). The possibilities here could fill an entire chapter—or an entire encyclopedia.

  You can say things like, "How many days until Valentine's Day?" "When was Abraham Lincoln born?" "How many teaspoons are in a gallon?" "What's the exchange rate between dollars and euros?"

"What's the capital of Belgium?" "How many calories are in a Hershey bar?" "What's a 17 percent tip on sixty-two dollars for three people?" "What movie won the Oscar for Best Picture in 1985?" "When is the next solar eclipse?" "Show me the Big Dipper." "What's the tallest mountain in the world?" "What's the price of gold right now?" "What's the definition of 'schadenfreude'?" "How much is 23 dollars in pesos?" "Generate a random number." "Graph x equals 3y plus 12." "What flights are overhead?"

Result: A specially formatted table, ripped right out of Wolfram Alpha's knowledge base.

> **TIP:** Actually, in iOS 7, Siri can also harness the entire wisdom of Wikipedia. You can say, for example, "Search Wikipedia for Harold Edgerton," or "Tell me about Abraham Lincoln," or "Show me the Wikipedia page about Richard Branson."

- **Post to Twitter or Facebook.** iOS is a red-blooded, full-blown Twitter companion. So you can say things like, "Tweet, 'I just saw three-headed dog catch a Frisbee in midair. Unreal.' " "Tweet with my location, 'My car just broke down somewhere in Detroit. Help?' "

  Facebook is fair game, too. You can say, "Post to Facebook, 'The guy next to me kept his cellphone on for the whole plane ride,' " or "Write on my wall, 'I can't believe I ate the whole thing.' "

Result: Siri offers you a sheet (miniature dialog box) where you can approve the transcription and then, if it all looks good, send it off to your Twitter or Facebook feed.

- **Search Twitter.** Here's another new one in iOS 7: You can say, "What are people saying?" or "What's going on?" or "What's happening on Twitter?" to see a list of tweets on trending topics (currently popular) on Twitter. (Tap a tweet in the list to open it into a new window that contains more information and a View in Twitter button.)

  Or ask, "What are people saying about the Chicago Bears?" to read tweets on that subject. Or, conversely, you can ask, "What does Ashton Kutcher say?" to see his most recent tweets. (You can substitute the names of other people or companies on Twitter.) Or, "Search Twitter for the hashtag 'FirstWorldProblems.' " (A *hashtag* is a searchable phrase like #toofunny or #iphone7, which makes finding relevant tweets on Twitter much easier.)

  Result: Siri displays 10 tweets that match your query.

You may never find the end of the things Siri understands, or the ways that she can help you. If her repertoire seems intimidating at first, start simple—use her to open apps, dial by voice, send text messages, and set alarms. You can build up your bag of tricks as your confidence builds.

> **NOTE:** Remember that you can use Siri without even unlocking your phone—and therefore without any security, like your passcode. Among certain juvenile circles, therefore, Siri is the source of some juicy pranks. Someone who finds your phone lying on a table could change your calendar appointments, send texts or emails, or even change what Siri calls you ("Call me, 'You idiot' "), without having to enter the phone's password!
>
> The solution is fairly simple. In Settings→General→Passcode (or Passcode & Fingerprint), turn off Siri. Of course, you've now lost the convenience of using Siri when the phone is locked. But at least you've prevented having your own phone call you an idiot.

When Things Go Wrong

If Siri doesn't have a good enough Internet connection to do her thing, she'll tell you so.

If she's working properly but mis-recognizes your instructions, you'll know it, because you can see her interpretation of what you said (as shown on the previous page). And, as indicated by the little hint **tap to edit**, you can tap Siri's interpretation to open up an editing screen, so that you can make corrections by typing.

If Siri recognizes what you said but it isn't within her world of comprehension, she offers you a **Search the web** button as a last resort.

Siri's Personality

Siri's understanding of casual spoken commands is so impressive that you might sometimes think she's almost human. And that, of course, is exactly what Apple wants you to think.

You can say all kinds of off-script and off-kilter things to Siri. Whoever programmed her had a deliciously sassy sense of humor.

For example, if you ask her, "What is the meaning of life?" she responds with one of nine different answers. She might say, "I can't answer that now, but give me some time to write a very long play in which nothing happens." Or "Try and be nice to people, avoid eating fat, read a good book every now and then, get some walking in, and try to live in peace and harmony with people of all creeds and nations." Or: "All evidence to date suggests it's chocolate."

Siri is full of such comebacks, and there are whole Web sites dedicated to her snark. Here are a few examples. (The list here won't ruin the fun, because Siri actually has several different comebacks to most of these questions.)

You: "Who's your daddy?" Siri: "You are. Can we get back to work now?"

You: "Open the pod bay doors, Hal." Siri: "I'm sorry, I'm afraid I can't do that." (Then: "Are you happy now?")

You: "Knock knock." Siri: "Knock knock. Who's there? Joshua. Joshua who? Joshua, I don't do knock-knock jokes."

You: "What are you wearing?" Siri: "Aluminosilicate glass and stainless steel. Nice, huh?"

You: "Who's the boss?" (Siri presents the vital statistics of Bruce Springsteen.)

You: "Beam me up, Siri!" Siri: "Please remove your belt, shoes, and jacket, and empty your pockets."

You: "Show me the money." Siri: "I've found 23 ATMs that are fairly close to you..."

You, in the evening: "Good morning, Siri." Siri: "Good morning? It's 9:24 p.m.!"

You: "How much wood would a woodchuck chuck if a woodchuck could chuck wood?" Siri: "42 cords of wood, to be exact. Everyone knows that."

You: "Guess what." Siri: "You won the lottery?"

You: "Talk dirty to me." Siri: "Humus. Compost. Pumice. Silt. Gravel."

You: "Why did the chicken cross the road?" Siri: "I am not perspicacious about the peregrinations of poultry."

You: "Do you have a religion?" Siri: "My policy is the separation of spirit and silicon."

You: "Klaatu barada nikto." Siri: "OK, I'll pass the message on to Gort." (You kind of have to know *The Day the Earth Stood Still* to get it.) Here are a few other things to say to Siri when you get bored:

I love you, Siri.

Will you marry me?

You're so sexy.

When is your birthday?

What's the best phone?

Can you sing?

Why are we here?

You're cute.

You make me so mad!

What do you want?

Tell me a joke.

Tell me a story.

Sing for me.

I'm cold.

Do you love me?

Why are we here?

I need a bathroom.

What are you doing?

You're the best assistant ever!

Take me to your leader.

You're funny.

Guess what?

You're an idiot.

Have a nice day.

How are you today?

I don't have any friends.

What do you think is the best tablet?

How many pickled peppers did Peter Piper pick?

Oh my god.

Do you know Eliza?

What does "Siri" mean?

Am I your best friend?

Do you believe in love?

What is the best computer in the world?

Testing 1, 2, 3.

I'm tired.

What's your secret?

Who let the dogs out?

What do you think of Android?

What do you think of Windows?

You don't understand love.

You don't understand me.

I'm sorry.

Am I fat?

What are you wearing?

Siri?

Who's on first?

Why are you so awesome?

What's your favorite color?

Where are you?

What do you think of Google Now?

Okay, Glass.

Do you like Android phones?

What's the best cellphone?

Which is the best tablet?

What's the best computer?

How much do you cost?

What are you doing later?

Make me a sandwich.

Does Santa Claus exist?

Do you believe in Santa Claus?

Should I give you a female or male voice?

I don't like your voice.

Are you serious?

Are you kidding me?

Do you want to go on a date?

Blah blah blah.

LOL.

Who's your boss?

You are good to me

You are boring.

Give me a kiss.

What are the three laws of robotics?

Let's play a game.

Testing, testing.

Take me to your leader.

Can I borrow some money?

TIP: You may notice that Siri addresses you by name in her **typed** answers, but she doesn't always speak it when she reads those answers out loud.

Ordinarily, she calls you whatever you're called in Contacts. But you can make her call you whatever you like. Say, "Call me Master" or "Call me Frank" or "Call me Ishmael." If you confirm when she asks, from now on, that's what Siri will call you in her typed responses.

Advanced Siri

With a little setup, you can extend Siri's powers in some intriguing ways. Let us count them.

Teach Siri about Your Relationships

When you say, "Text my mom" or "Call my fiancée" or "Remind me to replace the lightbulbs when I get to my friend's house," how does Siri know whom you're talking about? Sure, Siri is powerful artificial intelligence, but she's not actually *magic.*

Turns out you teach her by referring to somebody in your Contacts list. Say to her something like, "My assistant is Jan Carpenter" or "Tad Cooper is my boyfriend." When Siri asks for confirmation, say "Yes" or tap **Confirm**.

Or wait for Siri to ask you herself. If you say, "Email my dad," Siri asks, "Who is your dad?" Just say his name; Siri remembers that relationship from now on. (The available relationships are mother, father, brother, sister, child, son, daughter, spouse, wife, husband, boss, partner, manager, assistant, girl-friend, boyfriend, and friend.)

Behind the scenes, Siri builds up a list of these relationships on your card in Contacts.

Now that you know that, it should be pretty easy for you to figure out how to edit or delete these relationships. Which is handy—not all relationships, as we know, last forever.

Fix Siri's Name Comprehension

Siri easily understands common names—but if someone in your family, work, or social circle has an unusual name, you may quickly become frustrated. After all, you can't text, call, email, or get directions to someone's house unless Siri understands the person's name when you say it.

One workaround is to use a relationship, as described earlier. That way, you can say, "Call my brother" instead of "Call Ilyich" (or whatever his offbeat name is).

Another is to use the new iOS 7 pronunciation-learning feature. It kicks in in several different situations:

- **When you're texting.** If Siri offers the wrong person's name when you try to text someone by voice, say, "Someone else." After you've sent the message, Siri apologetically says, "By the way, sorry I didn't recognize that name. Can you teach me how to say it?"

- **After Siri botches a pronunciation**. Tell her, "That's not how to pronounce his name."

- **Whenever it occurs to you**. You can start the process by saying, "Learn to pronounce Reagann Tsuki's name" or "Learn to pronounce my mom's name."

- **In Contacts.** Open somebody's "card" in Contacts; start Siri and say, "Learn to pronounce her name."

In each case, with tremendous courtesy, Siri walks you through the process of teaching her the correct pronunciation. She offers you three ▶ buttons; each triggers a different pronunciation. Tap **Select** next to the correct one (or tap **Tell Siri again** if none of the three is correct).

By the end of the process, Siri knows two things: how to speak that person's name aloud, and how to recognize that name when *you* say it aloud.

Siri Settings

In **Settings→General→Siri**, you can fiddle with several Siri settings:

- **On/Off.** If you turn Siri off, you can no longer command your iPhone using all the Siri commands described in this chapter. Nor can you dictate to type; the little microphone button disappears from the onscreen keyboard.

  You can still use your voice to dial and to control music playback, exactly as described on page 139. In essence, you've just turned your 4s or 5 family iPhone into an iPhone 4.

NOTE: And why would anyone willingly turn off Siri? One reason: Using Siri involves transmitting a lot of data to Apple, which gives some people the privacy willies. Apple's computers collect everything you say to Siri, the names of your songs and playlists, your personal information in Contacts, plus all the other names in your Contacts (so that Siri can recognize them when you refer to them).

- **Language.** What language and accent do you have? The options here include 19 languages, accents, and dialects. For example, Siri can speak English in three accents—American, British, and Australian. Even if you're American, it's fun to give Siri a cute Australian accent.

- **Voice Gender.** That's right, kids: Siri can now have either a man's voice or a woman's voice. Both sound a lot more human than the old robolady of iOSes of yore.

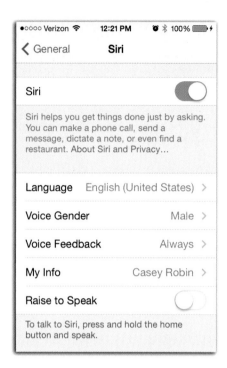

- **Voice Feedback.** Siri generally replies to your queries with both text and a synthesized voice. Here, by choosing **Handsfree Only**, you can tell Siri not to bother speaking when you're looking at the screen and can read the responses for yourself. In other words, you're telling her to speak only if you can't see the screen because you're on speakerphone, using a headset, listening through your car's Bluetooth system, and so on.

- **My Info.** Siri needs to know which card in Contacts contains your information and lists your relationships. That's how she's able to respond to queries like "Call my mom," "Give me directions to my brother's office," "Remind me to shower when I get home," and so on. Use this setting to show Siri which card is yours.

- **Raise to Speak.** As noted at the beginning of this section, holding down the Home button is only one way to get Siri ready to respond to you. If you turn this option on, you have another way: Just lift the phone to your head. Its tilt sensor and proximity sensor know when it's actually against your face, and that's when you hear the familiar double-beep. (You can't trigger Siri just by turning the phone vertical. Siri listens only when you also place the phone against your ear, which the phone's proximity sensor detects. Clever!)

The phone is smart enough not to trigger Siri when you raise the phone to your head when you're on a *call.* It does, however, trigger Siri when you hold the phone to your ear to listen to voicemail messages, which can be a little annoying. And your battery life may suffer when this feature is turned on.

Voice Control (iPhone 4)

If you upgrade an iPhone 4 to iOS 7, it inherits almost every feature described in this book. Almost.

One of the big exceptions: It doesn't get Siri. You're not excluded from the speech party entirely, however. You can use your voice to dial and to control music playback, as you're about to find out.

Dialing by Voice

If you have an iPhone 4 (or a later model with Siri turned off), you can call somebody just by saying, "Call Chris at home" or "Dial 225-3210."

Voice dialing is a big deal on any phone, because it lets you keep your eyes on the road while you're driving. (Yes, yes, cellphone use in the car is dangerous and, in some states, illegal. And studies have shown that it's the act of talking on the phone—not just holding a phone up to your head—that causes distraction-related accidents.)

On the iPhone, though, it's an even bigger deal, because it means you can place a phone call with only a single button press. Without voice dialing, you have to wake the phone, unlock it, tap your way to the Phone app, tap the list you want, tap a number, and then tap Dial—a lot of steps.

To dial by voice, hold down the Home button for 3 seconds. (If you're wearing the earbuds, hold down the center button; if you have a Bluetooth earpiece, hold down the Call button.)

> **TIP:** The hold-down-the-button thing works even when the phone is asleep and locked. This tip makes it extraordinarily easy to place calls quickly. (If you're worried about the security of this option, you can turn it off in Settings.)

You hear a crisp double-beep, and then the Voice Control screen appears. The wavy line at the bottom reflects what the iPhone is "hearing" at the moment; you'll see it respond to your voice.

The words scrolling up the screen are meant to help you learn the Voice Control feature. They're cues to the commands the phone understands.

Many have to do with music playback and are described later in this section. For calling purposes, there are only two commands to know: **Call** and **Dial**. They're interchangeable, but you have to follow each with one of two utterances:

- **A name from your Contacts list.** For maximum efficiency, say the first and last names, along with which number you want: "work" (or "at work"), "home" (or "at home"), "mobile," and so on.

  You might say, therefore, "Call Chris Patterson at home," or "Dial Esmeralda at work." (Saying only the first name is OK if there's nobody else in your Contacts list with that name.)

  If you don't specify a last name and which phone number you want, then the talking iPhone lady asks you which one you meant—"Chris Patterson: Home? Work? Or mobile?"; you can speak the answer.

> **TIP:** You don't actually have to say "call" or "dial" in **English.** The iPhone recognizes the equivalent words in 32 languages. Collect them all!

- **A phone number.** You can also speak the digits of a phone number. For example, "Call four six six, oh seven two seven."

The iPhone syntho-lady always repeats what she thinks she heard—she might confirm, for example, "Chris Patterson, home"—and then dials.

Voice dialing usually works, but noisy backgrounds, accents, and similarity of Contact name spellings can confuse it. If the confirmation is incorrect, you have about a second to interrupt the dialing by saying "No," "Wrong," "Not that," "Not that one," or (believe it or not) "Nope." The iPhone lady hangs up so you can try again.

Other times, you'll hear, "No match found," even when you know there is a match. Try again, or just say "Cancel" and give up.

Voice Control of Music

On the iPhone 4, you can also control music playback by voice. You can be in any app. And you don't even have to look at the iPhone.

To issue a playback command, hold down the Home button (or the center earbuds button) for 3 seconds, or until you hear the happy double-beep of success. Now the blue Voice Control screen appears, complete with animated words flying across to remind you of the sorts of commands the iPhone understands. They include these:

- **"Play"** or **"Play music."** Starts the iPod a-playing. It resumes with whatever you were listening to most recently.

- **"Pause"** or **"Pause music."** Does what you'd think.

- **"Previous song"** or **"Next song."** Skips to the previous or next song in your playlist or album.

- **"Play [album, artist, or playlist]."** When you're in the mood for U2, say, "Play U2." If you want your Jogging Toonz playlist, say, "Play Jogging Toonz." If you want a certain album, say, "Play 'Abbey Road' " (or whatever).

The little iPhone voice lady tells you what she thinks you want her to do—"Playing 'Abbey Road' "—and then the music begins. If she got it wrong—and she does fairly often—you can either press the Home button again and start over or just tap what you want.

- **"Shuffle."** Skips to a random new song.

- **"Next song"** or **"Previous song."** Handy if you're listening to a playlist.

- **"What's playing?"** or **"What song is this?"** or **"Who is this song by?"** or **"Who sings this song?"** The iPhone voice lady tells you what you're listening to: "Now playing 'Barbie Girl' by Aqua."

- **"Genius"** or **"Play more songs like this"** (or just **"Play more like this"**). All these commands use the Genius feature to choose a different song that's musically similar to the one you were just listening to (roughly the same tempo and rockiness).

- **"Cancel."** If you summoned the Voice Control screen but now you've changed your mind—maybe the song you were hating just got to a good part—say "Cancel" to go back to what you were doing.

> **TIP:** Dictation software—speak-to-type—may be built into the iPhone 4s and later, but it's also available for the iPhone 4 in the form of a free app: Dragon Dictation. It's not nearly as convenient, because you have to do your dictating in the app and then copy the transcription into your text message, email message, or whatever. But it's a lot better than nothing.

5

Voicemail, Texting & Other Phone Tricks

Once you've savored the exhilaration of making phone calls on the iPhone, you're ready to graduate to some of its fancier tricks: voicemail, text messages, cell-company features like caller ID and call forwarding, and a Bluetooth headset or car kit.

Visual Voicemail

On the iPhone, you don't *dial in* to check for answering-machine messages people have left for you. You don't enter a password. You don't sit through some Ambien-addled recorded lady saying, "You have...17...messages. To hear your messages, press 1. When you have finished, you may hang up...."

Instead, whenever somebody leaves you a message, the phone wakes up, and a notice on the screen lets you know who the message is from. You also hear a sound, unless you've turned that option off in Settings or turned on the silencer switch.

That's your cue to tap Home→Phone→Voicemail. There you see all your messages in a tidy chronological list. (The list shows the callers' names if they're in your Contacts list; otherwise it shows their numbers.) You can listen to them in any order—you're not forced to listen to three long-winded friends before discovering that there's an urgent message from your boss. It's a game-changer.

Setup

To access your voicemail, tap Phone on the Home screen, and then tap Voicemail on the Phone screen.

The very first time you visit this screen, the iPhone prompts you to make up a numeric password for your voicemail account—don't worry, you'll never have to enter it again—and to record a "Leave me a message" greeting.

You have two options for the outgoing greeting.

- **Default.** If you're microphone-shy, or if you're famous and you don't want stalkers and fans calling just to hear your famous voice, then use this option. It's a prerecorded, somewhat uptight female voice that says, "Your call has been forwarded to an automatic voice message system. 212-661-7837 is not available." ***Beep!***

- **Custom.** This option lets you record your own voice saying, for example, "You've reached my iPhone. You may begin drooling at the tone." Tap **Record**, hold the iPhone to your head, say your line, and then tap **Stop**.

  Check how it sounds by tapping **Play**.

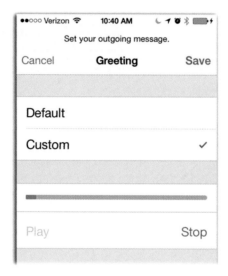

Then just wait for your fans to start leaving you messages!

Using Visual Voicemail

In the voicemail list, a blue dot (●) indicates a message you haven't yet played.

> **TIP:** You can work through your messages even when you're out of cellular range—on a plane, for example—because the recordings are stored on the iPhone itself.

In iOS 7, the Visual Voicemail controls have been thoroughly overhauled—and they're a lot clearer now. When you tap the name of a message, you instantly see the date and time it came on, plus the person's name (if it's in your Contacts) or the cellphone's registered city and state (if not). The

Play slider tells you how many seconds long the message is. And all the controls you need are right there, surrounding the message you tapped:

- ▶. Tap to listen to the message.

- **Speaker.** As the name "Visual Voicemail" suggests, you're *looking* at your voicemail list—which means you're *not* holding the phone up to your head. The first time people try using Visual Voicemail, therefore, they generally hear nothing!

  But if you hit Speaker before you tap the ▶ button, you can hear the playback *and* continue looking over the list.

NOTE: If you're listening through the earbuds, a Bluetooth earpiece, or a car kit, of course, you hear the message playing back through *that.* If you really want to listen through the iPhone's speaker instead, tap Audio and then Speaker. (You switch back the same way.)

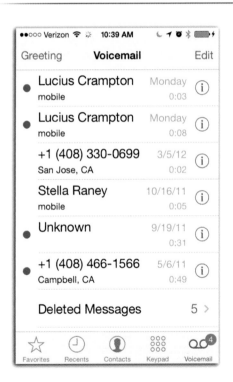
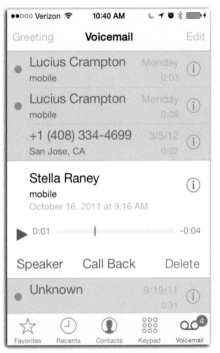

- **Call Back.** Tap Call Back to return the call. Very cool—you never even encounter the person's phone number.

- **Delete.** You might want to keep the list manageable by deleting old messages. To do that, tap a message's Delete button.

  If you have a lot of messages to delete, here's a faster way: Swipe across the first one's name right to left, and then tap Delete. The message disappears instantly. You can work down the list quickly this way.

  If you didn't know that trick, you could also do it the slow way: Tap Edit (upper right of the screen). Tap the ⊖ button next to a message's name, and then tap Delete to confirm. Tap the next ⊖ button and continue.

TIP: The iPhone hangs onto old messages for 30 days—even ones you've deleted. To listen to deleted messages that are still on the phone, scroll to the bottom of the list and then tap Deleted Messages.

On the Deleted screen, you can undelete a message that you actually don't want to lose yet (that is, move it back to the Voicemail screen) or tap Clear All to erase these messages for good.

- **Rewind, Fast Forward.** Drag the little vertical line in the scrubber bar (beneath the message) to skip backward or forward in the message. It's a great way to replay something you didn't catch the first time.

Even before you've expanded a message's row to view the Play, Speaker, Call Back, and Delete buttons, a few other Visual Voicemail buttons are awaiting your inspection:

- **Greeting.** Tap this button (upper-left corner) to record your voicemail greeting.

- **Call Details.** Tap ⓘ to open the Info screen—the Contacts card—for the message that was left for you.

  If it was left by somebody who's in your Contacts list, you can see *which* of that person's phone numbers the call came from (indicated in blue type), plus a gray ★ if that number is in your Favorites list. Oh, and you can add this person to your Favorites list at this point by tapping Add to Favorites (at the bottom of the screen).

  If the caller's number isn't in Contacts, then you're offered a Create New Contact button and an Add to Existing Contact button, so you can store it for future reference.

In both cases, you also have the option to return the call (right from the Info screen), fire off a text message, or place a FaceTime audio or video call.

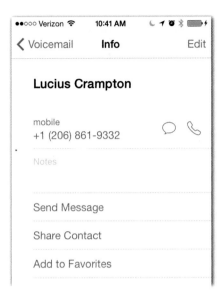

Dialing in for Messages

Gross and pre-iPhonish though it may sound, you can also dial in for your messages from another phone. (Hey, it could happen.)

To do that, dial your iPhone's number. Wait for the voicemail system to answer.

As your own voicemail greeting plays, dial * (or # if you have Verizon), your voicemail password, and then #.

You hear the Uptight Carrier Lady announce how many messages you have, and then she'll start playing them for you.

After you hear each message, she'll offer you the following options (but you don't have to wait for her to announce them):

- To delete the message, press 7.

- To save it, press 9.

- To replay it, press 4.

Conveniently enough, these keystrokes are the same on Verizon, Sprint, and AT&T.

TIP: If this whole Visual Voicemail thing freaks you out, you can also dial in for messages the old-fashioned way, right from the iPhone. Open the keypad and hold down the 1 key, just as though it were a speed-dial key on any normal phone.

After a moment, the phone connects; you're asked for your password, and then the messages begin to play back, just as described above.

Text Messages (SMS)

SMS stands for Short Messaging Service, but it's commonly just called texting. A text message is a very short note (under 160 characters—a sentence or two) that you shoot from one cellphone to another. What's so great about it?

- Like a phone call, it's immediate. You get the message off your chest right now.

- As with email, the recipient doesn't have to answer immediately. The message waits for him even when his phone is turned off.

- Unlike a phone call, it's nondisruptive. You can send someone a text message without worrying that he's in a movie, a meeting, or anywhere else where holding a phone up to his head and talking would be frowned upon. (And the other person can answer nondisruptively, too, by sending a text message *back.*)

- You have a written record of the exchange. There's no mistaking what the person meant. (Well, at least not because of sound quality. Understanding the texting shorthand that's evolved—"C U 2mrO," and so on—is another matter entirely.)

Some iPhone plans include unlimited texts. Some are capped at, say, 200 texts a month. Remember that you use up one of those 200 each time you send *or receive* a message.

And by the way, *picture and video messages* (known as MMS, or multimedia messaging service) count as regular text messages.

But whenever you're texting another iPhone owner (or iPad, or iPod Touch, or Mac), never mind that last part—all your texts are free, as described on page 154.

Receiving a Text Message

When you get an SMS, the iPhone plays a sound. It's a quick marimba riff, unless you've changed the standard sound or assigned a different text tone to this specific person.

The phone also displays the name or number of the sender *and* the message. Unless you've fooled around with the Notifications settings, the message appears at the top of the screen, disappearing momentarily on its own, so as not to interrupt what you're doing. (You can also flick it up and away if it's blocking what you were doing.)

Or, if the iPhone was asleep, it lights up long enough to display the message right on its Unlock screen (below, left). You can unlock the phone and jump directly to the message by swiping your finger *right across the message on the Lock screen.*

If you *have* changed the options in Notifications, then your text message might appear in a white bubble in the center of the screen, complete with Close and Reply buttons. If you turned off Show Preview, then you don't see the message itself—only the name or number of the sender. And if you've turned off View in Lock Screen, then, sure enough, the text message does *not* appear on the Lock screen.

> **TIP:** The Messages icon on the Home screen bears a little circled number "badge" letting you know how many new text messages are waiting for you.

Once you tap a message notification to open you see Apple's vision of what a text-message conversation should look like. Incoming text messages and your replies are displayed as though they're cartoon speech balloons (left).

 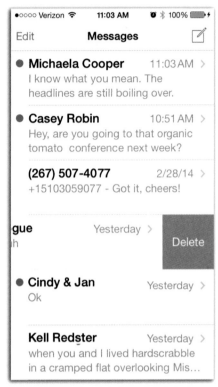

To respond to the message, tap in the text box at the bottom of the screen. The iPhone keyboard appears. Type away, or dictate a response, and then tap **Send**. Assuming your phone has cellular coverage, the message gets sent off immediately.

If your buddy replies, then the balloon-chat continues, scrolling up the screen. Don't forget to turn the iPhone 90 degrees for a bigger, wider keyboard!

And now, a selection of juicy Message tips:

- The last 50 exchanges appear here. If you want to see even older ones, scroll to the very top (which you can do by tapping the top edge of the screen) and tap **Load Earlier Messages**.

  And by the way—if the keyboard is blocking your view of the conversation, swipe downward to hide it.

- Links that people send you in text messages actually work. For example, if someone sends you a Web address, tap it with your finger to open it in Safari. If someone sends a street address, tap it to open it in Maps. And if someone sends a phone number, tap it to dial.

- If all this fussy typing is driving you nuts, you can always tap the big fat **Contact** button at the top of the screen. It produces a little strip of icons like ☎ (conclude the transaction by voice, with a phone call), ▢◁ (place a FaceTime video call), and ⓘ (open this person's full Contacts card, loaded with different ways to call, text, or email).

- Messages remembers the exact time that each text was sent or received. If you slide your finger leftward and hold it still, this hidden column of time stamps slides into view. Release your finger to snap them back.

The Text List

What's cool is that the iPhone retains all these exchanges. You can review them or resume them at any time by tapping Messages on the Home screen. A list of text message conversations appears; a blue dot indicates conversations that contain new messages (facing page, right).

> **TIP:** If you've sent a message to a certain group of people, you can address a new note to the same group by tapping the old message's row here.

The truth is, these listings represent *people,* not conversations. For example, if you had a text message exchange with Chris last week, then a quick way to send a new text message to Chris (even on a totally different subject) is to open that "conversation" and simply send a "reply." The iPhone saves you the administrative work of creating a new message, choosing a recipient, and so on.

> **TIP:** Hey, you can search text messages! At the very top of the list, there's a search box. You can actually find text inside your message collection.

If having these old exchanges hanging around presents a security (or marital) risk, you can delete them in either of two ways:

- **Delete an entire conversation.** *Swipe* away the conversation. At the list of conversations, swipe your finger *leftward* across the conversation's name. That makes the Delete confirmation button appear.

  Alternate method: Above the Messages list, tap Edit, then tap the next to the conversation you want to ditch, then tap the Delete confirmation button.

- **Delete just one text.** Open the conversation so that you're viewing the cascade of bubbles representing the texts back and forth.

  Now, this new iOS 7 technique is a little weird, but here goes: *Hold down your finger* on the individual message you want to delete (or double-tap it). When the little black bar of options appears, tap More.

  Now you can delete all the exchanges simultaneously (tap Delete All) or vaporize only particularly incriminating messages. To do that, tap the selection circles for the individual balloons you want to nuke, putting checks [✅] by them; then tap the 🗑 button to delete them all at once. Tap Delete Message to confirm.

NOTE: Interestingly, you can also *forward* some messages you've selected in this way. When you tap the Forward button (↪), a new outgoing text message appears, ready for you to specify the new recipient.

Sending a New Message

If you want to text somebody you've texted before, the quickest way, as noted above, is simply to resume one of the "conversations" already listed in the Messages list.

You can also tap a person's name in Contacts, or ⓘ next to a listing in Recents or Favorites, to open the Info screen; tap Send Message.

NOTE: In some cases, the iPhone shows you your *entire* Contacts list, even people with no cellphone numbers. But you can't text somebody who doesn't have a cellphone.

Actually, options to fire off text messages lurk all over the iPhone—anywhere you see the Share (⬆) button, which is frequently. The resulting Share screen includes options like Email, Twitter, Facebook—and Message. Tapping Message sends you back to Messages, where the photo, video, page, or other item is ready to send. (More on multimedia messages shortly.)

In other words, sending a text message to anyone who lives in your iPhone is only a couple of taps away.

NOTE: You can now tap that ⊕ button to add *another* recipient for this same message (or tap the 123 button to type in a phone number). Lather, rinse, and repeat as necessary; they'll all get the same message.

Yet another way to start: Tap the ✍ button at the top of the Messages screen.

In any case, the skinny little text message composition screen is waiting for you now. You're ready to type (or dictate) and send!

TIP: If you drag your finger down the screen, you *hide the keyboard.* Doing that makes much more of the screen available to display the text-message conversation.

Picture, Audio, or Video Messages

The iPhone can also send photos, video clips, and audio clips to other cellphones. Welcome to MMS (multimedia messaging service).

To send a photo or a video, tap the icon next to the box where you type your text messages. Two buttons appear: Take Photo or Video or Choose Existing.

If you want to transmit a photo or video that's already on your phone, tap **Choose Existing**; your Photos app opens automatically, showing all your photos and videos. Tap the one you want, and then tap **Choose**. If you choose **Take Photo or Video** instead, then your Camera app opens so you can take a new picture or snag a video clip.

In any case, you now return to your SMS conversation in progress—but now that photo or video appears inside the Send box. Type a caption or comment, if you like. Then tap **Send** to fire it off to your buddy.

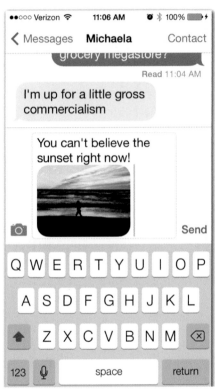

iMessages

This iOS feature should interest you—if it doesn't, in fact, make you giggle like a schoolgirl.

An iMessage looks and works exactly like a text message. You send iMessages and receive them in the same app (Messages). They show up in the same window. You can send the same kinds of things: text, photos, videos, contacts, map locations, whatever. You send and receive them using exactly the same techniques.

The big difference: iMessages are what your phone sends to other iPhones, iPads, iPod Touches, and Macs. If your iPhone determines that the address belongs to any **other** kind of phone, it automatically switches to sending regular old text messages.

So why would Apple reinvent the text-messaging wheel? Why did it create iMessages to replicate regular text messaging? Because iMessages offer some huge advantages over regular text messages:

- iMessages don't count as text messages! You don't have to pay for them. They look and work exactly like text messages, but they're transferred over the Internet (WiFi or cellular) instead of your cell company's voice airwaves. You can send and receive an unlimited number of them and never have to pay a penny more.

- When you're typing back and forth with somebody, you don't have to wonder whether, during a silence, they're typing a response to you or just ignoring you; when they're typing a response, you see an ellipsis (...), as you can see on the next page at left.

- You don't have to wonder if the other guy has received your message. A tiny, light-gray word "delivered" appears under each message you send, briefly, to let you know that the other guy's device received it.

- You can even turn on a "read receipt" feature that lets the other guy know when you've actually **seen** a message he sent. You'll see a notation that says, for example, "Read: 2:34 PM."

- Your history of iMessages shows up on all your i-gadgets; they're synchronized through your iCloud account. In other words, you can start a back-and-forth with somebody using your iPhone and later pick up your Mac laptop at home (in **its** Messages program) and carry right on from where you stopped.

  As a result, you always have a record of your iMessages. You have a copyable, searchable transcript on your computer.

You don't have to do anything special. Just go into Messages and create a text message as usual. If your recipient is using an Apple gadget running iOS 5 or later, or a Mac using OS X Mountain Lion or later, **and** has an iCloud account, **and** has turned on the iMessages feature, then your iPhone sends your message as an iMessage automatically. It somehow knows.

You'll know, too, because the light-gray text in the typing box says "iMessage" instead of "Text Message" (below, left). And each message you send shows up in a *blue* speech bubble instead of a *green* one. The Send button is blue, too.

In fact, when you're addressing the new text message, the names that appear in blue represent people with iMessages gadgets, so you know in advance who's cool and who's not (below, right). (The green names are those that do *not* have iMessage. The gray ones—well, your iPhone doesn't know yet.)

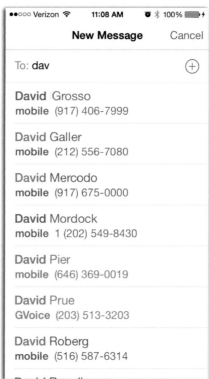

Text Messages: Details and Misc.

You might not think that something as simple as text messaging would involve a lot of fine print, but you'd be wrong.

Settings for Texts and iMessages

If you tap Settings→Messages, you'll stumble upon some intriguing messaging options:

- **iMessage.** This is the on/off switch for the entire iMessages feature. It's hard to imagine why you wouldn't want to avoid paying for text messages, but you know—whatever floats your boat.

- **Send Read Receipts.** When you turn this option on, your iMessage correspondents will know when you've seen their messages. A tiny word "Read" will appear beneath each sent message that you've actually seen. Turn this off only if it deprives you of the excuse for not responding promptly ("Hey, I never even saw your message!").

- **Send as SMS.** If iMessages is unavailable (meaning that you have no Internet connection at all), then your phone will send your message as a regular text message, via the regular cellphone voice network.

- **Send & Receive.** Tap here to specify what cellphone numbers and email addresses you want to register with iMessages. (Your laptop, obviously, does not have a phone number, which is why iMessages gives you the option of using an email address.)

  When people send iMessages to *you,* they can use any of the numbers or addresses you turn on here. That's the only time these numbers and addresses matter. *You* see the same messages exactly the same way on all of your Apple gadgets, no matter what email address or phone number the sender used for you.

  (If you scroll down on this Settings screen, you'll see the Start new conversations from options. This is where you specify which number or address others will see when *you* initiate the message. It really doesn't make much difference which one you choose.)

- **MMS Messaging.** MMS messages are like text messages—except that they can also include audio clips, video clips, or photos, as described in the following section. In the rare event that your cell company charges extra for these messages, you have an on/off switch here. If you turn it off, then you can send only plain text messages.

- **Group Messaging.** Suppose you're sending a message to three friends named A, B, and C (they have weird parents). When they reply to your message, the responses will appear in a Messages thread that's dedicated to this particular group (next page, left). It works only if *all* of you have turned on Group Messaging. (Note to the paranoid: It also means that everyone sees everyone else's phone numbers.)

- **Show Subject Field.** If email messages can have subject lines, why not text messages? Now, on certain newfangled phones (like yours), they can; the message arrives with a little dividing line between the subject and the body, offering your recipient a hint as to what it's about.

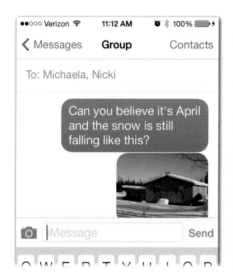

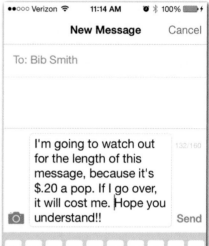

- **Character Count.** If a message is longer than 160 characters, the iPhone breaks it up into multiple messages. That's convenient, sure. But if your cellphone plan permits only a fixed number of messages a month, you could wind up sending (and spending) more than you intended.

  The Character Count feature can save you. When it's on, after your typing wraps to a second line, a little counter appears just above the Send button ("71/160," for example, as shown above at right). It tracks how many characters remain within your 160-character limit for one message. (Of course, if you're sending an iMessage, you don't care how long it is; there's no length limit.)

- **Blocked.** In iOS 7, Apple has introduced the option to block people who are harassing or depressing you with their texts or calls. Tap here to view the list of people in your Contacts app you've decided to block; tap Add New to add new people to the list.

Bonus Settings in a Place You Didn't Expect

Apple has stashed a few important text-messaging settings in Settings→ Notifications→Messages:

- **Alert Sound.** Tap here to choose a sound for incoming texts to play. (You can also choose a different sound for each person in your address book, as described on page 86.)

- **Show on Lock Screen.** Do you want received text messages and iMessages to appear on the screen of the phone when it's locked? If yes, then you can sneak reassuring glances at your phone without turning it fully on. If no, you maintain better protection against snoopers who find your phone on your desk.

- **Show Preview.** Usually, when a text message arrives, it wakes up your phone and shows itself. Which is great, as long as the message isn't private and the phone isn't lying on the table where everyone can see it. If you turn off Show Preview, though, you'll see who the message is from but not the actual text of the message (until you tap the notification banner or bubble).

- **Repeat Alerts.** If someone sends you a text message but you don't read it, the iPhone will remind you a couple more times that you have an unread text message. Or three times. Or five, or 10—whatever you choose here. (If you really don't want to be nagged about waiting messages, then turn this option off entirely.)

- **Show Alerts From.** This option is designed to give you some control over the flood of attention-getting bubbles that appear on your screen. If you choose Show Alerts From My Contacts, then you won't get that chime and bubble when total strangers send iMessages to you.

Capturing Messages and Files

In general, text messages are fleeting; most people have no idea how they might capture them and save them forever. Copy and Paste help with that. (So does the Google Voice service, but that's another conversation.)

Some of the stuff *in* those text messages is easy to captures, though. For example, if you're on the receiving end of a photo or a video, tap the small preview in the speech bubble. It opens at full-screen size so you can have a better look at it—and if it's a video, there's even a ▶ button so you can play it. Either way, if the picture or video is good enough to preserve, then tap the ⬆ button. You're offered a Save Image or Save Video button; tap to add the photo or video to your iPhone's collection.

If someone sends you contact information (a phone number, for example), you can add it to your address book. Just tap inside that bubble and then tap either Create New Contact or Add to Existing Contact.

If you'd like to preserve the actual text messages, you have a few options:

- **Copy them individually.** Double-tap a text bubble, and then tap Copy. At this point, you can paste that one message into, for example, an email message.

- **Forward them.** Double-tap a message to make the button bar appear. Tap More, and then tap the selection dots beside all the messages you want to pass on. Now you can tap the Forward ($\not\rightarrow$) button. All the selected messages go along for the ride in a single consolidated message to a new text-message addressee.

- **Save the iMessages.** If you have a Mac, then your iMessage messages (that is, notes to and from other Apple gadgets) show up in the Messages chat program. You can save them or copy them there.

> **TIP:** Behind the scenes, the Mac stores all your chat transcripts in a hidden folder, as special text files. To get there, press the Option key as you open the Go menu; choose Go→Library. The transcripts are in date-stamped folders in the Messages→Archive folder.

- **Use an app.** As you've probably figured out by now, there's no built-in way to save regular text messages in bulk. There are, however, apps that can do this for you, like DiskAid (for Windows) or iBackup Viewer (free for the Mac). They work from the invisible backup files that you create when you sync your phone with iTunes.

Free Text Messages

Text messaging is awesome. Paying for text messaging, not so much.

That's why iMessages is so great: It bypasses the cell companies' text-message network by sending messages over the Internet instead—but only when you're sending to fellow owners of Apple equipment.

Fortunately, there are all kinds of sneaky ways to do text messaging for free that *don't* require your correspondents to have iOS or OS X. Here are a couple of examples:

- **Textfree with Voice.** It's an app from the App Store that gives your iPhone its own phone number just for free text message or picture messages, so you can send and receive all you want without paying a cent. Incoming voice calls are free, too; you can buy minutes for outgoing calls.

- **WhatsApp.** Here's another app for free, iMessage-style texting— among all smartphones. The iPhone, Android, BlackBerry, Windows

Phone, Nokia Symbian, all together in glorious free texting (with pictures, videos, group chats, and more).

- **Google Voice.** Sign up for a free account. Google Voice has a million great features. But one of the best is that it lets you send and receive free text messages. You can do that from your computer (an amazingly useful feature, actually) at *voice.google.com*, or by using the free Google Voice app).

Chat Programs

The iPhone doesn't *come* with any chat programs, like AIM (AOL Instant Messenger), Yahoo Messenger, or MSN Messenger. But installing one yourself is simple enough.

If you're a hard-core chatter, though, what you really want is an all-in-one app like IM+ or Beejive IM. You get a single app that can conduct chats with people on just about every chat network known to man: GTalk, Yahoo, MSN/Live Messenger, AIM, iChat, ICQ, Myspace, Twitter, Facebook, Jabber, and Skype.

Call Waiting

Call waiting has been around for years. With a call-waiting feature, when you're on one phone call, you hear a beep indicating that someone else is calling in. You can tap the Flash key on your phone—if you know which one it is—to answer the second call while you put the first one on hold.

Some people don't use call waiting because it's rude to both callers. Others don't use it because they have no idea what the Flash key is.

On the iPhone, when a second call comes in, the phone rings (and/or vibrates) as usual, and the screen displays the name or number of the caller, just as it always does. Buttons on the screen, rejiggered in iOS 7, offer you three choices:

- **End Current Call.** Hangs up on the first call and takes the second one.

- **Answer (Hold Current Call).** This is the traditional call-waiting effect. You say, "Can you hold on a sec? I've got another call," to the first caller. The iPhone puts her on hold, and you connect to the second caller.

  At this point, you can jump back and forth between the two calls, or you can merge them into a conference call.

- **Decline Incoming Call.** The incoming call goes straight to voicemail. Your first caller has no idea that anything has happened.

If call waiting seems a bit disruptive, you can turn it off, at least on the AT&T iPhone (the switch is in Settings→Phone→Call Waiting). When call waiting is turned off, incoming calls go straight to voicemail when you're on the phone.

If you have T-Mobile, Sprint, or Verizon, then you can turn off call waiting only one call at a time; just dial *70 before you dial the number. You won't be disturbed by call waiting beeps while you're on that important call.

Call Forwarding

Here's a pretty cool feature you may not have even known you had. It lets you route all calls made to your iPhone number to a *different* number. How is this useful? Let us count the ways:

- **When you're home.** You can have your cellphone's calls ring your home number so you can use any extension in the house, and so you don't miss any calls while the iPhone is turned off or charging.

- **When you send your iPhone to Apple for battery replacement.** You can forward the calls you would have missed to your home or work phone number.

- **When you're overseas.** You can forward the number to one of the Web-based services that answers your voicemail and sends it to you as an email attachment (like Google Voice).

- **When you're going to be in a place with little or no cell coverage.** Let's say you're in Montana or Alaska. You can have your calls forwarded to your hotel or to a friend's cellphone. (Forwarded calls eat up your allotment of minutes, though.)

You have to turn on call forwarding while you're still in an area with cell coverage.

- **AT&T.** Tap Settings→Phone→Call Forwarding, turn call forwarding on, and then tap in the new phone number. That's all there is to it—your iPhone will no longer ring. At least not until you turn the same switch off again.

- **Verizon, Sprint.** On the dialing pad, dial *72, plus the number you're forwarding calls to. Then tap Call. (To turn off call forwarding, dial *73, and then tap Call.)

Caller ID

Caller ID is another classic cellphone feature. It's the one that displays the phone number of the incoming call (and sometimes the name of the caller).

The only thing worth noting about the iPhone's own implementation of caller ID is that you can prevent *your* number from appearing when you call *other* people's phones. From the Home screen, tap Settings→Phone→Show My Caller ID, and then tap the On/Off switch.

- **AT&T.** Tap Settings→Phone→Show My Caller ID, and then tap the On/Off switch.

- **Verizon, Sprint.** You can disable caller ID only for individual calls. For example, if you're calling your ex, you might not want your number to show up on his phone. Just dial *67 before you dial the number. (Caller ID turns on again for subsequent calls.)

Bluetooth Accessories

The iPhone has more antennas than an ant colony: for the cellular networks, for WiFi hotspots, for GPS, and for Bluetooth.

Bluetooth is a short-range *cable elimination* technology. It's designed to untether you from equipment that would ordinarily require a cord. Bluetooth crops up in computers (so you can print from a laptop to a Bluetooth printer), in game consoles (like Sony's wireless PlayStation controller), in fitness-tracking bands (like the UP band and Fitbit Flex), and above all, in cellphones.

There are all kinds of things Bluetooth *can* do in cellphones, like transmitting your music to a Bluetooth speaker, wirelessly syncing your address book from a computer, or letting the phone in your pocket serve as a wireless Internet antenna for your laptop. But most people use the iPhone's Bluetooth primarily for hands-free calling.

That is, it works with those tiny wireless Bluetooth earpieces, of the sort you see clipped to people's heads, as well as in cars with Bluetooth phone systems. If your car offers Bluetooth (it's an option on most car models), then you hear the other person's voice through your stereo speakers, and there's a microphone built into your steering wheel or rearview mirror. You keep your hands on the wheel the whole time.

Pairing with a Bluetooth Earpiece or Speaker

Pairing is the system of "marrying" a phone to a Bluetooth earpiece or speaker so that each works only with the other. If you didn't do this one-time pairing, then some other guy passing on the sidewalk might hear your conversation through *his* earpiece. And you probably wouldn't like that.

The pairing process is different for every cellphone and every Bluetooth earpiece. Usually it involves a sequence like this:

1. **On the earpiece, turn on Bluetooth. Make the earpiece or speaker dis-coverable.** *Discoverable* just means that your phone can "see" it. You'll have to consult the gadget's instructions to learn how to do so.

2. **On the iPhone, tap Settings→Bluetooth. Turn Bluetooth on.** The iPhone immediately begins searching for nearby Bluetooth equipment. If all goes well, you'll see the name of your earpiece or speaker show up on the screen.

3. **Tap the gadget's name. Type in the passcode, if necessary.** The *pass-code* is a number, usually four or six digits, that must be typed into the phone within about a minute. You have to enter this only once, during the initial pairing process. The idea is to prevent some evildoer sitting nearby in the airport lounge, for example, to secretly pair *his* earpiece with *your* iPhone.

   The user's manual for your earpiece should tell you what the pass-code is (if one is even required).

When you're using a Bluetooth earpiece or speaker (as a speakerphone), you *dial* using the iPhone itself. You usually use the iPhone's own volume controls, too. You generally press a button on the earpiece or speaker itself to answer an incoming call, to swap call-waiting calls, and to end a call.

If you're having any problems making a particular gadget work, Google it. Type "iphone jambox mini," for example. Chances are good that you'll find a write-up by somebody who's worked through the setup and made it work.

Bluetooth Car Systems

The iPhone works beautifully with Bluetooth car systems, too. The pairing procedure generally goes exactly as described above: You make the car discoverable, enter the passcode on the iPhone, and then make the connection.

Once you're paired up, you can answer an incoming call by pressing a button on your steering wheel, for example. You make calls either from the iPhone or, in some cars, by dialing the number on the car's own touchscreen.

> **NOTE:** When Bluetooth is turned on but the earpiece isn't, or when the earpiece isn't nearby, the * icon appears in gray. And when it's connected and working right, the earpiece's battery gauge appears on the iPhone's status bar.

Of course, studies show that it's the act of driving while conversing that causes accidents—not actually holding a phone. So the hands-free system is less for safety than for convenience and compliance with state laws.

Bluetooth 4.0

The trouble with Bluetooth has always been that it's a battery hog. Or, rather, it's a battery sipper, but since it's always on, your phone's battery drains much faster when Bluetooth is on.

That's why America's standards geeks came up with Bluetooth 4.0, also called Bluetooth Smart. Its very smart idea: It turns on only when necessary, then turns off again to save power. When you've paired your phone with a Bluetooth 4.0 gadget, you'll see the Bluetooth logo on your status bar (*) light up only when it's actually exchanging data with the gadget.

These products generally use a more direct method of pairing with your iPhone than the Settings method described above. When you open up the gadget's accompanying app, you're generally offered the chance to pair your phone to the gadget, right there where it makes sense. You're saved a detour to Settings.

Custom Ringtones

The iPhone comes with 25 creative and intriguing ringing sounds, from an old car horn to a peppy marimba lick. Page 514 shows you how to choose the one you want to hear when your phone rings. You can also buy ready-made pop-music ringtones from the wireless iTunes Store (read on).

But where's the fun in that? Surely you don't want to walk around listening to the same ringtones as the millions of *other* iPhone owners.

Fortunately, you can also make up *custom* ring sounds, either to use as your main iPhone ring or to assign to individual callers in your Contacts list. This section covers the two official ways of going about it—carving 30-second ringtone snippets out of pop songs and recording your own in GarageBand on a Mac—and points you to the two sneakier ways.

iTunes Ringtones

Apple began selling custom ringtones from its iTunes Store in 2007. Using simple audio tools in the iTunes program, you could buy a song for $1, choose a 30-second chunk, pay $1 more for the ringtone, and sync the result to your iPhone. It was a flop (at $1 for 30 seconds, is it any wonder?), and Apple quietly shut down that offering.

You can still buy canned pop-music ringtones, though—chosen by Apple or the record company, not you—for $1.30 each, from the iTunes Store. On your iPhone, open the iTunes app. Tap **More**, then **Tones**.

GarageBand Ringtones

If you have a Macintosh, then you can also create your own ringtones without paying anything to anyone—by using GarageBand, the music-editing program that comes on every new Mac (version '08 or later).

Start by building the ringtone itself. You can use GarageBand's Loops (prerecorded instrumental snippets designed to sound good together), for example, or sound you've recorded with a microphone. (There's nothing like the prerecorded sound of your spouse's voice barking out from the phone: "HONEY! PICK UP! IT'S ME!" every time your beloved calls.)

If you're not especially paranoid about record-company lawyers, you can also import any song at all into GarageBand—an MP3, AIFF, MIDI, or non–copy protected AAC file, for example—and adapt a piece of it into a ringtone. That's one way for conscientious objectors to escape the $1.30-per-ringtone surcharge.

In any case, once you have your audio laid out in GarageBand tracks, press the letter **C** key. That turns on the **Cycle strip**—the yellow bar in the ruler shown here. Drag the endpoints of this Cycle strip to determine the length of your ringtone (up to 40 seconds long).

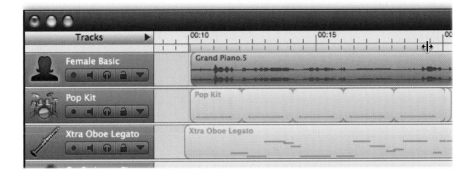

TIP: One feature that's blatantly missing on the iPhone is a "vibrate, **then** ring" option for incoming calls. That's where the phone first vibrates silently to get your attention and begins to ring only if you haven't responded after, say, 10 seconds.

GarageBand offers the solution: Create a ringtone that's silent for the first 10 seconds (drag the Cycle strip to the left of the music) and only **then** plays a sound. Then set your iPhone to vibrate and ring. When a call comes in, the phone plays the ringtone immediately as it vibrates—but you won't hear anything until after the silent portion of the ringtone has been "played."

Press the space bar to start and stop playback as you fiddle.

When everything sounds good, choose Share→Send Ringtone to iTunes. Next time you set up your iPhone sync, click the Ringtones tab in iTunes and schedule your newly minted ringtone for transfer to the phone.

TIP: There are two other, less-official ways to create ringtones. One method lets you snag a piece of any not-copy-protected song in your iTunes library. The process takes several steps, but it's free and doesn't require special software. Details are in the free PDF appendix on this book's "Missing CD" at *www.missingmanuals.com*.

The other is to use a program like Ringtone Recorder Pro, a $1 download from the App Store. It emails you a ringtone (for subsequent syncing from iTunes) from anything you can record with your iPhone's microphone—voices, music, any audio—which is a very cool idea.

Kiosk Mode, Large Type & Accessibility

If you were told the iPhone was one of the easiest phones in the world for a disabled person to use, you might spew your coffee. The thing has almost no physical keys! How would a blind person use it? It's a phone that rings! How would a deaf person use it?

You won't believe the lengths to which Apple has gone to make the iPhone usable for people with vision, hearing, or other physical impairments. If you're deaf, you can have the LED flash to get your attention. If you're blind, you can literally turn the screen off and operate *everything*—do your email, surf the Web, adjust settings, run apps—by tapping and letting the phone speak what you're touching, in whatever language your iPhone uses. It's pretty amazing.

You can also magnify the screen, reverse black for white (for better-contrast reading), set up custom vibrations for each person who might call you, and convert stereo music to mono (great if you're deaf in one ear).

Some of these features are useful even if you're not disabled—in particular, the LED flash, custom vibrations, and zooming. The kiosk mode is great for kids; it prevents them from exiting whatever app they're using now. And if you're disabled in the sense of being over 40, you might find the Large Text option especially handy when you can't find your reading glasses.

Finally, don't forget about Siri (Chapter 4). She may be the best friend a blind person's phone ever had.

Here's a rundown of the accessibility features in iOS 7. To turn on any of the features described here, open Settings→General→Accessibility.

 TIP: You can turn many of the iPhone's accessibility features on and off with a triple-click on the Home button. See page 183 for details.

VoiceOver

VoiceOver is the option that makes the iPhone speak everything you touch—even the little status gauges at the top of the screen.

On the VoiceOver settings pane, tap the On/Off switch to turn VoiceOver on. Because VoiceOver radically changes the way you control your phone, you must dismiss a warning to confirm that you know what you're doing. Immediately, you hear a female voice begin reading the names of the controls she sees on the screen.

You can adjust the **Speaking Rate** of the synthesized voice.

Now you're ready to start using the iPhone in VoiceOver mode. There's a lot to learn, and practice makes perfect, but here's the overview:

- **Tap something to hear it.** Tap icons, words, even status icons at the top; as you go, the voice tells you what you're tapping. "Messages." "Calendar." "Mail—14 new items." "45 percent battery power." You can tap the dots on the Home screen, and you'll hear, "Page 3 of 9."

  Once you've tapped a screen element, you can also flick your finger left or right—anywhere on the screen—to "walk" through everything on the screen, left to right, top to bottom.

TIP: A little black rectangle appears around whatever the voice is identifying. That's for the benefit of sighted people who might be helping you.

- **Double-tap the screen to "tap" it.** Ordinarily, you tap something on the screen to open it. But since single-tapping now means "speak this," you need a new way to open everything. So: To open something you've just heard identified, double-tap *anywhere on the screen.* (You don't have to wait for the voice to finish talking.)

TIP: Or do a *split tap.* Tap something to hear what it is—and with that finger still down, tap somewhere else with a different finger to open it.

There are all kinds of other special gestures in VoiceOver. Make the voice stop speaking with a *two-finger tap;* read everything, in sequence, from the top of the screen with a *two-finger upward flick;* scroll one page at a time with a *three-finger flick up or down;* go to the next or previous screen (Home, Stocks, and so on) with a *three-finger flick left or right;* and more.

Or try turning on Screen Curtain with a *three-finger triple-tap;* it blacks out the screen, giving you total privacy as well as a heck of a battery boost. (Repeat to turn the screen back on.)

On the VoiceOver settings screen, you'll find an expanded wealth of options for using the iPhone sightlessly. For example:

- **Speak Hints** makes the phone give you additional suggestions for operating something you've tapped. For example, instead of just saying "Safari," it says, "Safari. Double-tap to open."

- **Use Pitch Change** makes the phone talk in a higher voice when you're entering letters and a lower voice when you 're deleting them. It also uses a higher pitch when speaking the first item of a list, and a lower one when speaking the last item of a group. In both cases, this option is a great way to help you understand where you are in a list.

- **Use Sound Effects** helps you navigate by adding little clicks and chirps as you scroll, tap, and so on.

- **Use Compact Voice.** The "compact voice" is a starter voice. Its realism and vocabulary aren't as good as the "full voice," which you can download once you start using VoiceOver. But on older phones (the iPhone 4, for example), some people prefer the compact one because it's quicker to speak—less laggy.

- **Braille** lets the iPhone accept input from a Bluetooth Braille keyboard.

- **The Rotor** is a brilliant solution to a thorny problem. If you're blind, how are you supposed to control how VoiceOver reads to you? Do you have to keep burrowing into Settings to change the volume, speaking speed, punctuation verbosity, and so on?

   Not anymore. The Rotor is an imaginary dial. It appears when you twist two fingers on the screen as if you were turning an actual dial.

   And what are the options on this dial? That's up to you. Tap **Rotor** to get a list of options: **Characters**, **Words**, **Speech Rate**, **Volume**, **Punctuation**, **Zoom**, and so on.

   Once you've dialed up a setting, you can get VoiceOver to move from one item to another by flicking a finger up or down. For example, if you've chosen **Volume** from the Rotor, you make the playback volume louder or quieter with each flick up or down. If you've chosen Zoom, then each flick adjusts the screen magnification.

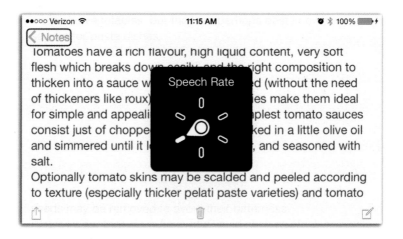

The Rotor is especially important if you're blind and using the Web. It lets you jump among Web page elements like pictures, headings, links, text boxes, and so on. Use the Rotor to choose, for example, images—then you can flick up and down from one picture to the next on that page.

- **Languages & Dialects.** Here's a list of languages and accents that the iPhone can speak to you. Tap Default Dialect to choose what accent you want to hear (American, British, Australian, and so on). Under Rotor Languages, tap Add New Language and then turn on all the languages that you might want your iPhone to use. Later, you can switch among them using the Rotor. (The Language option appears on the Rotor automatically if you've chosen more than one here.)

- **Typing Feedback** governs how the phone helps you figure out what you're typing. It can speak the individual letters you're striking, the words you've completed, or both.

- **Speak Notifications** makes the phone announce, with a spoken voice, when an alert or update message has appeared.

- **Navigate Images.** As VoiceOver reads to you what's on a Web page, how do you want it to handle pictures? It can say nothing about them (Never), it can read their names (Always), or it can read their names and whatever hidden Descriptions savvy Web designers have attached to them for the benefit of blind visitors.

- **Large Cursor.** This option fattens up the borders of the VoiceOver "cursor" (the box around whatever is highlighted) so you can see it better.

If you rely on VoiceOver for using your iPhone, then you should visit the more complete user guide at *http://support.apple.com/kb/HT3598*.

> **TIP:** VoiceOver is especially great at reading your iBooks out loud. Details are on page 332.

Zooming

The iPhone has one of the smallest screens of any computer on the market. Every now and then, you might need a little help reading small text or inspecting those tiny graphics.

If you turn on Zoom (in Settings→General→Accessibility), then you can magnify the screen whenever it's convenient, up to 500 percent. Of course, the screen image is now too big to fit the physical glass of the iPhone, so you'll need a way to scroll around on your virtual jumbo screen. Here's the scheme:

- **Turn zooming on or off** by tapping the screen with three fingers. The screen is now 200 percent of original size (below, left).

- **Pan around the virtual giant screen** by dragging with three fingers.

TIP: Once you begin a three-finger drag, you can lift two of your fingers. You can slide the remaining finger close to any screen border to continue scrolling in that direction—faster the closer you are to the edge.

- **Zoom in more or less** by double-tap/dragging with three fingers. It's like double-tapping, except that you leave your fingers down on the second tap—and drag them upward to zoom in more (up to 500 percent), or down to zoom out again.

Once again, you can lift two of your three fingers after the dragging has begun. That way, it's easier to see what you're doing.

When VoiceOver is turned on, three-finger tapping has its own meaning—"jump to top of screen." Until iOS 6 came along, therefore, you couldn't use Zoom while VoiceOver was on.

Now, however, you can, but you have to add an extra finger or tap to the usual VoiceOver gestures. For example, ordinarily, double-tapping with three fingers makes VoiceOver stop talking, but since that's the "zoom in" gesture, you must now *triple*-tap with three fingers to mute VoiceOver.

And what about VoiceOver's existing triple/three gesture, which turns the screen off? If Zoom is turned on, you must now triple-tap with *four* fingers to turn the screen off.

Invert Colors

By reversing the screen's colors black for white, like a film negative, you create a higher-contrast effect that some people find is easier on the eyes (facing page, right). To try it out, go to Settings→General→Accessibility and turn on Invert Colors. The other colors reverse, too—red for green, and so on.

Speak Selection

This convenient option adds a new Speak command to the buttons that appear whenever you highlight text in any app. Tap that button to make the phone read the selected text out loud. It can be an email message, a Web page, a text message—anything.

Speak Auto-Text

You know how the iPhone suggests a word as you type? This option in Settings→General→Accessibility makes the iPhone *speak* each suggestion. That effect has three benefits. First, of course, it helps blind people know what they're typing. Second, you don't have to take your eyes off the keyboard, which is great for speed and concentration. Third, if you're zoomed in, you may not be able to see the suggested word appear under your typed text—but now you still know what the suggestion is.

Larger Type

This option is the central control panel for iOS 7's new Dynamic Type feature. It's a game-changer if you have aging eyes—that is, if you often find the type on the screen too small.

Using the slider, you can choose a larger type size for all text the iPhone displays in apps like Mail, iBooks, Messages, and so on. This slider doesn't affect all the world's *other* apps—until their software companies update them to make them Dynamic Type-compatible. That day, when it comes, will be glorious. One slider to scale them all.

The switch at the top, **Larger Dynamic Type**, unlocks an even longer slider. That is, it makes it possible for you to make the text in all the Dynamic Type–compatible apps even larger.

Bold Text

The new design of iOS 7 has its fans and its detractors. But one thing is for sure: The new system font, Helvetica Neue Light, is a fairly light font. Its strokes are very thin; in some sizes and lighting conditions, it can even be hard to read.

But if you turn on **Bold Text** (and then tap **Continue** in the confirmation box), your iPhone restarts—and when it comes to, the fonts everywhere are slightly heavier: at the Home screen, in email, everywhere. And much easier to read with low light or aging eyesight.

It's one of the most useful features in iOS 7—and something almost nobody knows about.

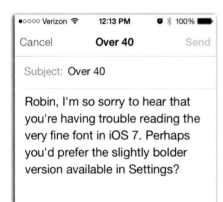

Increase Contrast

Here's yet another iOS 7 improvement for the benefit of people who have eyes.

This on/off switch doesn't really increase contrast. What it **does** do is eliminate the transparency of screens like the Control Center and the Notification Center. Their backgrounds are now opaque, rather than slightly see-through, so that text on them is much easier to read. (You can see the before and after here.)

Reduce Motion

What kind of killjoy would want to turn off the "parallax motion" of the Home screen background behind your icons? The effect is very subtle as it is!

In any case, you can if you want, thanks to this new button.

On/Off Labels

The Settings app teems with little tappable on/off switches, including this one. When something is turned on, the background of the switch is orange; when it's off, the background is white.

But if you're having trouble remembering that distinction, turn on this option. Now the background of each switch sprouts visible symbols to help you remember that orange means On (you see a | marking) and white means Off (you see a O marking).

Hearing Aids

A cellphone is bristling with wireless transmitters, which can cause inter-ference and static if you wear a hearing aid. But the iPhone offers a few solutions.

First, try holding the phone up to your ear normally when you're on a call. If the results aren't good, see if you can switch your hearing aid from M (acoustic coupling) mode to T mode (telecoil). If so, open Settings→General→Accessibility→Hearing Aids and turn on Hearing Aid mode (iPhone 5 and later), which makes it work better with T-model hearing aids.

(On the GSM [AT&T] iPhone 4 and 4s, Hearing Aid mode is for M mode only. It reduces the power of the phone's antennas, which might mean slower Internet speeds but also means less interference.)

This settings panel also lets you "pair" your phone with a Bluetooth hearing aid. These wireless hearing aids offer excellent sound but eat hungrily through battery charges.

Hearing aids bearing the "Made for iPhone" logo work especially well—they sound great and don't drain the battery.

Subtitles & Captioning

Occasionally, a movie you download or stream from the Internet offers subtitles, so you can understand the dialogue even if you can't hear it, the volume is turned down, or the actors are mumbling. This option turns on those subtitles automatically whenever they're available, so that you don't have to do that manually with each movie.

The **Style** option gives you control over the font, size, and background of those captions, complete with a preview. (Tap the ⊡ button to view the preview, and the sample caption, at full-screen size.) The **Custom** option even lets you dream up your own font, size, and color for the type; a new color and opacity of the caption background; and so on.

LED Flash for Alerts

If you're deaf, you know when the phone is ringing—because it vibrates, of course. But what if it's sitting on the desk, or it's over there charging? This option lets you know when you're getting a call, a text, or a notification by blinking the flash on the back of the phone—the very bright LED light.

Mono Audio

If you're deaf in one ear, then listening to any music that's a stereo mix can be frustrating; you might be missing half the orchestration or the vocals. When you turn on the **Mono Audio** option in **Settings→General→Accessibility**, the iPhone mixes everything down so that the left and right channels contain the same monaural playback. Now you can hear the entire mix in one ear.

Phone Noise Cancelation

iPhone models 5 and later have three microphones scattered around the body. In combination, they offer extremely good background-noise reduction when you're on a phone call. The microphones on the top and back, for example, listen to the wind, music, crowd noise, or other ambient sound and subtract that ambient noise from the sound going into the main phone mike.

You can turn that feature off here—if, for example, you experience a "pressure" in your ear when it's operating.

Balance Slider

The L/R slider lets you adjust the phone's stereo mix, in case one of your ears has better hearing than the other.

Guided Access (Kiosk Mode)

It's amazing how quickly even tiny tots can master the iPhone—and how easily they can muck things up with errant taps.

Guided Access solves that problem rather tidily. It's kiosk mode. That is, you can lock the phone into one app; the victim cannot switch out of it. You can even specify which *features* of that app are permitted. Never again will you find your Home screen icons accidentally rearranged or text messages accidentally deleted.

Guided Access is also great for helping out people with motor-control difficulties—or teenagers with self-control difficulties.

To turn on Guided Access, open Settings→General→Accessibility→Guided Access; turn the switch On.

Now a Set Passcode button appears. Tap it to specify a four-digit password. It ensures that only you, the wise parent or guardian, will be able to get the phone *out* of kiosk mode.

Now open the app you'll want to lock in place. Press the Home button three times fast. The Guided Access screen appears. At this point, you can proceed in any of three ways:

- **Declare some features off limits.** With your finger, draw a circle around each button, slider, and other control that you want to deactivate. You'll see the phone convert your circle to a tidy rectangle; you can drag its corners to adjust its size, drag inside the rectangle to move it, or tap the ⊗ to remove it if you change your mind or want to start again.

Once you enter Guided Access mode, the controls you've enclosed appear darkened (above, right). They no longer respond—and your phone-borrower can't get into trouble.

- **Change settings.** If you tap Options, you get a few additional controls. You can decide whether or not your little urchin is allowed to press the Sleep/Wake Button or the Volume Buttons when in Guided Access mode. You can turn Touch and Motion on or off, too. For example, if you want to hand the phone to your 2-year-old in the back seat to watch baby videos, you can disable the touchscreen altogether.

- **Begin kiosk mode.** Tap Start.

Later, when you get the phone back, and you want to use it normally, tri-ple-press the Home button again; enter your four-digit password. At this point, you can tap **Options** to change them, **Resume** to go back into kiosk mode, or **End** to return to the iPhone as you know it.

> **TIP:** If you use any of the other accessibility features described in this chapter, you may be dismayed to discover that you can no longer use the triple-clicking of the Home button to open the on/off buttons for those features. The triple-click has been taken over by Guided Access!
>
> Fortunately, Apple has already anticipated this problem. If you turn on **Accessibility Shortcut** on the Guided Access screen of Settings (see page 183), then triple-clicking produces the usual list of accessibility features—and Guided Access is on that list, too, ready to tap.

Switch Control

In iOS 7, Apple has made the iPhone available to another category of fans: those whose physical skills are limited to very simple gestures: puffing on an air pipe, pressing a foot switch, blinking an eye, or turning the head, for example. A hardware accessory called a *switch* lets you operate certain gadgets this way.

When you turn on Switch Control, the iPhone warns you that things are about to get very different. Tap **OK**.

Now the phone sequentially highlights one object on the screen after another; you're supposed to puff, tap, or blink at the right moment to say, "Yes, *this* one."

If you don't have a physical switch apparatus, you can use one nature gave you: your head. The iPhone's camera can detect when you turn your head left or right and can trigger various functions accordingly.

If you'd like to try it out, open **Settings→General→Accessibility→Switch Control**. Tap **Switches→Add New Switch→Camera→Left Head Movement**.

On this screen, you choose what a left head-turn will mean to your phone. The most obvious option is **Select Item**, which you could use in conjunc-tion with the sequential highlighting of controls on the screen. But you can also make it mean "press the Home button," "activate Siri," "adjust the volume," and so on.

Once you've made your selection, repeat that business for **Right Head Movement**.

When you return to the Switch Control screen, turn on **Switch Control**. Now your phone is watching you; whenever you turn your head left or right, it activates the control you set up. Pretty wild.

The controls here let you specify how fast the sequential highlighting proceeds, whether or not it pauses on the screen's first item, how many times the highlighting cycles through each screenful, and so on.

To turn off Switch Control, tap the on/off switch again. Or, if you're using some other app, triple-press the Home button to open the Accessibility shortcut panel. If you had the foresight to add Switch Control to its options (page 183), one tap does the trick.

Switch Control is a broad (and specialized) feature. To read more about it, open the Accessibility chapter of Apple's iPhone User Guide: *http://help. apple.com/iphone/7.*

AssistiveTouch

If you can't even hold the phone, you might have trouble shaking the phone (a shortcut for "Undo"); if you can't move your fingers, just adjusting the volume might be a challenge.

This feature is Apple's accessibility team at its most creative. When you turn AssistiveTouch on, you get a new, glowing white circle in a corner left of the screen (facing page, left).

You can drag this magic white ball anywhere on the edges of the screen, though; it remains onscreen all the time.

When you tap it, the white ball expands into the special palette shown on the facing page. It's offering four ways to trigger motions and gestures on the iPhone screen without requiring hand or multiple-finger movement. All you have to be able to do is tap with a single finger—or even a stylus held in your teeth or foot:

- **Siri.** Touch here when you want to speak to Siri (iPhone 4s and later). If you do, in fact, have trouble manipulating the phone, Siri is probably your best friend already—and now you don't even have to hold down the Home button to start her up.

- **Home.** You can tap here instead of pressing the physical Home button. (That's handy when your Home button gets sticky, too.)

- **Device.** Tap this button to open a palette of six functions that would otherwise require you to grasp the phone or push its tiny physical buttons (facing page, right). There's **Rotate Screen** (you can tap this instead of turning the phone 90 degrees), **Lock Screen** (instead of pressing the Sleep switch), **Volume Up** and **Volume Down** (instead of pressing the volume keys), and **Mute/Unmute** (instead of flipping the small Mute switch on the side).

If you tap **More**, you get some bonus buttons. They include **Shake** (does the same as shaking the phone to undo typing), **Screenshot** (as though you'd pressed the Sleep and Home buttons together), **Multitasking** (brings up the task switcher, as though you'd double-pressed the Home button), and **Gestures**.

 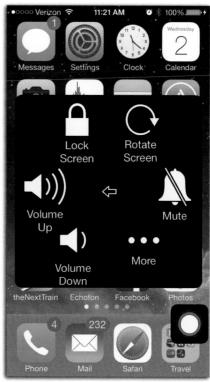

That **Gestures** button opens up a peculiar palette that depicts a hand holding up two, three, four, or five fingers. When you tap, for example, the three-finger icon, you get three blue circles on the screen. They move together. Drag one of them (with a stylus, for example), and the phone thinks you're dragging three fingers on its surface. Using this technique, you can operate apps that require multiple fingers dragging on the screen.

- **Favorites.** Impressively enough, you can actually define your own gestures. On the AssistiveTouch screen, tap **Create New Gesture** to draw your own gesture right on the screen, using one, two, three, four, or five fingers.

For example, suppose you're frustrated in Maps because you can't do the two-finger double-tap that means "zoom out." On the Create New Gesture screen, get somebody to do the two-finger double-tap for you. Tap **Save** and give the gesture a name—say, "2 double tap."

From now on, "2 double tap" shows up on the Favorites screen, ready to trigger with a single tap by a single finger or stylus.

> **TIP:** Apple starts you off with one predefined gesture in Favorites: pinch. That's the two-finger pinch or spread gesture you use to zoom in and out of photos, maps, Web pages, PDF documents, and so on. And now you can trigger it with only one finger; just drag either one of the two handles to stretch them apart. Drag the connecting line to move the point of stretchiness.

Home-Click Speed

If you have motor-control problems of any kind (sleep deprivation and overdoing it at the bachelor party come to mind), you might welcome this enhancement. It's an option to widen that time window for register-ing a double-press or triple-press of the Home button. If you choose **Slow** or **Slowest**, the phone accepts double- and triple-presses spaced far and farther apart, rather than interpreting them as individual presses a few sec-onds apart.

Incoming Calls

When a call comes in, where do you want it to go? Your headset? Directly to the speakerphone? Or the usual (headset unless there's no headset)? Here's where you make your choice.

Accessibility Shortcut

Burrowing all the way into the Settings→General→Accessibility screen is quite a slog when all you want to do is flip some feature on or off. Therefore, you get this handy shortcut: a fast triple-press of the Home button.

That action produces a little menu, in whatever app you're using, with on/off switches for the iPhone's various accessibility features.

It's up to you, however, to indicate which ones you want on that menu. That's why you're on this screen—to turn on the features you want to appear on the triple-press menu. Your options are VoiceOver, Invert Colors, Zoom, Switch Control, and AssistiveTouch.

 TIP: If you choose only one item here, then triple-pressing the Home button won't produce the menu of choices. It will just turn that one feature on or off.

6

The iPhone as iPod

Of all the iPhone's talents, its iPoddishness may be the most successful. This function, after all, gets the most impressive battery life (40 hours of playback). There's enough room on your phone to store thousands of songs. And iTunes Radio, new in iOS 7, means that you'll never run out of music to listen to—and you'll never have to pay a penny for it.

To enter iPod Land, open the Music app. On a new phone, it's at the lower-right corner of the screen.

 TIP: There's another way to get to the iPod mode. Just swipe upward from the bottom of the screen. That opens the Control Center, whose central feature is the music playback controls and a volume control.

List Land

The Music program begins with lists—lots of lists. The icons at the bottom of the screen represent your starter lists. You can rearrange or swap them, but you start out with Radio, Playlists, Artists, Songs, and More. Here's what they all do.

iTunes Radio

In iOS 7, Apple has given you an amazing gift: your own radio station. Your own *empire* of radio stations, in fact.

The new iTunes Radio service lets you listen to exactly the kind of music you want to hear. It doesn't just distinguish among genres like jazz or rock—your choices are more like "upbeat male vocals with driving brass section" versus "slow lovesick ballads with lots of strings."

You don't get to choose the exact songs or singers you want to hear; you have to trust iTunes Radio to choose a sequence of songs **based** on a song, singer, or music genre that you specify as a "seed." For example, if you choose Billy Joel as your "seed," you'll hear a lot of Billy Joel, but also a lot of other music that sounds more or less like his.

Here's something you can't do when you listen to real radio: Skip past a song you don't like. When you tap the ▶▶ button, iTunes Radio instantly skips to the next song it would have played. In fact, you can even tell it **Play More Like This** or **Never Play This Song** to shape your radio station's future.

In exchange for all this magic, you have to listen to the occasional ad between songs. Unless you subscribe to iTunes Match (page 485), that is, in which case you never hear any ads.

The idea of a "seed song"–based radio service isn't new, of course. It's the same idea as Pandora, a Web site and app that has offered precisely the same features for years. But iTunes Radio is built in, it's incorporated with Siri and the Control Center, and it's so nice to use. It's also part of Apple's larger ecosystem; that is, you can see your same set of "radio stations" on your Mac or PC (in the iTunes app), iPad, and Apple TV.

Playing iTunes Radio

The first time you open the Music app, you see a Welcome screen. Tap **Start Listening** to arrive at the main iTunes Radio app. (You may be asked to enter your Apple ID and password.)

Across the top, you get a horizontally scrolling set of "album covers." They represent ready-made "radio stations" that Apple has supplied for you. Tap the one called **iTunes Top 100: Pop**, for example, and your phone instantly begins playing the biggest current pop hits.

Below these, you see similar "album covers" for radio stations you've created yourself, as described below. Don't forget to scroll down to see them all.

The Now Playing Screen

As a station plays, you see a screen like the one shown below at right. It displays the cover picture for the song's album, the name of the song, band, and album name.

Here's what the controls do:

- ⟨. Return to the Start screen, where you can choose a different radio station.

- ⓘ. Opens the Info screen, described below.

- **Price.** Of course, Apple would be thrilled if you came across a song you liked so much you wanted to buy it. That's why the price button (**$1.29**, for example) is so prominent. When you tap it, the price changes to say **Buy Song**; tap again to download the song directly to your phone. Now you can listen to it again, on command, without being subject to the randomness of iTunes Radio.

- **Progress bar.** You can't fast-forward or rewind within a Radio song. This strip is just a graph that shows you where you are in the song. The numbers on either side show you how far you are into the song and how much is left to play.

- ★. Tap to find the **Play More Like This** and **Never Play This Song** buttons, which let you fine-tune your "radio station," tailoring it precisely to your tastes.

   The third button, **Add to iTunes Wish List**, means, "I liked this song; maybe I'll buy it later." When you get home to your Mac or PC, open the iTunes program, click **Store** at the top right, and then click **My Wish List** (in the list at right). Here's the list you've been quietly building with your taps on the **Add to iTunes Wish List** button. You can listen to 1-minute previews, buy the complete songs, or delete them from the list if you've changed your mind.

- **II/▶.** Yeah, here's another thing you can't do with regular radio: Pause.

- **▶▶.** This button doesn't actually mean "fast forward." It means "skip." You immediately hear the next song.

- **Volume slider.** Of course, you can also press the buttons on the left side of the phone.

Make Your Own Station

You can set up a new "radio station" of your own in either of two ways: by choosing one of Apple's canned, ready-to-use stations or by typing in a song or performer you like.

- **Prefab stations.** On the iTunes Radio screen, tap **New Station**. Boom: There's a huge list of music genres—Blues, Christian, Classical, Indie Rock, and so on. Tap one to see a list of prefab radio stations, ready to hear.

If you tap Jazz, for example, the options include **Bop, Early Jazz, Jazz Rock, Latin Jazz,** and **The Big Band Era**. Tap a name to listen a little bit. If you like what you hear, tap the tiny ➕ button to its right. You've just added a new "radio station" to the iTunes Radio main screen.

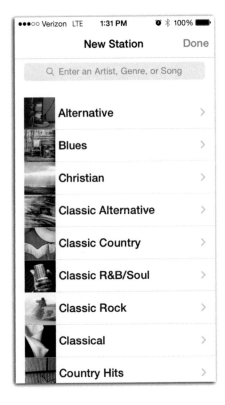

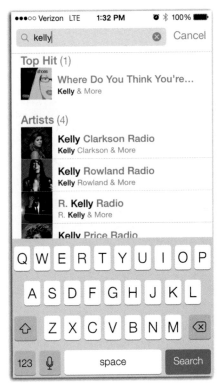

- **Type in a "seed."** Tap in the tiny search box at the top; the keyboard appears. Type in—or tap the microphone button 🎤 and speak—the name of a singer, band, song, or kind of music (*show tunes* or *a cappella*, for example).

  On the results screen, tap the entry that looks most promising ("A Cappella Radio," for example). You've just created a new station, and it begins instantly.

As your stations build up, they require more scrolling down the main iTunes Radio screen to find. But the ✚ button (to create a new station) is always there, always at the very bottom.

The Info Screen

If you tap the ⓘ button above the Now Playing screen, you're offered some options that give you more control over whatever's assaulting your ears:

- **☰**. This button opens the full list of songs from the album you're hearing right now. Each, of course, has a price button so that you can buy it. You can also read the album's reviews (**Reviews**) and see what other albums its fans have bought (**Related**).

- **Price.** Tap to buy the song and download it to your phone.

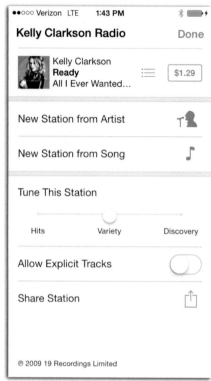

- **New Station from Artist, New Station from Song.** If a song comes on that you especially like, these buttons instantly create a new station that will play more music that sounds like this performer or this song. In effect, you get to branch your original station into one that's more finely tuned to a particular taste.

- **Tune This Station** (available for stations you've created). Do you want iTunes Radio to feed you the most popular songs within the category you've chosen? Or is it OK for it to play weirder, more obscure songs that you might not have heard before? Make your choice by adjusting this slider, from **Hits** (more mainstream) to **Discovery** (more out-there).

- **Add to My Stations** (available for Apple's suggested stations). Turns the current, Apple-selected station into one of your own.

- **Allow Explicit Tracks.** Turn this switch on if you're not easily offended by raunchy lyrics.

- **Share Station.** If you've created and fine-tuned a station so that it's truly amazing, you can bestow your superior taste on your friends by sending them a link to your station. Tap this button to produce the standard share sheet; you can send a station by AirDrop, text message, email, Twitter or Facebook.

Tap Done to close the Info screen.

Deleting or Editing a Station

On the main Radio screen, in the My Stations row, tap Edit. Tap the name of the station you want to mangle or obliterate.

Now you can rename your station or share it. Using the Play More Like This and Never Play This sections, you can add performers, songs, or genres that you do or don't want to be part of this station anymore.

Finally, if you scroll to the bottom, you can tap Delete Station to vaporize this ill-begotten station for good.

History

At the top of the main Radio screen, the History button opens a list of every song you've heard on each of your stations. It's an amazing way to find out the name of some great song whose name you didn't catch while it was playing.

This list also, of course, includes a Buy button for each of those songs.

Siri and iTunes Radio

One of the best ways to control iTunes Radio is barking orders at it. Luckily, Siri comes equipped to recognize a whole slew of new commands, all pertaining to iTunes Radio.

Here's a sampler; you don't have to use these precise wordings.

- **Play the radio.**
- **What song is this?**
- **Play more like this.**
- **Don't play this song again.**
- **Pause the music; resume the music; skip this song.**
- **Play Billy Joel Radio** or **Play some Kelly Clarkson.** (These must refer to a station you've already created.)

- Add this song to my Wish List.

- Stop the radio.

Playlists

A *playlist* is a group of songs you've placed together, in a sequence that makes sense to you. One might consist of party tunes; another might hold romantic dinnertime music; a third might be drum-heavy workout cuts.

In the olden days, you could create playlists only in the iTunes software. (And you still can. After you sync the iPhone with your computer, the playlists appear here.) These days, however, you can also create playlists right on the phone; read on.

Creating Playlists on the Phone

In the Music app, on the Playlists screen, tap **New Playlist**. Type a name for your new playlist (facing page, left), and then tap **Save**.

Now you're shown an alphabetical master list of songs. Tap each song you want to add to the new playlist (you don't have to tap the ⊕ button itself). Tap **Done** when you've added all the songs you want.

You arrive at the details screen for this playlist (facing page, center), where you can inspect or edit your handiwork. Tap **Edit** to rearrange the playlist songs or to delete some. Or tap **Playlists** to back out to the list of playlists, where your newly minted playlist is nestled.

> **TIP:** The ☁ icon means that you own this song, but it's not currently on your phone. You can still play it, but only when you're connected to the Internet. Tap the ☁ to download it to the phone for offline playback, or tap **Download All** to download all the online songs.

Whatever playlists you create (or edit) on the phone will wind up back on your computer, in iTunes, the next time you sync.

Using Playlists

To see what songs or videos are in a playlist, tap its name. (The > symbol in a Music menu always means "Tap to see what's in this list.") Or swipe rightward across its name.

Here you can use a standard iOS 7 convention: Anywhere you're asked to drill down from one list to another—from a playlist to the songs inside, for example—you can backtrack by *swiping from the left edge* of the phone into the screen.

Or do it the long way: Tap ‹ at the upper-left corner of the screen (or swipe that word to the left). That button's name always tells you what screen you just came from (Playlists, for example).

You now arrive at a Playlist details screen, where your tracks are listed for your inspection. To start playing a song once you see it in the Playlist list, tap it.

Tap **Edit**, if you like, to drag the songs into a new sequence or to delete some of them (above, right). Tap **Clear** (above, middle) if you want to choose a different set of songs within this playlist name, or tap **Delete** to get rid of the playlist altogether. (Tapping **Shuffle** starts them playing right now, in a random order.)

Genius Playlists

Apple's Genius playlist feature is supposed to analyze all your music and then, at the click of a button, create a playlist containing other songs from your library that "sound great" with one particular "seed" song. (Basically, it clumps songs by their degree of rockiness: soft-rock songs, harder rock, and so on.)

If you've used this feature in iTunes on your Mac or PC, and you've built up a Genius playlist or two, you'll also find those playlists on your iPhone. But you can make a Genius playlist right on the phone.

To do that, tap **Genius Playlist** at the top of the Playlist screen. Your list of all songs appears. (You can tap **Artists** or **Albums** and burrow through your songs that way, too.)

Tap the song you want to be the "seed"—the one you want the playlist to sound the most like. It starts to play—and if you let it run, you'll hear 24 more songs like it. You're listening to your new Genius playlist.

NOTE: That is, *if* you have enough music on the phone. If you don't have a lot of music, you may get the "This song does not have enough related songs" error message. Tap **OK** and then try a different song. Or just spend $500 on music.

At this point, the Genius Playlist screen lists the songs it's proposing for your new instant Genius playlist. If you consider this batch worth saving, tap **Save**. The new playlist now appears among your others on the Playlists screen, named after your seed song, bearing the ✸ logo to remind you that the phone created that wicked mix.

You can also tap **Refresh** to make the phone take another stab at building a similar group of songs, or **New** to start over with a different seed song.

Next time you sync, this playlist will return to the mother ship: iTunes.

If you spot a song you can't stand, you can either tap **Edit** and then delete it from the Genius playlist or tap **Refresh** to make the iPhone try again with a different assortment (based on the seed song).

TIP: There's another entity called a Genius *mix.* Unlike a Genius playlist, a mix is a never-ending "radio station." You have to create it in iTunes on your computer and then sync it to your phone. Once you do that, a new Genius button (⚛) appears in the Music app on your phone, providing access to your mixes.

Artists, Songs...

The other icons across the bottom of the Music screen include:

- **Artists.** This list identifies all the bands, orchestras, or singers in your collection. Even if you have only one song from a certain performer, it shows up here.

Once again, you drill down to the list of individual songs by tapping an artist's name. At that point, tap any song to begin playing it.

- **Songs.** Here's an alphabetical list of every song on your iPhone. Scroll or flick through it; use the index at the right side of the screen to jump to a letter of the alphabet; or scroll all the way to the top and type a song name, album name, podcast name, or band name into the search box. Tap anything to begin playing it.

> **TIP:** At the bottom of any of these lists, you'll see the total number of items *in* that list: "76 Songs," for example. At the top of the screen, you may see the Now Playing button, which opens up the playback screen of whatever is playing.
>
> Best of all, if you *drag all the way downward* on any list—Music, Podcasts, whatever—you'll see that a search box has been hiding from you, up off the top of the screen. It lets you search your audio stash by name (title, band, or album).

Other Lists

The icons at the bottom of the Music app—usually Radio, Playlists, Artists, and Songs—are only suggestions. You can slice and dice your music collection in all kinds of other listy ways, too: by Album, by Genre, by Composer, and so on.

To view some of the most useful secondary lists, tap the fifth icon, More. The More screen appears, listing a bunch of other ways to view your collection.

Here are your options:

- **Albums.** That's right, it's a list of all the CDs or downloaded albums from which your music collection is derived, complete with miniature pictures of the album art. Tap an album's name to see a list of songs that came from it; tap a song to start playing it.

- **Audiobooks.** One of the great pricey joys of life is listening to digital "books on tape" that you've bought from Audible.com. *If* you've bought any, this category appears, and they show up in this list. (Audiobooks you've ripped from CDs don't show up here—only ones you've downloaded from Audible.)

- **Compilations.** A *compilation* is one of those albums that's been put together from many different performers. You know: "Zither Hits of the 1600s," "Kazoo Classics," and so on. You're supposed to turn on the Compilation checkbox manually, in iTunes, to identify songs that belong together in this way. Once you've done that, all songs that belong to compilations you've created show up in this list..

- **Composers.** Here's your whole music collection sorted by composer—a crumb the iPhone creators have thrown to classical-music fans.

- **Shared.** This item appears only if you've turned on Home Sharing, so that you can listen to music that's sitting on a computer elsewhere in your house. Details later in this chapter.

- **Genres.** Tap this item to sort your collection by musical genre: Pop, Rock, World, Gospel, or whatever.

NOTE: There used to be entries here for iTunes U (lectures, lab reports, movies, and other educational materials supplied to the world by universities) and podcasts. They're gone now, because Apple would prefer that you download the dedicated iTunes U and Podcasts apps.

Customizing List Land

Now you know how to sort your collection by every conceivable criterion. But what if you like seeing your list of composers or albums? Are you really expected to open up the More screen every time you want to see your list sorted that way?

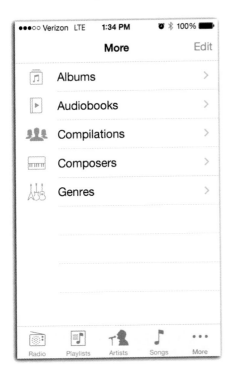

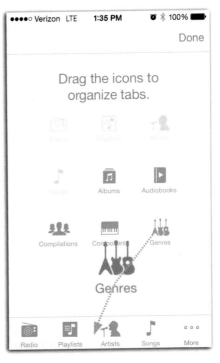

Fortunately, you can add the icons of these lists to the bottom of the main Music screen. You can replace any of the four starter categories (Radio, Playlists, Artists, Songs), so the lists you use most frequently are easier to open.

To renovate the four starter icons, tap **More** and then **Edit**. You arrive at the "Drag the icons to organize tabs" screen. Here's the complete list of music-sorting lists.

To replace one of the four starter icons at the bottom, drag an icon from the top half of the screen downward, directly onto the *existing* icon you want to replace. It lights up to show the success of your drag.

When you release your finger, the new icon has replaced the old one. Tap **Done**.

Oh, and while you're on the Edit screen: You can take this opportunity to *rearrange* the first four icons at the bottom. Drag them around with your finger. Fun for the whole family!

> **TIP:** Drag downward on any list in the Music app to reveal a hidden search box at the top.

The Album Mosaic

Anytime you're using the iPhone's Music personality, whether you're playing music or just flipping through your lists, you can rotate the iPhone 90 degrees in either direction—so it's in landscape orientation—to view a patchwork quilt of album art. (This is iOS 7's version of the old animated Cover Flow screen.)

Slide horizontally to scroll the album covers.

If you tap one, you get to see this view, complete with playback controls and a list of songs from that album. Tap a song to start playing it; tap the ▮▮ to pause. Tap the album cover to return to the mosaic and continue browsing. All of this goes away when you rotate the iPhone upright again.

So what, exactly, is this view for? You could argue that it's a unique way to browse your collection, to seek musical inspiration without having to stare at scrolling lists of text.

But you could also argue that it's just Apple's engineers showing off.

Playback Control: Now Playing

Whenever a song is playing, the Now Playing screen appears, offering all the controls you need to control music playback—some obvious and some not so obvious.

> **TIP:** Here's a non-obvious one: If the phone is asleep, double-press the Home button (or tap the Sleep switch). Why, look—playback controls, right on the Lock screen! You don't even have to wake or unlock the phone.

- **Return arrow.** At the top-left corner of the screen, the ❮ button means, "Return to the list whence this song came." It takes you back to the list of songs in this album, playlist, or whatever.

> **TIP:** You can also swipe to the right from the phone's left edge. In the Music app, that always means "go back."

- **Album list.** At the top-right corner, there's a ☰ icon that seems to say "list." Tap it to view a list of the other songs on *this* song's album (above, right). The track-listing screen offers two enjoyable activities. You can jump directly to another cut by tapping its name. Or you can check out the durations of the songs in this album.

> **TIP:** You can double-tap the big album art picture to open the track list, too. It's a bigger target.

- **Album art.** Most of the screen is filled with a bright, colorful shot of the original CD's album art. (If none is available—if you're listening to a song *you* wrote, for example—you see a big gray generic musical-note picture. You can drag or paste in an album-art graphic—one you found on the Web, for example—in iTunes.)

TIP: You can read the song's lyrics, superimposed right on the album art; see page 207.

- **Song info.** Center top: the artist name, track name, and album name.

- **Rating.** If you tap the song's name, it disappears. It's replaced by a row of five light-gray dots.

  This is your opportunity to *rate* the song, by tapping one of the five dots. If you tap dot number three, for example, the first three dots all turn into stars. You've just given that song three stars. When you next sync your iPhone with your computer, the ratings you've applied magically show up on the same songs in iTunes. (Tap the album cover to restore the song info and hide the rating.)

- **Scrubber.** This slider reveals two useful statistics: how much of the song you've heard, in minutes and seconds (at the left end) and how much time remains (at the right end).

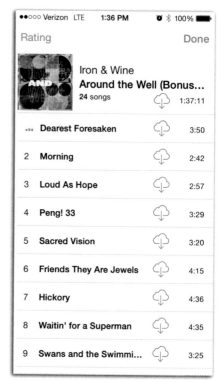

To operate the slider, drag the tiny, vertical-line handle with your finger. You can jump to any spot in the song this way. (Tapping directly on the spot you want to hear doesn't work.)

TIP: This is very cool: You can control the *speed* of the scrubbing, using this highly secret trick:

Drag the little handle *upward or downward;* the song title changes to show you the new scrubbing speed. As your finger slides farther from the handle, it says "Hi-Speed Scrubbing," then "Half-Speed Scrubbing," then "Quarter-Speed Scrubbing," then "Fine Scrubbing." The point is to get finer control over your scrubbing, making it easier to locate a specific spot in the tune.

- **Play/Pause button.** The Pause button beneath the album photo looks like this ‖ when the music is playing. If you do pause, then the button turns into the Play button (▶).

TIP: If you're wearing the earbuds, then pinching the microphone clicker serves the same purpose: It's a Play/Pause control.

Incidentally, when you plug in headphones, the iPhone's built-in speaker turns off, but when you unplug the headphones, your music pauses instead of switching abruptly back to the speaker.

- **Previous, Next (◀◀, ▶▶).** These buttons work exactly as they do on an iPod: Tap ◀◀ to skip to the beginning of this song (or, if you're already at the beginning, to the previous song). Tap ▶▶ to skip to the next song.

TIP: If you're wearing the earbuds, then you can pinch the clicker *twice* to skip to the next song.

If you hold down one of these buttons, you rewind or fast-forward. You hear the music speeding by, without turning the singer into a chipmunk. The rewinding or fast-forwarding accelerates if you keep holding the button down.

TIP: See the little scroll bar beneath the album art? You can also drag your finger across it to jump to any spot in the song.

- **Volume.** You can drag the round handle of this slider (bottom of the screen) to adjust the volume—or you can use the volume buttons on the left side of the phone.

TIP: If you use your iPhone for its iPod features a lot, don't miss the Control Center. It's the panel of controls that appears when you swipe up from the bottom of the screen. It includes playback controls, so you don't have to go to the Music app just to change tracks.

- **Repeat.** If you *really* love a certain album or playlist, you can command the iPhone to play it over and over again, beginning to end. Just tap the Repeat button.

  Now you're offered three looping options: Repeat Off (stop repeating), Repeat Song (loop this song endlessly), and Repeat All (repeat these songs over and over; it might instead say Repeat Album or Repeat Playlist).

- **Create.** And voilà: Another pop-up list of options. There's Genius Playlist (create a Genius playlist based on the song you're listening to, as described on page 194;) New Station from Artist; and New Station from Song. These create new iTunes Radio "stations," as described earlier in this chapter.

- **Shuffle.** Ordinarily, the iPhone plays the songs in an album sequentially, from beginning to end. But if you love surprises, tap here so it changes to say Shuffle All. Now the album plays in random order.

By the way, there's nothing to stop you from turning on Repeat *and* Shuffle, meaning that you'll hear the songs on the album played endlessly, but never in the same order twice.

TIP: Shake the whole iPhone to shuffle—that is, to start playing another random song. A little chime announces the phone's understanding of your action.

Voice Control

There's one more way to control your playback—a way that doesn't involve taking your eyes off the road or leaving whatever app you're using. You can control your music playback by voice command, using Siri. See Chapter 4.

Special Podcast/Audiobook Controls

When you're listening to a podcast or an audiobook, three new buttons replace the Loop, Genius, and Shuffle buttons described above:

- **15-second repeat (⟲).** What'd he say again? Tap to make the audio jump back 15 seconds so you can hear something you missed. Perfect when you've just been interrupted by an inquiry from a spouse, boss, or highway patrolman.

- **15-second skip (⟳).** Jump forward 15 seconds. Because, you know... ads happen.

- **1x Speed, 2x Speed, .5x Speed.** This feature may be God's gift to the audiobook or podcast fan: It changes how fast people are talking.

    Get through a podcast or audiobook faster when you're stuck with a slow droner; slow it down if it's a New York mile-a-minute chatterer. Each time you tap this button in the lower-right corner, the playback cycles through to the next speed.

> **TIP:** Along with the special podcast controls, you also get superimposed white text on the album art when you tap the screen. It displays a description of the episode, if the creators of the podcast bothered to supply one.

Multi(music)tasking

Once you're playing music, it keeps right on playing, even if you press the Home button and move on to do some other work on the iPhone. After all, the only thing more pleasurable than surfing the Web is surfing it with a Beach Boys soundtrack.

If you've got something else to do—like jogging, driving, or performing surgery—tap the Sleep/Wake switch to turn off the screen. The music keeps playing, but you'll save battery power.

> **TIP:** Even with the screen off, you can still adjust the music volume (use the volume buttons on the earbud clicker or the buttons on the side of the phone), pause the music (pinch the earbud clicker once), or advance to the next song (pinch it twice).

When a phone call comes in, the music fades, and you hear your chosen ringtone—through your earbuds, if you're wearing them. Squeeze the clicker on the earbud cord or tap the Sleep/Wake switch to answer the call. When the call ends, the music fades back in, right where it left off.

Speakers and Headphones

The iPhone's speaker is pretty darned good for such a tiny machine. But the world is full of better speakers—black and white Bluetooth wireless speakers, car stereo systems, hi-fi TVs, and fancy headphones. The iPhone is especially easy to use with them.

Bluetooth Wireless

You can now buy amazingly small, powerful Bluetooth stereo speakers that receive your iPhone's music from as far as 20 or 30 feet away—made by Jawbone, Bose, and others.

There are also Bluetooth *headphones.* But when you shop, make sure the headphones say "A2DP stereo"; the headsets for making office phone calls and so on don't play *music* over Bluetooth.)

Once you've bought your headphones or speakers, you have to introduce them to the iPhone—a process called *pairing.*

From the Home screen, tap Settings→Bluetooth. Turn Bluetooth on (below, left); you see the Searching ❊ animation as the iPhone wirelessly hunts for your headphones or speakers.

Grab them, turn them on, and start the pairing procedure, as described in the manual. Usually that means holding down a certain button until a tiny light starts flashing. At that point, the headphones' or speaker's name appears on the iPhone's screen (facing page, left).

> **TIP:** If the headphones or speakers require a one-time passcode—it's usually 0000, but check the manual—the iPhone's keyboard appears, so you can type it in.

A couple of seconds later, it says Connected; at this point, any sound that the iPhone would ordinarily play through its speakers or earbuds now plays through the wireless 'phones or speakers. Not just music—which, in general, sounds amazing—but chirps, game sounds, and so on. Oh, and phone calls.

If your headset has a microphone, too, you can even answer and make phone calls wirelessly. (There's an Answer button right on the headphones.)

Using Bluetooth wireless stereo does eat up your battery charge faster. But come on: listening to your music without wires, with the iPhone still in your pocket or bag? How cool is that?

AirPlay

There's another way to transmit audio wirelessly from the iPhone (and video, too). Apple came up with a technology called AirPlay; you can buy AirPlay speakers, amplifiers, and TV sets. The Apple TV may be the most famous AirPlay machine.

AirPlay is described on page 215, because most people use it to transmit video, not just audio. But the steps for transmitting to an AirPlay audio gadget are the same.

Switching Among Speakers

When your iPhone has a connection to a wireless sound source—a Bluetooth speaker or AirPlay receiver, for example—you need some way to direct the music playback to it.

The answer is the ⏏ button. It's on the Control Center (facing page, top right). When you tap it, the iPhone offers a button for each speaker (lower right); to switch, tap the one you want.

Instantly, the sound begins flowing from your other sound source. Use the same method to switch back to the iPhone's speakers when the time comes.

Familiar iPod Features

The iPhone has a long list of traditional iPod features for music playback. Most of these options all await in Settings→Music. (Shortcut: Tell Siri, "Open Music settings.")

Shake to Shuffle

If you turn this option on, then you can give the phone itself a quick shake to shuffle the current playlist, album, or all-music playback. That's great when you're jogging but just not feeling much inspiration from some lame ballad that's come on.

Sound Check

This feature smooths out the master volume levels of tracks from different albums, helping to compensate for differences in their recording levels. It doesn't deprive you of peaks and valleys in the music volume, of course—it affects only the baseline level.

EQ (Equalization)

Like any good music player, the iPhone offers an EQ function: a long list of presets, each of which affects your music differently by boosting or throttling various frequencies. One might bring out the bass to goose up your hip-hop tunes; another might emphasize the midrange for clearer vocals; and so on. "Late Night" is especially handy; it lowers the bass so it thuds less. Your downstairs neighbors love it.)

Volume Limit

It's now established fact: Listening to a lot of loud music through earphones can damage your hearing. Pump it up today, pay for it tomorrow.

Portable music players can be sinister that way, because in noisy places like planes and city streets, people turn up the volume much louder than they would in a quiet place, and they don't even realize how high they've cranked it.

That's why Apple created this volume slider. It lets you limit the maximum volume level of the music.

In fact, if you're a parent, you can even lock down this control on your child's iPhone; it can be bypassed only with a password. Set the volume slider here, and then, in Settings→General→Restrictions, turn on Volume Limit, as described on page 551.

Lyrics & Podcast Info

If you've pasted lyrics for a song into iTunes on your computer (or used one of the free automated lyrics-fetching programs—search "iTunes lyrics" in Google), you can make them appear on the iPhone screen during playback just by tapping the album art on the playback screen. (Scroll with a flick.) When you're listening to a podcast, its text description appears instead.

Group By Album Artist

Suppose you've bought a movie soundtrack album or compilation album with a different band on each track.

In iTunes, you can see all these songs listed in a group, thanks to a text field called Album Artist. (There you see the unifying title—the movie name, for example.)

When you turn on this option, the Music app consolidates all those artist names into a single new album-name entry in your Artists list. For example, you'll see an entry for "Apocalypse Now Soundtrack," which you can tap to see the individual '60s songs within it; the individual bands are no longer scattered alphabetically through the Artists list.

> **TIP:** Many soundtrack albums come with their Album Artist identified only as "Various Artists," and that's how your iPhone will group them. In iTunes, however, you can select all the songs on the album, choose File→Get Info, and change the Album Artist to something more descriptive, like the movie title. When you sync the results back to your phone, the album will show up in the proper spot in the Artists list.

Playing Music from Your Computer

Here's a trick you weren't expecting: You can store many terabytes of music on your Mac or PC upstairs—and play it on your phone in the kitchen downstairs.

This nifty bit of wireless magic is brought to you by Home Sharing, a feature of the iTunes program. To set it up, make sure your phone and computer are on the same WiFi network.

Then, in iTunes on the Mac or PC, open Preferences. Click Sharing, and turn on "Share my library on my local network." (You can share only certain playlists, if you like.) Turn on Require password and enter your Apple account (iCloud) password. Click OK.

Now pick up your phone. In Settings→Music, log into Home Sharing using the same Apple ID and password. Finally, open the Music app on the phone.

Tap **More**, tap **Shared**, and tap the name of your computer's iTunes library. (Later, when you want to return to listening to the stuff on the phone itself, tap that same **Shared** button, but this time tap the name of your phone.)

The iTunes Store

Just as you can buy apps using the App Store app, you can also browse, buy, and download songs, TV shows, and movies using the iTunes Store app. Anything you buy gets autosynced back to your computer's copy of iTunes when you get home. Whenever you hear somebody mention a buy-worthy song, for example, you can have it within a minute.

To begin, open the iTunes app. The store you see here is modeled on the App Store described in Chapter 8. This time, the buttons at the bottom of the screen include **Music**, **Movies**, **TV Shows**, **Search**, and **More**.

When you tap **Music**, **Movies**, or **TV Shows**, the screen offers further drill-ing-down buttons. For Music, for example, the scrolling horizontal rows of options might include **New Releases**, **Recent Releases**, **Singles**, and **Pre-Orders**.

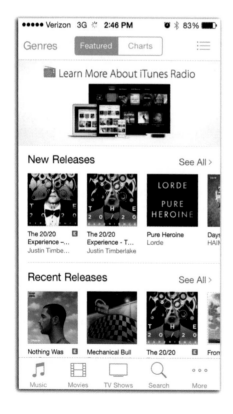
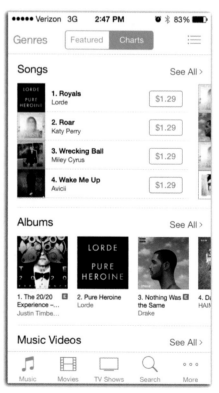

(Beneath each list is a **Redeem** button, which you can tap if you've been given an iTunes gift certificate or promo code; a **Send Gift** button, which lets you buy a song or video for someone else; and an **Apple ID** button, which can show you your current credit balance.)

TIP: You can't buy TV shows or movies on the cellular network—just in WiFi hotspots. That's your cell company's way of saying, "We don't want you jamming up our precious cellular network with your hefty video downloads, bucko."

Note, by the way, that you can *rent* movies from the store instead of buying them outright. You pay only $3, $4, or $5 to rent (instead of $10 to $16 to buy). But once you start watching, you have only 24 hours to finish; after that, the movie deletes itself from your phone. (If you like, you can sync it to your Mac or PC to continue watching in iTunes—still within 24 hours.)

To search for something in particular, tap **Search**. The keyboard appears. Type what you're looking for: the name of a song, movie, show, performer, or album, for example. At any time, you can stop typing and tap the name of a match to see its details. You can use the buttons across the top to restrict the search to one category (just songs or movies, for example).

All of these tools eventually take you to the details page of an album, song, or movie. It closely resembles the details page of an app in the App Store—you get an Info page, a page of customer ratings and reviews, and a Related tab that suggests similar masterpieces.

For a song, tap its name to hear an instant 90-second preview (tap again to stop). For a TV show or movie, tap ▶ to watch the ad or the sneak preview.

If you're sold, tap the price button to buy the song, show, or album (and tap **BUY** to confirm). Enter your Apple ID password when you're asked. (For movies, you can choose either **Buy** or **Rent**, priced accordingly.) At this point, your iPhone downloads the music or video you bought.

Purchased Items

Anything you buy from the iTunes Store winds up in the appropriate app on your iPhone. Open the Videos app to see your TV shows and movies or the Music app to see your songs.

You can also inspect them from within the iTunes Store app; tap **More** and then **Purchased**.

If you do that (and then tap the relevant category, like **Music** or **Movies**), you get a pair of tabs:

- **All.** Here's a list of everything you've bought from iTunes, on your iPhone or any other Apple machine.

- **Not On This iPhone.** This is the cool part. Here you see not just the files on the iPhone in your hand, but things you've bought on other Apple gadgets—an album you bought on your iPad, for example, or a song you downloaded to your iPod Touch. (This assumes that you're using the same Apple ID on all your gizmos.)

  The beauty of this arrangement, of course, is that you can tap the name of something that's Not On This iPhone—and then download it. No extra charge.

TIP: If you prefer, you can direct your phone to download those purchases that you make on other gadgets automatically, without your having to tap **Not On This iPhone**. Visit **Settings→iTunes & App Store**, and turn on the switches for **Music**, **Apps**, and/or **Books** under **Automatic Downloads**. If you also turn on **Use Cellular Data**, then your phone will do this auto-downloading when you're in any 3G or LTE cellular Internet area, not just in a WiFi hotspot.

More in "More"

The Purchased option may be the most useful one hanging out in the More section. But tapping **More** at the bottom of the screen also offers these options:

- **Audiobooks.** This means you, Audible.com fans. Listen to your books.

- **Tones.** You can buy ready-made ringtones on this page—30-second slices of pop songs. (Don't ask what sense it makes to pay $1.30 for 30 seconds of a song, when you could buy the whole song for the same price.)

- **Genius.** Apple offers a list of music, movies, and TV shows for sale that it thinks you'll like, based on stuff you already have.

- **Podcasts.** Browse for thousands of free, and delightful, podcasts (commercial and homemade downloadable "radio shows" and "TV shows"). If you've installed Apple's Podcasts app, this item doesn't appear.

- **Downloads.** Shows you a progress bar for anything you've started to download. Also shows you anything that's queued up to download but hasn't started yet.

TIP: If you tap Edit, you'll see that you can replace any of the four iTunes Store bottom-row icons with one of the More buttons (Audiobooks, Tones, and so on). The procedure is exactly like the one described on page 197.

So you've downloaded one of the store's millions of songs, podcasts, TV shows, music videos, ringtones, or movies directly to your phone. Next time you sync, that song will swim **upstream** to your Mac or PC, where it will be safely backed up in iTunes. (And if you lost your connection before the iPhone was finished downloading, your Mac or PC will finish the job automatically. Cool.)

The Videos App

The iPhone has a separate app for playing TV shows, movies, and other videos. It's called, of all things, Videos.

If you can't figure out how to operate this app, then you shouldn't be allowed to have an iPhone. It's got three tabs: Movies, TV Shows, and Music Videos (or whatever video types you actually have).

NOTE: If you've turned on Home Sharing (page 534), a tab appears here called Shared. It's where you see your computers listed so that you can view the videos contained on them instead of on your phone.

Tap to see the thumbnails of your videos; tap a video to see its plot summary, year of release, and so on. If it's a TV series, tap an episode in that series, if necessary. Either way, tap ▶ to begin watching.

NOTE: If you see a ☁ icon on this screen, it means that this bought or rented movie is not actually on your phone. If you have a good WiFi signal, you can watch it right now by streaming it (instead of downloading it to your phone).

If you don't see that icon, then an Edit button appears instead. Tap it, and then tap the ✪, to delete it.

When you're playing video, anything else on the screen is distracting, so Apple hides the video playback controls. Tap the screen once to make them appear, and again to make them disappear.

Here's what they do:

- **Done.** Tap this button, in the top-left corner, to stop playback and return to the master list of videos.

- **Scroll slider.** This progress indicator (top of the screen) is exactly like the one you see when you're playing music. You see the elapsed time, the remaining time, and a white, round handle that you can drag to jump forward or back in the video.

> **TIP:** Drag your finger farther (up or down) from the handle to choose a faster or slower scrubbing speed.

- **Zoom/Unzoom.** In the top-right corner, a little ◤ or ◥ button appears if the video's shape doesn't exactly match your screen. (The iPhone 5 family's screen is a perfect match for most hi-def TV shows, so the button appears less often.) Tap it to adjust the zoom level of the video, as described on the next page.

- **Play/Pause (▶/❚❚).** These buttons (and the earbud clicker) do the same thing to video as they do to music: alternate playing and pausing.

- **Previous, Next (◄◄, ►►I).** Hold down your finger to rewind or fast-forward the video. The longer you hold, the faster the zipping. (When you fast-forward, you even get to hear the sped-up audio.)

  If you're watching a movie from the iTunes Store, you may be surprised to discover that it comes with predefined chapter markers, just like a DVD. Internally, it's divided up into scenes. To see them, stop playback (tap Done); on the movie page, tap Chapters. Tap a chapter name to skip to that chapter marker—or tap ▶ to return to your original spot.

TIP: If you're wearing the earbuds, you can pinch the clicker *twice* to skip to the next chapter, or *three times* to go back a chapter.

- **Volume.** You can drag the round handle of this slider (bottom of the screen) to adjust the volume—or you can use the volume buttons on the left side of the phone.

- **Language ().** You won't see this button often. But when you do, it summons subtitle and alternate-language soundtrack options, just like a DVD player.

- **AirPlay (⬛).** This symbol appears if you have an Apple TV (or another AirPlay-compatible electronic). Tap it to send your video playback to the TV, as described on page 214.

> **TIP:** To delete a video, swipe leftward across its name in the Videos list; tap Delete to confirm. (You can always re-download it, of course.)

Zoom/Unzoom

The iPhone's screen is bright, vibrant, and stunningly sharp. Sometimes, however, it's not the right shape for videos.

Pre-HDTV shows are squarish, not rectangular. So when you watch older TV shows on a rectangular screen, you get black letterbox columns on either side of the picture.

Movies have the opposite problem. They're usually **too** wide for the iPhone screen. So when you watch movies, you may wind up with **horizontal** letterbox bars above and below the picture.

Some people are fine with that. After all, HDTVs have the same problem. At least when letterbox bars are onscreen, you know you're seeing the complete composition of the scene the director intended.

Other people can't stand letterboxing. You're already watching on a pretty small screen; why sacrifice some of that precious area to black bars?

Fortunately, the iPhone gives you a choice. If you double-tap the video as it plays, you zoom in, magnifying the image so it fills the entire screen. Or, if the playback controls are visible, you can also tap ▨ or ▨.

Of course, now you're not seeing the entire original composition. You lose the top and bottom of old TV scenes, or the left and right edges of movie scenes.

Fortunately, if this effect chops off something important—some text, for example—the original letterbox view is just another double-tap away.

(As noted above, no zooming happens if the source material is already a perfect fit for the iPhone's screen shape.)

TV Output

When you crave a screen bigger than 3 or 4 inches, you can play your iPhone's videos on a regular TV. All you need is the right cable.

If you have the iPhone 4s or later, you can use the Apple Digital AV Adapter. It carries both audio and video over a single cable (an HDMI cable).

It *mirrors* what's on the phone: your Home screen, email, Safari, and everything else. (Photos and presentations appear on your TV in pure, "video outputted" form, without any controls or other window clutter.)

AirPlay

If you have an iPhone 4s or later, you have an even juicier option available to you: wireless projection, thanks to a feature called AirPlay. It transmits music or hi-def video (with audio) from your iPhone to an Apple TV (or another AirPlay-equipped receiver) across the room. It's a fantastic way to send slideshows, movies, presentations, games, FaceTime calls, and Web sites to your TV for a larger audience to enjoy. Whatever's on the screen gets sent to your Apple TV, even if you rotate the phone partway through.

AirPlay receivers include the Apple TV (version 2 or later), as well as speakers, stereos, and audio receivers from Denon, Marantz, JBL, iHome, and other companies.

To make AirPlay work, make sure the phone and the AirPlay receiver are on the same WiFi network. Then, when you're playing a video or even music, tap ◻ at the bottom of the screen.

Or, if you just want to show what's on the iPhone's regular operating screens (not video), like the Home screen or an app, swipe up to open the Control Center.

Tap ◻ to see a list of available AirPlay receivers, as illustrated above. If you have an Apple TV, turn its Mirroring switch **On**.

That's it! Everything on the iPhone screen now appears on the TV or sound system. (The phone's status bar displays the ◻ icon, so you don't wander off and forget that every move you make is visible to the entire crowd in the living room.)

> **TIP:** You can even turn a *Mac* into an AirPlay receiver. A $13 program called Reflector (*reflectorapp.com*) lets you view the iPhone's live image on the Mac's screen—and hear its sound.
>
> You can opt to see a frame around the image, representing the body of the phone itself. There's also a **Record** command, so you can create a movie of whatever you're doing on the phone.
>
> Reflector is great for trainers, teachers, or product demonstrators. And if you have a projector connected to the Mac, it's a fantastic way to project your iPhone onto a screen that's even bigger yet.

7

Camera, Photos & Video

This chapter is all about the iPhone's ability to display photos copied over from your computer, to take new pictures with its built-in camera, and to capture videos. You've probably never seen pictures and movies look this good on a pocket gadget. The iPhone screen is bright, the colors are vivid, and the super-high pixel density makes every shot of your life look cracklin' sharp.

With each new version of the iPhone, Apple improves its camera—and on the iPhone 5s, it's unbelievably good. There's no optical zoom, but otherwise, the photos *can* look every bit as good as what you'd get from a dedicated camera. And the hi-def videos are indistinguishable from what you'd get out of a camcorder. They're even auto-stabilized.

The Camera App

The little hole on the back of the iPhone, in the upper-left corner, is its camera.

On the latest iPhones, it's pretty impressive, at least for a cellphone cam. The iPhone 5s, for example, has two LED flashes, takes excellent 8-megapixel photos, can shoot 10 shots a second, and does amazingly well in low light.

The earlier iPhone models' cameras aren't quite as good, but they're still fine as long as your subject is still and well lit. Action shots may come out blurry, and dim-light shots come out rather grainy.

Now that you know what you're in for, here's how it works.

Firing Up the Camera

For years, the usual ritual for opening up the Camera app was tapping its icon on the Home screen.

And that still works. Unfortunately, photographic opportunities are frequently fleeting; by the time you fish the phone from your pocket, wake it up, slide your finger to unlock it, press the Home button, find the Camera app, and wait for it to load, the magic moment may be gone forever.

Fortunately, there's a much quicker way to get to the Camera app when the phone is asleep:

1. **Press the Home button or Sleep switch to wake the phone.** A very faint  button appears at the lower-right corner of the screen.

2. **Flick the** 📷 **button upward**.

   The Camera app opens directly. This trick shaves an unbelievable amount of time off the old get-to-the-camera method.

> **TIP:** This Camera shortcut bypasses the "enter password" screen (if you've put a password or fingerprint restriction on your phone). Any random stranger who picks up your phone can jump directly into picture-taking mode.
>
> Said stranger can't do much damage, though. She can take new photos, or delete the new photos taken during her session—but the photos you've *already* taken are off limits, and the features that could damage your reputation (editing, emailing, and posting photos) are unavailable in the Camera app. You have to open the Photos app to get to those—and that requires the phone password.

The first time you use the camera, you may be asked if it's OK to *geotag* your shots (record where you were when you took them). Unless you're a burglar or are having an affair, tap OK.

> **TIP:** Of course, there's a hands-free way to fire up the Camera app, too: Tell Siri, "Open camera."

The Five Modes of Camera

The Camera app in iOS 7 has been thoroughly made over. By swiping your finger horizontally anywhere on the screen, you switch among its modes:

- **Slo-Mo** (iPhone 5s only). Wow, what gorgeousness! You get a video filmed at 120 frames a second—so it plays back at one-quarter the speed, incredibly smoothly. Fantastic for sports, tender smiles, and cannonballs in the pool.

- **Video.** Here's your basic camcorder mode.

- **Photo.** This is the primary mode for taking pictures. It's the one Camera chooses automatically when it opens.

- **Square.** You might wonder why Apple would go to the trouble of designating a whole special camera mode to taking square, not rectangular, pictures. Answer: Instagram, the crazy-popular app that takes square pictures and was sold to Facebook for $1 billion.

- **Pano.** Choose this mode to capture super wide-angle panoramic photos (iPhone 4s and later).

All of these modes are described in this chapter, but in a more logical order: still photos first, then video modes.

Still Photos

Most people, most of the time, use the Camera app to take still photos.

It's a pretty great experience. At 3.5 or 4 inches, the iPhone's screen is an absolutely huge digital-camera viewfinder. You can turn it 90 degrees for a wider or taller shot, if you like.

Tap to Set the Focus and Exposure

All right: You've opened the Camera app, and it's set to Photos. See the yellow box that appears briefly on the screen?

It's telling you where the iPhone will focus, the area it examines to calculate the overall brightness of the photo (exposure), and the portion that will determine the overall *white balance* of the scene (that is, the color cast).

If you're taking a picture of people, the iPhone's software tries to lock in on a face—up to 10 faces, actually—and calculate focus and exposure so that *they* look right (iPhone 4s and later).

But sometimes, there are no faces—and dead center may not the most important part of the photo. The cool thing is that you can *tap* somewhere

Tap the sky to make it correctly exposed, even if the beach is now too dark.

Tap the dark beach to brighten it up, although that also brightens up the sky.

else in the scene to move that white square—to recalculate the focus, exposure, and white balance.

Here's when you might want to do this tapping:

- **When the whole image looks too dark or too bright.** If you tap a *dark* part of the scene, the whole photo brightens up; if you tap a *bright* part, the whole photo darkens a bit. You're telling the camera, "Redo your calculations so *this* part has the best exposure; I don't really care if the rest of the picture gets brighter or darker."

- **When the scene has a color cast.** If the photo looks, for example, a little bluish or yellowish, tap a different spot in the scene—the one you care most about. The iPhone recomputes its assessment of the white balance.

- **When you're in macro mode.** If the foreground object is very close to the lens—4 to 8 inches away—the iPhone automatically goes into *macro* (super closeup) mode. In this mode, you can do something really cool: You can *defocus the background.* The background goes soft, slightly blurry, just like the professional photos you see in magazines. Just make sure you tap the foreground object.

Locking Focus and Exposure

The iPhone likes to focus and calculate the exposure before it shoots. Yeah—cameras are funny that way.

That tendency, however, can get in your way when you're shooting something that moves fast. Horse races, divers. Pets. Kids on merry-go-rounds, kids on slides, kids in your house. By the time the camera has calculated the focus and exposure, which takes about a second, you've lost the shot.

Therefore, Apple provides an advanced feature that's common on professional cameras but rare on phones: Auto-Exposure Lock and Autofocus Lock. They let you set up the focus and exposure in advance so that there's zero lag when you finally snap the shot.

To use this feature, point the camera at something that has the **same distance and lighting** as the subject-to-be. For example, focus at the base of the merry-go-round that's directly below where your daughter's horse will be. Or point at the bottom of the water slide before your son is ready to go.

Now hold down your finger on that spot on the iPhone's screen until you see the yellow square blink twice. When you lift your finger, the phrase "AE/AF Lock" appears to tell you that you've now locked in exposure and autofocus. (You can tap again to unlock it if you change your mind.)

Now you can snap photos, rapid-fire, without ever having to wait while your iPhone rethinks focus and exposure.

The Flash

The iPhone has what, in the cellphone industry, is called a flash. It's actually just a very bright LED light on the back. You can make it turn on momentarily, providing a small boost of illumination when the lights are low. (That's a **small** boost—it won't do anything for subjects more than a few feet away.)

iPhone 5 (single flash, too white)   iPhone 5s (dual flash, closer to true skin tone)

The iPhone 5s, in fact, has *two* LED flashes: one white, one amber. They go off simultaneously, with their strengths mixed properly so that the flashes' light matches the color temperature of the scene. (You might notice that before the 5s takes the picture, it flashes once *before* the shot is captured. That's the camera's opportunity to *measure* the light color of the scene.)

Nobody's ever done this dual-flash trick before, and it makes a huge difference in the quality of your flash photos. (Especially skin tones, which may be why Apple calls the feature "True Tone.")

No matter which model you have, the flash comes set to Auto. It will turn on automatically when the scene is too dark, in the iPhone's opinion. But if you tap the ⚡ icon when it says Auto, two other options pop out: On (the flash will turn on no matter what the lighting conditions) and Off (the flash will not fire, no matter what).

> **TIP:** If you open the Control Center (page 37) and tap the flashlight icon (🔦), the phone's flash LED turns on and stays on. It's great when you want to see your key in the door or read the tiny type in a program or a menu.

Zooming In

The iPhone has a zoom, which can help bring you "closer" to the subject— but it's a *digital* zoom. It doesn't work like a real camera's optical zoom, which actually moves lenses to blow up the scene. Instead, it basically just blows up the image, making everything bigger, and slightly degrading the picture quality in the process.

To zoom in like this, *spread two fingers* on the screen. As you spread, a zoom slider appears; you can also drag the handle in the slider, or tap **+** or **–**, for more precise zooming.

Sometimes, getting closer to the action is worth the subtle image-quality sacrifice.

The "Rule of Thirds" Grid

The Rule of Thirds, long held as gospel by painters and photographers, suggests that you imagine a tic-tac-toe grid superimposed on your frame. Then, as you frame the shot, you should position the important parts of the photo on those lines, or better yet, at their intersections.

According to the Rule of Thirds, this setup creates a stronger composition than putting everything in dead center, which is most people's instinct.

Now, it's really a *Guideline* of Thirds, or a *Consideration* of Thirds; plenty of photographs are, in fact, strongest when the subject is centered.

But if you want to know where those magic intersections are so that you can at least *consider* the Rule of Thirds, you have to duck into the Settings→Photos & Camera screen to turn it on. Turn on Grid.

From now on, the phone displays the tic-tac-toe grid on your viewfinder, for your composition pleasure. (It's not part of the photo.) You turn it off the same way.

High Dynamic Range (HDR)

Digital cameras have come a long way, but in one regard, they're still pathetic: Compared with the human eye, they still have terrible *dynamic range.*

That's a reference to the scale of bright and dark spots in a single scene. If you see someone standing in front of a bright window, you can probably make out who it is. But in a photo, that person will be a solid black silhouette. The camera doesn't have enough dynamic range to handle both the bright background and the person standing in front of it.

Sure, you could adjust the exposure so that the person's face is lit—but in the process, you'd brighten the background into a nuclear-white rectangle.

Until the world's cameras are as sensitive as our eyes, we can make do with HDR (high dynamic range) photography. That's when the camera takes three photos (or even more)—one each at dark, medium, and light exposure settings. Then software combines the best parts of all three, bringing details to both the shadows and the highlights.

Believe it or not, your iPhone has a built-in HDR feature. It's not as amazing as what an HDR guru can do in Photoshop—for one thing, you have zero control over how the images are combined, how many are combined, or how much of each is combined. And sometimes, the HDR version of the photo looks **worse** than the original.

TIP: Should the phone save a standard shot in addition to the HDR shot? That's up to you. In **Settings→Photos & Camera**, you'll find the on/off switch for **Keep Normal Photo**.

But often, an HDR photo does indeed show more detail in both bright and dark areas than a single shot would. In the iPhone shot at left, the sky is blown out—pure white. In the shot at right, the HDR feature brings back the lost streaks of color.

To use HDR, tap **HDR Off** at the top of the screen (unless it already says **HDR On**). Take your best shot.

When you inspect your photos later in the Photos app, you'll know which ones were taken with HDR turned on; when you tap the photo, you'll see the HDR logo at the upper-left corner.

Taking the Shot

All right. You've opened the Camera app. You've set up the focus, exposure, flash, grid, HDR, and zoom. If, in fact, your subject hasn't already left the scene, you can now take the picture.

You can do that in any of three ways:

- Tap the shutter (●) button.

NOTE: Before iOS 7, the iPhone didn't record the image until the instant you took your finger *off* the screen. But in iOS 7, holding your button down on the button triggers burst mode—10 frames a second (at least on recent iPhone models).

- Press either of the physical Volume buttons on the left edge of the phone.

  This option is fantastic. If you hold the phone with the volume buttons at the top, those buttons are right where the shutter button would be on a real camera. Pressing one feels more natural than, and doesn't shake the camera as much as, tapping the onscreen ● button.

NOTE: Before iOS 7, only the Volume Up button worked as a shutter button. Now you can press *either* the Up or Down button. Progress!

- Press a volume button on your earbuds clicker—a great way to trigger the shutter without jiggling the phone in the process, and a more convenient way to take "selfies" when the phone is at arm's length.

NOTE: The iPhone knows which way you're holding the phone, thanks to its built-in gyroscope. The "which way is up" information accompanies the photo; any Apple photo-viewing app (like iPhoto, Aperture, or the iPhone's own Photos app) will therefore display your photo right-side up. If you use a volume key as a shutter button, that's lucky because, technically, you're holding the phone upside-down.

Unfortunately, Windows photo software isn't so well informed. Photos you take with the volume keys up will appear upside-down on a PC. Of course, you can always flip a photo right-side-up before you send it, right on the phone, using the Edit controls described later in this chapter.

Either way, if the phone isn't muted, you hear the *snap!* sound of a picture successfully taken.

You get to admire your work for only about half a second—and then the photo slurps itself into the thumbnail icon at the corner of the screen.

To review the photo you just took, tap that thumbnail icon at the corner of the screen. (You can no longer swipe across the screen to review your photos, since that gesture now means "change camera modes.")

To look at other pictures you've taken, tap Camera Roll at the top of the screen. (Camera Roll refers to pictures you've shot with the iPhone, as opposed to pictures from your computer.)

This is your opportunity to choose a photo (or many) for emailing, texting, posting to Facebook, and so on; tap Select, tap the photos you want, and then tap the Share button (⬆). See page 243.

TIP: For details on copying your iPhone photos and videos back to your Mac or PC, see page 467.

To return to taking pictures, tap Done.

TIP: If it seems as though the iPhone 5s's camera seems to do better in dim light than previous phones, it's not your imagination.

This camera has an image stabilizer that helps compensate for small hand shakes when you take pictures in low light. It has a bigger sensor inside with bigger pixel sensors, so it soaks up more light. It has a larger aperture (f/2.2), which lets in more light. And in low light, unbeknownst to you, it actually snaps four images in a row, and then combines the sharpest areas of each individual shot into one gloriously sharp unified whole.

Burst Mode (iPhone 5s)

In iOS 7, every iPhone model snaps photos over and over if you keep your finger pressed on the ● button or a volume key.

But the iPhone 5s takes them *quickly*—10 shots a second. That's a fantastic feature when you're trying to study something that happens very fast: a golf swing, a pet trick, a toddler sitting still.

All you have to do is keep your finger pressed on the ● button or the volume key. A counter rapidly increments, showing you how many shots you've fired off.

Now, the iPhone 5s isn't the first camera (or phone) with a burst mode. But it's the first to help you **clean up the mess** afterward—the hassle of hand-inspecting all 230 photos you shot, trying to find the ones worth keeping.

Tap the lower-left thumbnail to view your burst shot. To help keep you sane, the iPhone depicts it as a single photo, with the phrase "Burst (72 photos)" (or whatever) in the corner of the screen. (In the Camera Roll, its thumbnail bears multiple frames, as though it's a stack of slides.)

Here's where it gets cool.

If you tap **Favorites**, you see all frames of the burst in a horizontally scrolling row. Underneath, you see an even smaller "filmstrip" of them—and a few of them are marked with dots.

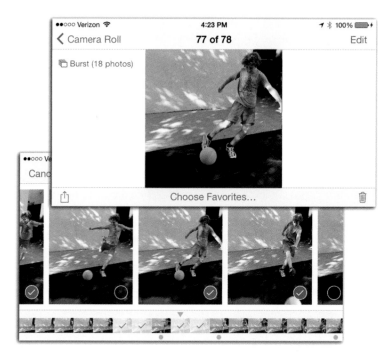

These are the ones the iPhone has decided are the keepers. It does that by studying the clarity or blur of each shot, examining how much one frame is different from those around it, and even skipping past shots where somebody's eyes are closed. Tap the marked thumbnails to see if you approve of the iPhone's selections.

Whether you do or not, you should work through the larger thumbnails in the burst, tapping each one you want to keep. (The small circle in the corner sprouts a blue checkmark.)

When you tap **Done,** the frames you selected become regular, standalone shots in your Camera Roll. The original burst remains in the roll, too, though, so you can always return later to extract a different set of frames.

Self-Portraits (the Front Camera)

The iPhone has a second camera, right there on the front, above the screen. The point, of course, is that you can use the screen itself as a viewfinder to frame yourself, experiment with your expression, and check your teeth.

To activate the front camera, open the Camera app, and then tap the ⟳ icon. Suddenly, you see yourself on the screen. Frame the shot, and then tap the ● button to take the photo.

Now, don't get your expectations too high. The front camera is not the back camera. It's much lower resolution: 640 × 480 pixels on the iPhone 4 and 4s, not even enough for a small print, and 1.2 megapixels (1280 × 960) on the iPhone 5, 5c, and 5s. There's no flash. You can't zoom.

But when your goal is a well-framed self-portrait that you'll use on the screen—in an email or on a Web page, for example, where high resolution isn't very important—then having the front-camera option is better than not having it.

> **TIP:** It's not impossible to take a self-portrait using the better camera on the back; you just need a self-timer app. For example, just.SelfTimer is simple, it offers a choice of countdown lengths, and it's free.

Square Photos

No longer do you have to download a special app just to take perfectly square photos, the way all the cool kids do these days. Just swipe across the screen until you enter Square mode.

In square mode, the photos the Camera app takes are square (2448 × 2448 pixels) instead of rectangular (4 × 3 proportions, 3246 × 2448 pixels on most iPhones). Otherwise, everything you've read in this chapter, and will read, is exactly the same in Square mode.

Filters

Square photos weren't the only influence that Apple felt from the popularity of Facebook's Instagram app. It also became clear that the masses want *filters*: special effects that degrade the color of your photo in artsy ways. (They can affect either square or regular photos.) And now, in iOS 7, you, too, can make your pictures look old, washed-out, or oversaturated.

If you have an iPhone 5 or later, you can turn on the filter *before* you take the shot, so you can see how it'll look. If you have an older phone, you can apply the filter only after you've taken the shot.

Filter Before You Shoot

To view your options, tap the ⊗ icon. You see a tic-tac-toe board of eight color filters (and black-and-white filters); None is always in the center.

Tap a filter thumbnail to try it on for size. In essence, each turns your photo into a variation of black-and-white or plays with its saturation (color intensity, dialing it up or down). If you find one that looks good, take the shot as usual.

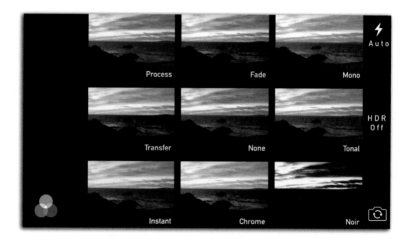

To turn off the filters, tap the ⊗ icon again and tap None.

NOTE: You can always unfilter a filtered shot later, if you prefer the original. Just tap the ⊗ icon to open the palette of filters—and this time, tap None.

Filter After You Shoot

No matter which iPhone model you have, you can apply a filter to any photo you've already taken.

Open the Photos app (it's described later in this chapter), find the photo you want, tap **Edit**, and tap the ⬡ icon. Find the filter you like, tap it, tap **Apply**, and then tap **Save**.

> **TIP:** It may look like you've just filtered that picture forever. But in fact, you can return to it later and apply the **None** filter to it, thereby restoring it to its original pristine condition.

Panoramas

Here's one of the best camera features of the iPhone: panoramic photographs. The iPhone now lets you capture a 240-degree, ultra-wide-angle, 28-megapixel photo by swinging the phone around you in an arc. The phone creates the panorama in real time (you don't have to line up the sections yourself). Next time you're standing at the edge of the Grand

Canyon—or anything else that requires a *really* wide angle—keep this feature in mind. (It's available on the iPhone 4s and later models.)

> **TIP:** On the iPhone 5s, the improved Panorama mode smoothly adjusts the exposure of the scene as you pan. That fixes one of the most frustrating aspects of other cameras, which use the same exposure all the way across their panoramas; you discover that the sunlit part of the scene is blown out and the shadowy parts are way too dark.

Once you've opened the Camera app, swipe leftward until you reach Pano mode, as shown here at left.

> **TIP:** The big white arrow tells you which way to move the phone. But you can reverse it (the direction) just by tapping it (the arrow) before you begin.

Tap the ⊙ button (or press a volume key). Now, as instructed by the screen, swing the phone around you—smoothly and slowly, please.

As you go, the screen gives you three kinds of feedback:

- It says, "Slow down" if you start swinging too fast. Truth is, as far as the iPhone is concerned, the slower, the better.

- It says, "Move up" or "Move down" if you're not keeping the phone level. Use the big white arrow itself like a carpenter's level; you'll leave the center line if you're not staying level as you move your arm.

- The preview of your finished panorama builds itself as you move. That is, you're seeing the final product, in miniature, while you're still taking it.

You'll probably find that 240 degrees—the maximum—is a *really* wide angle. You'll feel twisted at the waist like taffy. But in fact, you can end the panorama at any stage, just by tapping the ⊙ button.

When you do finally tap the ⦿ button, you'll find that the iPhone has taken a very wide, amazingly seamless photograph at very high resolution (16 to 28 megabytes—over 10,000 pixels wide). If a panorama is *too* wide, you can crop it, as described later in this chapter.

If you snap a real winner, you can print it out at a local graphics shop, frame it, and hang it above the entire length of your living-room couch.

The Photos App

Once you've taken some photos, or copied them to your phone from your computer (see Chapter 13), you'll have some pictures ready to view. Presenting them, sharing them, editing them, and slideshowing them is the job of the Photos app. This app, too, has had a long, profound visit from the Makeover Fairy.

TIP: The Photos app is fully rotational. That is, you can turn the phone 90 degrees. Whether you're viewing a list, a screen full of thumbnails, or an individual photo, the image on the screen rotates, too, for easier admiring. (Unless, of course, you've turned on the rotation lock.)

At the bottom of the Photos app screen, three tabs lie in wait: Photos, Shared, and Albums. The next few sections explain what they do.

TIP: In general, you can use the new "go back" gesture—swipe in from the left border of the phone—to go back one screen when navigating the Photos app. Weirdly, it doesn't seem to work in the Photos tab—only in the Shared and Albums screens.

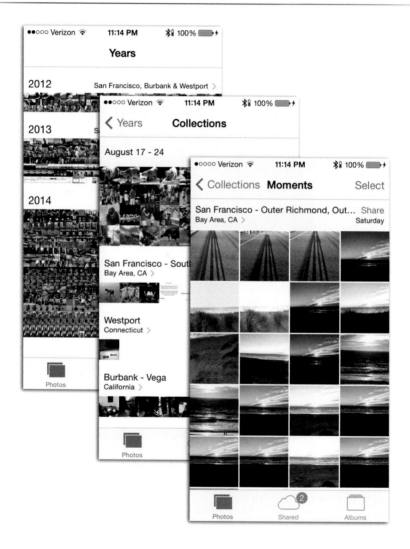

The Photos Tab

In the olden days (before September 2013), the Photos app displayed all your photos—thousands of them—in one endless, hopeless, scrolling mass. If you were hunting for a particular shot, you had to study the thumbnails with an electronic microscope to find it.

Now, though, iOS 7 groups them intelligently into sets that are easy to navigate. Here they are, from smallest to largest.

- **Moments.** A *moment* is a group of photos you took in one place at one time—for example, all the shots at the picnic by the lake. The phone even uses its own GPS to give each moment a name: "San Francisco, California (Union Square)," for example.

TIP: If you tap a Moment's name, a map opens up; little photo thumbnails show exactly where these pictures were taken. Slick!

- **Collections.** Put a bunch of moments together, and what do you get? A collection. Here again, the phone tries to study the times and places of your photo taking—but this time, it puts them into groups that might span a few days and several locations. You might discover that your entire spring vacation is a single collection, for example.

- **Years.** If you "zoom out" of your photos far enough, you wind up viewing them by year: 2013, 2014, and so on.

To "zoom in" from larger groupings to smaller ones (Years→Collections→Moments), just tap each pile of thumbnails. If you tap a thumbnail on the Moments screen, you open that photo for viewing.

TIP: When you first open a photo, it appears on a white background. Tap the photo to change the background to black, which often makes your photos' colors look better.

To "zoom out" again, tap the grouping name at top left (Years, for example).

TIP: If you've opened a single photo for examination, you can retreat to the *moment* it came from by pinching with two fingers.

The Albums Tab

(Yes, it's true: The Shared tab is actually the second tab. But we're skipping over it for now, because the Albums tab is so much like the Photos tab just described.)

The Albums tab is a lot like what iOS used to look like. It's a scrolling list of photo collections like these:

- **Camera Roll.** First on the list is Camera Roll, which means "pictures you've taken with the iPhone."

- **My Photo Stream.** Here are the last 1,000 photos you've taken or imported, as described later in this chapter.

- **Panoramas, Videos.** As a convenience to you, these categories give you one-tap shopping for all the panoramas and movies you've taken with the phone.

- **Events** means *all* the photos you've selected to copy from your Mac or PC.

  After that is the list of *albums* you've brought over from the computer. (An album is the photo equivalent of a playlist. It's a subset of photos, in a sequence you've selected.)

- **Faces.** Both iPhoto and Aperture, Apple's Mac photography programs, have features that let you identify, by name, the people whose faces are in your photos. Once you've given the software a running

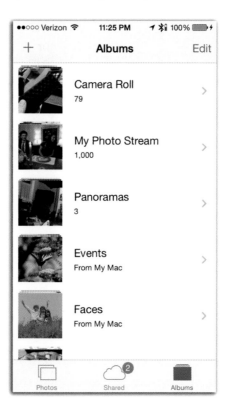

start, it can find those people in the rest of your photo collection automatically. That's handy every now and then—when you need a photo of your kid for a school project, for example.

Here you'll find a list of everyone whose faces you identified on your Mac—and every picture of that person.

NOTE: The Faces and Places categories of iOS 6 have otherwise disappeared. (Places, if you think about it, has been incorporated into Moments.)

- **Albums.** Finally, you get a list of albums—whatever you've copied to the phone from your Mac or PC.

As you'd guess, you can drill down from any of these groupings to a screen full of thumbnails, and from there to an individual photo.

TIP: If you hold your finger down on the photo or even its thumbnail, a Copy button appears. That's one way to prepare for pasting a single photo into an email message, an MMS (picture or video) message to another phone, and so on.

Flicking, Rotating, Zooming, Panning

Once a photo is open at full size, you have your chance to perform the four most famous and most dazzling tricks of the iPhone: flicking, rotating, zooming, and panning a photo.

- **Flicking** right to left is how you advance to the next picture or movie in the batch. (Flick from left to right to view the *previous* photo.)

- **Rotating** is what you do when a horizontal photo or video appears on the upright iPhone, which makes the photo look small and fills most of the screen with blackness.

  Just turn the iPhone 90 degrees in either direction. Like magic, the photo itself rotates and enlarges to fill its new, wider canvas. No taps required. (This doesn't work when the phone is flat on its back—on a table, for example. It has to be more or less upright. It also doesn't work when Portrait Orientation is locked.)

  This trick also works the other way: You can make a *vertical* photo fit better when you hold the iPhone horizontally. Just turn the iPhone upright.

- **Zooming** a photo means magnifying it, and it's a blast. One quick way is to double-tap the photo; the iPhone zooms in on the portion you tapped, doubling its size.

  Another technique is to use the two-finger spread, which gives you more control over what gets magnified and by how much.

  (The iPhone doesn't store the giganto 20-megapixel originals you took with your fancy camera—only scaled-down, iPhone-sized versions—so you can't zoom in more than about three times the original size.)

  Once you've spread a photo bigger, you can then pinch to scale it down again. Or just double-tap to restore the original size. (You don't have to restore a photo to original size before advancing to the next one, though; if you flick enough times, you'll pull the next photo onto the screen.)

- **Panning** means moving a photo around on the screen after you've zoomed in. Just drag your finger to do that; no scroll bars are necessary.

TIP: When the iPhone is rotated, all the controls and gestures reorient themselves. For example, flicking right to left still brings on the next photo, even if you're now holding the iPhone the wide way.

Deleting Photos

If some photo no longer meets your exacting standards, you can delete it. But this action is trickier than you may think.

- **If you took the picture using the iPhone,** no sweat. Open the photo; tap 🗑. When you tap Delete Photo, that picture is gone.

- **If the photo was synced to the iPhone from your computer,** well, that's life. The iPhone remains a *mirror* of what's on the computer. In other words, you can't delete the photo right on the phone. Instead, delete it from the original album on your computer (which does *not* mean deleting it from the computer altogether). The next time you sync the iPhone, the photo disappears from it, too.

Photo Controls

If you tap the screen once, some useful controls appear. They remain on the screen for only a couple of seconds, so as not to ruin the majesty of your photo, so act now.

- **Album name.** You can return to the thumbnails page by tapping the screen once, which summons the playback controls, and then tapping the album name in the upper-left corner.

- **Photo number.** The top of the screen says "88 of 405," for example, meaning that this is the 88th photo out of 405 in the set.

- **Edit.** This button is the gateway to the iPhone's photo-editing features, described later in this chapter.

- **Share icon.** Tap the ⬆ button in the lower left if you want to do something more with this photo than just stare at it. You can use it as your iPhone's wallpaper, print it, copy it, text it, send it by email, use it as somebody's headshot in your Contacts list, post it on Twitter or Facebook, and so on. These options are all described in the next sections.

The Share sheet also includes an option to begin a slideshow, as described next.

Slideshows

A slideshow is a great way to show off your photos and videos. You can turn a set of photos, or the Camera Roll itself, into a slideshow by tapping the ⬆ button to open the Share sheet and then tapping Slideshow.

You have a surprising amount of control over your slideshow, too. But beware: The controls are split up between two locations. Some of them appear when you first tap Slideshow, as shown here:

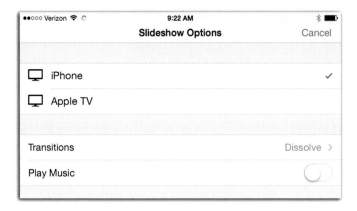

- **TV or phone.** Where do you want the slideshow? On your phone or on your TV? (This option appears only if you have an Apple TV.)

- **Transitions.** What kind of crossfade or special effect do you want the phone to create in the blend from one photo to the next? You're offered five choices—Dissolve, Cube, Ripple, Wipe Across, Wipe Down. (Dissolve is the least tacky one.)

- **Play Music.** Would you like tunes with that? If you want background music, turn this switch on.

- **Music.** Finally, tap the Music pop-up menu to choose a song from your music collection.

The other set of controls is buried in Settings→Photos & Camera:

- **Play Each Slide For.** You can specify how many seconds each photo hangs around.

- **Repeat.** Makes the slideshow play over and over again until you stop it manually.

- **Shuffle.** Randomizes the sequence of photos within the chosen album.

While the slideshow is going on, tapping the screen stops the show, freezing it on the current photo. If you open the Share sheet and tap Slideshow again, you resume the slideshow from the photo where you stopped.

You must let each video play to its conclusion if you want the show to continue. (Or tap to interrupt a particularly boring video, swipe to the next photo or video, and start the slideshow again from there.)

You can feel free to turn the iPhone 90 degrees to accommodate landscape-orientation photos as they come up; the slideshow keeps right on going.

Copying/Sending/Deleting in Batches

In iOS 7, it's easy to send several pictures in a single email; paste them as a group into another program; print them all at once; post some online; paste them into an outgoing MMS message; or delete them en masse.

How you do so, however, depends on where you start.

- **A Moment.** You can't choose batches of photos when you're looking at a Year or a Collection. But every single Moment bears a Share button next to its name.

  When you tap it, you get a choice: Share this moment (send or post the entire batch) or Share some photos (you'll be offered a page of thumbnails, so you can choose only a lucky few).

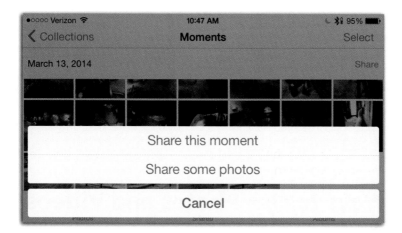

- **Photos from the Albums tab.** If you begin instead on a page of thumbnails from the Albums tab, you can tap Share and then individually select the photos you want to send. With each tap, a ✅ appears, meaning, "OK, this one will be included." (Tap again to remove the checkmark.)

Either way, the next thing you see is the Share sheet described on page 294. It presents a choice of buttons: AirDrop, Message, Mail, iCloud (meaning a photo stream), Facebook, Flickr, Copy, and Print.

All of these options are described below.

> **NOTE:** The Mail option doesn't appear if you've chosen more than five photos. That's because five is the maximum for sending as email attachments. More than that and the attachment will be too big for most email systems.

Starting from the Albums tab gains you a couple of additional options, by the way. First, there's a 🗑 button, so that you can **delete** a bunch of photos at once. (You can delete only photos or videos you've taken **with the iPhone**—not ones you transferred from your computer.)

And there's a button called Add To. It lets you put the selected photos into one of your albums—a great way to organize a huge batch you've shot on vacation, for example.

You're now offered an Add to Album screen. Tap the album into which you want to move these pictures. (If albums are dimmed, that's because they've been synced from your Mac or PC. You're not allowed to mess with them. The list shows only albums you've created on the phone.)

This list also includes a New Album button; you're asked to type out the name you want for the new album and then tap Save.

> **NOTE:** These buttons don't actually move photos out of their original albums. You're creating *aliases* of them—pointers to the original photos. If you edit or delete a photo from one album, it's edited or deleted from all of them.

To **delete** an album you created on the phone, start on the main Albums tab. Tap Edit, and then tap the button next to the album you want to delete.

14 Ways to Use Photos and Videos

It's great that the iPhone has one of the best cameras on any cellphone. But what's even greater is that it *is* a cellphone. It's online. So once you've taken a picture, you can *do* something with it right away. Mail it, text it, post it to Facebook or Twitter, use it as wallpaper—all right from the iPhone.

That's all useful when you're out shopping and want to seek your spouse's opinion on something you're about to buy. It's handy when you want to remember the parking-garage section where you parked ("4 South"). It's great when you want to give your Twitter fans a glimpse of whatever hell or heaven you're experiencing at the moment.

Once you've opened a photo (or selected a few), tap the ⬆ button.

Now you have a bunch of "send my photo here" options—Apple supplies about a dozen of them, but others may come along in time. (If you don't see them all, swipe to the left to change screens.)

AirDrop

So very cool: You can shoot a photo, or several, to any nearby iPhone, iPad, or iPod Touch—wirelessly, securely, conveniently, and instantly. See page 296 for the step-by-steps.

Message

You can also send a photo or video as a *picture or video message.* It winds up on the screen of the other guy's cellphone.

That's a delicious feature, almost handier than sending a photo by email. After all, your friends and relatives don't sit in front of their computers all day and all night (unless they're serious geeks).

Tap **Message** and then specify the phone number of the recipient; if you're sending by iMessage, the email address also works. Or choose someone from your Contacts list. Then type a little note, tap **Send**, and off it goes.

Mail

The iPhone automatically compresses, rotates, and attaches the photo or video clip to a new outgoing message. All you have to do is address it and hit **Send**. You're asked how much you want the photo *scaled down* from its original size. Tap **Small**, **Medium**, **Large**, or **Actual Size**, using the megabyte indicator as a guide.

Why is this necessary? Because many email systems won't accept attachments larger than 5 megabytes; even four "actual size" photos taken with the iPhone would be too big to send by email. The Size button you tap controls how big the photo will be on the receiving end—and how long the message will take to send.

In general, when you send **Small**, the photo will arrive in the recipient's message window about the size of a brownie. A **Medium** image will fill the email window. **Large** will fill your recipient's computer screen. And **Actual**

Size is intended for making printouts. It sends the full, multimegabyte originals (2592 × 1936 on the iPhone 4 and 4s; 3264 × 2448 on the iPhone 5 family).

TIP: Using the steps on page 241, you can send up to five photos at once.

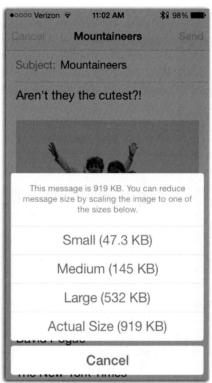

iCloud

This option really means "photo stream." It lets you add new photos to one of your photo streams (read on), with a little comment.

Photo Stream

This special feature of iOS has two faces. There's My Photo Stream, in which every picture you take magically winds up duplicated on every Apple gadget you own; and then there are the **Shared** Photo Streams, in which you "publish" sets of pictures to other people's phones, tablets, or computers, or even post them as free Web galleries. In iOS 7, those people can contribute their own photos to your streams, too.

Photo streams get a special writeup that begins on page 250.

Twitter, Facebook, Flickr

If you've told your iPhone what your name and password are (in **Settings→ Twitter** or **Settings→Facebook** or **Settings→Flickr**), then posting a photo from your phone to your Twitter feed or Facebook wall is ridiculously simple.

Open the photo; tap the ⬆ button; tap **Twitter, Facebook**, or **Flickr**. You're offered the chance to type a message that accompanies your photo, as shown below. (As usual with Twitter, you have a maximum of 140 characters for your message. Fewer, actually, because some of your characters are eaten up by the link to the photo.) You can also tap **Add Location** if you want Twitterites or Facebookers to know where the photo was taken.

> **NOTE:** The Add Location option is available only if you've permitted Twitter or Facebook to use your location information, which you set up in **Settings→Privacy→Location Services**.

If you're posting to Facebook or Flickr, you can also indicate whom you're sharing this item with—just your friends, everyone, and so on—by tapping **Audience** beneath the photo thumbnail. Flickr also offers a chance to specify which of your Flickr photo sets you want to post to.

When you tap **Send** or **Post**, your photo, and your accompanying tweet or post, zoom off to Twitter, Facebook, or Flickr for all to enjoy.

Copy

The Copy button puts the photo onto the Clipboard, ready for pasting into another app (an outgoing Mail message, for example). Once you've opened an app that can, in fact, accept pasted graphics, double-tap to make the **Paste** button appear.

Slideshow

Tap this button to begin a slideshow of the current photo batch, as described on page 239.

AirPlay

This button offers a list of nearby AirPlay gadgets—the only one you've probably heard of is Apple TV—so that you can display the current photo on your TV or another screen.

Assign to Contact

If you're viewing a photo of somebody who's listed in Contacts, then you can use it (or part of it) as her headshot. After that, her photo appears on your screen every time she calls.

You can add a photo to a contact from either direction: starting with the photo, or starting with the person's "card" open in Contacts.

- **Within the Photos app.** Open a picture. Tap the ⬆ button, and then tap Assign to Contact.

  Your address book list pops up. Tap the name of the person who goes with this photo.

  Now you see a preview of what the photo will look like when that person calls. This is the Move and Scale screen. You want to crop the photo and shift it in the frame so only *that person* is visible (if it's a group shot)—in fact, just the face.

  Start by enlarging the photo: Spread your thumb and forefinger against the glass. As you go, *shift* the photo's placement in the round frame with a one-finger drag. When you've got the person correctly centered, tap Choose.

- **Start on somebody's Contacts card.** Using this method, you don't have to begin the process from the photo.

  Just open the card, tap Edit, and then tap Add Photo. Now you have a choice: Take Photo (if that person is with you) or Choose Photo (hunt through your photo collection until you find a good one). Tap it, do your thing on the Move and Scale screen, and off you go.

Use as Wallpaper

Wallpaper, in the world of iOS, refers to the background photo that appears in either of two places: the Home screen (plastered behind your app icons) or the Lock screen (which appears every time you wake the iPhone).

You can replace Apple's standard photos with one of your photos or with a different one of Apple's. You go at this task in either of two ways:

- **Start in Settings.** From the Home screen, tap Settings→Wallpapers & Brightness. (Or tell Siri, "Open wallpaper settings.")

  Now you see miniatures of the two places you can install wallpaper— the Lock screen and the Home screen (facing page, left). Each shows what you've got installed there as wallpaper at the moment.

  These aren't separate buttons; that is, this isn't the place to indicate which screen (Lock or Home) you're redecorating. Just tap once on the whole thing to move on.

  When you tap that picture, you're shown a list of photo sources you can use as backgrounds. Under Apple Wallpaper, you get two categories worth noticing.

The **Dynamic** wallpapers all look like soft-focus bubbles against solid-color backgrounds. Once you've installed the wallpaper, these bubbles actually *move*, rising and falling on your Lock screen or on your Home behind your icons. Yes, animated wallpaper has finally come to the iPhone.

The Stills category is a bunch of lovely nature photography. It doesn't move.

Scroll down a little, and you'll find your own photos, in the form of the **Camera Roll**, **Photo Stream**, **Panoramas**, and **Albums** categories, as described earlier in this chapter.

All these pictures show up as thumbnail miniatures; tap one to see what it looks like at full size. If it looks good, tap **Set**.

Now the iPhone wants to know which of the two places you want to use this wallpaper; tap **Set Lock Screen**, **Set Home Screen**, or **Set Both** (if you want the same picture in both places).

- **Start in the Photos app.** The task of applying one of your own photos to your Home or Lock screen can also begin in the Photos app. Open one of your photos, as described in the previous pages. Tap ⬆, and then tap **Use as Wallpaper**.

  You're now offered the Move and Scale screen so you can fit your rectangular photo within the rectangular wallpaper "frame." Pinch or spread to enlarge the shot; drag your finger on the screen to scroll and center it.

  Finally, tap **Set**. Here again, you specify where you want to use this wallpaper; tap **Set Lock Screen**, **Set Home Screen**, or **Set Both** (if you want the same picture in both places).

When it's all over, you'll discover something that's just so Apple: In iOS 7, your wallpaper—whichever one you chose—appears to be *floating behind* your screen. If you look closely as you tilt the phone left and right, up or down, you can see this sneaky special parallax effect. The phone's sensors know how you're tilting it, so the wallpaper actually moves, simulating a parallax (shifting angle) effect.

Print

You can print a photo easily enough, provided that you've hooked up your iPhone to a compatible printer. Once you've opened the photo, tap the ⬆ button and then tap **Print**. The rest goes down as described on page 293.

My Photo Stream

iCloud is Apple's free suite of online services. It's described in Chapter 14—but for an iPhone shutterbug, its most interesting feature by far is My Photo Stream.

The concept is simple: Every time a new photo enters your life—when you take a picture with your iPhone or import one onto your computer—it gets added to your Photo Stream. From there, it appears automatically on all your *other* iCloud machines.

Photo Stream doesn't sync over the cellular airwaves. It sends photos around only when you're in a WiFi hotspot or connected to a wired network.

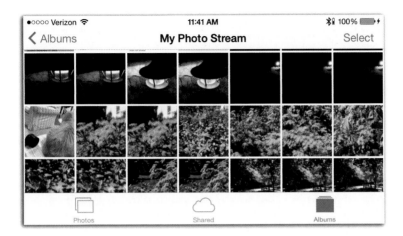

Using Photo Stream means all kinds of good things:

- Your photos are always backed up. Lose your iPhone? No big-gie—when you buy a new one, your latest 1,000 photos appear on it automatically.

- Any pictures you take with your iPhone appear automatically on your computer. You don't have to connect any cables or sync anything yourself.

TIP: Actually, there's one exception. Suppose you take a photo and then look it over while you're still in the Camera app. You hate it. You delete it.

In that case, the photo will never become part of your Photo Stream, because you deleted it while you were still in the Camera app.

A similar rule holds true with edits: If you edit a photo you've just taken, those edits become part of the Photo Stream copy. But if you take a photo, leave the Camera app, and *later* edit it, then the Photo Stream gets the original copy only.

Here's a sneaky one: You can drag favorite photos into your Photo Stream from your computer's photo stash—a quick, easy way to get pictures from your computer onto your iPhone.

To get started with Photo Stream on your iPhone, you need an iCloud account (Chapter 14). You also have to turn **on** Photo Stream, which you do in Settings→iCloud. (You should also turn it on using the iCloud control panel on your computers. That's in System Preferences on your Mac, or in the Control Panel of Windows.) Give your phone some time in a WiFi hotspot to form its initial slurping-in of all your most recent photos.

Once Photo Stream is up and running, here's how to use it.

On the iPhone (or iPad or iPod Touch)

Open your Photos app. Tap the tab at the bottom called Albums; in the list of albums, tap My Photo Stream. Inside are the photos that have entered your life most recently.

Now, Apple realizes that your i-gadget doesn't have nearly as much storage available as your Mac or PC; you can't yet buy an iPhone with 750 gigabytes of storage. That's why, on your iPhone/iPad/iPod, your My Photo Stream consists of just the last 1,000 photos. (There's another limitation, too: The iCloud servers store your photos for 30 days. As long as your gadgets go online at least once a month, they'll remain current with the Photo Stream.)

Ordinarily, the oldest of the 1,000 photos in your Photo Stream scroll away forever as new photos come in. But you can rescue the best ones from that fate—by saving them into your Camera Roll, where they're free from the risk of automatic deletion.

To rescue a bunch at a time, open My Photo Stream so you're looking over the thumbnails. Tap Select, and then tap the thumbnails of the photos you want to preserve. Once they're selected, tap Add To (and then choose one of your phone's albums); or tap the Save button and tap Save to Camera Roll.

Or, if you're viewing one open picture in My Photo Stream, tap the ⬆ button; on the Share sheet, tap Save to Camera Roll.

> **NOTE:** Most people think of the Camera Roll as the set of pictures taken **by the iPhone**. And usually, that's true. But when you use this Save to Camera Roll command, you're violating that sacred definition. You're adding other pictures—perhaps taken by **other cameras**—into the set of iPhone photos. Somehow, life will go on.

That's it. Now the photos you rescued appear in **both** your Photo Stream, where they will eventually disappear, **and** in your Camera Roll or your albums, where they're safe until you delete them manually.

On the Mac or PC

In iPhoto or Aperture (Mac), your Photo Stream photos appear in a new album called, of course, Photo Stream. On a Windows PC, you get a Photo Stream folder in your Pictures folder.

On the computer, you don't have to worry about that 30-day, 1,000-photo business. Once pictures appear here, they're here until you delete them.

This, in its way, is one of the best features in all of iCloudland, because it means you don't have to sync your iPhone over a USB cable to get your photos onto your computer. It all happens automatically, wirelessly, over WiFi.

> **TIP:** You can also drag photos *into* your Photo Stream from your computer. That's a quick, easy way to get them onto your iPhone wirelessly. On the Mac, drag the photos into the Photo Stream album (within iPhoto or Aperture), and choose whether you want them dropped into your main Photo Stream or one of your shared ones. In Windows, drag them into the Photo Stream Uploads folder, which you designate in the iCloud Control Panel.

On the Apple TV

When you're viewing your photos on an Apple TV, an album appears there called Photo Stream. There they are, ready for showing on the big plasma. You can use your Photo Stream in an Apple TV screen saver, too.

Deleting Photos from the Photo Stream

You can't choose what photos go into the Photo Stream. *Every* picture you take with the iPhone goes into it. *Every* photo you bring into your computer goes into it. Every photo you save on your iPhone from an app like Twitter goes into it. Every screenshot you make goes into it.

And remember, the same 1,000 photos appear on all of your Apple gadgets (assuming you've turned on Photo Stream on each one). You might think you're taking a private picture with your phone, forgetting that your spouse or parent will see it seconds later on the iPad. It's only a matter of time before Photo Stream gets some politician in big trouble.

Even if you delete a photo from your iPhone's Camera Roll, it's too late. The Photo Stream version is already out there, replicated across all your i-gadgets and computers.

Fortunately, you can delete photos from your Photo Stream. Just select the thumbnail of the photo you want to delete, and then tap the Trash icon (🗑). The confirmation box warns you that you're about to delete the photo from all your Apple machines (and, for shared streams, the machines of everyone who's subscribed to your photographic output).

If you haven't saved it to a different album or roll, it's gone for good when you tap Delete Photo.

> **TIP:** If you use iPhoto or Aperture, don't forget that these programs offer an Auto-Import feature in their Preferences. That is, any photo that appears in the Photo Stream album automatically gets imported into the program's permanent collection. In the event of an Embarrassing Photo Stream Mistake, don't forget to delete that auto-imported copy of the incriminating photos, too.

Shared Photo Streams

A *shared* Photo Stream lets you send photos or videos to *other* people's gadgets. After a party or some other get-together, you could send your best shots to everyone who attended; after a trip, you could post your photographic memories for anyone who might care.

The lucky recipients can post comments about your pix, click a "like" button to indicate their enthusiasm, or even submit pictures and videos of their own (a new iOS 7 feature). It's like having a tiny Instagram network of your very own, consisting solely of people you invite.

In designing this feature, Apple had quite a challenge. There's a lot of back-and-forth among multiple people, sharing multiple photos, so Shared Photo Streams can get a little complicated. Stay calm and keep hands and feet inside the tram at all times.

Here's how it works.

> **TIP:** Well, here's how it works *if* your equipment meets the requirements. Photo Streams can show up on an iPhone, iPad, or iPod Touch with iOS 5.1 or later; on a Mac with OS X Lion v10.7.3 or later and iPhoto 9.2.2 or Aperture 3.2.3 or later; on a PC with Windows 7 or Windows Vista (Service Pack 2) and the iCloud Control Panel 1.1 or later for Windows; or on an Apple TV (2nd generation) with Software Update 5.0 or later.
>
> You also have to *turn on* the Photo Stream feature. On an iOS gadget, the switch is in Settings→iCloud→Photos. On the Mac, it's in System Preferences→iCloud. On a Windows PC, it's in the iCloud Control Panel for Windows (a free download from Apple's Web site).

Create a Shared Photo Stream

To share some of your masterpieces with your adoring fans, proceed like this:

1. **Create the empty stream.** Open the Photos app. On the Shared tab, scroll to the bottom of the list (if necessary) and tap New Shared Stream.

2. **Name the new stream.** In the Shared Stream box, name the Photo Stream ("Bday Fun" or whatever). Tap Next.

3. **Specify the audience.** You're now asked for the email addresses of your lucky audience members; enter their addresses in the "To:" box just as you would an outgoing email address. For your convenience, a list of recent sharees appears below the "To:" box.

   When that's done, tap Create. You return to the list of Shared Streams, where your newly named stream appears at the top. It is, however, completely empty.

4. **Pour some photos or movies into the stream.** Tap your new, empty stream's name. Then, on the "No Items" screen, tap the **+** button to

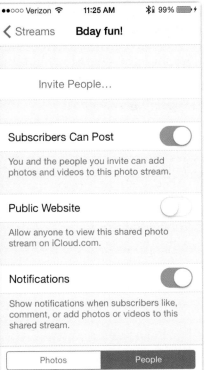

burrow through your photos and videos—you can use any of the three tabs (Photos, Shared, Albums)—to select the material you want to share. Tap their thumbnails so that they sprout checkmarks (facing page, left), and then tap Done.

A little box appears, so that you can type up a description.

5. **Type a little description of the new batch.** In theory, you and other people can add to this stream later. That's why you're offered the chance to caption each new batch.

   Once that's done, tap Post.

The thumbnails of the shared photos and videos appear before you—and the **+** button is there, too, in case you want to add more pictures later.

 TIP: You can easily *remove* photos from the stream, too. On this screen of thumbnails, tap Select; tap the thumbnails you want to nuke; tap 🗑; confirm by tapping Delete Photo.

Adjusting a Stream's Settings

Before you set your stream free, tap the People tab at the bottom of the screen. Here are a few important options to establish for this stream:

- **Invite People.** This list identifies everyone with whom you've shared the stream. To add a new subscriber, tap Invite People. To delete a subscriber, tap the name and then (at the bottom of the contact card) tap Remove Subscriber.

- **Subscribers Can Post**. This is the hot new iOS 7 feature: your subscribers can now contribute photos and videos to your stream. That's a fantastic feature when the stream contains pictures of an event where there was a crowd: a wedding, show, concert, picnic, badminton tournament. Now everyone who was there can enhance the gallery with shots taken from their own points of view with their own phones or cameras.

- **Public Website.** If you turn on Public Website, then even people who aren't members of the Apple cult will be able to see these photos. The invitees will get an email containing a Web address. It links to a hidden page on the iCloud Web site that contains your published photos (facing page, left).

  When you turn this switch on, the Web address of your new gallery appears in light-gray type. Tap Share Link for a selection of methods for sending the link to people: by Message, Mail, Twitter, Facebook, AirDrop, and so on.

What they'll see is a mosaic of pictures, laid out in a grid on a single sort of Web poster (below, right). Your fans can download their favorites by clicking the ☁ button. (You can't add comments or "like" photos on the Web, however.)

TIP: If you click one of these medium-sized photos, you enter slideshow mode, in which one photo at a time fills your Web browser window. Click the arrow buttons to move through them.

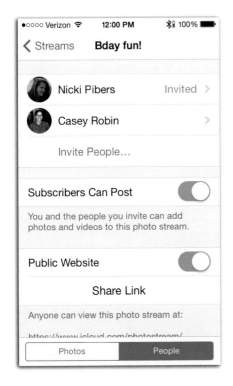

- **Notifications.** If this switch is on, then your phone will show a banner each time someone adds photos or videos to your stream, clicks the "Like" button for a photo, or leaves a comment.

- **Delete Photo Stream.** That's right: If the whole thing gets out of hand, you can slam the door in your subscribers' faces by making the entire stream disappear.

Read on to see what it's like to be the person whose email address you entered.

Receiving a Photo Stream on Your Gadget

When other people share Photo Streams with *you,* your phone makes a little warble, and a notification banner appears: "[Your buddy's name] invited you to join '[name of shared photo batch]'."

Simultaneously, a badge like (❷) appears on the Photos app icon and on the Shared tab within Photos, letting you know how many streams have come your way.

> **TIP:** If you have iPhoto or Aperture on a Mac, an invitation to accept the stream appears there, too.

As you'd guess, you can tap the new stream's name to see what's inside it; tap **Accept** if you're sure (below, left).

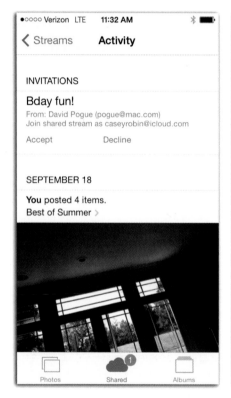 

Once you're subscribed, you view the photos and movies as you would any album—with a couple of differences. First, you can tap **Add a comment** to make worshipful or snarky remarks, or tap the **Like** smiley to offer your silent support (above, right).

You can also snag a copy of somebody's published photo or video for yourself. With the photo before you, tap the ⬆ button to see the usual sharing options—and tap Save to Camera Roll. Now the picture or video isn't some virtual online wisp—it's a solid, tangible electronic copy in your own photo pool.

If your buddy has turned on Subscribers Can Post for this stream, you can send your own photos and clips into the stream; everybody who's subscribed to it (and, of course, its owner) will see them.

To do that, tap the + button on the stream's page of thumbnails; choose your photos and movies; tap Done; add a little comment about them; and tap Post.

Fun with Shared Photo Streams

Once you've created a shared Photo Stream, you can update it or modify it in all kinds of ways:

- **Add new photos or movies to it.** In Photos, open the shared Photo Stream, whether it's one you created or one you've subscribed to. Tap the + button. Now you can browse your whole world of photos, tapping to add them to the Photo Stream already in progress.

- **Remove things from it.** In Photos, open the shared Photo Stream. Tap Select, tap the item(s) you want to delete, and then tap the Trash icon (🗑) (and confirm with a tap on Delete Photo(s).

- **Delete an entire shared Photo Stream.** Tap the People tab below an open photo stream, scroll down, tap Delete Photo Stream, and confirm by tapping Delete.

- **Change who's invited, change the name.** The People tab is also where you can add to the list of email addresses (tap Invite People), remove someone (tap the name, and then tap Remove Subscriber), rename the stream, or turn off Public Website to dismantle the Web version of this gallery.

At any time, you can tap the Shared tab in the Photos app. Here, for your amusement, is a visual record of everything that's gone on in Shared Photo Stream Land: photos you've posted, photos other people have posted, comments back and forth, "likes," and so on. It's your personal photographic Facebook.

Editing Photos

Yes, kids, it's true: You can crop and edit your pictures right on the phone. The tools Apple gives you aren't exactly Photoshop, but at least you don't need to download some app just to touch up a promising picture.

To edit a photo, tap its thumbnail (anywhere in the Photos app) to open it. Tap **Edit** in the upper right.

Now you get five buttons across the bottom. Their names aren't shown, but their functions are Rotate, Auto-Enhance, Filters, Remove Red-Eye, and Crop. Read on.

Rotate (⟳)

Tap this button to rotate the photo 90 degrees.

> **TIP:** You can rotate the photo in smaller amounts when you enter Crop mode, as described below—to straighten a tilted horizon, for example.

Auto-Enhance (✦)

When you tap this magical, do-it-all button, the iPhone analyzes the relative brightness of all the pixels in your photo and attempts to "balance" it. After a moment, the app adjusts the brightness and contrast and intensifies dull or grayish-looking areas. Usually, the pictures look richer and more vivid as a result.

You may find that Auto-Enhance has little effect on some photos, only minimally improves others, and totally rescues a few. In any case, if you don't care for the result, you can tap the ✦ button again to turn Auto-Enhance off.

Filters (◉)

Filters, new in iOS 7, are effects that make a photo black-and-white, over-saturated, or washed-out. If you have an iPhone 5 or later, you can apply a filter as you take the picture (page 230); no matter which phone you have, though, you can apply a filter to an existing photo here.

Tap the ◉ button to view a horizontally scrolling row of filter buttons. Tap each to see what it looks like on your photo; finish up by tapping **Apply** or **Cancel**. (You can always restore the photo's original look later—by returning to this screen and tapping **None**.)

Remove Red-Eye (👁)

Red eye is a common problem in flash photography. This creepy, possessed look—devilish, glowing-red pupils in your subjects' eyes—has ruined many an otherwise great photo.

Red eye is caused by light reflected back from eyes. The bright light of your flash illuminates the blood-red retinal tissue at the back of the eyes. That's why red-eye problems are worse when you shoot pictures in a dim room: Your subjects' pupils are dilated, allowing even *more* light from your flash to reach their retinas.

When you tap this button, a message says, "Tap each red-eye." Do what it says: Tap with your finger inside each eye that has the problem. The app turns the red in each eye to black.

TIP: It usually helps to zoom in first. Use the usual two-finger spread technique.

Crop (⌗)

Cropping means shaving off unnecessary portions of a photo. Usually, you crop a photo to improve its composition—adjusting where the subject appears within the frame of the picture. Often, a photo has more impact if it's cropped tightly around the subject, especially in portraits. Or maybe you want to crop out wasted space, like big expanses of background sky. You can even chop a former romantic interest out of an otherwise perfect family portrait.

Cropping is also very useful if your photo needs to have a certain *aspect ratio* (length-to-width proportion), like 8 × 10 or 5 × 7.

To crop a photo you've opened, tap the ⊡ button. A white tic-tac-toe grid appears on your photo, just in case you want to crop according to the Rule of Thirds.

Drag inward on any edge or corner. The part of the photo that iPhoto will eventually trim away is dimmed out. You can re-center the photo within your cropping frame by dragging any part of the photo, inside or outside of the white grid. Adjust the frame and drag the photo until everything looks just right.

TIP: In Cropping mode, you can also straighten or fine-tune the rotation of a picture. Place two fingers on the screen and twist them. Who knew?

Ordinarily, you can draw a cropping rectangle of any size and proportions, freehand. But if you tap the **Aspect** button, you get a choice of nine canned proportions: Square, 3 × 2, 3 × 5, 4 × 3, and so on. They make the app limit the cropping frame to preset proportions.

The Aspect feature is especially important if you plan to order prints of your photos. Prints come only in standard photo sizes: 4 × 6, 5 × 7, 8 × 10, and so on. But unless you crop them, the iPhone's photos are all 3 × 2, which doesn't divide evenly into most standard print photograph sizes. Limiting your cropping to one of these standard sizes guarantees that your cropped photos will fit perfectly into Kodak prints. (If you don't constrain your cropping this way, then Kodak—not you—will decide how to crop them to fit.)

TIP: The Original option here maintains the proportions of the original photo even as you make the grid smaller.

The iPhone's Aspect feature doesn't work like the one in iPhoto, Picasa, Photoshop, or any other app. When you tap one of the preset sizes, the cropping frame jumps to those proportions—but it doesn't **stay** that way. If you start to drag the frame edges again, you're back to freehand.

In other words, the trick is to get the frame **almost** the way you want it, and **then** tap the Aspect button. If your cropping frame is a little too big or small, you'll have to drag to adjust it and then use the Aspect button again.

Saving Your Changes

Once you've rotated, cropped, auto-enhanced, or de-red-eyed a photo, tap the Save button in the upper-right corner. You've just immortalized your changes to the photo. If you send the picture off your phone—message or email it, or sync it to your Mac or PC—it arrives in its edited condition.

What's especially convenient, though, is that the Photos app never forgets the original photo. At any time, hours or years later, you can return to the Edit screen and undo the changes you've made. You can recrop the photo back to its original size, for example, or turn off the Auto-Enhance button. In other words, your changes are never really permanent.

> **TIP:** If you sync your photos to iPhoto or Aperture on the Mac, they show up in their edited condition. Yet, amazingly, you can undo or modify the edits there! The original photo is still lurking behind the edited version. You can use your Mac's Crop tool to adjust the crop, for example. Or you can use iPhoto's Revert to Original command to throw away **all** the edits you made to the original photo while it was on the iPhone.

Geotagging

Mention to a geek that a gadget has both GPS and a camera, and there's only one possible reaction: "Does it do **geotagging?**"

Geotagging means "embedding your latitude and longitude information into a photo or video when you take it." After all, every digital picture you've ever taken comes with its time and date embedded in its file; why not its location?

The good news is that the iPhone can geotag every photo and movie you take. How you use this information, however, is a bit trickier. The iPhone doesn't geotag unless all the following conditions are true:

- **The location feature on your phone is turned on.** On the Home screen, tap Settings→General→Location Services. Make sure Camera is turned **On**.

- **The phone knows where it is.** If you're indoors, the GPS chip in the iPhone probably can't get a fix on the satellites overhead. And if you're not near cellular towers or WiFi base stations, then even the pseudo-GPS may not be able to triangulate your location.

- **You've given permission.** The first time you use the iPhone's camera, a peculiar message appears, asking if it's allowed to use your location information. In this case, it's asking, "Do you want to geotag your pictures?" If you tap **OK**, then the iPhone's geographic coordinates will be embedded in each photo you take.

OK, so suppose all of this is true, and the geotagging feature is working. How will you know? Well, the new Moments feature can put geotagging to work right on the phone. You can open a map and see all the photos you took in that spot, as described on page 235.

You can also transfer the photos to your computer, where your likelihood of being able to see the geotag information depends on what photo-viewing software you're using. For example:

- When you've selected a photo in iPhoto (on the Mac), you can press ⌘-I to view the Photo Info panel. At the very bottom, you'll see the photo's spot on a map.

- Once you've posted your geotagged photos on Flickr.com (the world's largest photo-sharing site), people can use the Explore menu to search for them by location, or even see them clustered on a world map.

- If you import your photos into Picasa (for Windows), then you can choose Tools→Geotag→View in Google Earth to see a picture's location on the map (if the free Google Earth program is installed on your computer, that is).

Or choose **Tools→Geotag→Export to Google Earth File** to create a .kmz file, which you can send to a friend. When opened, this file opens Google Earth (if it's on your friend's computer) and displays a miniature of the picture in the right place on the map.

Recording Video

You can record video as well as still photos. And not just crummy, jerky, microscopic cellphone video, either—it's smooth (30 frames per second), sharp, colorful video that does surprisingly well in low light. It's probably the best-looking video a cellphone can take.

On the iPhone 4s and later, the video is the best flavor of high definition (1080p)—and it's even stabilized to prevent hand jerkiness, just like a real camcorder is. The 5s even offers a gorgeous, 120-frames-per-second *slow-motion* mode that turns even frenzied action into graceful, liquidy visual ballet.

Using video is almost exactly like taking stills. Pop into the Camera app. Swipe to the right until you've selected the Video mode. You can hold the iPhone either vertically or horizontally; it doesn't care if your video is tall and thin or wide and squat.

TIP: When you switch from still-photo mode to video, you may notice that the video image on the screen suddenly jumps bigger, as though it's zooming in. And it's true: The iPhone is oddly more "zoomed in" in camcorder mode than in camera mode.

Tap to compute focus, exposure, and white balance, as described on the previous pages. (You can even hold your finger down to trigger the exposure and focus locks, as described earlier.)

Then tap Record (⦿)—or press a volume key on the edge of the phone—and you're rolling! As you film, a time counter ticks away at the top.

Things To Do While You're Rolling

Once you've begun capturing video, don't think your work is done. You can have all kinds of fun during the recording. For example:

- **Change focus.** You can change focus while you're filming, which is great when you're panning from a nearby object to a distant one. Refocusing is automatic, just as it is on regular camcorders—but you can also force a refocusing (for example, when the phone's focusing on the wrong thing) by tapping in your "viewfinder" to specify a new focus point. The iPhone recalculates the focus, white balance, and exposure at that point, just as it does when you're taking stills.

- **Zoom in (iPhone 5, 5c, and 5s).** For the first time in iPhone history, you can now zoom in while you're filming, up to 3x actual size. Just spread two fingers on the screen, like you would to magnify a photo. Pinch two fingers to zoom out again.

> **TIP:** Once you start to zoom, a zoom *slider* appears on the screen. It's much easier to zoom smoothly by dragging its handle than it is to use a two-finger pinch or spread.
>
> So here's a smart idea: Zoom in slightly before you start recording, so that the zoom slider appears on the screen. Then, during the shot, drag its handle to zoom in, as smoothly as you like.

- **Take a still photo.** Here's something the iPhone 5 family can do that even your digital camera probably can't: You can snap still photos while you're capturing video. Just tap the ⦿ shutter button that appears while you're filming. Awesome.

> **NOTE:** The pictures you take while filming don't have the same dimensions as the ones you take in Photo mode. These have 16:9 proportions, just like the video; they're not as tall as still photos.

When you're finished recording, tap the red Stop button (⦿). The iPhone stops recording and plays a chime; it's ready to record another shot.

There's no easier-to-use camcorder on earth. And, man, what a lot of capacity! Each individual shot can be one hour long—and on the 64-giga-byte iPhone, you can record *34 hours* of video. Which ought to be just about long enough to capture the entire elementary-school talent show.

The Front Camera

You can film yourself, too. Just tap the ⧉ icon before you film to make the iPhone use its front-mounted camera, so that the screen shows you. The iPhone 4 and 4s give you fairly poor video resolution (640 × 480 pix-els); the iPhone 5 family manages 720p. That's not as high definition as the back camera, but it's still high definition.

The Video Light

You know the LED "flash" on the back of the phone? You can use it as a video light, too, supplying some illumination to subjects within about 5 feet or so. Just tap the ⚡ icon and then tap On. The light remains on until you tap to turn it off (or you exit the Camera app).

> **TIP:** You can turn the video light on and off even in the middle of a shot. In fact, you can turn the video light on even when you're not filming—great when you need a little help reading a restaurant menu in tiny type by candlelight. Swipe up from the bottom of the screen to open the Control Center, and then tap the flashlight icon.

Slow-Motion Video (iPhone 5s)

If you have a 5s, you're a lucky duck: Your Camera app has an additional mode called Slo-Mo. (Swipe the screen all the way to the right until Slo-Mo is selected.)

Capturing video in this mode is exactly like capturing video the regular way—but behind the scenes, the phone is recording 120 frames a second instead of the usual 30.

When you open the captured movie to watch it, you'll see something star-tling and beautiful: The clip plays at full speed for 1 second, slows down to quarter speed, and, for the final second, accelerates back to full speed. It's a great way to study sports action, cannonball dives, and shades of expression in a growing smile.

What you may not realize, however, is that you can adjust where the slo-mo effect begins and ends in the clip. When you open the video for play-back, a strange kind of ruler track appears above it. Drag the vertical handles inward or outward to change the spot where the slow motion begins and ends. (Use the thick white vertical bar in the "filmstrip" at top to scrub through the clip to see where you are.)

NOTE: When you transfer the video to your Mac or PC (Chapter 13), you may be disappointed to discover that the video plays at only normal speed. If that happens, it's because the computer's playback software hasn't been updated to recognize the slow-motion effect.

There's an easy solution: Send the video to your computer by email, or by using any of the buttons on the Share sheet—AirDrop, Mail, Message, YouTube, Facebook, Vimeo, and so on. When you do that, the slo-mo plays back just the way it does on your phone.

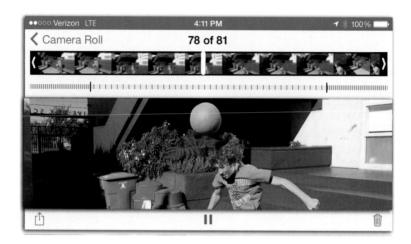

Trimming a Video

To review what you just shot, tap the ⬚ thumbnail icon at the lower corner of the screen. You've just opened up the video playback screen. Tap the big ▶ button to play back the video you just shot.

What's really cool, though, is that you can *edit* this video right on the phone. You can trim off the dead air at the beginning and the end.

To do that, tap the screen to make the scroll bar appear at the top (if you don't already see it). Then drag the < and > markers (currently at the outer ends of the little filmstrip) inward so that they turn yellow. Adjust them, hitting ▶ to see the effect as you go.

When you've positioned the handles so that they isolate the good stuff, tap Trim.

Finally, tap either Trim Original (meaning "shorten the original clip permanently") or Save as New Clip (meaning "leave the original untouched, and spin out the shortened version as a separate video").

iMovie for iPhone

Of course, there's more to editing than just snipping dead air from the ends of a clip. That's why Apple made iMovie for iPhone. It's free on a new iPhone, or $5 if it didn't come with your phone.

Either way, it lets you trim and rearrange video clips, add music and credits, drop in photos with zooming and crossfades, and then post the whole thing directly to YouTube.

Sure, the whole concept sounds a little ridiculous—video editing on a phone? You might as well introduce Microsoft Excel for Toaster Ovens.

But you watch. The way life goes, some all-iPhone production will win at Cannes next year.

If the idea appeals to you, the app waits in the App Store—and you can get instructions for using it by tapping the ⑦ icon and then tapping More Help.

Uploading Your Video to YouTube, MMS, or Email

Now, here's something not every cellphone can do: Film a movie, edit out the boring parts, and then upload it to YouTube—right from the phone!

Call up the video, if it's not already on the screen before you. Tap the ⬆️ button. The Share sheet offers some familiar choices:

- **Message, Mail.** The iPhone compresses the video so that it's small enough to send as an email or text-message attachment (smaller dimensions, lower picture quality). Then it attaches the clip to an outgoing text message or email message; it's your job to address it.

- **YouTube.** The iPhone asks for your YouTube account name and password. Next it wants a title, description, and *tags* (searchable keywords like "funny" or "babies").

  It also wants to know if the video will be in standard definition or high definition (and it gives the approximate size of the file). You should also pick a Category (Autos & Vehicles, Comedy, Education, or whatever).

  Finally, choose from Public (anyone online can search for and view your video), Unlisted (only people who have the link can view this video), or Private (only specific YouTube users can view). When everything looks good, tap Publish.

  After the upload is complete, you're offered the chance to see the video as it now appears on YouTube, or to Tell a Friend (that is, to email the YouTube link to a pal). Both are excellent ways to admire your masterful cinematography.

- **Facebook, Vimeo.** You're supposed to have set up your name and password in Settings for Facebook and for Vimeo (a video site a lot like YouTube, but classier, with a greater emphasis on quality and artistry).

  If you've done that, then all you have to do, when posting a video, is specify a caption or a description, a video size, and who your audience is (public, private, and so on). Once you tap Post, your video gets sent on to the great cinema on the Web.

Capturing the Screen

Let's say you want to write a book about the iPhone. (Hey, it could happen.) How are you supposed to illustrate that book? How can you take pictures of what's on the screen?

The trick is very simple: Start by getting the screen just the way you want it, even if that means holding your finger down on an onscreen button or a keyboard key. Now hold down the **Home** button, and while it's down, press the Sleep switch at the top of the phone. (Yes, you may need to invite some friends over to help you execute this multiple-finger move.)

But that's all there is to it. The screen flashes white. Now, if you go to the Photos program and open up the Camera Roll, you see a crisp, colorful pixel image, in PNG format, of whatever was on the screen. (Its resolution matches the screen: 480 × 320 pixels on the iPhone 3GS, 960 × 640 on the iPhone 4 or 4s, 1136 × 640 on the iPhone 5 family.)

At this point, you can send it by email (to illustrate a request for help, for example, or to send a screen from Maps to a friend who's driving your way); sync it with your computer (to add it to your Mac or Windows photo collection); or designate it as the iPhone's wallpaper (to confuse the heck out of its owner).

TIP: In some corners of iOS 7, there's no way to take a screenshot like this. For example, when the phone is ringing, pressing the screenshot button combination sends the call to voicemail instead of capturing the screen image.

In those situations, you may have to rely on a program like Reflector, described on page 216—and take a screenshot on the *Mac*.

8

All About Apps

App is short for *application,* meaning software program, and the App Store is a single, centralized catalog of every authorized iPhone add-on program in the world. In fact, it's the *only* place where you can get new programs (at least without hacking your phone).

You hear people talking about downsides to this approach: Apple's stifling the competition; Apple's taking a 30 percent cut of every program sold; Apple's maintaining veto power over programs it doesn't like.

But there are some enormous benefits, too. First, there's one central place to look for apps. Second, Apple checks out every program to make sure it's decent and runs decently. Third, the store is beautifully integrated with the iPhone itself.

There's an incredible wealth of software in the App Store. These programs can turn the iPhone into an instant-message tool, a pocket Internet radio, a medical reference, a musical keyboard, a time and expense tracker, a TV remote control, a photo editor, a recipe box, a tip calculator, a restaurant finder, a teleprompter, and so on. And games—thousands of dazzling handheld games, some with smooth 3-D graphics and tilt control.

It's so much stuff—a million apps, 50 billion downloads—that the challenge now is just finding your way through it. Thank goodness for those Most Popular lists.

Two Ways to the App Store

You can get to the App Store in two ways: from the phone itself, or from your computer's copy of the iTunes software.

Using iTunes offers a much easier browsing and shopping experience, of course, because you've got a mouse, a keyboard, and that big screen. But downloading straight to the iPhone, without ever involving the computer, is wicked convenient when you're out and about.

Shopping from the Phone

To check out iOS 7's redesigned App Store from your iPhone, tap the App Store icon. You arrive at the colorful, scrolling wonder of the store itself.

The layout of the first tap, Featured, is pretty clear: You can scroll vertically to see different categories, like Editors' Choices and Collections, and horizontally to see more apps within each category.

The top row might say, "Best New Apps." Scroll that row sideways to see the apps that Apple is recommending (or tap See All to see all the new apps).

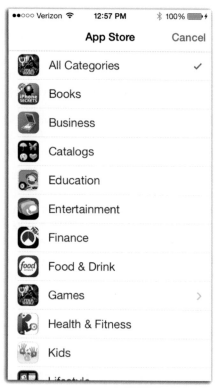

Tap Top Charts to reveal a list of the 100 most popular programs at the moment, ranked by how many people have downloaded them. There are actually three lists here: the most popular *free* programs, the most popular ones that cost money, and which apps have made the most money, even if they haven't sold the most copies.

- **Near Me,** new in iOS 7, lists apps that are popular—yes, near you. It uses your location to check for geographically relevant apps. Usually, this concept is most useful when you're at a public institution: a museum, baseball arena, and so on. You may also see the newspaper apps for whatever town you're in, or local bus and subway apps.

NOTE: The Near Me tab replaces the old Genius tab, whose purpose was to propose apps that you might like based on others you've downloaded.

- **Search.** Scrolling through those massive lists is a fun way to stumble onto cool things. But as the number of iPhone programs grows into the hundreds of thousands, viewing by list begins to get awfully unwieldy.

  Fortunately, you can also *search* the catalog, which is a very efficient way to go if you know what you're looking for (either the name of a program, the kind of program, or the software company that made it). Tap in the search box to make the keyboard appear. As you type, the list shrinks so that it's showing you only the matches. You might type *tetris,* or *piano,* or *Disney,* or whatever.

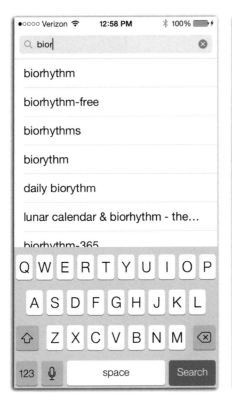
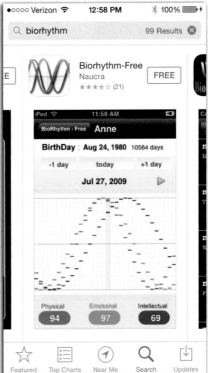

Tap anything in the results list (previous page, left) to see a series of "cards," one for each matching app. You can swipe horizontally to scroll through them. Tap one to view its details screen, as described below.

- **Updates.** Unlike its buddies, this button isn't intended to help you navigate the catalog. Instead, it lets you know when one of the programs you've *already* installed is available in a newer version. Details in a moment.

- **Categories.** This button isn't at the bottom; it's at the top left on the Featured and Top Charts screens described above. It shows the entire catalog, organized by category: Books, Business, Education, Entertainment, Finance, Games, and so on. Tap a category to see what's in it.

About a third of the App Store's programs are free; the rest are usually under $5. A few, intended for professionals (pilots, for example), can cost a lot more.

The App Details Page

No matter which button was your starting point, eventually you wind up at an app's details screen. There's a description, a horizontally scrolling set of screenshots, info about the author, the date posted, the version number, a page of related and similar apps, and so on.

You can also tap the **Reviews** link to dig beyond the average star rating into the *actual* written reviews from people who've already tried the thing.

Why are the ratings so important? Because the App Store's goodies aren't equally good. Remember, these programs come from a huge variety of people—teenagers in Hungary, professional firms in Silicon Valley, college kids goofing around on weekends—and just because they made it into the store doesn't mean they're worth the money (or even the time to download).

Sometimes a program has a low score because it's just not designed well or it doesn't do what it's advertised to do. And sometimes, of course, it's a little buggy.

If you decide something is worth getting, scroll back to the top of the page and tap its price button. It may say, for example, **FREE** or **$0.99**.

TIP: If you see a little **+** sign on the price button, it means that the app works well on both the iPad and the iPhone.

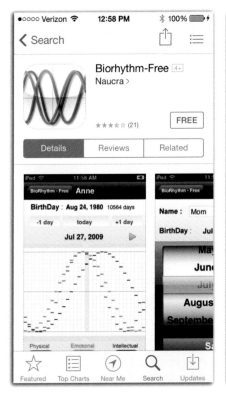

If you've previously bought it, either on this iPhone or another Apple touchscreen gadget, the button just says **INSTALL**; you don't have to buy it again. If, in fact, this app is already on your iPhone, then the button says **OPEN** (handy!).

Once you tap the price and then **INSTALL APP**, you've committed to downloading the program. There are only a few things that may stand in your way:

- **A request for your iTunes account info.** You can't use the App Store without an iTunes account—even if you're just downloading free stuff. If you've ever bought anything from the iTunes Store, signed up for an iCloud account, or bought anything from Apple online, then you already have an iTunes account (an Apple ID, meaning your email address and password).

  The iPhone asks you to enter your iTunes account name and password the first time you access the App Store and periodically thereafter, just to make sure some marauding child in your household can't run up your bill without your knowledge. Mercifully, you no longer have to enter your Apple ID information just to download an *update* to an app you already own.

- **A file size over 100 megabytes.** Most iPhone apps are pretty small—small enough to download directly to the phone, even over a cellular connection. If a program is bigger than 100 MB, though, you can't download it over the cellular airwaves, a policy no doubt intended to soothe nerves at AT&T, Sprint, T-Mobile, and Verizon, whose networks could be choked with 200 million iPhoners downloading huge files.

  Instead, over-100-meg files are available only when you're on a WiFi connection. Of course, you can also download them to your computer and sync them from there, as described later in this chapter.

Once you begin downloading a file, a tiny progress circle next to the app's name fills in to indicate the download's progress. (Tap the square Stop button inside the circle to cancel the download.) When the downloading is done, tap the OPEN button to launch it and try it out.

Two Welcome Notes about Backups

Especially when you've paid good money for your iPhone apps, you might worry about what would happen if your phone got lost or stolen, or if someone (maybe you) accidentally deleted one of your precious downloads.

You don't have to worry, for two reasons.

First, the next time you sync your iPhone with your computer, iTunes asks if you want the newly purchased apps backed up onto your computer. If you click Transfer, then the programs eventually show up on the Applications tab in iTunes.

Second, here's a handy little fact about the App Store: It remembers what you've already bought. You can re-download a purchased program at any time, on any of your iPhones, iPads, or iPod Touches, without having to pay for it again.

TIP: If some program doesn't download properly on the iPhone, don't sweat it. Go into iTunes on your computer and choose Store→Check for Available Downloads. And if a program does download to the phone but doesn't transfer to iTunes, choose File→Transfer Purchases from "iPhone". These two commands straighten things out, clear up the accounting, and make all well with your two copies of each app (iPhone + computer).

Shopping in iTunes

You can also download new programs to your computer using iTunes and then sync them over to the phone. By all means, use this method whenever you can. It's much more efficient to use a mouse, a keyboard, and a full screen.

In iTunes, click **iTunes Store** (top right). At the top of the window, click **App Store**. Now the screen fills with starting points for your quest, matching what you'd see on the phone: Best New Apps, Best New Games, and so on.

Or use the search box at top right.

From here, the experience is the same as it is on the phone. Drill down to the **Details** page for a program, read its description and reviews, look at its photos, and so on. Click the price button to download and, at the next sync, install it.

> **TIP:** The little **+** symbol on some price buttons indicates a hybrid app— one that will run on both the iPhone and the iPad.

Organizing Your Apps

As you add new apps to your iPhone, it sprouts new Home screens as necessary to accommodate them all, up to a grand total of 11 screens. On an iPhone 5, 5c, or 5s, that's 224 icons—and yet you can actually go all the way up to many thousands of apps, thanks to the miracle of *folders.*

That multiple-Home screen business can get a little unwieldy, but a couple of tools can help you manage. First, you can just use Siri to open an app, without ever having to know where it is ("Open Angry Birds").

Second, the Spotlight search feature can pluck the program you want out of your haystack, as described on page 68.

Third, you can organize your apps into folders, which greatly alleviates the agony of TMHSS (Too Many Home Screens Syndrome).

It's worth taking the time to arrange the icons on your Home screens into logical categories, tidy folders, or at least a sensible sequence.

You can do that either on the phone itself or in iTunes on your computer. (That's a far quicker and easier method, but of course it works only when your phone is actually connected to the Mac or PC.)

Rearranging/Deleting Apps Using iTunes

To fiddle with the layout of your Home screens with the least amount of hassle, connect the iPhone to your computer using the white charging cable or over WiFi. Open iTunes.

Click your iPhone's name at the top right, and then click the **Apps** tab at the top of the screen. You see the display on the facing page.

From here, it's all mouse power:

- For each listed app, click the button so that it says either **Install** (if the app isn't already on your phone) or **Remove** (if it is; at that point, the button changes to say **Will Remove**). In other words, it's possible to store hundreds of apps in iTunes but load only some of them onto your iPhone.

- Click one of the Home screen miniatures on the right list to indicate which screen you want to edit. It gets big. Now you can drag the app icons to rearrange them on that page. (Click the gray background to close the life-size image.)

- Beneath the Home screen miniatures, iTunes displays similar mockups of each folder on your phone. Because they're visible here, all of them, all the time, it's very easy to put icons into them—and to work with the multiple "pages" within each folder (read on).

- It's fine to drag an app onto a different page mockup. You can organize your icons on these Home screens by category, frequency of use, color, or whatever tickles your fancy. (The **+** button above each pile of mockups means, "Click to install an additional Home screen.")

- You can drag the page mockups around to rearrange *them,* too.

- To delete an app from the iPhone, point to its icon and click the ✖ that appears. (You can't delete the original iPhone apps like Safari and Mail.)

- Create a folder by dragging one app's icon on top of another (see page 284 for more on folders).

When your design spurt is complete, click Sync in the lower-right corner of the screen.

Rearranging/Deleting Apps Right on the Phone

You can also redesign your Home screens right on the iPhone, which is handy when you don't happen to be wired up to a computer.

To enter this Home screen editing mode, hold your finger down on any icon until, after about a second, the icons begin to—what's the correct term?—*wiggle.* (That's got to be a first in user-interface history.)

At this point, you can rearrange your icons by dragging them around the glass into a new order; other icons scoot aside to make room.

To create an additional Home screen, drag a wiggling icon to the right edge of the screen; keep your finger down. The first Home screen slides off to the left, leaving you on a new, blank one, where you can deposit the icon. You can create up to 11 Home screens in this way.

You may have noticed that, while your icons are wiggling, most of them also sprout little ⊗'s. That's how you *delete* a program you don't need anymore: Tap that ⊗. You'll be asked if you're sure; if so, it says bye-bye.

(You can't delete one of Apple's preinstalled apps, so no ⊗ appears on those icons. If they really bug you, you can drag the little-used Apple apps into a folder somewhere. In iOS 7, you can even drag the Newsstand icon into a folder, praise be.)

When everything looks good, press the Home button to stop the wiggling.

Restoring the Home Screen

If you ever need to undo all the damage you've done, tap Settings→General→ Reset→Reset Home Screen Layout. That function preserves any new programs you've installed, but it consolidates them. If you'd put 10 programs on each of four Home screens, you wind up with only two screens, each packed with 20 icons. Any leftover blank pages are eliminated. This function also places all your downloaded apps in alphabetical order.

Folders

Folders are so useful on your Mac or PC—so why not use them on your phone? Folders let you organize your apps, de-emphasize the ones you don't use often, and restore order to that dizzying display of icons.

It used to be that each iPhone folder could hold only 12 app icons. And since there are so many icons per Home screen page, and only 11 Home page screens maximum, there was a fixed limit of how many icons your phone could display.

Not anymore. In iOS 7, each folder can have many pages of its own (although each displays only nine icons now). A single folder, in other words, can contain as many apps as you want—and therefore, only memory limits how many apps you can fit onto your phone.

Setting Up Folders on the iPhone

To create and edit folders, you must always begin by entering Home screen editing mode. That is, hold your finger down on any icon until all the icons begin to wiggle.

Drag one app onto another…   …and a new folder is born. Rename it here.

Now, to create a folder, drag one app's icon on top of another. The software puts both of them into a new folder and gives it a proposed name, which you can change at this point. If they're the same kind of app, iOS even tries to figure out what category they both belong to—and names the new folder accordingly ("Music," "Photos," "Kid Games," or whatever).

You're welcome to add more apps to this folder. Tap the Home-screen background to close the folder, then (while the icons are still wiggling) drag another app onto the folder's icon. Lather, rinse, repeat.

If one of your folders has more than nine apps in it, iOS 7 creates a second "page" for the folder—and a third, a fourth, and so on. You can move apps around within the pages, and otherwise master your new multipage folder domain.

You can scroll the folder "pages" by swiping sideways, just as you can scroll the full-size Home pages. The only limit to how many icons a folder can hold is your tolerance for absurdity.

 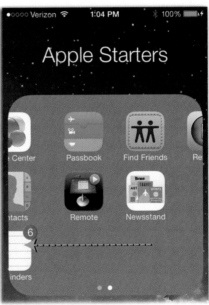

Once you've created a folder or two, they're easy to rename, move, delete, and so on. (Again, you can do all of the following *only in icon-wiggling editing mode.*) Like this:

- **Take an app out of a folder** by dragging its icon anywhere else on the Home screen. The other icons scoot aside to make room, just as they do when you move them from one Home screen to another.

- **Move a folder around** by dragging, as you would any other icon.

TIP: You can drag a folder icon onto the Dock, too, just as you would any app. Now you've got a popup subfolder full of your favorite apps—on the Dock, which is present on every Home screen. That's a very useful feature; it multiplies the handiness of the Dock itself.

- **Rename a folder** by opening it (tapping it). At this point, the folder's name box is ready for editing.

- **Move an icon from one folder "page" to another** by dragging it to the edge of the folder, waiting with your finger down until the page "changes," and then releasing your finger in the right spot.

- **Delete a folder** by removing all of its contents. The folder disappears automatically.

When you're finished manipulating your folders, press the Home button to exit Home screen editing mode—and stop all the wiggling madness.

Setting Up Folders in iTunes

It's actually faster and easier to set up your folders within iTunes, on your Mac or PC, where you have a mouse and a big screen to help you. Connect your iPhone to your computer (by cable or WiFi), open iTunes, click the iPhone's name at top right, and then click the **Apps** tab at the top. You see something like the illustration on page 281.

To create a folder, click a Home page miniature to expand it; now drag one app's icon on top of another, exactly as you'd do on the iPhone. The software puts both of them into a single new folder. As on the iPhone, the phone proposes a folder name; an editing bar also appears so that you can type a custom name you prefer.

Once you've got a folder, you can open it just by double-clicking. It expands to life size, revealing its contents. Now you can edit the folder's name, drag the icons around inside it, or drag an app right out of the folder window and onto another Home page (or another folder on it). Just keep your finger down on the mouse button or trackpad, no matter how long it takes, until the new Home page or folder page opens.

Below the Home pages, you'll discover that each of your app folders now has an app-management screen mockup of its own, complete with a horizontally scrolling set of pages. That's so you can move the "pages" around, organize the apps within them, and so on.

If you remove all the apps from a folder, the folder disappears.

App Preferences

If you're wondering where you can change an iPhone app's settings, consider backing out to the Home screen and then tapping Settings. Apple encourages programmers to add their programs' settings *here,* way down below the bottom of the iPhone's own Settings screen.

Some programmers ignore the advice and build the settings right into their apps, where they're a little easier to find. But if you don't see them there, now you know where else to look.

App Updates

When a circled number (like ❷) appears on the App Store's icon on the Home screen, or on the Updates icon within the App Store program, that's Apple's way of letting you know that a program you already own has been updated. Apple knows which programs you've bought—and notifies you automatically when new, improved versions are released. Which is remarkably often; software companies constantly fix bugs and add new features.

Manual Updates

When you tap Updates, you're shown a list of the programs with waiting updates. A tiny What's New arrow lets you know what the changes are—new features, perhaps, or some bug fixes. And when you tap a program's name, you go to its details screen, where you can remind yourself of what the app does, and where you can read other people's reviews of this new version.

You can download one app's update, or, with a tap on the Update All button, all of them...no charge.

> **NOTE:** You can also download your updates from iTunes. Click Apps in the Source list (under the Library heading); the lower edge of the window lets you know if there are updated versions of your programs waiting and offers buttons that let you download the updates individually or all at once.

Automatic Updates

If you have a lot of apps, you may come to feel as though you're spending your whole life downloading updates. They descend like locusts, every single day, demanding your attention.

That's why, in iOS 7, Apple finally blessed us with the automatic update-downloading option. Now your phone can download and install updated versions of your apps quietly and automatically in the background.

To turn on this feature, open **Settings→iTunes & App Store**. Under Automatic Downloads, turn on **Updates**. (If you'd prefer that the phone wait to do this downloading until it's in a WiFi hotspot—to avoid eating up your monthly cellular data-plan allotment—turn off **Use Cellular Data**.)

From now on, the task of manually approving each app's update is off your to-do list forever. Only a blue dot next to an app's name on the Home screen lets you know that it's been updated.

TIP: Fortunately, the iPhone also keeps a tidy record of every app it's updated, and what that update gives you. Open the App Store app; tap the **Updates** tab. There's your list, sorted chronologically. Tap an app's row to read what was new in the update you've already received.

How to Find Good Apps

If the Featured, What's Hot, and Charts lists aren't getting you inspired, there are all kinds of Web sites dedicated to reviewing and recommending iPhone apps. There's *appcraver.com*, and *whatsoniphone.com*, and on and on.

But if you've never dug into iPhone apps before, you should at the very least try out some of the superstars, the big dogs that almost everybody has.

Here are a few—a very few, a drop in the bucket at the tip of the iceberg—meant only to suggest the infinite variety that's available from the App Store:

- **Apple Apps (free).** The first time you open the App Store, you're offered a set of free Apple apps that Apple thinks you might like: iBooks, iTunes U, Podcasts, Find My Friends, and Find My iPhone. With one tap, you can grab this whole set.

- **Google Maps (free).** Google Maps is a replacement for the built-in Maps app. It's much, *much* better than the built-in Maps program— even Apple has admitted that. Among other things, it offers Street View (you can actually see a photo of almost any address and "look around" you), it incorporates the Zagat guides for restaurants, and it's unbelievably smart about knowing what you're trying to type into the search box. Usually, about three letters is all you need to type before the app guesses what you mean.

- **FlightTrack Pro ($10).** Incredible. Shows every detail of every flight: gate, time delayed, airline phone number, where the flight is on the map, and more. Knows more—and knows it sooner—than the actual airlines do.

- **Google Mobile (free).** Speak to search Google's maps. Includes Google Goggles: Point the phone's camera at a book, DVD, wine bottle, logo, painting, landmark, or bit of text, and the hyper-intelligent app recognizes it and displays information about it from the Web.

- **YouTube (free).** In iOS 7, there's no built-in YouTube player. (You can thank the rising tensions between Apple and Google for that.) Fortunately, Google offers its own, free, nearly identical app.

- **Ocarina ($1).** A bona fide wind instrument. Blow into the microphone, learn the fingerings of the four "holes" on the glass screen...beautiful music.

- **Fake Calls ($1).** When you tap this icon on your Home screen, in about 10 seconds, your phone rings. It's a fake call—from anyone you've selected in advance. The simulation of the iPhone's traditional incoming-call screen is perfect. Ideal for extricating yourself from difficult situations, like meetings or bad dates.

- **Line2 (free).** Gives your iPhone a second phone line with its own number—one that makes or receives calls over WiFi when you're in a hotspot (no cellular minutes!), or over your regular carrier when you're not. Unlimited texting, unlimited calling, $10 a month.

- **Echofon (free).** Most free Twitter apps are a bit on the baffling side. This one is simple and clean.

- **SoundHound (free).** Beats Shazam at its own game. Hold this app up to a song that's playing on the radio, or even hum or sing the song, and the app miraculously identifies the song and offers you lyrics. It's faster than Shazam, too.

- **Bump (free).** If you and another iPhone owner both have this app, you just bump your phones together to exchange business cards (or photos, or other files).

- **Instagram (free)** has a bunch of filter effects, as iOS 7's Camera app now does, too. But the real magic is in the way it's designed to share your photos. You sign up to receive Instagrams from Facebook or Twitter folk. They (the photos, not the folk) show up right in the app, scrolling up like a photographic Twitter feed. Seeing what other people are doing every day with their cameraphones and creative urges is really inspirational.

Other essentials: Angry Birds and its sequel, Bad Piggies. Skype. Netflix. Hipmunk (finds flights). The New York Times, of course. The Amazon Kindle book reader, B&N eReader. Dictionary. Facebook. TED. Mint.com. Scrabble. Keynote Remote (controls your Keynote presentations from the phone). Remote (yes, another one, also from Apple—turns the iPhone into a WiFi, whole-house *remote control* for your Mac or PC's music playback—and for Apple TV.

Foursquare. Pandora. Yelp. Flickr. Instant-messaging (AIM, Yahoo Messenger, IM+, or Beejive IM). Yahoo Weather (absolutely gorgeous).

Happy apping!

Multitasking

You don't have to exit one program before opening the next. The iPhone is, more or less, a multitasking phone now.

The big benefit here is speed. You can duck out of what you're doing, check some other app, and return to where you left off—without having to wait for your apps to close and then reopen, and without having to reconstruct how you had things when you left.

Switching out of a program doesn't actually close it. In iOS 7, all apps are capable of running in the background. (In iOS 6, only certain kinds of apps were allowed to keep chugging away in the background: Internet audio, GPS navigation, Internet phone apps like Skype, and notifications.)

Apple's reluctance to offer full-blown multitasking was battery life. If every app was running simultaneously, it'd wolf down your battery juice.

In iOS 7, Apple thinks it's solved that problem—by putting two kinds of limits in place:

- **iOS 7's limits.** Not all apps run full-speed, full-bore in the background. iOS 7 attempts to use some logic about which ones get the processor's attention. For example, apps that really need constant updating, like Facebook or Twitter, get refreshed every few seconds; apps that don't rely on constant Internet updates get to nap for a while in the background.

    In deciding which apps get background attention, iOS 7 studies things like how good your phone's Internet connection is and what time you traditionally use a certain app (so that your favorite newspaper's app is ready with the latest articles when you open it).

- **Your own limits.** You can't control which apps *run* in the background, but you can control which ones *download new data* in the background. In Settings→General→Background App Refresh, you'll find a list of every app that may want to update itself in the background. In an effort to make your battery last longer, you can turn off background updating for the apps you don't really care about; you can even turn off all background updating using the master switch at the top.

The App Switcher

From the day the app concept was invented, the iPhone desperately needed a handy way to switch among open apps. Maybe you want to copy something from Safari (on the Web) into Mail (a message you're writing). Maybe you want to refer to your frequent flyer number (in Notes) as you're using an airline's check-in app. Maybe you want to adjust something in Settings and then get back to whatever you were doing.

The key to switching apps is this: *Double-press the Home button.*

In iOS 7, what happens next has had some radical cosmetic surgery. Whatever is on the screen gets replaced by the new, improved app switcher.

You still see a horizontally scrolling row of icons, representing the open apps. But above them, you now see shrunken-down images of their *screens.* You can actually see what's going on in each open app. In fact, sometimes, that's all you need; you can refer to another app's screen in this view, without actually having to switch *into* that app.

When you scroll horizontally to look through your recently opened apps (they appear in chronological order), you may notice that the icons and their screens seem to scroll at different speeds. It's a little odd at first, but you get the point: They're actually moving so that the icon is always centered under its much larger screen.

TIP: Thoughtfully enough, the app switcher always puts the *previous app* front and center when you first double-press the Home button. For example, if you're in Safari but you were using Mail a minute ago, Mail appears centered in the app switcher. That makes life easier if you're doing a lot of jumping back and forth between two particular apps; one tap takes you into the previous app.

When you tap an app's icon or screen in the app switcher, you open that app.

Force Quitting an App

The task switcher lets you manually exit an app, closing it down. To do that, flick the unwanted app's mini-screen upward, so that it flies up off the top of the screen (facing page, right).

(The app will return to the lineup the next time you open it from the Home screen; it's not really gone.)

Now, you'll need this gesture only rarely. It's not as though you're supposed to quit every app when you're finished using it, as you might on a PC. The iPhone is perfectly capable of managing its own memory situation. You may see dozens of apps in the app switcher, but you'll never sense that your phone is bogging down as a result.

Instead, the force-quitting gesture is intended for use when an app is acting glitchy and simply needs to be restarted.

AirPrint: Printing from the Phone

The very phrase "printing from the phone" might seem a little peculiar. How do you print from a gadget that's smaller than a Hershey bar—a gadget without any jacks for connecting a printer?

Wirelessly, of course.

You can send printouts from your phone to any printer that's connected to your Mac or PC on the same WiFi network if you have a piece of software like Printopia ($20).

Or you can use the iPhone's built-in AirPrint technology, which can send printouts directly to a WiFi printer without requiring a Mac or a PC.

Not just any WiFi printer, though—only those that recognize AirPrint. A lot of recent Canon, Epson, HP, and Lexmark printers work with AirPrint; you can see a list of them on Apple's Web site, here: *http://support.apple.com/kb/HT4356*.

Not all apps can print. Of the built-in Apple programs, only iBooks, Mail, Photos, Notes, and Safari offer Print commands. Those apps contain what most people want to print most of the time: PDF documents (iBooks), email messages, driving directions from the Web, and so on. Plenty of non-Apple apps work with AirPrint, too.

To use AirPrint, start by tapping the ⬆ button; tap **Print**. You're offered a **Select Printer** option. Tap it to introduce the phone to your printer, whose name should appear automatically. Now you can adjust the printing options (number of copies, page range)—and when you finally tap **Print**, your printout shoots wirelessly to the printer, exactly as though your phone and printer were wired together.

The Share Sheet

Every app is different, of course. But all of them have certain things in common; otherwise, you'd go out of your mind.

One of them is the Share sheet. It's your headquarters for sending stuff off your phone: to other apps, to other phones, to the Internet, to a printer. And this, too, has had a big makeover in iOS 7. It's now made up of several icon rows, each of which can scroll horizontally. (From top to bottom, you could title these rows What to Share, Send by AirDrop, Send to an App, and Send to Anything Else.)

The Share sheet pops up whenever you tap the Share button (⬆) that appears in many, many apps: Maps, Photos, Safari, Notes, Voice Memos, Contacts, and so on.

The buttons you see depend on the app in question; you may see only two options here, or you may see a dozen. But here are some of the options you'll see most often:

- **AirDrop.** This new iOS 7 feature lets you shoot stuff directly from iPhone to iPhone (or to iPad or iPod Touch). Keep reading.

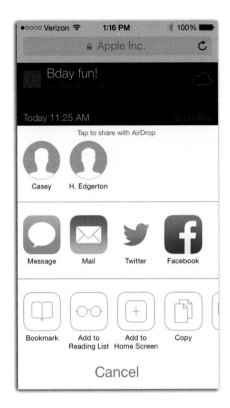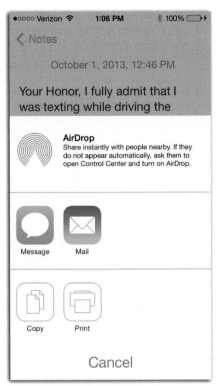

- **Message** and **Mail** attach whatever you're sending (a photo, a video, a map, a Web page, whatever) to a text message or outgoing email.

- **Twitter** and **Facebook** let you post a picture, video, or text bit to your Twitter or Facebook accounts. (First, you'll be asked to compose or edit the caption, indicate your audience, and so on.) For photos, you also get a Flickr option.

- **Copy** puts the material on the Clipboard, ready to paste somewhere.

- **AirPlay** sends the photos, music, or video wirelessly to an AirPlay receiver connected to your TV or stereo system, like an Apple TV.

- **Print.** Sends the selected material to an AirPrint-compatible printer, as described above.

You may see other options here; for example, when you've opened a photo, you get a special row of neighboring photos across the top of the Share sheet so that you can choose additional pictures to go along for the ride. And you get options like Assign to Contact and Use as Wallpaper, which work beautifully for photos but wouldn't make much sense for, say, a map.

AirDrop

It's an iOS 7 headline feature: AirDrop, a way to shoot things from one phone or tablet to another—wirelessly, instantly, easily, encryptedly, without requiring names, passwords, or settings-up. It's much faster than emailing or text-messaging, since you don't have to know (or type) the other guy's address. It's available on the iPhone 5 and later.

> **NOTE:** Even though there's an OS X feature called AirDrop, it's exclusively for sending files between Macs. You can't shoot files between iPhones and Macs.

The kinds of things you can transmit are pictures and videos from the Photos app, people's info cards from Contacts, directions (or your current location) from Maps, pages from Notes, Web addresses from Safari, electronic tickets from Passbook, apps you like in the App Store, song and video listings from the iTunes app), radio stations (iTunes Radio), and so on. As time goes on, more and more non-Apple apps will offer AirDrop, too.

Behind the scenes, AirDrop uses Bluetooth (to find nearby gadgets within about 30 feet) and a private, temporary WiFi mini-network (to transfer the file). Both sender and receiver have Bluetooth and WiFi turned on.

The process goes like this:

1. **Find a willing recipient.** You can't send anything with AirDrop unless the receiving phone or tablet is running iOS 7 or later—and is awake. And only recent models work with AirDrop: iPhone 5 or later, fourth-generation iPad or later, any iPad mini, and fifth-generation iPod Touch or later.

   In other words, most AirDrop exchanges begin with your saying, "Hey, do you have iOS 7?"

2. **Open the item you want to share. Tap the Share button (⬆).** If your app doesn't have a ⬆ button, then you can't use AirDrop.

   When the Share sheet appears, within a few seconds, you see something that would have awed the masses in 1975: small circular photos of everyone nearby. (Or at least everyone with iOS 7. Or at least everyone among them who's ***open to receiving*** AirDrop transmissions, as described below.)

3. **Tap the icon of the person you want to share with.** In about a second, a message appears on the recipient's screen, conveying your offer to transmit something good—and, when it makes sense, showing a picture of it (right).

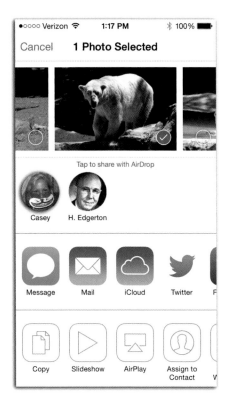 

At this point, it's up to your recipients. If they tap Accept, then the transfer begins (and ends); whatever you sent them opens up automatically in the relevant app. You'll know that AirDrop was successful because the word Sent appears on your screen.

9

The Built-In Apps

Your Home screen comes already loaded with the icons of about 25 programs. These are the essentials; eventually, of course, you'll fill that Home screen with apps you install yourself. The starter apps include gateways to the Internet (Safari), communications tools (Phone, Messages, Mail, Contacts), visual records of your life (Photos, Camera), shopping centers (iTunes, App Store), and entertainment (Music, Videos).

Those core apps get special treatment in the other chapters. This chapter covers the secondary programs, in alphabetical order: Calculator, Calendar, Clock, Compass, Find My Friends, Game Center, iBooks, Maps, Newsstand, Notes, Passbook, Reminders, Stocks, Voice Memos, and Weather.

Calculator

The iPhone wouldn't be much of a computer without a calculator, now, would it? And here it is, your everyday calculator—with a secret twist.

> **NOTE:** On a new iPhone, the Calculator sits in a folder called Extras. But it's much faster to tell Siri, "Open the calculator" or to tap the Calculator button on the Control Center.

In Calculator's basic four-function mode, you can tap out equations (like **15.4 × 300 =**) to see the answer at the top. (You can **paste** things you've copied into here, too; just hold your finger down until the Paste button

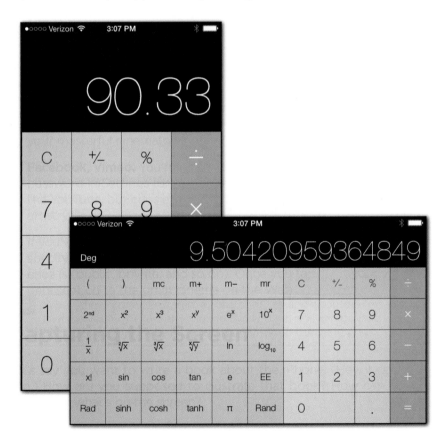

appears.) Apple took the memory function out of the basic calculator in iOS 7, but you do get a +/– button; its function is to change the currently displayed number from positive to negative, or vice versa.

> **TIP:** When you tap one of the operators (like ×, +, –, or ÷) it sprouts a black outline to help you remember which operation is in progress. Let's see an ordinary calculator do *that!*

Now the twist: If you rotate the iPhone 90 degrees in either direction, the Calculator morphs into a full-blown HP *scientific* calculator, complete with trigonometry, logarithmic functions, a memory function, exponents, roots beyond the square root, and so on. Go wild, ye engineers and physicists!

> **TIP:** If you make a mistake while entering a number, swipe horizontally across the numerical display (either direction). Each swipe backspaces over the rightmost digit.

Calendar

What kind of digital companion would the iPhone be if it didn't have a calendar program? And not only does it have a calendar—it has a completely overhauled one. In iOS 7, it's barely recognizable as the iPhone's traditional calendar.

And it syncs. If you maintain your life's schedule on a Mac (in Calendar or Entourage) or a PC (in Outlook), then you already have your calendar on your iPhone. Make a change in one place, and it changes in the other, every time you sync over the USB cable.

Better yet, if you have an iCloud account or work for a company with an Exchange server (Chapters 14 and 15), then your calendar can be synchronized with your computer *automatically,* wirelessly, over the air.

Or you can use Calendar all by itself.

> **TIP:** The Calendar icon on the Home screen shows what looks like one of those paper Page-a-Day calendar pads. But if you look closely, you'll see a sweet touch: It actually shows *today's* day and date.

Day View

When you open Calendar, you're shown today's schedule, broken down by time slot. After about a second, as a courtesy to you, the iOS 7 calendar auto-scrolls to the next appointment in your day. (Or, if you're checking out some other day, it auto-scrolls to the first thing on that day.)

You can navigate to other days' schedules in any of three ways:

- **Swipe horizontally across the Day screen** to see the previous or next day.

- **Tap a date at the top** to see another day this week.

- **Swipe across the dates at the top** to jump to another week.

If the date you want to check is further away than a week or two, though, it might make more sense to pop into Month view, described next.

Month View

Month view, of course, shows the entire month at a glance. What's handy in the iOS 7 incarnation is that you can scroll the month vertically, thereby scanning the entire year in a few seconds.

To get there from Day view, tap the name of the month (like **March 2014**) at the top left.

Of course, your little phone screen is too small to show you what's written on each calendar square; all you get is a gray dot on any date where you've scheduled an appointment.

Tap that dot to jump back into Day view and read your schedule.

Year View

If you're in Month view, you can "zoom out" yet another level—to Year view. It's a simple, vertically scrolling map of the year's months. Tap the name of the year (top left) to see it.

From there, tap a month block to open it back into Month view.

TIP: In all three of these views—Day, Month, Year—you can tap **Today** (bottom left) to return to today's date.

Week View

The most useful view yet may be the fourth one: the scrolling Week view, like the one shown here.

No button opens this view; instead, turn the phone 90 degrees so that it's in landscape mode. Here you can swipe sideways to move to earlier or later dates. Swipe up or down to move through the hours of the day.

NOTE: What Apple calls "Week" view doesn't actually show the whole week. But on the wider screens of the iPhone 5, 5c, and 5s, at least, it comes pretty close.

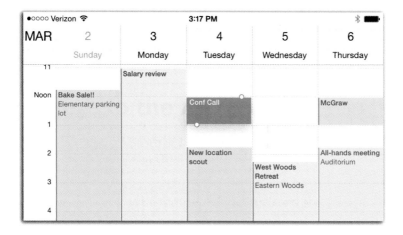

Making an Appointment (Day, Month View)

The basic calendar is easy to figure out. After all, with the exception of one unfortunate Gregorian incident, we've been using calendars successfully for centuries.

Even so, recording an event on this calendar is quite a bit more flexible than entering one on, say, one of those "Hunks of the Midwest Police Stations" paper calendars.

Start by tapping the $+$ (top-right corner of the screen). The Add Event screen pops up, filled with tappable lines of information. Tap one (like Starts/Ends or Repeat) to open a configuration screen for that element.

For example:

- **Title/Location.** Name your appointment here. For example, you might type *Fly to Phoenix.*

  The second line, called Location, makes a lot of sense. If you think about it, almost everyone needs to record *where* a meeting is to take place. You might type a reminder for yourself like *My place,* a specific address like *212 East 23rd,* a contact phone number, or a flight number.

  Use the keyboard as usual.

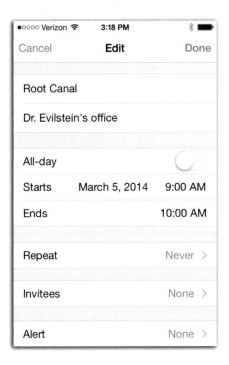

- **Starts/Ends.** On this screen, tap **Starts**, and then indicate the starting time for this appointment, using the four spinning dials at the bottom of the screen. The first sets the date; the second, the hour; the third, the minute; the fourth, AM or PM. If only real alarm clocks were so much fun!

  Then tap **Ends**, and repeat the process to schedule the ending time. (The iPhone helpfully presets the Ends time to one hour later.)

  An **All-day** event, of course, has no specific time of day: a holiday, a birthday, a book deadline. When you turn this option on, the Starts and Ends times disappear. The event appears at the top of the list for that day.

> **TIP:** Calendar can handle multiday appointments, too, like trips away. Turn on All-day—and then use the Starts and Ends controls to specify beginning and ending *dates.* On the iPhone, you'll see it as a list item that repeats on every day's square. Back on your computer, you'll see it as a banner stretching across the Month view.

Appointment, with start and end times   *All-day event*

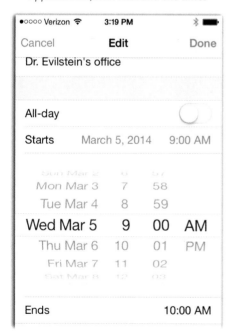 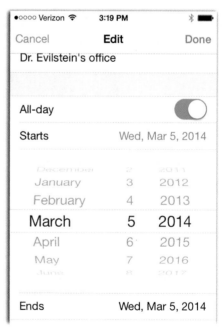

- **Repeat.** The screen here contains common options for recurring events: every day, every week, and so on. It starts out saying **Never**.

Once you've tapped a selection, you return to the Edit screen. Now you can tap the **End Repeat** button to specify when this event should *stop* repeating. If you leave the setting at **Never**, then you're stuck seeing this event repeating on your calendar until the end of time (a good choice for recording, say, your anniversary, especially if your spouse might be consulting the same calendar).

In other situations, you may prefer to tap **On Date** and spin the three dials (month, day, year) to specify an ending date, which is useful for car and mortgage payments.

Tap **Add Event** to return to the editing screen.

- **Invitees.** If you have an iCloud, Exchange, or CalDAV account, you can invite people to an event—a meeting, a party, whatever—and track their responses, right there on your phone (or any iCloud gadget). When you tap **Invitees**, you get an Add Invitees screen, where you can type in the email addresses of your lucky guests. (Or tap ⊕ to choose them from your Contacts list.)

  Later, when you tap **Done**, the phone fires off email invitations to those guests. It contains buttons for them to click: Accept, Decline, and Maybe. You get to see their responses right here in the Details of your calendar event.

  As icing on the cake, your guests (at least those hip enough to be using iOS 5 or later) will see a pop-up reminder on their phones when the time comes for the party to get started.

- **Alert.** This screen tells Calendar how to notify you when a certain appointment is about to begin. Calendar can send any of four kinds of flags to get your attention. Tap how much notice you want: 5, 15, or 30 minutes before the big moment; an hour or two before; a day or two before; a week before; or on the day of the event.

NOTE: For all-day events like birthdays, you get a smaller but very useful list of choices: "On day of event (9 AM)," "1 day before (9 AM)," "2 days before (9 AM)," and "1 week before."

When you tap **Add Event** and return to the main Add Event screen, you see that a new line, called **Second Alert**, has sprouted up beneath the first Alert line. This line lets you schedule a *second* warning for your appointment, which can occur either before or after the first one. Think of it as a backup alarm for events of extra urgency.

Once you've scheduled these alerts, you'll see a message appear on the screen at the appointed time(s). (Even if the phone was asleep, it appears briefly.) You'll also hear a chirpy alarm sound.

> **TIP:** The iPhone doesn't play the sound if you turned off Calendar Alerts in **Settings→Sounds**. It also doesn't play if you silenced the phone with the silencer switch on the side.

- **Calendar.** Tap here to specify which color-coded *calendar* (category, like Home, Kids, or Work) this appointment belongs to. Turn to page 311 for details on the calendar concept.

- **URL.** Here's a spot where you can record the Web address of some online site that provides more information about this event.

- **Notes.** Here's your chance to customize your calendar event. You can type any text you want in the Notes area—driving directions, contact phone numbers, a call history, or whatever. Tap Done when you're finished.

When you've completed filling in all these blanks, tap Done. Your newly scheduled event now shows up on the calendar.

Making an Appointment (Day View, Week View)

As noted earlier, turning the phone 90 degrees opens up a new, widescreen, scrolling Week view of your life.

In both Day view and Week view, you can *hold your finger down on a time slot* to add a new, 1-hour appointment right there. You're asked to enter a name and, if you like, location for this new appointment. Tap Done. You can always edit this appointment's details or duration later, as described next—but this quick-and-dirty technique saves the effort of tapping in Start and End times.

Editing, Rescheduling, Deleting Events (Long Way)

To examine the details of an appointment in the calendar, tap it once. The Event Details screen appears, filled with the details you previously established.

To edit any of these characteristics, tap Edit. You return to what looks like a clone of the Add Event screen.

Here you can change the name, time, alarm, repeat schedule, calendar category, or any other detail of the event, just the way you set them up to begin with.

This time, there's a red **Delete Event** button at the bottom. That's the only way to erase an appointment from your calendar. (You can't erase events created by other people—Facebook birthdays, meetings on shared calendars, and so on—only appointments *you* created.)

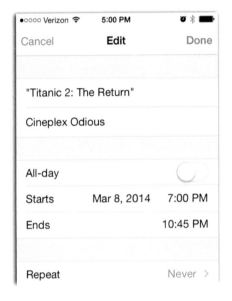
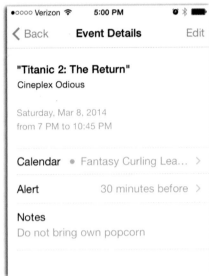

Editing and Rescheduling Events (Fun Way)

In Day or Week views, you can ***drag an appointment's block*** to another time slot or even another day. Just hold your finger down on the appoint-

ment's bubble for about a second—until it darkens—before you start to drag. It's a lot quicker and more fluid than having to edit in a dialog box.

You can also change the **duration** of an appointment in Day and Week views. Hold your finger down on its colored block for about a second; when you let go, small, round handles appear.

You can drag those tiny handles up or down to make the block taller or shorter, in effect making it start or end at a different time.

Whether you drag the whole block, the top edge, or the bottom edge, the iPhone thoughtfully displays ":15," ":30," or ":45" on the left-side time ruler to let you know where you'll be when you let go.

The Calendar (Category) Concept

A **calendar,** in Apple's somewhat confusing terminology, is a color-coded subset—a **category**—into which you can place various appointments. They can be anything you like. One person might have calendars called Home, Work, and TV Reminders. Another might have Me, Spouse 'n' Me, and The Kidz. A small business could have categories called Deductible Travel, R&D, and R&R.

You can create and edit calendar categories right on the iPhone, in your desktop calendar program, or (if you're an iCloud member) at *www.icloud. com* when you're at your computer; all your categories and color-codings show up on the iPhone automatically.

At any time, on the iPhone, you can choose which subset of categories you want to see. Just tap Calendars at the bottom of Day, Month, or Year view. You arrive at the big color-coded list of your categories (next page, left). As you can see, it's subdivided according to your accounts: your Gmail categories, your Yahoo categories, your iCloud categories, and so on. There's even a Facebook option, if you've set up your Facebook account, so that you can see your Facebook calendar entries and friends' birthdays right on the main calendar.

This screen exists partly as a reference, a cheat sheet to help you remember what color goes with which category, and partly as a tappable subset chooser. That is, you can tap a category's name to hide or show all of its appointments on the calendar. A checkmark means you're seeing its appointments. (The All [Account Name] button turns on or off all of that account's categories at once.)

If you tap Edit, a little > appears next to each calendar's name. If you tap it, you're offered a screen where you can change the calendar's name, color, and list of people who can see it—or scroll all the way down to see the **Delete Calendar** button.

The Edit Calendars screen also offers an **Add Calendar** button. It's the key to creating, naming, and colorizing a new calendar on the phone. (Whatever changes you make to your calendar categories on the phone will be synced back to your Mac or PC.)

> **TIP:** You can set up real-time, wireless connections to calendars published on the Web in the CalDAV format—notably your Yahoo or Google calendar. Just tap your way to **Settings→Mail, Contacts, Calendars→Add Account**. Here you can tap **iCloud, Exchange, Gmail, Yahoo, AOL**, or **Outlook.com** to set up your account. (You can also tap **Other→Add CalDAV Account** to fill in the details of a less well-known calendar server.)

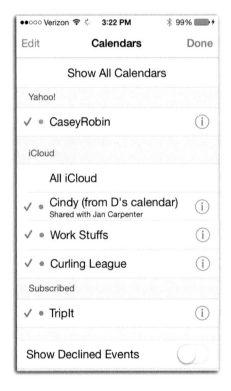

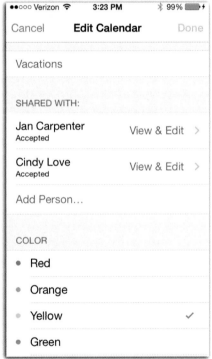

Now you have a two-way synced calendar between your iPhone and (in this case) your online calendar. To read about other ways of syncing the iPhone with online calendars, including read-only .ics files (like sports-team schedules), download the PDF appendix called "Syncing Calendar with .ics Files" from this book's "Missing CD" page (which you'll find at *www.missingmanuals.com*).

You can share an iCloud calendar with other iCloud members, which is fantastic for families and small businesses who need to coordinate. Tap **Calendars**, tap **Edit**, and then tap the calendar to share. Tap **Add Person** and enter the person's name. Your invitees get invitations by email; with one click, they've added your appointments to their calendars. They can make changes, too.

You can also share a calendar with anyone (not just iCloud members) in a "look, don't touch" condition. Tap **Calendars**, tap **Edit**, then tap the calendar to share. Turn on **Public Calendar**; tap **Share Link** to open the Share sheet for sending the link. Most calendar apps understand the calendar link that your phone sends.

Search

The search box at the top of the screen is iOS 7's version of the old List view. It's better, though, because as you type into it, you pare down the list of all calendar events from all time; only events whose names match what you've typed show up. Tap one to jump to its block on the corresponding Day view.

Next time you're sure you made an appointment with Harvey but you can't remember the date, keep this search feature in mind.

 If the iOS 7 calendar strikes you as fairly stripped-down, you're not alone. You might want to consider some calendar apps that have more features and power, like Fantastical or Tempo.

Clock

It's not just a clock—it's more like a time factory. Hiding behind this single icon on the Home screen are four programs: a world clock, an alarm clock, a stopwatch, and a countdown timer.

 The app icon itself is an accurate clock. It shows the time! Isn't that cute?

World Clock

When you tap **World Clock** on the Clock screen, you start out with only one clock, showing the current time in Apple's own Cupertino, California.

The neat part is that you can open up *several* of these clocks and set each one to show the time in a different city. The result looks like the row of clocks in a hotel lobby, making you seem Swiss and precise.

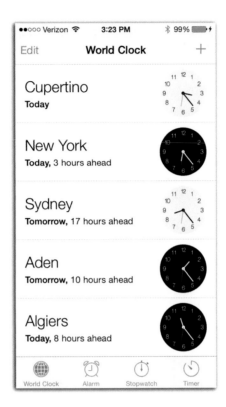

By checking these clocks, you'll know what time it is in some remote city, so you don't wake somebody up at what turns out to be 3 a.m.

To specify which city's time appears on the clock, tap + at the upper-right corner. Scroll to the city you want, or tap its first letter in the index at the right side to save scrolling, or tap in the search box at the top and type the name of a major city. As you type, matching city names appear; tap the one whose time you want to track.

As soon as you tap a city name, you return to the World Clock display. The color of the clock indicates whether it's daytime (white) or night (black).

TIP: Tap any row—the city name or the clock—to switch the display between analog and digital displays of the times.

You can scroll the list of clocks. You're not limited to four or five, although only that many fit on the screen at once.

TIP: Only the world's major cities are in the iPhone's database. If you're trying to track the time in Squirrel Cheeks, New Mexico, add a major city in the same time zone instead—like Albuquerque.

To edit the list of clocks, tap **Edit**. Delete a city clock by tapping ⊖ and then **Delete**, or drag clocks up or down using the ≡ as a handle. Then tap **Done**.

Alarm

If you travel much, this feature could turn out to be one of your iPhone's most useful functions. It's reliable, it's programmable, and it even wakes *the phone* first, if necessary, to wake *you.*

To set an alarm, tap **Alarm** at the bottom of the Clock screen. You're shown the list of alarms you've already created, even if none are currently set to go off (below, left). You could create a 6:30 a.m. alarm for weekdays and an 11:30 a.m. alarm for weekends.

To create a new alarm, tap + to open the **Add Alarm** screen (below, right).

TIP: But really, you should *not* bother setting alarms using this manual technique. Instead, you'll save a lot of time and steps by using Siri. Just say, "Set my alarm for 7:30 a.m." (or whatever time you want).

You have several options here:

- **Repeat.** Tap to specify what days this alarm rings. You can specify, for example, Mondays, Wednesdays, and Fridays by tapping those three buttons. (Tap a day-of-the-week button again to turn off its check-mark.) Tap **Back** when you're done. (If you choose Saturdays and Sundays, iOS 7 is smart enough to call that "Weekends.")

- **Label.** Tap to give this alarm a description, like "Get dressed for wedding." That message appears on the screen when the alarm goes off.

- **Sound.** Choose what sound you want to ring. You can choose from any of the iPhone's ringtone sounds, any you've added yourself—or, best of all, **Pick a Song**. That's right—you can wake to the music of your choice.

- **Snooze.** If this option is on, then at the appointed time, the alarm message on the screen offers you a **tap to snooze** button. Tap it for 10 more minutes of sleep, at which point the iPhone tries again to get your attention. (It gives you a countdown in the meantime.)

- **Time dials.** Spin these three vertical wheels—hour, minute, AM/PM—to specify the time you want the alarm to go off.

When you finally tap **Save**, you return to the Alarm screen, which lists your new alarm. Just tap the On/Off switch to cancel an alarm. It stays in the list, though, so you can quickly reactivate it another day, without having to redo the whole thing. You can tap ＋ to set another alarm, if you like.

Note, too, that the 🕐 icon appears in the status bar at the top of the iPhone screen. That's your indicator that the alarm is set.

To delete or edit an alarm, tap **Edit**. Tap ⊖ and then **Delete** to get rid of an alarm completely, or tap the alarm's name to return to the setup screen, where you can make changes to the time, name, sound, and so on.

So what happens when the alarm goes off? The iPhone wakes itself up, if it was asleep. A message appears on the screen, identifying the alarm and the time.

And, of course, the sound rings. This alarm is one of the only iPhone sounds that you'll hear *even if the silencer switch is turned on.* Apple figures that if you've gone to the trouble of setting an alarm, you probably *really* want to know about it, even if you forget to turn the ringer back on.

In that case, the screen says slide to stop alarm.

To cut the ringing short, tap **OK** or **Snooze**, or press the Sleep switch, or tap a volume button. After the alarm plays (or you cut it short), its On/Off switch goes to Off (on the Alarm screen).

> **TIP:** Oddly enough, flipping the silencer switch isn't the same thing as turning the volume all the way down to zero.
>
> If you just turn on the iPhone's silencer switch, then the alarm will ring **and** vibrate. If you choose None as the alarm sound, it won't ring **or** vibrate.
>
> But if you press the Volume Down key all the way to zero, then whatever alarm you've set becomes a silent, **vibrating** alarm. It can be a subtle cue that it's time to wrap up your speech, conclude a meeting, or end a date so you can get home to watch *American Idol.*

Stopwatch

You've never met a more beautiful stopwatch than this one. Tap **Start** to begin timing something: a runner, a train, a long-winded person who's arguing with you.

While the digits are flying by, you can tap **Lap** as often as you like. Each time, the list at the bottom identifies how much time elapsed since the

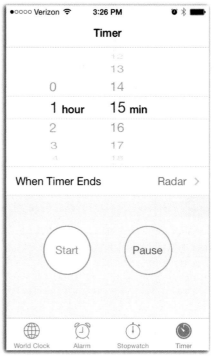

last time you tapped Lap. It's a way for you to compare, for example, how much time a runner is spending on each lap around a track.

(The tiny digits at the **very** top measure the current lap.)

You can do other things on the iPhone while the stopwatch is counting, by the way. In fact, the timer keeps ticking away even when the iPhone is asleep! As a result, you can time long-term events, like how long it takes an ice sculpture to melt, the time it takes for a bean seed to sprout, or the length of a Michael Bay movie.

Tap Stop to freeze the counter; tap Start to resume the timing. If you tap Reset, you reset the counter to zero and erase all the lap times.

Timer

The fourth Clock mini-app is a countdown timer. You input a starting time, and it counts down to zero.

Countdown timers are everywhere in life. They measure the periods in sports and games, cooking times in the kitchen, penalties on *The Amazing Race*. But on the iPhone, the timer has an especially handy function: It can turn off the music or video after a specified amount of time. In short, it's a sleep timer that plays you to sleep and then shuts off to save power.

To set the timer, open the Clock app and then tap Timer. Spin the two dials to specify the number of hours and minutes you want to count down.

Then tap the When Timer Ends control to set up what happens when the timer reaches 0:00. Most of the options here are ringtone sounds, so you'll have an audible cue that the time's up. The last one, though, Stop Playing, is the aforementioned sleep timer. It stops audio and video playback at the appointed time, so that you (and the iPhone) can go to sleep. Tap Set.

Finally, tap Start. Big clock digits count down toward zero. While it's in progress, you can do other things on the iPhone, change the When Timer Ends settings, or just hit Cancel to forget the whole thing.

> **TIP:** It's much faster and simpler to use Siri to start, pause, and resume the Timer. See page 119.

Compass

Yeah, yeah: WiFi, camera, Bluetooth, music, touchscreen, tilt sensor—all phones have that stuff these days. But the iPhone still has something the also-rans lack: a magnetic-field sensor known as a magnetometer, which is even better known as a compass.

When you open the Compass app, you get exactly what you'd expect: a classic Boy Scout wilderness compass that always points north.

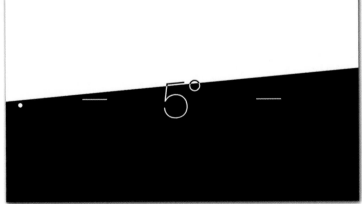

Except it does a few things the Boy Scout compasses never did. Like displaying a digital readout of your heading (previous page) or displaying your precise geographic coordinates at the bottom, or offering a choice of *true* north (the "top" point of the Earth's rotational axis) or *magnetic* north (the spot traditional compasses point to, which is about 11 degrees away from true north). (You do that in Settings→Compass.)

The very first time you use the Compass app (or anytime you're standing near something big and metal—or magnetic, like stereo speakers), you get the little message shown below (left). It's telling you to de-confuse the compass by rotating the phone completely, so that the entire ring fills in. (Yes, you look like a deranged person, but it's good exercise.)

Once the compass is working, hold it roughly parallel to the ground, and then read it like...a compass.

For many people, the real power of the compass isn't even on display here. It's when you're using the Maps program. (You can jump directly from Compass to Maps by tapping the coordinates below the compass dial.)

The compass powers the map-orientation feature—the one that shows you not just where you are on the map, but which way you're facing. That's a rather critical detail when you're lost in a city, trying to find a new address, or emerging from the subway with no idea which way to walk.

But there's more magic yet. People who write iPhone programs can tap into the compass's information, too, and use it in clever new ways. There's an "augmented reality" app called New York Nearest Subway, for example. By using the compass, GPS, and tilt-sensor information, it knows exactly where you are, which way you're facing, and how you're holding the phone—and so it superimposes, in real time, arrows that show you where to find the nearest New York subway stop and which line it's on. Freaky.

The Carpenter's Level

In iOS 7, this app has a secret identity: It doubles as a carpenter's level. That's right: The next time you need to hang a picture, or prop up a wobbly table, or raise a barn, you'll now know when you've got things perfectly horizontal or perfectly vertical.

From the Compass screen, swipe to the left to reveal the new level. It measures all three dimensions:

- **Right/left.** Hold the iPhone upright (against a picture you're hanging, say), and tilt it left and right. When it's perfectly upright, the readout says 0 degrees, and the bottom half of the screen turns green.

- **Forward/back.** Hold the phone upright and tip it away from or toward you. Once again, "0 degrees" and green means "level."

- **Perfectly flat.** Hold the phone on its back, screen facing the sky. When the two circles merge, you'll know you've got it perfectly level. You could, for example, put the iPhone on a table you're trying to adjust, using its gauge to know how close you're getting as you wedge something under its short leg.

TIP: Level doesn't have to be the zero point. You can tilt the phone to any angle and declare *that* to be the zero point—by tapping the the screen.

Game Center

The iPhone is an accomplished gaming device, the equal of Sony's PlayStation Portable or Nintendo's DS. iPhone features like the accelerometer and touchscreen are perfect for a multitude of games, from first-person shoot-'em-ups to casual games that require nothing more complicated than dragging a tile across the iPhone's screen. Game makers have responded to the iPhone—on the App Store, the Games category is one of the most active sections, with tens of thousands of games available.

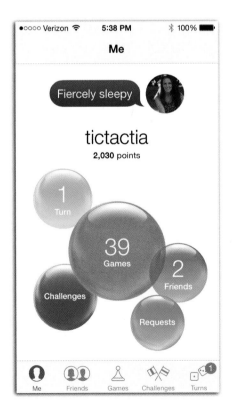
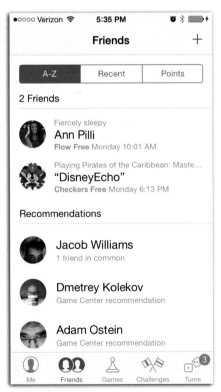

To help fan the flames of iPhone gaming, Apple created Game Center in 2010 as a way for iOS device owners to compare scores with their friends and to challenge buddies to games. In iOS 7, it's had a complete make-over: Out with the green felt gaming tables, in with white backgrounds and bright bubbles.

Here's what you can expect when you launch Game Center.

Getting Started

You have to sign up for Game Center before you can use it, but the process is simple: Just enter your Apple ID and password.

You'll be asked to create a nickname—"AngriestBird" or "BobSmith2000," for example. On the next screen, you can make this nickname public, so that it can appear on the leaderboards (scoreboards that show the highest point winners) for iOS games; you can also use this nickname when you play multiplayer apps like Super Stickman Golf against other people.

That public profile includes a photo of yourself; you can grab one from your photo library or shoot it from within Game Center itself using the iPhone's front-facing camera. You also have space to write a little description of yourself, like the bio line in Twitter.

Once all that's in place, the Me tab in Game Center displays your nickname, that clever little phrase you wrote, and your picture (previous page, left). Beneath that, multicolored spheres display the number of Game Center-compatible games you own, the number of Game Center friends you have, and—perhaps most significantly—the number of points you've accrued from your gaming activities.

Points and Achievements

Points play a leading role in Game Center. They're what you earn from racking up achievements in Game Center–compatible apps. Smash enough blocks in Angry Birds Seasons, or build a certain number of floors in Tiny Tower, and you unlock achievements in those games; those achievements translate to points, which show up in your Game Center profile.

Those points also provide a way to measure yourself against your friends. On Game Center's Friends tab, you can tap the name of one of your friends. You get a choice of three bubbles: the Games your friends play, the names of **their** Friends, and the number of Points they've tallied. That points view features a side-by-side comparison showing your respective accomplishments in commonly played games, so you can settle once and for all who's tops at Tiny Wings. (Game Center also shows the points your friends have racked up in games you **don't** own, which is Apple's way of suggesting that maybe you should download more games.)

Making Friends

Of course, before you can compare your scores with your friends, you have to *have* some friends. Tap the + button in the upper-right corner of the Friends screen to open the Friend Request page, where you can invite someone to be your Game Center buddy using his nickname, Facebook account, or email address. (In fact, Game Center thoughtfully offers you a list of Facebook contacts who are already on Game Center.)

But what if you don't have any existing friends, or at least none that you know are on Game Center? Tap Upload My Contacts. The app sends your address book to Apple's master computers, so it can match you up with strangers who have the same games you do. Tapping one of those names takes you to a page that shows common friends, if any, and a Send Friend Request button.

You can also find gaming companions through your other Game Center friends. Just tap on a name in the list of your current friends, and then select the Friends view on their page to see who *they* hang out with in Game Center when they're not matching scores with you.

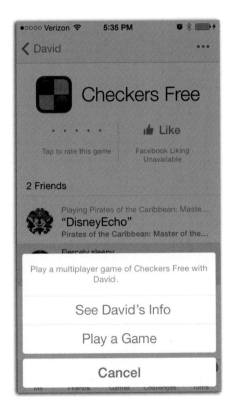

Finding Games

Game Center can also help you find games to play—specifically, games that are designed to tie in with Game Center. The **Recommended** section at the top of the Games tab lists suggested games. Game Center bases these recommendations on what you already own, what your friends play, and popular App Store downloads. Selecting a game in the Recommendations list shows you leaderboards, achievements you can unlock, and which of your friends are playing the game. You can download the app right from this screen.

You can also buy games directly from the list of games your friends play within the Friends tab. Tap a game name to see your friends' rankings, or tap the price tag to download the game directly.

Playing Games

All right. Suppose, then, that you've downloaded some games (easy) and you have some friends (it could happen). You're ready to play!

Tap the **Games** tab, tap the game you want, and then tap the player you want to challenge (previous page, left).

Or start on the **Friends** tab. Tap the friend, tap his **Games** bubble, and then tap the game you want.

Game Center hands you off to the game itself—a different app—so that your online adventure can begin. (Usually you'll see an option for Network play or Internet play; that's the one you want.)

iBooks

iBooks is Apple's ebook reading program. It turns the iPhone into a sort of pocket-sized Kindle. With iBooks, you can carry around dozens or hundreds of books in your pocket, which, in the pre-ebook days, would have drawn some funny looks in public.

Most people think of iBooks as a reader for books that Apple sells on its iTunes bookstore—bestsellers and current fiction, for example—and it does that very well. But you can also load it up with your own PDF documents, as well as thousands of free, older, out-of-copyright books.

> **TIP:** iBooks is very cool and all. But in the interest of fairness, it's worth noting that Amazon's free Kindle app, and Barnes & Noble's free B&N eReader app, are much the same thing—but offer much bigger book libraries at lower prices than Apple's.

Downloading Books

To shop the iBooks bookstore, open the iBooks app. Tap **Store** in the upper-right corner. Here's the literary equivalent of the App Store, complete with the icons across the bottom. Tap **Featured** to see what Apple is plugging this week; **Top Charts** to see this week's bestsellers, including what's on *The New York Times* Best Seller list (note that there's a special row for *free* books); **Top Authors**; **Search** to search by name; and **Purchased** to see what you've bought.

> **TIP:** Once you've bought a book from Apple, you can download it again on other iPhones, iPod Touches, iPads, and (someday, when Apple releases the necessary reader software), Macs and PCs. Buy once, read many times. That's the purpose of the **Not On This iPhone** tab, which appears when you tap **Purchased**.

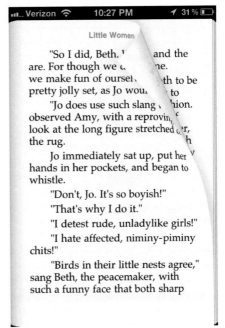

Once you find a book that looks good, you can tap **Sample** to download a free chapter, read ratings and reviews, or tap the price itself to buy the book and download it straight to the phone.

PDFs and ePub Files

Apple's bookstore isn't the only way to get books. You can also load up your ebook reader from your computer, feeding it with PDF documents and ePub files.

ePub is the normal iBooks format. It's a very popular standard for ebook readers, Apple's and otherwise. The only difference between ePub documents you create and the ones Apple sells is that Apple's are copy protected.

As usual, iTunes is the most convenient loading dock for files bound for your iPhone. Open the program on your Mac or PC. Click your iPhone's name (when it's connected) and then click Books. Here you'll see all the books, PDF documents, and ePub files that you've slated for transfer.

To add to this set, just drag files off of your desktop and directly into this window.

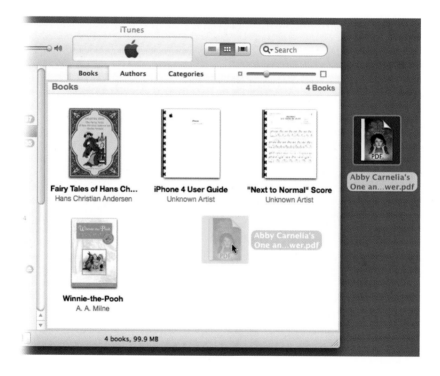

And where are you supposed to get all these files? Well, PDF documents are everywhere—people send them as attachments, and you can turn any document into a PDF file. (For example, on the Mac, in any program, choose File→Print; in the resulting dialog box, click PDF→Save as PDF.)

TIP: If you get a PDF document as an email attachment, then adding it to iBooks is even easier. Tap the attachment to open it; now tap Open in iBooks in the corner of the page. (The iPhone may not be able to open really huge PDFs, though.)

But free ebooks in ePub format are everywhere, too. There are 33,000 free downloadable books at *gutenberg.org*, for example, and over a million at *books.google.com*—oldies, but classic oldies, with lots of Mark Twain, Agatha Christie, Herman Melville, H.G. Wells, and so on. (Lots of these are available in the Free pages of Apple's own iBook store, too.)

TIP: You'll discover that these freebie books usually come with generic-looking covers. But once you've dragged them into iTunes, it's easy to add a good-looking cover. Use *images.google.com* to search for the book's title. Right-click (or Control-click) the cover image in your Web browser; from the shortcut menu, choose **Copy Image**. In iTunes, in Library mode, choose Books from the top-left pop-up menu. Right-click (or Control-click) the generic book; choose **Get Info**; click **Artwork**; and paste the cover you copied. Now that cover will sync over to the iPhone along with the book.

Once you've got books in iTunes, connect the iPhone, choose its name at top right, click the **Books** tab at top, and turn on the checkboxes of the books you want to transfer.

Your Library

Once you've supplied your iBooks app with some reading material, the fun begins. When you open the app, you see a handsome wooden bookshelf with your own personal library represented as little book covers. Mostly what you'll do here is tap a book to open it. But there are all kinds of other activities waiting for you:

- You can reorganize your bookshelf. Tap **Edit**. Hold down your finger on a book until it swells with pride, and then drag it into a new spot.

- If you drag your finger down, you reveal a ☰ icon, which switches the book-cover view to a much more boring (but more compact) list view. (Buttons at the bottom let you sort the list by author, title, category, and so on.) And there's a search box, too, which lets you search your books' titles—helpful if you have an enormous library.

- Tap **Edit** if you want to delete a book, or a bunch of them. To do that, tap each book thumbnail that you want to target for termination; observe how they sprout ✓ marks. Then tap **Delete**. Of course, deleting a book from the phone doesn't delete your safety copy in iTunes or online.

  In Edit mode, once you've tapped a book to select it (or tapped several), the **Move** button becomes available. When you tap it, you get the Collections screen shown below. The idea is that you can create subfolders for your books, called **collections.** You might have one for school, one for work, and a third for somebody who shares your phone, for example. Tap an existing collection to move the selected titles, or tap **New** to create and name a new collection.

> **TIP:** To switch your bookshelf view among collections, tap the collection's name. It's the top-center button, which starts out saying **Books** or **PDFs**.

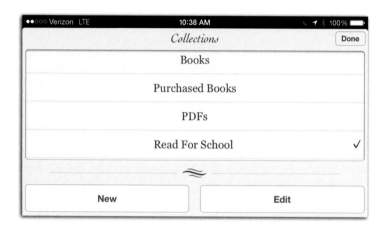

- If you've loaded some PDF documents, then you can switch between the **Books** and **PDFs** bookshelves by tapping the top-center button to open the Collections screen.

Reading

But come on—you're a reader, not a librarian. Here's how you read an ebook.

Open the book or PDF by tapping the book cover. Now the book opens, ready for you to read. Looks great, doesn't it? (If you're returning to a book you've been reading, iBooks remembers your place.)

> **TIP:** Turn the phone 90 degrees for a wider column of text. The whole page image rotates with you.

In general, reading is simple: Just read. Turn the page by tapping the edge of the page—or swiping your finger across the page. (If you swipe slowly, you can actually see the "paper" bending over—in fact, you can see through to the "ink" on the other side of the page! Amaze your friends.)

You can tap or swipe the left edge (to go back a page) or the right edge (to go forward).

TIP: This is Rotation Lock's big moment. When you want to read lying down, you can prevent the text from rotating 90 degrees using Rotation Lock (page 39).

But if you tap a page, a row of additional controls appears:

- **Library** takes you back to the bookshelf view.

- ☰ opens the Table of Contents. The chapter or page names are "live"— you can tap one to jump there.

- ₐA lets you change the type size. That's a huge feature for people with tired or over-40 eyes. And it's something paper books definitely can't do.

  The same pop-out panel offers a **Fonts** button, where you can choose from five different typefaces for your book, as well as a **Themes** button, which lets you specify whether the page itself is white, black (with white text, for nighttime reading), or Sepia (off-white).

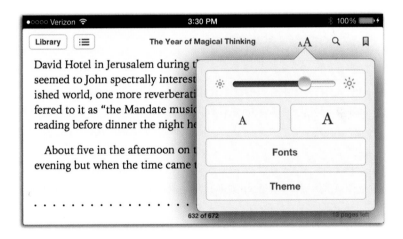

Finally, this panel offers a screen-brightness slider. That's a nice touch, because the brightness of the screen makes a big difference in the comfort of your reading. (This is the same control you'd find in the Control Center or in Settings.)

- **Q** opens the search box. It lets you search for text within the book you're reading, which can be extremely useful. As a bonus, there are also **Search Web** and **Search Wikipedia** buttons so you can hop online to learn more about something you've just read.

- **🔖** adds a bookmark to the current page. This isn't like a physical bookmark, where there's only one in the whole book; you can use it to flag as many pages, for as many reasons, as you like.

- **Page dots.** At the bottom of the screen, the horizontal dots represent the chapters of your book. Tap or drag the slider to jump around in the book; as you drag, a pop-up indicator shows you what page number you're scrolling to. (If you've magnified the font size, of course, then your book consumes more pages.)

> **TIP:** An iBook can include pictures and even videos. Double-tap a picture in a book to zoom in on it.

When you're reading a PDF document, by the way, you can do something you can't do when reading regular books: zoom in and out using the usual two-finger pinch-and-spread gestures. Very handy indeed.

> **TIP:** On the other hand, here are some features that **don't** work in PDF files (only ebooks): font and type-size changes, page-turn animations, sepia or black backgrounds, highlighting, and notes.

Notes, Bookmarks, Highlighting, Dictionary

Here are some more stunts that you'd have trouble pulling off in a printed book. If you *double-tap* a word, or *hold your finger down* on a word, you get a bar that offers these options:

- **Define.** Opens up a graceful, elegant page from iBooks' built-in dictionary. You know—in the unlikely event that you encounter a word you don't know.

- **Highlight.** Adds tinted, transparent highlighting, or underlining, to the word you tapped. For best results, don't tap the Highlight button until you've first grabbed the blue dot handles and dragged them to enclose the entire passage you want highlighted.

  Once you tap Highlight, the buttons change into a special Highlight bar (below, middle). The first button opens a *third* row of buttons (bottom), so that you can specify which highlight color you want. (The final button designates underlining.)

The second button (middle) removes highlighting. The third lets you add a note, as described next. (The ▶ button returns you to the *first* button bar, the one shown here at top.)

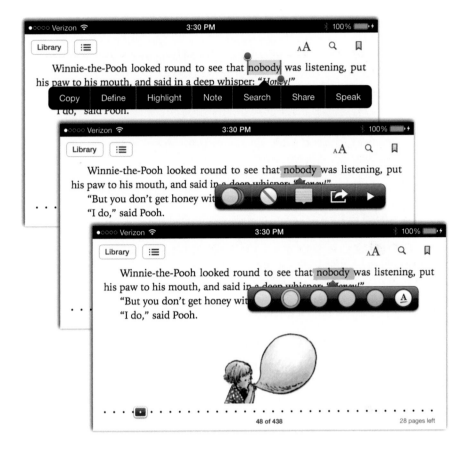

Once you've selected a highlighting color from the third bar, you can go to town, dragging across more passages; each time, the highlighting appears without your having to plod through all the button-bar sequences shown here.

To stop highlighting stuff, double-tap a word, tap **Highlight**, but this time tap the "no highlighting" button.

- **Note.** This feature creates highlighting on the selected passage *and* opens an empty colored sticky note, complete with keyboard, so you can type in your own annotations. When you tap **Done**, your note collapses down to a tiny yellow Post-it peeking out from the right edge of the margin. Tap to reopen it.

To delete a note, tap the highlighted text. Tap **Remove Note**.

- **Search** opens the same search box that you'd get by tapping the Q icon—except this time, the highlighted word is already filled in, saving you a bit of typing.

- **Share** opens the Share sheet (page 294) so you can send the high-lighted material to somebody else by message or email (or copy it to your Clipboard for pasting into another app).

- **Speak** reads the highlighted passage aloud. Thank you, Siri!

There are a couple of cool things going on with your bookmarks, notes, and highlighting, by the way. Once you've added them to your book, they're magically and wirelessly synced to any other copies of that book—on other gadgets, like the iPad or iPod Touch, other iPhones, or even Macs running OS X "Mavericks" or later. Very handy indeed.

Furthermore, if you tap the ☰ button to open the Table of Contents, you'll see the **Bookmarks** and **Notes** tabs. Each presents a tidy list of all your bookmarked pages, notes, and highlighted passages. You can tap ↱ to print or email them, or tap one of the listings to jump to the relevant page.

> **TIP:** iBooks can actually read to you! Just turn on VoiceOver (see page 168, which also explains some of the other changes in your lifestyle that are required when VoiceOver is turned on).
>
> Then open a book. Tap the first line (to get the highlighting off the buttons).
>
> Now swipe down the page with two fingers to make the iPhone start reading the book to you, out loud, with a synthesized voice. It even turns the pages automatically and keeps going until you tap with two fingers to stop it.
>
> Yes, this is exactly the feature that debuted in the Amazon Kindle and was then removed when publishers screamed bloody murder—but somehow, so far, Apple has gotten away with it.

iBooks Settings

If you've embraced the simple joy of reading electronic books the size of a chalkboard eraser, then you deserve to know where to make settings changes: in **Settings→iBooks**. Here are the options waiting there:

- **Full Justification.** Ordinarily, iBooks presents text with fully justified margins (left). Turn this on if you prefer ragged right margins (right).

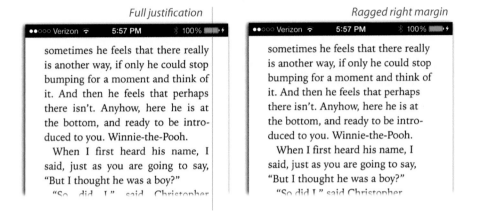

- **Auto-hyphenation.** Sometimes, typesetting looks better if hyphens allow partial words to appear at the right edge of each line. Especially if you've also turned on Full Justification.

- **Both Margins Advance.** Usually, tapping the right edge of the screen turns to the next page, and tapping the left edge turns *back* a page. If you turn on this option, tapping *either* edge of the screen opens the next page. That can be handy if you're a lefty, for example.

- **Sync Bookmarks, Sync Collections.** Turn these on if you'd like your bookmarks and book collections to be synced with your other Apple gadgets.

- **Online Audio and Video.** A few books contain links to video or audio clips online. This option comes set to Off, because video and audio can eat up your monthly cellular data allotment like a hungry teenager.

Maps

Here it is, folks: the feature that made international headlines: the Maps app.

From its birth in 2007, the iPhone always came with Google Maps—an excellent mapping and navigation app. (Apple wrote it, but Google provided the maps and navigation data.) But in iOS 6, Apple replaced it with a new mapping system of its own.

Why? Apple says Google was withholding features like spoken turn-by-turn directions and smoothly drawn (vector-based) map images. Furthermore, as the rivalry intensified, Apple no longer wanted to share the super-valuable *data* generated by all those millions of moving iPhones with Google.

Unfortunately, in its initial version, the databases underlying the Maps app had a lot of problems. They didn't include nearly as many points of interest (buildings, stores, landmarks) as Google. Addresses were sometimes wrong.

Apple promised to keep working on Maps until it was all fixed, but in the meantime, in a remarkable apology letter, CEO Tim Cook recommended using one of its rivals. By far the best one is Google Maps. It's free, it's amazingly smart (it knows what address you mean after you type only a few letters), it has public transportation details, live traffic reports, Street View (you can see photos of most addresses, and even "look around" you), and, of course, Google's far superior maps and data.

All right—you've been warned. It may still take some time before Apple's Maps is complete and reliable.

But some of its features are pretty great. And while Apple's cartographical elves keep working on cleaning up the underlying maps, the software itself has been blessed with plenty of improvements in iOS 7. For example, your maps now go full screen, edge to edge (you can bring back the buttons and controls by tapping). And if you have a Mac (running OS X "Mavericks"), you can look up a destination on the Mac and then send the directions wirelessly to your phone.

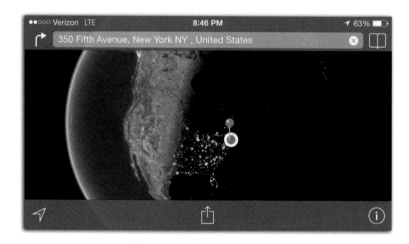

Here's what you have to look forward to.

Meet Maps

The underlying geographical database may need work, but Maps, the app itself, is a thing of beauty.

It lets you type in any address or point of interest in the U.S. or many other countries and see it plotted on a map, with turn-by-turn driving directions, just like a $300 windshield GPS unit. It also gives you a live national Yellow Pages business directory and real-time traffic-jam alerts. You have a choice of a street-map diagram or actual aerial photos, taken by satellite.

And Maps offers Flyover, an amazing aerial, 360-degree 3-D view of major cities.

Maps Basics

When you open Maps, you see a blue dot that represents your current location. Double-tap to zoom in, over and over again, until you're seeing actual city blocks. You can also pinch or spread two fingers to shrink or magnify the view. Drag or flick to scroll around the map.

To zoom *out* again, you can use the rare ***two-finger double-tap.***

At any time, you can tap the ⓘ button in the corner of the screen to open a secret panel of options. Here you can tap your choice of amazing map views: **Standard** (street-map illustration), **Satellite** (stunning aerial photos), or **Hybrid** (photos superimposed with street names).

There's no guarantee that the Satellite view provides a very ***recent*** photo—different parts of the Maps database use photography taken at different times—but it's still very cool.

NOTE: You'll know when you've zoomed in to the resolution limits of Apple's satellite imagery; it will just stop zooming. Do some two-finger double-taps to back out.

You can twist two fingers to rotate the map. (A compass icon at top right helps you keep your bearings; you can tap it to restore the map's usual north-is-up orientation.) And if you drag two fingers up the screen, you tilt the map into 3-D view, which makes it look more like you're surveying the map at an angle instead of straight down. (The **3D** button "lights up.")

Finding Yourself

If any phone can tell you where you are, it's the iPhone. It has not one, not two, but ***three*** ways to determine your location.

- **GPS.** First, the iPhone contains a traditional GPS chip, of the sort that's found in automotive navigation units from Garmin, TomTom, and others.

    Don't expect it to work as well as those car units, though. This is a cellphone, for goodness' sake—not some much bigger, single-purpose, dedicated-GPS car unit.

    Still, if the iPhone has a good view of the sky, and isn't confounded by skyscrapers or the metal of your car, then it can do a decent job of consulting the 24 satellites that make up the Global Positioning System and determining its own location.

    And if it can't see the sky, the iPhone has two fallback location features.

- **Wi-Fi Positioning System.** Metropolitan areas today are blanketed by overlapping WiFi signals. At a typical Manhattan intersection, you might be in range of 20 base stations. Each one broadcasts its own name and unique network address (its ***MAC address***—nothing to do with Mac computers) once every second. Although you'd need to be within 150 feet or so to actually get onto the Internet, a laptop or phone can detect this beacon signal from up to 1,500 feet away.

Imagine if you could correlate all those beacon signals with their physical locations. Why, you'd be able to simulate GPS—without the GPS!

So for years, all those millions of iPhones have been quietly logging all those WiFi signals, noting their network addresses and locations. (The iPhone never has to **connect** to these base stations. It's just reading the one-way beacon signals.)

At this point, Apple's database knows about millions of hotspots—and the precise longitude and latitude of each.

So if the iPhone can't get a fix on GPS, it sniffs for WiFi base stations. If it finds any, it transmits their IDs back to Apple (via cellular network)—which looks up those network addresses and sends coordinates back to the phone.

That accuracy is good to within only 100 feet, and of course the system fails completely once you're out of populated areas. On the other hand, it works indoors, which GPS definitely doesn't.

- **Google's cellular triangulation system.** Finally, as a last resort, the iPhone can check its proximity to the cellphone towers around you. Software from Google works a lot like the WiFi location system, but it relies upon its knowledge of cellular towers' locations rather than WiFi base stations. The accuracy isn't as good as GPS—you're lucky if it puts you within a block or two of your actual location—but it's something.

TIP: The iPhone's location circuits eat into battery power. To shut them down when you're not using them, open Settings→Privacy and turn off Location Services.

All right—now that you know how the iPhone gets its location information, here's how you can use it. Its first trick is to show you where you are.

Tap the ➹ at the bottom of the Maps screen. The button turns white, indicating that the iPhone is consulting its various references to figure out where you are. You show up as a blue pushpin that moves with you; pulsing rings help draw your eye to it. That's the iPhone saying, "OK, pal, I've got you. You're **here.**" It keeps tracking until you tap the ➹ enough times to turn it off.

Orienting the Map

It's great to see a blue pin on the map, and all—but how do you know which way you're facing? Thanks to the built-in magnetometer (compass), the map can orient itself for you.

Just tap the ➤ button twice. The map spins so that the direction you're facing is upward, and the ➤ icon points straight up. A "flashlight beam" emanates from your blue dot; its width indicates the iPhone's degree of confidence. (The narrower the beam, the surer it is.)

Searching the Maps

You're not always interested in finding out where you are; often, you know that much perfectly well. Instead, you want to see where something *else* is.

Now, the following paragraphs guide you through using the search box at the top of Maps. But frankly, if you use it, you're a sucker. If you have an iPhone 4s or later, it's *much* quicker to use Siri to specify what you want to find.

You can say, for example, "Show me the map of Detroit" or "Show me the closest Starbucks" or "Give me directions to 200 West 79th Street in New York." Siri shows you that spot on a map; tap to jump into the Maps app.

If you must use the search box, though, here's how it works: Tap in the search box to summon the iPhone keyboard. (If there's already something in the box, tap ✕ to clear it out.) Here's what Maps can find for you:

- **An address.** You can skip the periods (and usually the commas, too). And you can use abbreviations. Typing *710 w end ave ny ny* will find 710 West End Avenue, New York, New York. (In this and any of the other examples, you can type a Zip code instead of a city and a state.)

- **An intersection.** Type *57th and lexington, ny ny.* Maps will find the spot where East 57th Street crosses Lexington Avenue in New York City.

- **A city.** Type *chicago il* to see that city. You can zoom in from there.

- **A Zip code or a neighborhood.** Type *10024* or *greenwich village.*

- **A point of interest.** Type *washington monument* or *niagara falls.*

- **A business type.** Type *drugstores in albany ny* or *hospitals in roanoke va.*

When Maps finds a specific address, an animated, red-topped pushpin comes flying down onto its precise spot on the map. A bubble identifies the location by name.

Tap outside the bubble to hide it. Tap the map pin to bring the bubble back. Tap the 🚗 icon for instant driving directions.

TIP: Or walking directions. You choose whether you mostly walk or drive (and therefore which Maps suggests) in Settings→Maps.

Tap the > to open the Location page; read on.

The Location Page

Once you've found something on the map—your current position, say, or something you've searched for—you can drop a pin there for future reference. Tap the ⓘ button; when the page slides up, tap Drop a Pin. A blue pushpin appears. (You can drag the pin to move it, if your aim wasn't exact.)

TIP: You can also drop a pin by holding your finger down on the right spot.

There are also the red pushpins that represent addresses you've looked up. And there are the tiny icons that represent restaurants, stores, and other establishments in Apple's (actually Yelp's) database.

All of these pushpins and nano-icons are tappable. You get a little label that identifies it. And if you tap the > on that label, you open a details screen called the Location page.

Here links let you bookmark the spot, get directions, add it to Contacts, or share it with other people (via AirDrop, email, text message, Facebook, or Twitter). Often, what you're after are the **Directions to here** and **Directions from here** links ("here" meaning your current location).

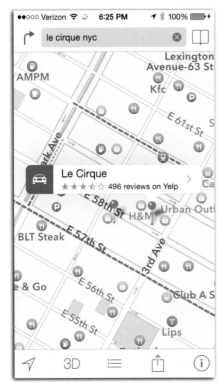
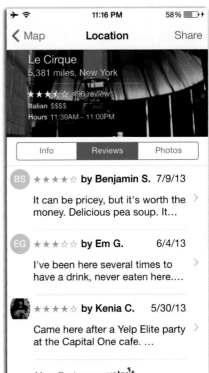

If this is the location for a restaurant or a business, you might strike gold: The Location page might offer several screens full of useful information, courtesy of Yelp.com. You'll see customer reviews, photos, hours of operation, delivery and reservation information, and so on.

The Location screen also offers the new **Popular Apps Nearby** link. It lists apps that other people have downloaded in the vicinity. Sometimes there's no rhyme or reason to them, but sometimes you'll discover a gem that pertains to the place you're scoping out: a guide app, for example.

Finding Friends and Businesses

Maps is also plugged into your Contacts list, which makes it especially easy to find a friend's house (or just to see how ritzy his neighborhood is).

Instead of typing an address into the empty search bar, tap ⬚ at the right end of it. You arrive at the **Bookmarks/Recents/Contacts** screen, containing three lists that can save you a lot of typing.

Two of them are described in the next section. But if you tap **Contacts**, you see your master address book (Chapter 3). Tap a name. In a flash, Maps drops a red, animated pushpin onto the map to identify that address.

> **TIP:** As you type, the iPhone displays a list of matching names. Tap the one you want to find on the map.

That pushpin business also comes into play when you use Maps as a glorified national Yellow Pages. If you type, for example, **pharmacy 60609**, then those red pushpins show you all the drugstores in that Chicago Zip code. It's a great way to find a gas station, a cash machine, or a hospital in a pinch. Tap a pushpin to see the name of the corresponding business.

As usual, you can tap the ⟩ button in the map pin's label bubble to open a details screen. If you've searched for a friend, then you see the corresponding Contacts card. If you've searched for a business, then you get a screen containing its phone number, address, Web site, and so on; often, you get a beautiful page of Yelp information (photos, reviews, ratings).

Remember that you can tap a Web address to open it or tap a phone number to dial it. ("Hello, what time do you close today?")

In both cases, you get two useful buttons, labeled **Directions To Here** and **Directions From Here**. You also get buttons like **Add to Bookmarks** and **Create New Contact**, which save this address for instant recall (read on). The Share Location is a great way to text a friend the address for a restaurant where you're supposed to meet.

Bookmarks and Recents

Let's face it: The iPhone's tiny keyboard can be a little fussy. One nice thing about Maps is the way it tries to eliminate typing at every step.

If you tap ⬚ at the right end of the search bar, for example, you get the **Bookmarks/Recents/Contacts** screen—three lists that spare you from having to type stuff.

- **Bookmarks** are addresses you've flagged for later use by tapping **Add to Bookmarks**, an option that appears whenever you tap the ⟩ in a pushpin's label. For sure you should bookmark your home and workplace. That will make it much easier to request driving directions.

- **Recents** are searches you've conducted. You'd be surprised at how often you want to call up the same spot again later—and now you can, just by tapping its name in this list. You can also tap **Clear** to empty the list (if, for example, you intend to elope and don't want your parents to find out).

- **Contacts** is your iPhone address book. One tap maps out where someone lives.

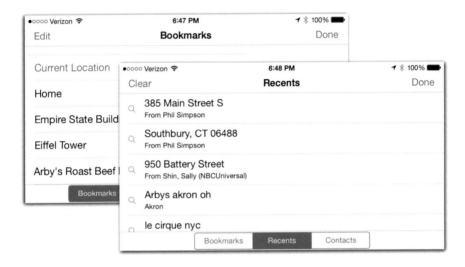

Tap **Done** to back out without choosing a destination. Or tap a destination to see it on the map.

Directions

If you tap the ↱ button next to the search bar, you get *two* search bars: one labeled **Start** and the other, **End**. Plug in two addresses—the Start address may already say "Current Location"—and let Maps guide you from the first to the second. You can use any of the address shortcuts on page 338, or you can tap ▢ to specify a bookmark, a recent search, or a name in Contacts. (Or, after performing any search that produces a pushpin, you can tap ❯ in its label bubble and then tap **Directions To Here** or **Directions From Here** on the details screen.)

> **TIP:** If you tap the ↻ button, you swap the Start and End points. That's a great way to find your way back after a trip.

Amazingly, you also see buttons for 🚌 (public transportation) and 🚶 (walking) directions. Alas, the 🚌 button doesn't actually give you bus and train info, as you might expect; instead, it presents a page from the App Store that offers other people's train- and bus-schedule apps, relevant to the city of your search, for downloading.

When everything looks good, tap Start. In just a moment, Maps displays an overview of the route you're about to drive. In fact, it usually proposes several different routes. They're labeled with little tags: Route 1, Route 2, and Route 3, for example.

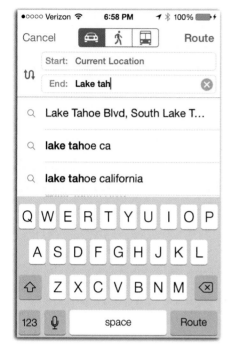

If you tap one of these tags, the top of the screen lets you know the distance and estimated time for that option and identifies the main roads you'll be on.

Tap the Route label you want and then tap Start to see the first driving instruction.

The map zooms into the actual road you'll be traveling, which looks like it's been drawn in with blue highlighter, and Navigation mode begins.

Navigation Mode

When the iPhone is guiding you to a location, Maps behaves exactly like a windshield GPS unit, but better looking and with less clutter to distract you. You see a simplified map of the world around you, complete with the outlines of buildings, with huge white directional banners that tell you how to turn next, and onto what street. Siri's familiar voice speaks the same information at the right times, so you don't even have to look at the screen.

Even if you hit the Sleep switch to lock the phone, the map stays on the screen and the navigation, complete with voice announcements, continues. (It continues even if you switch to another app; return to Maps by tapping the banner at the top of the screen.)

If you do tap the Maps screen, however, a few extra controls appear. The top bar shows your projected arrival time, plus the remaining distance and time. It also offers the **End** button, which makes the navigation stop. Tap **End** when you suddenly recognize where you are, for example, and don't need Siri's opinion anymore.

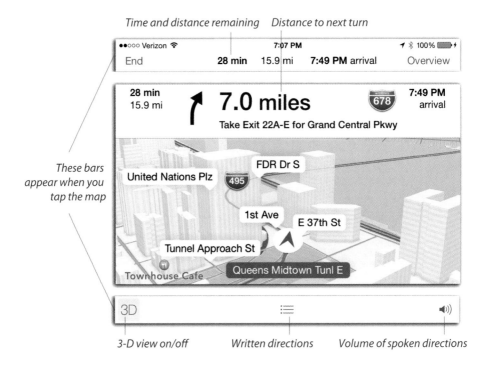

At the bottom, these buttons await:

- **List view (⊟).** Tap to get a written list of turn-by-turn instructions.

- **Overview.** The Navigation mode is meant to be a hands-free, distraction-free guidance system only. While Maps is guiding you, you can't zoom in and out, nor can you pan the map to look ahead at upcoming turns or to inspect alternate routes. (In iOS 7, you can twist two fingers to turn the map, but it snaps back as soon as you let go.)

But if you tap Overview in the upper-right corner, your entire planned route shrinks down to fit on a single screen. Now you see your entire route, and you can zoom, turn, and pan. To return to the navigation screen, tap Resume.

- ◀)). You can adjust the volume of Siri's speaking voice as she gives you driving directions by tapping here. Choose Low, Medium, or Loud Volume, or turn off her voice prompts altogether with No Voice.

Tap the screen to hide these additional controls once again.

Night Mode

If the phone's ambient light sensor decides that it's dark in your car, it switches to a dimmer, grayer version of the map. It wouldn't want to distract you, after all. When there's light, it brightens back up again.

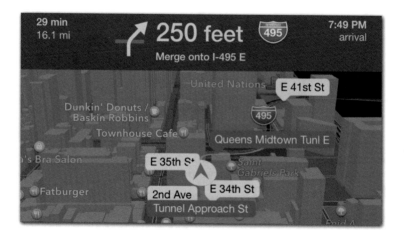

Passenger-Navigation Mode

Navigation mode is designed with your safety in mind—it's fully automated. You're not supposed to interact with the phone at all; you're supposed to listen to the voice, maybe glance at the map for the next turn, but otherwise keep your paws on the wheel.

There's another navigation mode, however, that few people even know exists. It's for use when your passenger is using the phone to direct you. As a result, it doesn't offer spoken directions. Since your passenger is doing the back-seat driving, Siri has the good sense to shut up.

This mode does, however, let you—or, rather, your passenger—zoom in and out, scan ahead, rotate the map, and so on.

In the same vein, you don't see individual issues on your Newsstand book-shelf. You see *one* cover for each magazine; other issues are inside it. A blue dot appears beneath the cover to let you know that a new issue has arrived.

Notes

The Notes app is the iPhone's answer to a word processor. It's simple in the extreme—there's no option to format the text, for example. (In iOS 7, you don't even have a choice of three typefaces.)

Still, it's nice to be able to jot down—or dictate—lists, reminders, and brain-storms. You can email them to yourself when you're finished—or sync them right to your Mac or PC.

The first time you open Notes, you see what looks like a blank white page. (The yellow, lined legal pad has been banished from iOS 7.) Tap to make the keyboard appear so you can begin typing.

TIP: You can get a much larger, widescreen keyboard by rotating the phone 90 degrees.

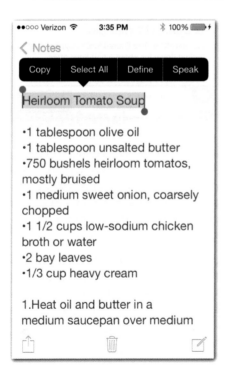

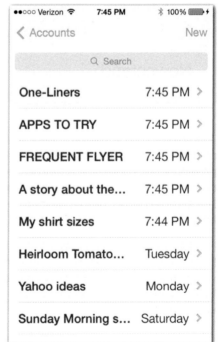

When you're finished with a note for now, tap Done. The keyboard goes away, and a New button appears at the top right. It opens a new note.

Whenever you put away the keyboard by tapping Done, a handy row of icons appears at the bottom of your Notes page. The rundown:

- ⤴. Tap to print your note, copy it, or send it to someone by email, text message, or AirDrop. For example, if you tap Mail, the iPhone creates a new outgoing message, pastes the first line of the note into the subject line, and pastes the note's text into the body. Address the note, edit the body if necessary, and hit Send. The iPhone returns you to Notes.

- 🗑. Tap to delete the current note. After you confirm your decision, the note vanishes.

- ☑ starts a new blank note.

As you create more pages, the Notes button (top left) becomes more useful. It's your table of contents for the Notes pad. (And in iOS 7, it's the only way you have to jump from one note to another, since the arrow buttons are gone now.)

> **TIP** You can swipe rightward to jump from an open note back to the list.

This list displays the first lines of your notes (most recent at the top), along with the time or date you last edited them. To open a note, tap its name. To delete a note, swipe across its name, right to left, and then confirm by tapping Delete.

There's a search box hiding here, too. Drag down on the Notes list to bring the Spotlight box into view. Tap it to open the keyboard. You can now search all your notes instantly—not just their titles, but also the text inside them.

Syncing Notes

The real beauty of this app is that it can synchronize your collection of Notes with all kinds of other Apple gear—other iPhones, iPads, iPod Touches, and Mountain Lion or later Macs—so the same notes are waiting for you everywhere you look. Just make sure Notes is turned on in Settings→Mail, Contacts, Calendars→iCloud on each phone or tablet, and in System Preferences→iCloud on your Mac. The rest is automatic.

Notes Accounts

Your notes can also sync wirelessly with the Notes modules on Google, Yahoo, AOL, Exchange, or another IMAP email account. To set this up, open **Settings→Mail, Contacts, Calendars**. Tap the account you want (iCloud, Gmail, Yahoo, AOL, or whatever); finally, turn the Notes switch **On**.

That should do it. Now your notes are synced nearly instantly, wirelessly, both directions.

NOTE: One catch: Notes you create at *gmail.com*, *aol.com*, or *yahoo.com* don't wind up on the phone. Those accounts sync wirelessly in one direction only: *from* the iPhone to the Web site, where the notes arrive in a Notes folder. (There's no problem, however, if you get your AOL or Gmail mail in an email program like Outlook, Entourage, or Apple Mail. Then it's two-way syncing as usual.)

At this point, an **Accounts** button appears at the top-left corner of the table-of-contents screen. Tap it to see your note sets from Google, Yahoo, AOL, Exchange, iCloud, or an IMAP email account.

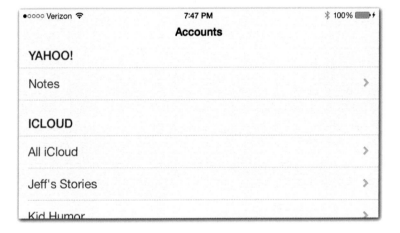

If you've created Notes folders in OS X on your Mac (Mountain Lion or later), then you see those folders here, too.

All of this makes life a little more complex, of course. For example, when you create a note, you have to worry about which account it's about to go into. To do that, be sure to specify an account name (and a folder within it, if necessary) *before* you create the new note.

Passbook

This app is designed to store, in one place, every form of ticket that uses a barcode. For most people, that means airline boarding passes. But, occasionally, you may find a Passbook-compatible theater or sports admission pass, loyalty card, coupon, movie ticket, and so on. At the moment, there's a separate app for each one of these, which means a lot of fussing and hunting every time you want to find the relevant barcode screen.

What's cool is that Passbook uses both its own clock and GPS to know when the time and place are right. For example, when you arrive at the airport, a notification appears on your Lock screen. Each time you have to show your boarding pass as you work through the stages of airport security, you can wake your phone and swipe across that notification; your boarding pass barcode appears instantly. You're spared having to unlock your phone (enter its password), hunt for the airline app, log in, and fiddle your way to the boarding pass.

The hardest part might be finding things to put *into* Passbook. Apple says that someday there will be a "Send to Passbook" button on the Web site or a confirmation email when you buy the ticket.

For now, you can visit the App Store and search for ***passbook*** to find apps that work with Passbook—big airlines, Fandango (movie tickets), Starbucks, Walgreens, Ticketmaster, and Major League Baseball are among the compatible apps. In some, you're supposed to open the app to view the barcode *first* and put it into Passbook from there. For example, in most airline apps, you call up the boarding-pass screen and then tap **Add.**

Once your barcodes have successfully landed in Passbook, the rest is pure fun. When you arrive at the theater or stadium or airport, the Lock screen displays an alert. Swipe it to open the barcode in Passbook. You can put the entire phone under the ticket-taker's scanner.

Tap the ⓘ button in the corner to read the details—and to delete a ticket after you've used it (tap **Delete**). That details screen also offers a **Show On Lock Screen** on/off switch, in case you *don't* want Passbook to hand you your ticket as you arrive.

Reminders

Reminders not only records your life's little tasks, but it also reminds you about them, either when the right time comes or when you come to the right place. For example, it can remind you to water the plants as soon as you get home.

If you have an iCloud account, your reminders sync across all your gadgets. Create or check off a task on your iPhone, and you'll also find it created or checked off on your iPad, iPod Touch, Mac (thanks to Calendar), PC (thanks to Outlook or Exchange), and so on.

> **TIP:** Reminders sync wirelessly with anything your iCloud account knows about: the iCal, Calendar, or BusyCal programs on your Mac, Outlook on the PC, and so on.

Siri and Reminders are a match made in heaven. "Remind me to file the Jenkins report when I get to work." "Remind me to set the TiVo for tonight at 8." "Remind me about Timmy's soccer game a week from Saturday." "Add waffles to my Groceries list."

To record a new task the manual way, tap the blank line beneath your existing reminders. Type your reminder (or dictate it). Tap the ⓘ to set up the details, described below; tap Done when you're finished.

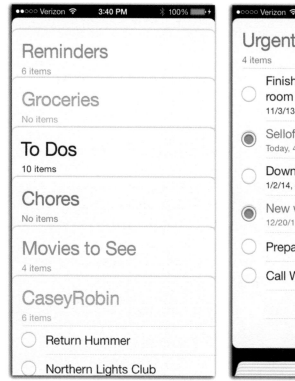
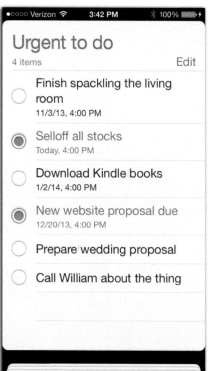

As you go through life completing tasks, tap the circle next to each one. A checked-off to-do remains in place until the next time you visit its list. At that point, it disappears. It's moved into a separate list called Completed.

But when you want to take pride in how much you've accomplished, you can tap Show Completed to bring your checked-off tasks back into view.

Other stuff you can do:

- **Delete a to-do item altogether, as though it never existed.** Swipe leftward across its name, and then tap Delete to confirm.

- **Delete a bunch of items in a row.** Tap Edit. Tap each ⊖ icon, and then tap Delete to confirm.

- **Rearrange a list so the items appear in a different order.** Tap Edit, and then drag the ☰ handle up or down.

The Details Screen

If you tap ⓘ next to an item's name, you arrive at the Details screen. Here you can set up a reminder that will pop up at a certain time or place, create an auto-repeating schedule, file this item into a different to-do list with its own name, add notes to this item, or delete it. Here are your options, one by one (below, left):

- **Remind me on a day.** Here you can set up the phone to chime at a certain date and time (tap whatever it says now to bring up the "time wheel").

- **Repeat.** Reminders can remind you about things that recur in your life, like quarterly tax payments, haircuts, and anniversaries. Tap Repeat if you want this reminder to appear every day, week, two weeks, month, or year.

- **Remind me at a location.** If you turn on this amazing feature, then the phone will use its location circuits to remind you of this item

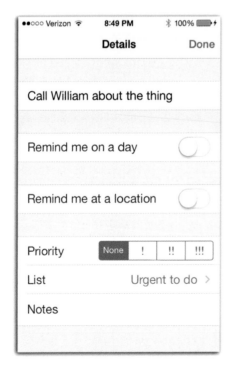

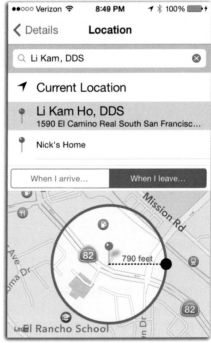

when you arrive at a certain place or leave a certain place. The phone proposes "Current Location"—wherever you are at the moment. That's handy if, for example, you're dropping off your dry cleaning and want to remember to pick it up the next time you're driving by.

But you can also choose Home or Work (your home or work addresses, as you've set them up in Contacts). Or you can use the search box at the top, either to type (or dictate) a street address or to search your own Contacts list.

NOTE: If you choose someone with *multiple* addresses, you're shown all of them; tap the one you want.

Once you've specified an address, the Location screen shows a map. The diameter of the blue circle, new in iOS 7, shows the area where your presence will trigger the appearance of the reminder on your screen (facing page, right).

TIP: You can adjust the size of this "geofence" by dragging the black handle to adjust the size of the circle. In effect, you're telling the iPhone how close you have to be to the specified address for the reminder to pop up. You can adjust the circle's radius anywhere from 328 feet ("Remind me when I'm in that store") to 1,500 miles ("Remind me when I'm in that country").

The final step here is to tap either When I leave or When I arrive.

Later, the phone will remind you at the appointed time or as you approach (or leave) the appointed address, which is fairly mind-blowing the first few times it happens.

NOTE: If you set up *both* a time reminder *and* a location reminder, then your iPhone uses whichever event happens first. That is, if you ask to be reminded at 3 p.m. today and "When I arrive at the office," then you'll get the reminder when you get to the office—or at 3 p.m., if that time rolls around before you make it to work.

- **Priority.** Tap one of these buttons to specify whether this item has low, medium, or high priority—or None. In some of the calendar programs that sync with Reminders, you can sort your task list by priority.

- **List.** Tap here to assign this to-do to a different reminder list (read on).

- **Notes.** Here's a handy box where you can record freehand notes about this item: an address, a phone number, details of any kind.

To exit the Details screen, tap Details (or swipe to the right).

The List of Lists

Believe it or not, you can create **more than one** to-do list, each with its own name: a groceries list, kids' chores, a running tally of expenses, and so on. It's a great way to log what you eat if you're on a diet, or to keep a list of movies people recommend.

If you share an iCloud account with another family member, you might create a different Reminders list for each person. (Of course, now you run the risk that your spouse might sneakily add items to **your** to-do list!)

If you have an Exchange account, one of your lists can be synced to your corporate Tasks list. It doesn't offer all the features of the other lists in Reminders, but at least it's kept tidy and separate.

> **TIP:** You can use Siri to add things to individual lists by name. You can say, for example, "Add low-fat cottage cheese to the Groceries list."
>
> Siri can also find these reminders later, saving you a lot of navigation. You can say, "Find my reminder about dosage instructions," for example.

Once you've created some lists, you can easily switch among them. Just tap an open list's name to collapse it, returning to the list of lists. At that point you can tap the title of a different list to open it.

> **TIP:** When you're viewing the list of lists, you can rearrange them by dragging their title bars up or down.

To create a new list, begin at the list of lists (facing page, left). Tap the New List button. If you have multiple accounts that offer reminder features, you're asked to specify which one will receive this new list (facing page, bottom right). Now your jobs begin:

Your jobs:

1. **Enter a name for the list.** When you tap the light-gray letters New List, the keyboard appears to help you out (facing page, top right).

2. **Tap a colored dot.** This will be the color of the list's title font and also of the "checked-off" circles once the list is under way.

3. **Tap Done.** Now you can tap the first blank line and enter the first item in the list.

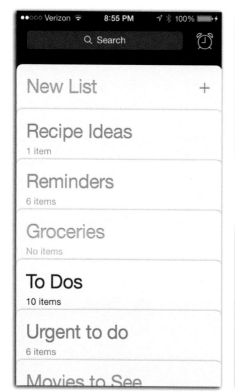

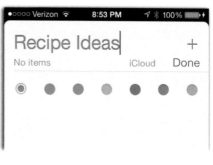

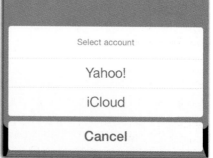

To delete a list, tap **Edit** and then tap **Delete List**.

Later, you can assign a task to a different list by tapping **List** on its Details screen.

The Secret Scheduled List

If you really do wind up using Reminders as a to-do list, you might be gratified to discover that the app also offers a secret, invisible list. It's the Scheduled list: a consolidated list of every item, from all your lists, to which you've given a deadline.

To view this secret list, begin at the list of lists (close whichever list is open). Tug down so that the search box appears. Tap the alarm clock next to the search box.

Now you're seeing the list of all items, from all lists, with times and dates associated with them.

To close the Scheduled list, tap its title as you would to close any other list.

Stocks

This one's for you, big-time day trader. The Stocks app tracks the rise and fall of the stocks in your portfolio by downloading the very latest stock prices.

(All right, maybe not the **very** latest. The price info may be delayed as much as 20 minutes, which is typical of free stock-info services.)

When you first fire it up, Stocks shows you a handful of sample high-tech stocks—or, rather, their abbreviations. (They stand for the Dow Jones Industrial Index, the NASDAQ Index, the S&P 500 Index, Apple, Google, and Yahoo.)

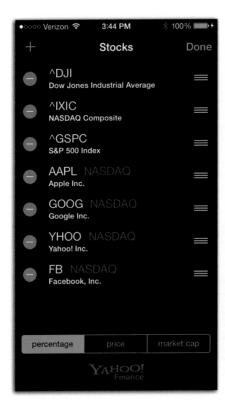

Next to each, you see its current share price, and next to *that,* you see how much that price has gone up or down today. As a handy visual gauge to how elated or depressed you should be, this final number appears on a **green** background if it's gone up, or a **red** one if it's gone down. Tap this number to cycle the display from a percentage to a dollar amount to current market capitalization ("120.3B," meaning $120.3 billion total corporate value).

When you tap a stock, the bottom part of the screen shows some handy data. Swipe horizontally to cycle among three different displays:

- **A table of statistics.** A capsule summary of today's price and volume statistics for this stock.

- **A table of relevant headlines,** courtesy of Yahoo Finance. Tap a headline to read the article—or tap and hold to add it, or all the articles, to your Safari Reading List (page 395).

- **A graph of the stock's price.** It starts out showing you the graph of the current year. But by tapping the headings above the chart, you can zoom in or out from one day (**1D**) to three months (**3M**) to two years (**2Y**).

Landscape View

If you turn the iPhone sideways, you get a much bigger, more detailed, widescreen graph of the stock in question. (Flick horizontally to view the previous or next stock.)

Better yet, you can pinch with two fingers or two thumbs to isolate a certain time period; a pop-up label shows you how much of a bath you took (or how much of a windfall you received) during the interval you highlighted. Cool!

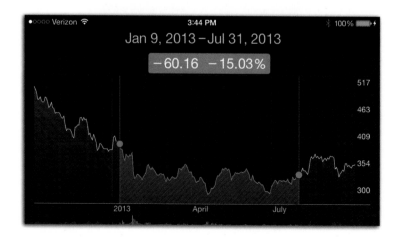

Customizing Your Portfolio

It's fairly unlikely that **your** stock portfolio contains just Apple, Google, and Yahoo. Fortunately, you can customize the list of stocks to reflect the companies you **do** own (or want to track).

To edit the list, tap the :≡ button in the lower-right corner. You arrive at the editing screen, where the following choices await:

- **Delete a stock** by tapping the ⊖ button and then the Delete confirmation button.

- **Rearrange the list** by dragging the grip strips on the right side.

- **Add a stock** by tapping the + button in the top-left corner; the Add Stock screen and the keyboard appear.

    You're not expected to know every stock-symbol abbreviation. Type in the company's **name,** and then tap Search. The iPhone shows you, above the keyboard, a scrolling list of companies with matching names. Tap the one you want to track. You return to the stocks-list editing screen.

- **Choose %, Price, or Numbers.** By tapping the buttons at the bottom, you can specify how you want to see the changes in stock prices in the far-right column: as *percentages* ("+0.65%"), *numbers* ("+2.23") or as *market cap*. (Here, you're simply choosing which number starts out appearing on the main stock screen. As noted earlier, you can easily cycle among these three stats by tapping them.)

When you're finished setting up your stock list, tap Done.

Voice Memos

This audio app, radically redesigned in iOS 7, is ideal for recording lectures, musical performances, notes to self, and cute child utterances. You'll probably be very surprised at how good the microphone is, even from a distance.

The best part: When you sync your iPhone, all of your voice recordings get copied back to the Mac or PC automatically. You'll find them in iTunes, in a folder called Voice Memos.

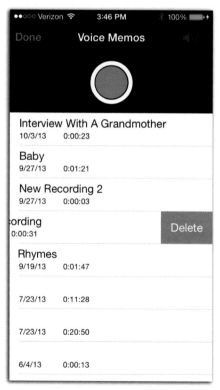

Start by doing a "Testing, testing" check, and make sure the VU meter's needle is moving. (If it's not, maybe the iPhone thinks you're recording from the wrong source—a Bluetooth headset, for example.)

Tap the round, red Record button (or click your earbud clicker) to start recording. A little ding signals the start (and stop) of the session—unless you've turned the phone's volume all the way down (you sneak!).

In the iOS 7 redesign, you get to watch the actual sound waves as the recording proceeds. You can pause at any time by pressing the Stop button (⏺) and then continue the same recording with another tap on the round red button.

> **TIP:** The built-in mike records in mono. But it records in stereo if you connect a stereo mike (to the headphone jack or charging jack).

You can also switch out of the app to do other work. A red banner across the top of the screen reminds you that you're still recording. You can even *switch the screen off* by tapping the Sleep switch; the recording goes on! (You can make *very* long recordings with this thing. Let it run all day, if you like. Even your most long-winded friends can be immortalized.)

Tap **Done** when you're sure the recording session is over. You're asked to type a name for the new recording ("Chris's First Words," "Orch Concert," whatever). Tap **OK**.

Below the recording controls, the list of your recordings appears. When you tap one, a convenient set of controls appears. (They look a lot like the ones that appear when you tap a voicemail message in the Phone app.) Here's what you can do here (facing page, left):

- **[Recording name].** Tap the name to edit or rename it.

- **▶.** Tap to play the recording. You can pause with a tap on the **II** button.

> **TIP:** As a recording plays back, you can tap the ◀) icon at the top of the screen to mute the sound.

- **Rewind, Fast Forward**. Drag the little vertical line in the scrubber bar to skip backward or forward in the recording. It's a great way to skip over the boring pleasantries.

- **🗑.** Tap to get rid of a recording (you'll be asked to confirm).

- **⬆.** Tap to open the standard Share sheet. It gives you the chance to send your recording to someone else by AirDrop, email, or MMS.

Editing Your Recording

You might not guess that such a tiny, self-effacing app actually offers some basic editing functions, but it does. Tap a recording and then tap **Edit** to open its Edit screen.

The main thing you'll do here is trim off the beginning or end of your audio clip. That, of course, is where you'll usually find "dead air" or microphone fumbling before the good stuff starts playing. (You can't otherwise edit the sound; for example, you can't copy or paste bits or cut a chunk out of the middle.)

To trim the bookends of your clip, tap the Trim button (⎑). At this point, the beginning and end of the recording are marked by vertical red lines; these are your trim points. Drag them inward to isolate the part of the clip you want to keep. The app thoughtfully magnifies the sound waves whenever you're dragging, to help with precision. Play the sound as necessary to guide you (▶).

Tap **Trim** to lock in your changes. But be careful: There's no Undo, and the part you chopped off is gone forever.

Weather

This little app, redesigned in iOS 7, shows a handy current-conditions display for your city (or any other city). Handy—and lovely; the weather display is actually animated. Clouds drift by, rain falls gently. If it's nighttime in the city you're looking up, you might see a beautiful starscape.

The current temperature is shown nice and big; the table below shows the cloud-versus-sun forecast, as well as the high and low temperatures.

You don't even have to tell the app what weather you want; it uses your location and assumes you want the *local* weather forecast.

There are three places you can tap or swipe:

- **Tap the current temperature** to replace it with a table of handy stats: humidity, chance of rain, wind speed, and "feels like" (that is, wind chill or heat index).

- **Swipe horizontally across the hourly forecast** to scroll later in the day.

- **Swipe horizontally anywhere else** to view the weather for other cities (if you've set them up). The tiny dots beneath the display correspond to the number of cities you've set up—and the white bold one indicates where you are in the sequence.

  The first city—the screen at far left—is always the city you're *in right now.* The iPhone uses GPS to figure out where you are.

The City List

It's easy to get the weather for other cities—great if you're going to be traveling, or if you're wondering how life is for distant relations.

When you tap the ☰ button at the lower-right corner, the screen collapses into a list of your preprogrammed cities (facing page, right).

You can tap one to open its weather screen. You can delete one by swiping leftward across it (and then tapping Delete). You can drag them up or down into a new order (leave your finger down for one second before you drag each time). You can switch between centigrade and Fahrenheit by tapping the C/F button.

Or you can scroll to the bottom (if necessary) and tap ⊕ to enter a new city.

Here you're asked to type a city, a Zip code, or an airport abbreviation (like JFK for New York's John F. Kennedy airport). You can specify any reasonably sized city on earth. (Remember to check before you travel!)

When you tap Search, you're shown a list of matching cities; tap the one you want to track. When you return to the configuration screen, you can also specify whether you prefer degrees Celsius or degrees Fahrenheit. Tap Done.

There's nothing else to tap here except the ☒! icon at lower left. It fires up the Safari browser, which loads itself with Yahoo's information page about that city. Depending on the city, you might see a City Guide, city news, city photos, and more.

If you've added more than one city to the list, by the way, just flick your finger right or left to flip through the weather screens for the different cities.

More Standard Apps

This book describes every app that comes on your iPhone. But Apple has another suite of useful programs for you to download. And they're free.

To find them, scroll down to Collections on the first page of the App Store. Tap **Apps Made by Apple**. You'll find links to these apps:

- **Pages** is, believe it or not, a word processing/page-layout program.

- **Numbers** is Apple's spreadsheet program.

- **Keynote** is Apple's version of PowerPoint. It lets you make slideshow presentations from your iPhone.

- **iPhoto** is great for editing, touching up, and presenting your photos.

- **iMovie.** A video-editing program on your cellphone? Yes, with all the basics: rearranging clips; adding music, crossfades, and credits.

- **GarageBand** is a pocket music studio.

- **iBooks** is described on page 324.

- **iTunes U** is a catalog of 600,000 free courses by professors at colleges, museums, and libraries all over the world. This app lets you browse the catalog, watch and read the course materials.

- **Podcasts** is an app dedicated to, yes, playing podcasts.

- **Find My Friends** lets you see where your friends and family members are on a map (with their permission, of course).

- **Find My iPhone** is useful when you want to find *other* missing Apple gadgets (Macs, iPads, iPod Touches, iPhones).

- **iTunes Movie Trailers** shows you previews for upcoming movies.

- **Apple Store** lets you buy things from the Apple Store: either online (and stuff gets shipped to you) or at physical Apple Stores. In that case, the app lets you walk into the store, scan a product's barcode with your phone ($100 or less), tap Buy, and walk out. You don't interact with a salesperson, see a cash register, or pull out your wallet.

- **Remote** lets you control playback of the copy of iTunes that's running on your Mac or PC.

- **Keynote Remote** lets you use your phone as a remote control for a Mac that's running Apple's Keynote presentation program. It does more than advance the slides; it shows you your private notes for each slide and gives you a preview of the slide coming up next.

10

Getting Online

The iPhone's concept as an all-screen machine is a curse and a blessing. You may curse it when you're trying to type text, wishing you had real keys. But when you're online—oh, baby. That's when the Web comes to life, looming larger and clearer than you'd think possible on a cellphone. That's when you see real email, full-blown YouTube videos, hyper-clear Google maps, and all kinds of Internet goodness, right in your hand.

And it's fast, too, at least if you have an iPhone 5, 5c, or 5s. And you're in one of the cities covered by 4G LTE cellular towers. And the gods are smiling.

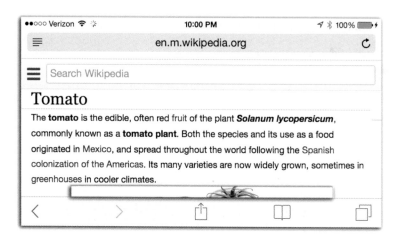

A Tale of Two Connections

The iPhone can get onto the Internet using either of two methods—two kinds of wireless networks. Which kind you're on makes a huge difference to your iPhone experience; there's nothing worse than having to wait until the next ice age for some Web page to arrive when you need the information *now.*

Cellular Networks

Once you've accepted the miracle that a cellphone can transmit your voice wirelessly, it's not much of a stretch to realize that it can also transmit your data. Cellphone carriers (Verizon, AT&T, and so on) maintain separate networks for voice and for Internet data—and every year, they spend billions of dollars trying to make those Internet networks faster. Over the years, they've come up with data networks like these:

- **Old, slow cellular network.** The earliest, slowest cellular Internet connections were called things like EDGE (AT&T) or 1xRTT (Verizon and Sprint). The good part is that these networks are almost everywhere, so your iPhone can get online almost anywhere you can make a phone call. You'll know when you're on one of these slow networks because your status bar bears a symbol like **E** or **O**.

  The bad news is that it's slow. *Dog* slow—dial-up slow.

  You can't be on a phone call while you're online using EDGE or 1xRTT, either.

- **3G cellular networks.** The world wasn't happy with those slow networks, so the carriers spent several years building faster systems called *3G* networks. (3G stands for "third generation." The ancient analog cellphones were the first generation; EDGE-type networks were the second.) Geeks refer to the 3G network standard by its official name: HSDPA, for High-Speed Downlink Packet Access.

  Life is much sweeter on 3G. Web pages that take 2 minutes to appear using EDGE or 1xRTT show up in about 20 seconds. Email downloads much faster, especially when there are attachments involved. Voice calls sound better, too, even when the signal strength is very low, since the iPhone's 3G radio can communicate with multiple towers at once.

  Oh, and on AT&T or T-Mobile, you can talk on the phone and use the Internet simultaneously, which can be very handy indeed.

- **"4G" networks.** AT&T enhanced HSDPA, made it faster using a technology called HSPA+ (High-Speed Packet Access), and calls it 4G. (You'll know when you're on one; your status bar says **4G**.) But nobody else recognizes HSPA+ as real 4G, which is why AT&T feels fine advertising "the nation's largest 4G network." The other carriers aren't even measuring that network type.

- **4G LTE networks.** Now *this* is 4G.

  An LTE network (Long-Term Evolution), offered in major cities by all four carriers, gives you amazing speeds—in many cases, faster than your broadband Internet at home. When your status bar says **LTE**, it's *fantastic.*

  But LTE is not all sunshine and bunnies; it has two huge downsides.

  First: coverage. In an attempt to serve the most people with the least effort, cell companies always bring LTE service to the big cities first. LTE coverage is available in dozens of U.S. cities, which is a good start. But that still leaves most of the country, including huge chunks of several entire states, without any 4G coverage at all. For example, here's Verizon's LTE coverage map. AT&T has about half as many cities; Sprint and T-Mobile have only a handful. Whenever you're outside the high-speed areas, your iPhone falls back to the slower speeds.

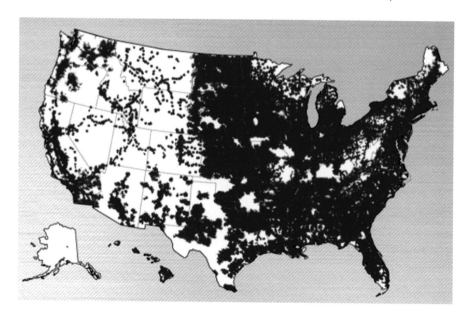

The second big problem with LTE is that, to receive its signal, a phone's circuitry uses a lot of power. That's why the iPhone 5 family models are bigger than their predecessors; they need beefier batteries.

WiFi Hotspots

WiFi, known to geeks as 802.11, is wireless networking, the same technology that gets laptops online at high speed in any WiFi **hotspot.**

Hotspots are everywhere these days: in homes, offices, coffee shops, hotels, airports, and thousands of other places. Unfortunately, a hotspot is a bubble about 300 feet across; once you wander out of it, you're off the Internet. So WiFi is for people who are sitting still.

> **TIP:** At *www.jiwire.com*, you can type an address or a city and find out exactly where to find the closest WiFi hotspots. Or, quicker yet: Open Maps on your iPhone and type in, for example, **wifi austin tx** or **wifi 06902.** Pushpins on the map show you the closest WiFi hotspots.

When you're in a WiFi hotspot, your iPhone usually gets a **very** fast connection to the Internet, as though it's connected to a cable modem or DSL. And when you're online this way, you can make phone calls and surf the Internet simultaneously. And why not? Your iPhone's WiFi and cellular antennas are independent.

(Over cellular connections, only the AT&T iPhone lets you talk and get online simultaneously.)

The iPhone looks for a WiFi connection first and considers connecting to a cellular network only if there's no WiFi. You'll always know which kind of network you're on, thanks to the icons on the status bar: you'll see either 📶 for WiFi, or one of the cellular icons (**E**, °, **3G**, **4G**, or **LTE**).

Or "No service" if there's nothing available at all.

And how much faster is one than the next? Well, network speeds are measured in kilobits and megabits per second (which isn't the same as the more familiar **kilobytes** and **megabytes** per second; divide by 8 to get those).

The EDGE/1xRTT network is supposed to deliver data from 70 to 200 kbps, depending on your distance from the cell towers. 3G gets 300 to 700 kbps. A WiFi hotspot can spit out 650 to 2,100 kbps. And 4G LTE can deliver speeds as fast as 20 Mbps on the iPhone 5. You'll rarely get speeds near the high ends—but even so, you can see that there's quite a difference.

The bottom line: LTE and WiFi are **awesome.** EDGE/1xRTT—not so much.

Sequence of Connections

The iPhone isn't online all the time. To save battery power, it opens the connection only on demand: when you check email, request a Web page, and so on. At that point, the iPhone tries to get online following this sequence:

- **First, it sniffs around for a WiFi network** that you've used before. If it finds one, it connects quietly and automatically. You're not asked for permission, a password, or anything else.

- **If the iPhone can't find a previous hotspot,** but it detects a *new* hotspot, a message appears (below, left). It displays any new hotspots' names; tap the one you want. (If you see a 🔒 icon, then that hotspot is password-protected.)

 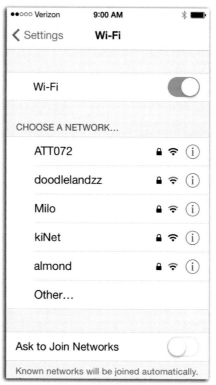

- **If the iPhone can't find any WiFi hotspots to join,** or if you don't join any, it connects to the cellular network, like 3G or LTE.

Silencing the "Want to Join?" Messages

Sometimes, you might be bombarded by those "Do you want to join?" messages at a time when you have no need to be online. You might want the iPhone to stop bugging you—to *stop* offering WiFi hotspots. In that situation, from the Home screen, tap Settings→Wi-Fi (or tell Siri, "Open WiFi settings"), and then turn off Ask to Join Networks. When this option is off, the iPhone never interrupts your work by bounding in, wagging its tail, and dropping the name of a new network at your feet. In this case, to get onto a new network, you have to visit the aforementioned Settings screen and select it, as described next.

The List of Hotspots

At some street corners in big cities, WiFi signals bleeding out of apartment buildings sometimes give you a choice of 20 or 30 hotspots to join. But whenever the iPhone invites you to join a hotspot, it suggests only a couple of them: the ones with the strongest signal and, if possible, no password requirement.

But you might sometimes want to see the complete list of available hotspots—maybe because the iPhone-suggested hotspot is flaky. To see the full list, from the Home screen, open Settings→Wi-Fi. Tap the one you want to join, as shown on the previous page at right.

> **TIP:** Tap ⓘ next to a hotspot's name to view an info sheet for techies. it shows your IP address, subnet mask, router address, and other delicious stats. Even mere mortals, however, will sometimes enjoy the Forget this Network button. It removes this hotspot from the list, which is handy if you've moved away and don't need to be reminded of the high speed that was once yours.

Commercial Hotspots

Tapping the name of the hotspot you want to join is generally all you have to do—if it's a home WiFi network. Unfortunately, joining a *commercial* WiFi hotspot—one that requires a credit-card number (in a hotel room or an airport, for example)—requires more than just connecting to it. You also have to *sign into* it, exactly as you'd do if you were using a laptop.

To do that, return to the Home screen and open Safari. You'll see the "Enter your payment information" screen, either immediately or as soon as you try to open a Web page of your choice.

Supply your credit-card information or (if you have a membership to this WiFi chain, like Boingo or T-Mobile) your name and password. Tap Submit or Proceed, try *not* to contemplate the cost, and enjoy your surfing.

Mercifully, the iPhone memorizes your password. The next time you use this hotspot, you won't have to enter it again.

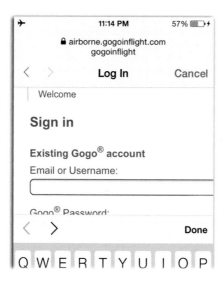

Airplane Mode and WiFi Off Mode

To save even more battery power, you can turn off all three of the iPhone's network connections in one fell swoop. You can also turn off WiFi alone.

- **To turn all radios off.** In Airplane mode, you turn off *all* wireless circuitry: Bluetooth, WiFi, and cellular. Now you can't make calls or get
  onto the Internet. You're saving power, however, and also complying
  with regulations that ban cellphones in flight.

  The short way: Swipe up from the bottom of the screen; on the Control Center, tap ✈ so it turns white. (The long way: Open Settings,
  turn on Airplane Mode.)

- **To turn WiFi on or off.** Swipe up; on the Control Center, tap 🛜 so it's
  no longer white. (You can also switch it in Settings→Wi-Fi.)

TIP: Once you've turned on Airplane mode, you can actually turn Wi-Fi back **on** again. Why on earth? Because some flights offer WiFi. You need a way to turn WiFi **on,** but your cellular circuitry **off.**

Conversely, you sometimes might want to do the opposite: turn **off** WiFi, but leave cellular **on.** Why? Because sometimes, the iPhone bizarrely won't get online at all. It's struggling to use a WiFi network that, for one reason or another, isn't connecting to the Internet. By turning WiFi off, you force the iPhone to use its cell connection—which may be slower, but at least it works!

In Airplane mode, anything that requires voice or Internet access—text messages, Web, email, and so on—triggers a message: "Turn off Airplane Mode or use WiFi to access data." Tap either OK (to back out of your decision) or Settings (to turn off Airplane mode and get online).

You can, however, enjoy all the other iPhone features: Music, Camera, and so on. You can also work with stuff you've **already** downloaded to the phone, like email, voicemail messages, and Web pages you've saved in the Reading List.

Personal Hotspot (Tethering)

Tethering means using your iPhone as a glorified Internet antenna, so that your laptops, iPod Touches, iPads, game consoles, and other Internet-connectables can get online. (The other gadgets can connect to the phone over a WiFi connection, a Bluetooth connection, or a USB cable.) In fact, several laptops and other gadgets can all share the iPhone's connection simultaneously. Your phone becomes a personal cellular router, like a MiFi.

That's incredibly convenient. Many other app phones have it, but Apple's execution is especially nice. For example, the hotspot shuts itself off 90 seconds after the last laptop disconnects. That's hugely important, because a personal hotspot is a merciless battery drain.

The hotspot feature generally costs $20 a month extra, which buys only 2 gigabytes of data for all those laptops (that's in addition to your existing iPhone data plan). Think email, not YouTube. Additional gigabytes are $20 per month each.

To get this feature, you have to sign up for it by calling your cellular company or visiting its Web site (if you didn't already do that when you signed up for service).

Turning On the Hotspot

On the phone, open **Settings→General→Cellular→Personal Hotspot** (or tell Siri, "Open cellular settings").

> **TIP:** Once you've turned on Personal Hotspot for the first time, you won't have to drill down as far to get to it. A new **Personal Hotspot** item appears right there on the main Settings screen from now on.

The Personal Hotspot screen contains details on connecting other computers. It also has the master on/off switch. Turn Personal Hotspot **On**.

(If you see a button that says **Set Up Personal Hotspot**, it means you haven't yet added the monthly tethering fee to your cellular plan. Contact your wireless carrier to get that change made to your account.)

You have to use a password for your personal hotspot; it's to ensure that people sitting nearby can't surf using your connection and run up your cell bill. The software proposes a password, but you can edit it and make up one of your own. (It has to be at least eight characters long and contain letters, numbers, and punctuation. Don't worry—your laptop or other WiFi gadget can memorize it for you.)

Your laptops and other gadgets can connect to the Internet using any of three connections to the iPhone: WiFi, Bluetooth, or a USB cable. The USB connection ("tethering") is always available, but you can't share your connection over WiFi or Bluetooth unless those iPhone antennas are turned on (duh).

If one or both (WiFi or Bluetooth) are turned off, a message appears to let you know—and offers to turn them on for you. To save battery power, turn on only what you need.

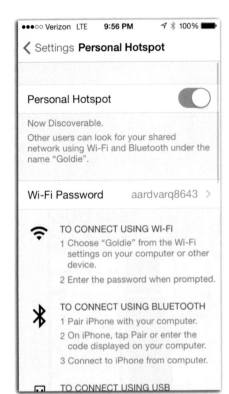

Connecting via WiFi

After about 15 seconds, the iPhone shows up on your laptop or other gadget as though it's a WiFi network. Just choose the iPhone's name from your computer's WiFi hotspot menu (on the Mac, it's the 🛜 menu). Enter the password, and bam—your laptop is now online, using the iPhone as an antenna. On the Mac, the 🛜 menu changes to look like this: 🔄.

> **TIP:** Sometimes, your iPhone's name doesn't show up in your laptop's WiFi menu. If you're having that trouble, do this: On the phone, turn Personal Hotspot off and then on again. Wait about 20 seconds without leaving the Personal Hotspot screen; by then, your iPhone's name should appear. (And remember: If nobody connects to the phone within 90 seconds of your leaving the Personal Hotspot screen, the hotspot turns itself off to save battery.)

You can leave the iPhone in your pocket or purse. You'll surf away on your laptop, baffling every Internet-less soul around you. Your laptop can now use email, the Web, chat programs—anything it could do in a real WiFi hotspot (just a little slower).

Connecting via Bluetooth

There's no compelling reason to use Bluetooth instead of WiFi, especially since Bluetooth slows down your Internet connection. But anyway.

To connect wirelessly over Bluetooth, you first have to *pair* your laptop with the phone—a one-time procedure. It varies by laptop. For example:

- **OS X.** On the Mac, open System Preferences→Bluetooth. Click the **+** button in the lower-left corner; when your iPhone's name shows up in the list, click it and then click Continue. After a moment, a huge six-digit number appears on both the Mac screen and the iPhone screen; on the phone, tap Pair, and on the Mac, click Continue and then Quit.

> **TIP:** You can make life a lot easier later if, before you click Quit, you turn on "Show Bluetooth status in the menu bar." You'll see why in a moment.

- **Windows 7 or 8.** Open the Start menu; type *Bluetooth.* Click Add a Bluetooth Device. When your iPhone's name shows up in the list, click it and then click Next. After a moment, a huge six-digit number appears on both the PC screen and the iPhone screen; on the phone, tap Pair, and on the PC, tap Close.

Now, the pairing business is a one-time operation, but you still have to connect to the phone manually each time you want to go online.

- **On the Mac,** click the ☀ icon in the menu bar (which appears there because you wisely followed the preceding tip). Choose iPhone→ Connect to Network. (The menu lists whatever your actual iPhone's name is, which might not be "iPhone.")

- **In Windows,** click the ☀ icon on the system tray and connect to the iPhone.

Connecting via USB Cable

If you can connect your laptop to your iPhone using the white charging cable, you should. Tethering eats up a lot of the phone's battery power, so keeping it plugged into the laptop means you won't wind up with a dead phone when you're finished surfing.

Once You're Connected

On the iPhone, a blue bar appears at the top of the screen to make you aware that the laptop is connected; in fact, it shows how many laptops or other gadgets are connected at the moment, via any of the three connection methods. (You can tap that bar to open the Personal Hotspot screen in Settings.)

Most carriers won't let more than five people connect through a single iPhone.

If you have AT&T or T-Mobile, you can still use all the functions of the iPhone, including making calls and even surfing the Web, while it's channeling your laptop's Internet connection.

If you have Verizon or Sprint, your iPhone can't handle Internet connections and voice calls simultaneously. So if a phone call comes in, the iPhone suspends the hotspot feature until you're finished talking; when you hang up (or if you decline the call), all connected gadgets regain their Internet connections automatically.

Turning Off Personal Hotspot

If you're connected wirelessly to the iPhone, the Personal Hotspot feature is a battery hog. It'll cut your iPhone's battery longevity in half. That's why, if no laptops are connected for 90 seconds, the iPhone turns the hotspot off automatically.

You can also turn off the hotspot manually, just the way you'd expect: In Settings→Personal Hotspot, tap Off.

Turning Personal Hotspot Back On

About 90 seconds after the last gadget stops using the hotspot, your iPhone shuts off the feature to save its own battery. To fire it back up again later, open Settings and tap Personal Hotspot. That's it—just visit the Personal Hotspot screen to make the iPhone resume broadcasting its WiFi or Bluetooth network to your laptops and other gadgets.

Twitter and Facebook

Twitter, of course, is a free service (sign up at *twitter.com*) that lets you send out short messages, like text messages, to anyone who wants to get them from you. Twitter is a fantastic way for people to spread news, links, thoughts, and observations directly to the people who care—incredibly quickly.

And Facebook is—well, Facebook. One billion people sharing their personal details and thoughts can't be wrong, right?

These services are woven into the built-in iPhone apps.

Start by visiting **Settings→Twitter** or **Settings→Facebook**. Here you can enter your account name and password or sign up for an account. Here, too, you're offered the chance to download the actual Twitter or Facebook apps. You can also tap **Update Contacts**, which attempts to add the Twitter or Facebook addresses of everybody in your Contacts app to their information cards. For details, see page 86.

Once you've set up Twitter in this way, you'll find some nifty buttons built into your other apps, for one-tap tweeting or Facebook posting. For example, the Share button (⬆) appears in Photos, Maps, Safari, and other apps, making it easy to post a photo, location, or Web page. Siri understands commands like "Tweet" and "Post to Facebook," too, so you can broadcast when the spirit moves you. (The **Tweet** and **Post** buttons are no longer in the Notification Center, however.)

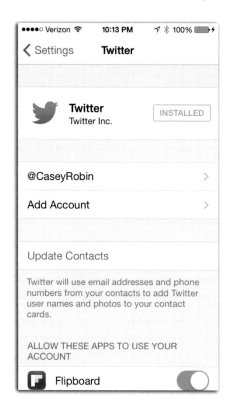

In each case, you wind up at a small tweet sheet or Facebook sheet, as shown on page 246. Here you can add a comment to the link or photo, or attach your current location, or (for Facebook) specify who's allowed to see this post—Everyone or Friends, for example.

For Twitter posts, you'll notice that the keyboard at that point offers dedicated @ and # keys. (The # is for creating hashtags—searchable keywords on a tweet like #iphone5sbugs—that Twitter fans can use when searching for tweets about certain topics. And the @ precedes every Twitter person's address—@pogue, for example.)

11

The Web

The iPhone's Web browser is Safari, a lite version of the same one that comes with every Mac. It's fast, simple to use, and very pretty indeed. You see the real deal—the actual fonts, graphics, and layouts—not the stripped-down, bare-bones mini-Web on cellphones of years gone by.

In iOS 7, Safari has been substantially revamped and revised. It's still not quite as good as surfing the Web on, you know, a laptop. But it's getting closer.

Safari Tour

The Web on the iPhone can be either fast (when you're in a WiFi hotspot or on LTE), medium (in a 3G or 4G coverage area) or excruciating (on the EDGE cellular network). Even so, some Web is usually better than none.

TIP: You don't have to wait for a Web page to load entirely. You can zoom in, scroll, and begin reading the text even when only part of the page has appeared.

Safari has most of the features of a desktop Web browser: bookmarks, autocomplete (for Web addresses), scrolling shortcuts, cookies, a pop-up ad blocker, password memorization, and so on. (It's missing niceties like streaming music, Java, Flash, and other plug-ins.)

Here's a quick tour of the main screen elements, starting from the upper right:

- **Search/address bar.** In iOS 7, a single, unified box serves as both the address bar and the search bar at the top of the screen. (That's the trend these days. Desktop-computer browsers like Chrome and Safari on the Mac work that way, too.)

  This white box is where you enter the *URL* (Web address) for a page you want to visit. ("URL" is short for the even-less-self-explanatory *Uniform Resource Locator.*) For example, if you type *amazon.com*, tapping Go takes you to that Web site.

  But this is also where you search the Web. If you type anything else, like *cashmere sweaters* or just *amazon*, tapping Go gives you the Google search results for that phrase.

  In general, it's handy to have a combined address bar/search bar. Unfortunately, it means that you can no longer leave off the .com when you're typing an address—a longtime advantage of Safari's smart address bar.

> **TIP:** Fortunately, Apple has made it up to you in iOS 7: If you hold your finger down briefly on the keyboard's period key, you get a pop-up palette of Web-address suffixes (.org, .edu, and so on). Luckily, *.com* starts out selected—so just release your finger to type it in. In other words, the entire process for typing in *.com* goes like this: Hold finger on period key; release.

- **✗, ↻ (Stop, Reload).** Tap ✗ to interrupt the downloading of a Web page you've just requested (if you've made a mistake, for instance, or if it's taking too long).

  Once a page has finished loading, the ✗ button turns into a ↻ (reload) button. Click it if a page doesn't look or work quite right. Safari redownloads the Web page and reinterprets its text and graphics.

- **‹, › (Back, Forward).** Tap ‹ to revisit the page you were just on. Once you've tapped ‹, you can then tap › to return to the page you were on *before* you tapped the ‹ button.

- ⬆ **(Share/Bookmark).** When you're on an especially useful page, tap this button. It offers every conceivable choice for commemorating the page: Mail, Message, Twitter, Facebook, Bookmark, Add to Reading List, Add to Home Screen, Copy, Print, and AirDrop. See page 294 for details.

- 📖 **(Bookmarks).** This button brings up your list of saved bookmarks—and much more. Here, too, are your History list, your Favorites, your Reading List, and links recommended by the people you follow on Twitter. You can read about these elements later in this chapter.

- 🗐 **(Page Juggler).** Safari can keep multiple Web pages open, just like any other browser. Page 402 has the details.

Zooming and Scrolling

In the early days, these two gestures—zooming in on Web pages and then scrolling around them—probably sold more people on the iPhone than any other demonstration. It all happens with a fluid animation, and a responsiveness to your finger taps, that's positively addicting.

When you first open a Web page, you get to see the *entire thing,* so you can get the lay of the land.

At this point, of course, you're looking at .004-point type, which is too small to read unless you're a microbe. So the next step is to magnify the *part* of the page you want to read.

The iPhone offers three ways to do that:

- **Rotate the iPhone.** Turn the device 90 degrees in either direction. The iPhone rotates and magnifies the image to fill the wider view. Often, this simple act is enough to make tiny type big enough to read.

- **Do the two-finger spread.** Put two fingers on the glass and slide them apart. The Web page stretches before your very eyes, growing larger. Then you can pinch to shrink the page back down again. (Most people do several spreads or several pinches in a row to achieve the degree of zoom they want.)

- **Double-tap.** Safari is intelligent enough to recognize different *chunks* of a Web page. One article might represent a chunk. A photograph might qualify as a chunk. When you double-tap a chunk, Safari magnifies *just that chunk* to fill the whole screen. It's smart and useful.

  Double-tap again to zoom back out.

Once you've zoomed out to the proper degree, you can then scroll around the page by dragging or flicking with a finger. You don't have to worry about "clicking a link" by accident; if your finger's in motion, Safari ignores the tapping action, even if you happen to land on a link.

Double-tap

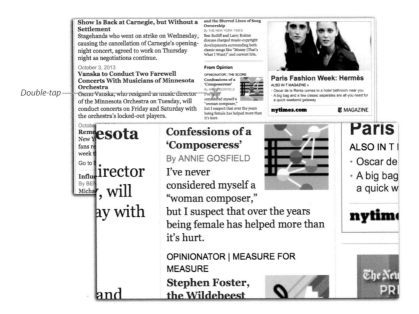

By the way, you'll occasionally encounter a *frame* (a column of text) on a page—an area that scrolls independently of the main page. The iPhone has a secret, undocumented method for scrolling one of these frames without scrolling the whole page: the *two-finger drag.* Try it out.

Full-Screen Mode

In creating iOS 7, Apple recognized that all those bars and controls—address bar, toolbar, status bar, button bar and so on—eat up screen space. Now, on a phone, the screen is pretty small to begin with; most people would rather dedicate that space to showing more *Web.*

So in iOS 7, Safari automatically enters *full-screen mode* the instant you start to *scroll down* a page. (There's no longer a full-screen *button.* And this full-screen business happens no matter how you're holding the phone —upright or sideways.)

In full-screen mode, all of those controls and toolbars vanish. Now the *entire* iPhone screen is filled with Web goodness, as shown on these pages.

You can bring the controls back in any of these ways:

- Scroll *up* a little bit.

- Return to the top or bottom of a Web page.

- Navigate to a different page.

And enjoy Safari's dedication to trying to get out of your way. More people should be like that.

Typing a Web Address

As on a computer, this Web browser offers several tools for navigating the Web: the address bar, bookmarks, the History list, and good old link-tapping. These pages cover each of these methods in turn, along with the Reading List and Web Clips.

The address/search bar is the strip at the top of the screen where you type in a Web page's address. And it so happens that *four* of the iPhone's greatest tips and shortcuts all have to do with this important navigational tool:

- **Insta-scroll to the top.** You can jump directly to the address bar, no matter how far down a page you've scrolled, just by tapping the very top edge of the screen (that is, the status bar). That "tap the top" trick is timely, too, when a Web site is designed to *hide* the address bar.

- **Don't delete.** There *is* a ⊗ button at the right end of the address bar whose purpose is to erase the entire current address so you can type another one. (Tap inside the address bar to make it, and the keyboard, appear.) But the ⊗ button is for suckers.

  Instead, whenever the address bar is open for typing, *just type.* Forget that there's already a URL there. The iPhone is smart enough to figure out that you want to *replace* that Web address with a new one.

- **Don't type http://www.** Safari is also smart enough to know that most Web addresses use that format—so you can leave that stuff out, and it will supply them automatically. Instead of *http://www.cnn.com*, for example, you can just type *cnn.com* (or tap its name in the suggestions list) and hit Go.

- **Don't type .com, .net, .org, or .edu either.** Safari's canned URL choices can save you four keyboard taps apiece. To see their secret menu, hold your finger down on the *period key* on the keyboard. Then tap the common suffix you want. (Or, if you want .com, just release your finger without moving it.)

Otherwise, this address bar works just like the one in any other Web browser. Tap inside it to make the keyboard appear. (Once more: If the address bar is hidden, then tap the top edge of the iPhone screen.)

Tap the blue **Go** key when you're finished typing the address. That's your Enter key. (Or tap **Cancel** to hide the keyboard *without* "pressing Enter.")

Autocomplete Suggestions

In iOS 7, that address bar is also the search box. Just tap into it and type your search phrase (or speak it, using Siri).

To save you time and fiddling, Safari instantly produces a drop-down menu filled with suggestions that could spare you some typing—things it guesses you might be looking for. If you see the address you're trying to type, then by all means tap it instead of typing out the rest of the URL. The time you save could be your own:

- **Top Hits.** The Top Hits are Safari's best guesses at what you're looking for. They're the sites on your bookmarks and History lists that you've visited most often (and that match what you've typed so far).

  Try tapping one of the Top Hits sometime. You'll discover, to your amazement, that that site appears almost instantly. It doesn't seem to have to load. That's because, as a favor to you, Safari quietly down-loads the Top Hits in the background, while you're still entering your search term, all to save you time.

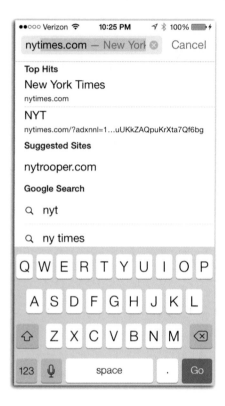

- **Suggested Sites.** Occasionally, you'll see another proposed site or two here: Suggested Sites. It's yet another site that Safari supposes you might be trying to reach, based on what you've typed so far and what sites other people visit.

- **Google Search.** The next category of suggestions: a list of search terms you *might* be typing, based on how popular those searches are on Google. For example, if you type *chick,* this section proposes things like *chicken recipes, chick fil a,* and *chicken pox.* It's just trying to save you a little typing; if none of these tappable choices is the one you want, ignore them and continue typing.

- **Bookmarks and History.** Here Safari offers matching selections from Web sites you've bookmarked or recently visited. Again, it's trying save you typing if it can.

- **On This Page.** Here's how you search for certain text *on the page you're reading.*

  Once you've started typing, under the On This Page heading, you see a listing called Find "chic" (or whatever you've typed so far), shown here at left. Tap that line to jump to the first appearance of that text on the page; then use the ⟨ and ⟩ buttons to jump from one match to the next. Tap Done to return to your regularly scheduled browsing.

TIP: Suppose you've started typing a search term. Safari pipes up with its usual list of suggestions. At this point, if you drag up or down the screen, you hide the keyboard—so you can see the suggestions that were hidden behind it.

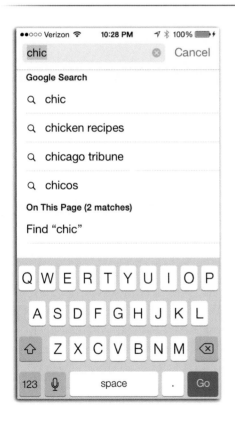

Now then. If, among all of these Safari labor-saving suggestions, you don't see what you're looking for, then maybe you really do have to search the Web. Tap the big blue Go button in the corner.

You can tell the iPhone to use a Yahoo or Bing search instead of Google, if you like. From the Home screen, tap Settings→Safari→Search Engine.

TIP: If you've set your search options to use Google, there are all kinds of cool things you can type here—special terms that tell Google, "I want *information,* not Web-page matches."

You can type a movie name and Zip code or city/state (*Titanic Returns 10024*) to get a list of today's showtimes in theaters near you. Get the forecast by typing *weather chicago* or *weather 60609.* Stock quotes: Type the symbol (*AMZN*). Dictionary definitions: *define schadenfreude.* Unit conversions: *liters in 5 gallons.* Currency conversions: *25 usd in euros.* Then tap Go to get instant results.

Bookmarks

Bookmarks, of course, are Web sites you might want to visit again without having to remember and type their URLs.

To see the list of bookmarks on your phone, tap ⬚ at the bottom of the screen. You see the master list of bookmarks (acing page, left). They're organized in folders, or even folders *within* folders.

Tapping a folder shows you what's inside (facing page, right), and tapping a bookmark begins opening the corresponding Web site.

NOTE: Actually, what you see when you tap ⬚ are *three* tabs at the top: ⬚ (Bookmarks), ◯◯ (Reading List), and @ Twitter Links). The latter two are described later in this chapter.

You might be surprised to discover that Safari already seems to be pre-stocked with bookmarks—that, amazingly, are interesting and useful to *you* in particular! How did it know?

Easy—it copied your existing desktop computer's browser bookmarks from Internet Explorer (Windows) or Safari (Macintosh) when you synced the iPhone (Chapter 13), or when you turned on Safari syncing through iCloud. Sneaky, eh?

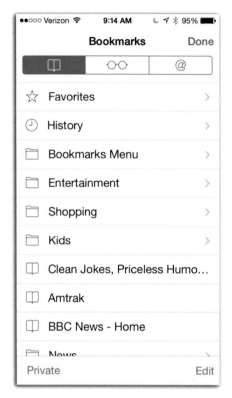

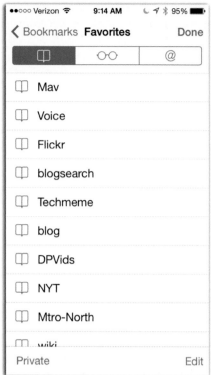

Creating New Bookmarks

You can add new bookmarks right on the phone. Any work you do here is copied **back** to your computer the next time you sync the two machines—or instantaneously, if you've turned on iCloud bookmark syncing.

When you find a Web page you might like to visit again, tap the ⬆ button to reveal the options shown on the next page at left; then tap Bookmark. The Add Bookmark screen appears (right).

You have two tasks here:

- **Type a better name.** In the top box, you can type a shorter or clearer name for the page. Instead of "Bass, Trout & Tackle—the Web's Premier Resource for the Avid Outdoorsman," you can just call it "Fish fun."

  The box below this one identifies the underlying URL, which is independent of what you've **named** your bookmark. You can't edit this one.

- **Specify where to file this bookmark.** If you tap Bookmarks >, you open Safari's hierarchical list of bookmark folders, which organize your bookmarked sites. Tap the folder where you want to file the new bookmark so you'll know where to find it later.

> **TIP:** Here's a site worth bookmarking: *http://google.com/gwt/n*. It gives you a bare-bones, superfast version of the Web, provided by Google for the benefit of people on slow connections (like EDGE). You can opt to hide graphics for even more speed. Yeah, the iPhone's browser is glorious and all—but sometimes you'd rather have fast than pretty.

Editing Bookmarks and Folders

It's easy enough to massage your Bookmarks list within Safari—to delete favorites that aren't so favorite anymore, to make new folders, to rearrange the list, to rename a folder or a bookmark, and so on.

The techniques are the same for editing bookmark *folders* as editing the bookmarks themselves—after the first step. To edit the folder list, start by opening the Bookmarks (tap the ⬚ button), and then tap Edit.

To edit the bookmarks themselves, tap ⬚, tap a folder, and *then* tap Edit. Now you can get organized:

- **Delete something.** Tap ⊖ next to a folder or a bookmark, and then tap Delete to confirm.

- **Rearrange the list.** Drag the grip strip (≡) up or down in the list to move the folders or bookmarks around. (You can't move or delete the top two folders—Favorites and History.)

- **Edit a name and location.** Tap a folder or a bookmark name. If you tap a folder, you arrive at the Edit Folder screen; you can edit the folder's name and which folder it's inside of. If you tap a bookmark, Edit Bookmark lets you edit the name and the URL it points to.

  Tap Done when you're finished.

- **Create a folder.** Tap New Folder in the lower-left corner of the Edit Folders screen. You're offered the chance to type a name for it and to specify where you want to file it (that is, in which *other* folder).

Tap Done when you're finished.

The Reading List

The Reading List is a handy list of Web pages you want to read later. Unlike a bookmark, it stores entire pages, so you can read them later even when you don't have an Internet connection (on the subway or on a plane, for example).

The Reading List also keeps track of what you've read. You can use the Show All/Show Unread button at the bottom of the screen to view everything—or just what you haven't yet read.

> **TIP:** To make matters even sweeter, iCloud synchronizes your Reading List on your Mac, iPhone, iPad, and so on—as long as you've turned on bookmark syncing. It's as though the Web always keeps your place.

To add a page to the Reading List, tap the ⬆️ button and then tap **Add to Reading List** (below, left). Or just hold your finger down on a link until a set of buttons appears, including **Add to Reading List**.

Once you've added a page to the Reading List, you can get to it by tapping 📖, and then tapping the Reading List tab at the top (◯◯). Tap an item on your list to open and read it.

By the way, some Web pages require a hefty amount of data to download, what with photos and all. If you're worried about Reading List downloads eating up your monthly data allotment, you can visit **Settings→Safari** and turn off **Use Cellular Data**. Now you'll be able to download Reading List pages only when you're on WiFi, but at least there's no risk of going over your monthly cellular-data allotment.

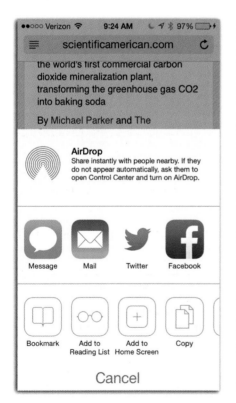

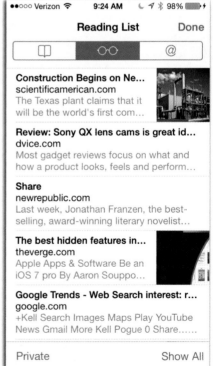

Shared Links

There's a third tab button on the Bookmarks screen, too: @. That's the Shared Links button.

It lists every tweet from Twitter that contains a link. The idea is to make it easier for you to explore the sites that your Twitter friends are recommending; all of their great Web finds are collected in one handy place.

> **TIP:** In Safari, "shared links" has another meaning, too: the ⬆️ makes it easy to share the URL of a particularly juicy Web page. On the Share sheet (facing page, left), you get a Copy button, so you can copy and paste Web addresses. It also offers links for Mail (the iPhone's email program opens, a new outgoing message ready), Message (text message), Twitter (the tweet sheet shown on page 246 appears) and Facebook.

Web Clips

If there's a certain Web site you visit all the time, like every day, then even the four taps necessary to open it in the usual way (Home, Safari, Bookmarks, your site's name) can seem like a lot of red tape. That's why Apple made it simple to add the icon of a certain Web page right to your Home screen. It's a shortcut that Apple calls a Web clip.

Start by opening the page in question. Tap ⬆️ at the bottom of the screen. In the button list, tap Add to Home Screen. Now you're offered the chance to edit the icon's name; finally, tap Add.

When you return to your Home screen, you'll see the new icon. You can move it around, drag it to a different Home screen, and so on, exactly as you would any other app.

Or, to delete it, touch its icon until all the Home icons begin to wiggle. Tap the Web Clip's ✖️ badge to remove its icon.

> **TIP:** You can turn *part* of a Web page into one of these Web Clips, too. You might want quick access to The New York Times' "Most emailed" list, or the bestselling children's books on Amazon, or the most-viewed video on YouTube, or the box scores for a certain sports league.
>
> All you have to do is zoom and scroll the page in Safari *before* you tap ⬆️, isolating the section you want. Later, when you open the Web Clip, you'll see exactly the part of the Web page you wanted.

The History List

Behind the scenes, Safari keeps track of the Web sites you've visited in the past week or so, neatly organized into subfolders like This Evening and Yesterday. It's a great feature when you can't recall the address for a Web site you visited recently—or when you remember it had a long, complicated address and you get the psychiatric condition known as iPhone Keyboard Dread.

To see the list of recent sites, tap ⬜, and then tap the History folder, whose icon bears a 🕐 to make sure you know it's special. Once the History list appears, just tap a bookmark to revisit that Web page.

Erasing the History List

Some people find it creepy that Safari maintains a complete list of every Web site they've seen recently, right there in plain view of any family member or coworker who wanders by. They'd just as soon their wife/husband/boss/parent/kid not know what Web sites they've been visiting.

You can't delete just one particularly incriminating History listing. You can, however, delete the *entire* History menu, thus erasing all your tracks. To do that, tap Clear; confirm by tapping Clear History.

You've just rewritten History.

Tapping Links

On the iPhone, not all links take you to other Web pages. If you tap an email address, it opens up the Mail app (Chapter 12) and creates a preaddressed outgoing message. If you tap a phone number you find online, the iPhone calls it for you. There's even such a thing as a **map** link, which opens the Maps app.

Each of these links, in other words, takes you out of Safari. If you want to return to your Web browsing, then you have to return to the Home screen, or the task switcher, and tap Safari. The page you had open is still there, waiting.

 TIP: If you hold your finger on a link for a moment—touching rather than tapping—a handy sliding panel appears. At the top, you see the full Web address that link will open. And there are some useful buttons: Open, Open in New Page, Add to Reading List, and Copy (meaning "copy the link address"). Oh, and there's also Cancel.

Saving Graphics

If you find a picture online that you wish you could keep forever, you have two choices. You could stare at it until you've memorized it, or you could save it.

To do that, touch the image for about a second. A sheet appears, just like the one that appears when you hold your finger down on a regular link.

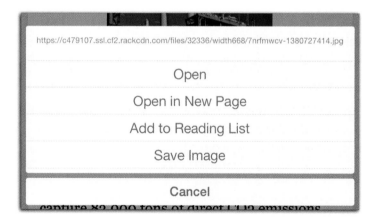

If you tap Save Image, then the iPhone thoughtfully deposits a copy of the image in your Camera Roll so it will be copied back to your Mac or PC at the next sync opportunity. If you tap Copy, then you nab a *link* to that graphic, which you can now paste it into another program.

Saved Passwords & Credit Cards

On the real Safari—on the Mac or PC—a feature called AutoFill saves you an awful lot of typing. It fills out your name and address automatically when you're ordering something online. It stores your passwords so you don't have to re-enter them every time you visit passworded sites.

On the iPhone, where you're typing on glass, the convenience of AutoFill goes to a whole new level.

And in iOS 7, there's a whole new level above that level. Now the phone can memorize your credit card information, making it much easier to buy stuff online. And thanks to iCloud syncing, all those passwords and credit cards can auto-store themselves on all your other Apple gadgetry.

> **TIP:** Here's the obligatory speech about security. You know: If your iPhone is stolen, and you haven't protected it with a password or a fingerprint, then the bad guy could see your bank account if the password has been stored, and so on. You've been warned.

To turn on AutoFill, visit Settings→Safari→Passwords & AutoFill. Here's what you find (facing page, left):

- **Use Contact Info.** Turn this On. Then tap My Info. From the address book, find your own listing. You've just told Safari *which* name, address, city, state, Zip code, and phone number belong to you.

  From now on, whenever you're asked to input your address, phone number, and so on, you'll see an AutoFill button at the top of the keyboard. Tap it to make Safari auto-enter all those details, saving you no end of typing. (It works on *most* sites.) If there are extra blanks that AutoFill doesn't fill, then you can tap the Previous and Next buttons to move your cursor from one to the next instead of tapping and scrolling manually.

- **Names & Passwords** lets Safari fill in your user name and passwords when you visit sites that require you to log in (Google, Amazon, and so on). You can tap Yes (a good idea for your PTA or library account), Never for this Website (a good idea for your bank), or Not Now (you'll be asked again next time).

You can also tap Saved Passwords to view a list of the memorized names and passwords.

- **Always Show.** Some Web sites discourage you from saving your passwords. Banks, for example; they'd rather not worry about a pick-pocket stealing your phone and then logging into your bank account because the password was memorized. But if you turn on Always Allow, Safari saves all passwords anyway.

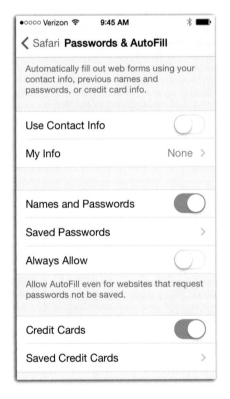
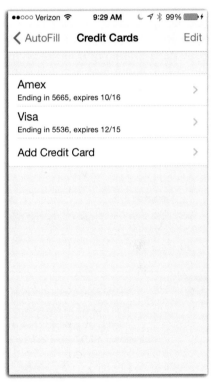

- **Credit Cards.** Turn on Credit Cards, of course, if you'd like Safari to memorize your charge card info. To enter your card details, tap Saved Credit Cards (where you see a list of them) and then Add Credit Card. Gracefully enough, Safari stores your name *and* your card number *and* its expiration date.

When you buy something online, iOS 7 offers an Autofill Credit Card button. When you tap it, Safari asks you first which credit card you want to use, if you've stored more than one (it displays the last four digits for your reference). Tap it, and boom: Safari cheerfully fills in the credit card information, saving you time and hassle.

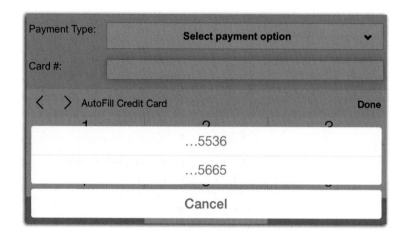

By the way: You'll notice that there's nowhere to store the little three-digit security code (four digits for American Express), sometimes called the CSC, CVV, or CV2 code. Nor does Safari attempt to fill that in; you always have to enter the CV2 code manually.

That's one last safeguard against a kid, a spouse, a parent, or a thief using your phone for an online shopping spree when you're not around.

TIP: Once you've stored all of these passwords and credit cards, it sure would be nice if you didn't have to enter them into other Apple gadgets, wouldn't it? Your Mac, your iPad, and so on?

Fortunately, the iCloud service can synchronize this information to Safari running on other Apple machines. Page 478 has the details.

Manipulating Multiple Pages

Like any other self-respecting browser, Safari can keep multiple pages open at once, making it easy for you to switch among them. You can think of it as a miniature version of tabbed browsing, a feature of browsers like Safari Senior, Firefox, Chrome, and Internet Explorer. Tabbed browsing keeps a bunch of Web pages open simultaneously.

One advantage of this arrangement is that you can start reading one Web page while the others load into their own tabs in the background.

To Open a New Window

Tap the ⬓ button in the lower right. The Web page seems to duck backward, bowing to you in 3-D space. Tap the + button.

You now arrive at iOS 7's new Favorites page (below, left). Here are one-tap icons for all the sites you've designated as Favorites. Tap one to open it. Or, in the address bar at the top, enter an address. Or use a bookmark. (More on the Favorites page in a moment.)

TIP: Alternatively, hold your finger down on a link instead of tapping it. You get a choice of three commands, one of which is Open in New Page.

Sometimes Safari sprouts a new window *automatically* when you click a link. That's because the link you tapped is programmed to open in a new window. To return to the original window, read on.

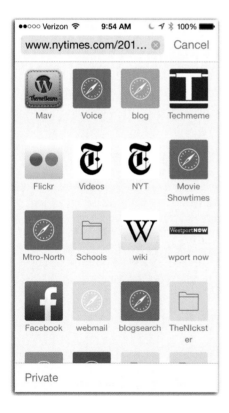

To Switch among Windows

Tap ⬚ again. Now you see something like the 3-D floating pages shown above at right.

These, of course, are all of your open windows. You can work with them like this:

- **Close a window** by tapping the X in the corner—or by swiping a page away to the left. It slides away into the void; the only thing missing is a falling sound effect like, "Oh nooooooooooooooo!"

- **Rearrange these windows** by dragging them up or down with your finger.

- **Open a window** to full screen by tapping it.

You can open a third window, and a fourth, and so on, and jump among them, using these two techniques.

iCloud Tabs

The iPhone can auto-open whatever browser windows and tabs you had open on another Apple gadget, like a Mac or an iPad. Thanks to the miracle of iCloud syncing, the last windows and tabs you had open on that other gadget (even if the gadget is turned off) show up here.

The concept is to unify your Macs and i-gadgets into one glorious, seamless Web-browsing experience. You're reading three browser windows and tabs on your phone—why not resume on the big screen when you get home and sit down in front of your Mac?

You won't see these tabs unless the other gadgets have iOS 6 or later and the other Macs have OS X Mountain Lion or later. And, of course, Safari has to be turned on in **System Preferences→iCloud** on the Mac, or **Settings→iCloud** on the phone or tablet.

To see these tabs, tap ⬚ to open your sharply angled view of open Safari windows. Scroll to the bottom. There they are: your iCloud tabs, sorted into headings that correspond to your other Apple gadgets.

The Favorites Page

You can never close all your Safari windows. The app will never let you get past the final page, always lurking behind the others: the Favorites page, new in iOS 7 (previous page, left).

This is the new starting point. It's what you first see when you tap the + button. It's like a page of visual bookmarks.

In fact, if you see a bunch of icons here already, it's because your phone has synced them over from Safari on a Mac; whatever sites are on your Bookmarks *bar* become icons on this bookmark *page.*

You can edit this Favorites page, of course:

- **Rearrange them** as you would Home screen icons. That is, hold your finger down on an icon momentarily and then drag it to a new spot.

- **Remove or rename a Favorites icon.** Favorites are actually just bookmarks. So you can edit, move, or delete them just as you would any bookmark. (Tap the ⬚ to open your Bookmarks screen. Make sure that you're on the ⬚ tab, so that your list of folders is showing. Tap Favorites, then Edit. Tap ⊖ for a site you want to delete, and then tap Delete.)

> **TIP:** You can create folders *inside* the Favorites folder, too. Whenever the Favorites screen appears, you'll see these subfolders listed as further sources of speed-dial Web sites.

- **Add a Favorites icon.** When you find a page you'd like to add to the Favorites screen, tap ⬆. On the Share sheet, tap Bookmark. The phone proposes putting the new bookmark into the Favorites *folder,* which means that it will show up on the Favorites *screen.* Tap Save.

> **TIP:** It's worth noting, by the way, that you don't have to use the Favorites folder of bookmarks as the one whose contents appear on the Favorites screen. In Settings→Safari→Favorites, a list of all your Bookmarks folders appears. Whichever one you select there becomes your new Favorites folder, even if its name isn't "Favorites."

Reader

How can people read Web articles when there's Times-Square blinking going on all around them? Fortunately, you'll never have to put up with that again.

The Reader button in the address bar (☰) is amazing. With one tap, it eliminates *everything* from the Web page you're reading except the text and photos. No ads, toolbars, blinking, links, banners, promos, or anything else.

The text is also changed to a clean, clear font and size, and the background is made plain white. Basically, it makes any Web page look like a printed book page, and it's glorious. Below: the before and after. Which looks easier to read?

To exit Reader, tap ☰ again. Best. Feature. Ever.

The fine print: Reader doesn't appear until the page has fully loaded. It doesn't appear on "front page" pages, like the *nytimes.com* home page—only when you've opened an article within. It may not appear on sites that are already specially designed for access by cellphones.

Web Security

Safari on the iPhone isn't meant to be a full-blown Web browser like the one on your desktop computer, but it comes surprisingly close—especially when it comes to privacy and security. Cookies, pop-up blockers, parental controls...they're all here, for your paranoid pleasure.

Pop-Up Blocker

The world's smarmiest advertisers like to inundate us with pop-up and pop-under ads—nasty little windows that appear in front of the browser window, or, worse, behind it, waiting to jump out the moment you close your window. Fortunately, Safari comes set to block those pop-ups so you don't see them. It's a war out there—but at least you now have some ammunition.

The thing is, though, pop-ups are sometimes legitimate (and not ads)—notices of new banking features, seating charts on ticket-sales sites, warnings that the instructions for using a site have changed, and so on. Safari can't tell these from ads—and it stifles them, too. So if a site you trust says, "Please turn off pop-up blockers and reload this page," then you know you're probably missing out on a *useful* pop-up message.

In those situations, you can turn off the pop-up blocker. The on/off switch is in Settings→Safari.

Password Suggestions

New in iOS 7: When you're signing up for a new account on some Web site, and you tap inside the box where you're supposed to make up a password, Safari now offers to make up a password for you. It's a doozy, too, along the lines of 23k2k4-29cs8-58384-ckk3322.

Now, don't freak out. You're not expected to remember that. Safari will, of course, memorize it for you (and sync it to your other Apple computers). Meanwhile, you've got yourself a unique, nearly uncrackable password.

Cookies

Cookies are something like Web page preference files. Certain Web sites—particularly commercial ones like Amazon.com—deposit them on your hard drive like little bookmarks so they'll remember you the next time you visit. Ever notice how Amazon.com greets you with, "Welcome, Chris" (or whatever your name is)? It's reading its own cookie, left behind on your hard drive (or in this case, on your iPhone).

Most cookies are perfectly innocuous—and, in fact, are extremely useful, because they help Web sites remember your tastes. Cookies also spare you the effort of having to type in your name, address, and so on every time you visit these Web sites.

But fear is widespread, and the media fan the flames with tales of sinister cookies that track your movement on the Web. If you're worried about invasions of privacy, Safari is ready to protect you.

From the Home screen, tap Settings→Safari→Block Cookies. The options here are like a paranoia gauge. If you click Always, you create an acrylic shield around your iPhone. No cookies can come in, and no cookie information can go out. You'll probably find the Web a very inconvenient place; you'll have to re-enter your information upon every visit, and some Web sites may not work properly at all. The **Never** option means, "Oh, what the heck—just gimme all of them."

A good compromise is **From third parties and advertisers**, which accepts cookies from sites you *want* to visit, but blocks cookies deposited on your phone by sites you're not actually visiting—cookies an especially evil banner ad gives you, for example.

The **Settings→Safari** screen also offers a **Clear History** button, as well as a **Clear History and Data** button. It deletes all the cookies you've accumulated so far, as well as your phone's *cache.*

The cache is a patch of the iPhone's storage area where pieces of Web pages you visit—graphics, for example—are retained. The idea is that the next time you visit the same page, the iPhone won't have to download those bits again. It already has them on board, so the page appears much faster.

If you worry that your cache eats up space, poses a security risk, or is confusing some page (and preventing the most recent version of the page from appearing), then tap **Clear History** to erase it and start over.

Private Browsing

Private Browsing lets you surf without adding any pages to your History list, searches to your Google search suggestions, passwords to Safari's saved password list, or autofill entries to Safari's memory. You might want to turn on Private Browsing before you start visiting Web sites that would, you know, raise interesting questions with your spouse, parents, or boss.

Until iOS 7 came along, you had to dig three screens deep in Settings to turn Private Browsing on or off—a detour to a totally different app.

Not anymore. Now, when you want to start leaving no tracks, tap the ⊞ button to open your Bookmarks screen; tap **Private** at the bottom-left corner. A duplicate **Private** button awaits when you tap the ⧉ button.

(When you tap **Private**, Safari may ask you what to do about pages you already have open. You can **Close All** or **Keep All**. If you choose Keep All, those pages remain open; only the new pages you visit won't be remembered.)

From now on, Safari records nothing while you surf.

When you're ready to browse "publicly" again, turn Private Browsing off once more. Safari resumes taking note of the pages you visit—but it never remembers the ones you opened while in Private.

In other words, what happens in Private Browsing stays in Private Browsing.

Parental Controls

If your child (or employee) is old enough to have an iPhone but not old enough for the seedier side of the Web, then don't miss the Restrictions feature in Settings. The iPhone makes no attempt to separate the good Web sites from the bad—but it *can* remove the Safari icon from the iPhone altogether so that no Web browsing is possible at all. See page 549 for instructions.

12

Email

Email on your iPhone offers full formatting, fonts, graphics, and choice of type size; file attachments like Word, Excel, PowerPoint, PDF, Pages, Numbers, photos, and (in iOS 7) even .zip compressed files; and compatibility with Yahoo Mail, Gmail, AOL Mail, iCloud mail, corporate Exchange mail, and any standard email account. Dude, if you want a more satisfying portable email machine than this one, buy a laptop.

This chapter covers the basic email experience. If you've gotten yourself hooked up with iCloud or Exchange ActiveSync, see Chapters 14 and 15 for details.

Setting Up Your Account

If you play your cards right, you won't **have** to set up your email account on the phone. The first time you set up the iPhone to sync with your computer (Chapter 13), you're offered the chance to **sync** your Mac's or PC's mail with the phone. That doesn't mean it copies actual messages—only the email settings, so the iPhone is ready to start downloading mail.

You're offered this option if your Mac's mail program is Mail or Outlook/Entourage, or if your PC's mail program is Outlook, Outlook Express, or Windows Mail.

But what if you don't use one of those email programs? No sweat. You can also plug the necessary settings right into the iPhone.

Free Email Accounts

If you have a free email account from Google, AOL, Outlook, or Yahoo; an iCloud account (Chapter 14); or a Microsoft Exchange account run by your employer (Chapter 15), then setup on the iPhone is easy.

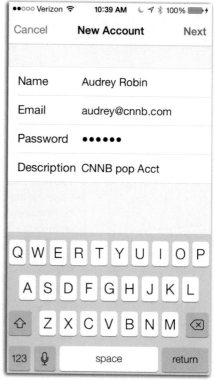

From the Home screen, tap Settings→Mail, Contacts, Calendars→Add Account. Tap the colorful logo that corresponds to the kind of account you have (Google, Yahoo, or whatever).

Now you land on the account-information screen. Tap into each of the blanks and, when the keyboard appears, type the requested info: for example, your name, email address, account password, and a description (that one's optional). Tap Next.

Now, depending on the kind of account you specified, you may be shown the list of non-email data that the iPhone can show you (from iCloud, Google, Yahoo, Exchange, and so on): Mail, Contacts, calendars, Reminders, and Notes. Turn off the ones you don't want synced to your phone, and then tap Save.

Your email account is ready to go!

 TIP: If you don't have one of these free accounts, they're worth having, if only as a backup to your regular account. They can help with spam filtering, too, since the iPhone doesn't offer any. To sign up, go to Google.com, Yahoo.com, AOL.com, or iCloud.com.

POP3 and IMAP Accounts

Those freebie, brand-name, Web-based accounts are super-easy to set up. But they're not the whole ball of wax. Millions of people have more generic email accounts, perhaps supplied by their employers or Internet providers. They're generally one of two types:

- **POP accounts** are the oldest, most compatible, and most common type on the Internet. (POP stands for Post Office Protocol, but this won't be on the test.) A POP account can make life complicated if you check your mail on more than one machine (say, a PC and an iPhone), as you'll discover shortly.

  A POP server transfers incoming mail to your computer (or iPhone) before you read it, which works fine as long as you're using *only that machine* to access your email.

- **IMAP accounts** (Internet Message Access Protocol) are newer and have more features than POP servers, and they're quickly putting POP out to pasture. IMAP servers keep all your mail online, rather than making you store it on your computer; as a result, you can access the same mail from any computer (or phone). IMAP servers remember which messages you've read and sent, and they even keep track of how you've filed messages into mail folders. (Those free Yahoo email accounts are IMAP accounts, and so are Apple's iCloud accounts and corporate Exchange accounts. Gmail accounts *can* be IMAP, too.)

TIP: The iPhone generally copies your IMAP messages onto the phone itself, so you can work on your email even when you're not online. You can, in fact, control where these messages are stored (in which mail folder). To see this, open Settings→Mail, Contacts, Calendars→[your IMAP account name]→[your IMAP account name again]→Advanced. See? You can specify where your drafts, sent messages, and deleted messages wind up on the phone.

The iPhone can communicate with both kinds of accounts, with varying degrees of completeness.

If you haven't opted to have your account-setup information transferred automatically to the iPhone from your Mac or PC, then you can set it up manually on the phone.

Tap your way to Settings→Mail, Contacts, Calendars→Add Account. Tap Other, tap Add Mail Account, and then enter your name, email address, password, and an optional description. Tap Next.

Apple's software attempts to figure out which kind of account you have (POP or IMAP) by the email address. If it can't make that determination, then you arrive at a second screen, where you're asked for such juicy details as the Host Name for Incoming and Outgoing Mail servers. (This is also where you tap either IMAP or POP, to tell the iPhone what sort of account it's dealing with.)

If you don't know this stuff offhand, you'll have to ask your Internet provider, corporate tech-support person, or next-door teenager to help you. When you're finished, tap Save.

To delete an account, open Settings→Mail, Contacts, Calendars→[account name]. At the bottom of the screen, you'll find the Delete Account button.

TIP: You can make, rename, or delete IMAP or Exchange mailboxes (mail folders) right on the phone.

View the mailbox list for the account and then tap Edit. Tap New Mailbox to create a new folder. To edit an existing mailbox, tap its name; you can then rename it, tap the Mailbox Location folder to move it, or tap Delete Mailbox. Tap Save to finish up.

Downloading Mail

If you have "push" email (Yahoo, iCloud, or Exchange), then your iPhone doesn't **check** for messages; new messages show up on your iPhone **as they arrive,** around the clock.

If you have any other kind of account, then the iPhone checks for new messages automatically on a schedule—every 15, 30, or 60 minutes. It also checks for new messages each time you open the Mail program, or whenever you **drag downward** on the Inbox list.

> **TIP:** There actually is a sneaky way to turn a Gmail account into a "push" account: Disguise it as an Exchange account. For complete steps, see the free PDF appendix to this chapter, "Setting Up Push Email for Gmail." It's on this book's "Missing CD" page at *www. missingmanuals.com*.

You can adjust the frequency of these automatic checks or turn off the "push" feature (because it uses up your battery faster) in Settings; see page 520.

When new mail arrives, you'll know it at a glance; all the Notification Center options work well in Mail. For example, if your phone is off, you can tap the Sleep or Home button to view the sender, subject, and the first line of the message right on the Lock screen. (Swipe across one, right there on the Lock screen, to jump to it in Mail.)

You'll also hear the iPhone's little "You've got mail" sound, unless you've turned that off in Settings.

If your phone is on, then a new message can alert you by appearing briefly at the top of the screen, without disturbing your work.

At the Home screen, Mail's icon sprouts a circled number that tells you how many new messages are waiting. If you have more than one email account, it shows you the **total** number of new messages, from all accounts.

If you routinely leave a lot of unread messages in your inbox, and so you don't really care about this "badge," you can turn it off. In fact, you can now turn it off on a per-account basis, which is great if one of your accounts is sort of a junk account that you keep as a spare. Tap Settings→Notification Center→Mail→[account name]→Badge App Icon.)

In any case, once you know you have mail, tap Mail on the Home screen to start reading it.

The Mail app, more than any other app, is designed to be a series of nested lists. You start out seeing a list of accounts; tap one to see a list of folders; tap one for a list of messages; tap one to open the actual message.

To **backtrack** through these lists, you can tap the button in the upper-left corner over and over again—or you can use the new iOS 7 technique: **swipe rightward** across the screen. That's a bigger target and more fun.

The Unified Inbox

If you have more than one email address, you're in luck. The iPhone offers a **unified inbox**—an option that displays all the incoming messages from all your accounts in a single place. (If you don't see it—if Mail opened up to some other screen—keep swiping rightward, backing up a screen at a time, until you do.)

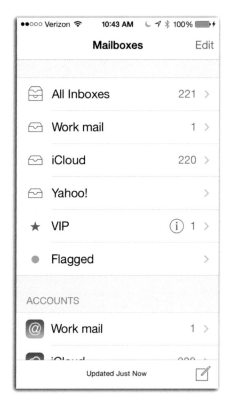

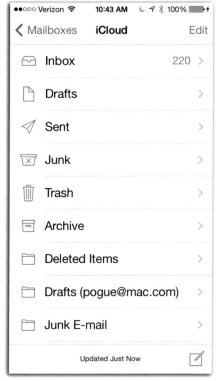

This Mailboxes page has two sections:

- **Unified inboxes (and other unified folders).** To see all the incoming messages in one unified box, tap All Inboxes. You can also view the inbox for any *individual* account in the top section (facing page, left).

  This part of the main Mail list also offers unified folders for VIPs and Flagged messages, which are described below.

  But what you may not realize is that, in iOS 7, you can add *other* unified folders to this section. You can, for example, add a folder called Unread, which contains only new messages from *all* accounts. (That's not the same thing as All Inboxes, because your inbox can contain messages you *have* read but haven't deleted or filed.)

  You can also add a unified folder showing all messages where you were either the To or CC addressee; this folder won't include any mail where your name appeared on the BCC (blind carbon-copy) line, like mailing lists and, often, spam.

  You can also add an Attachments folder here (messages with files attached), or unified folders that contain All Drafts, All Sent, or All Trash. ("All" means "from all accounts.")

  To hide or show these special uni-folders, tap Edit, then tap the selection circles beside the names of the folders you want to appear. (You can also take this opportunity to drag them up or down into a pleasing sequence.) Tap Done.

- **Accounts.** Farther down the Mailboxes screen, you see your accounts listed again. Tap one to view the traditional mail folders: Inbox, Drafts (emails written but not sent), Sent, Trash, and any folders you've created yourself (Family, Little League, Old Stuff, whatever), as shown on the facing page at right. If you have a Yahoo, iCloud, Exchange, or another IMAP account, then the iPhone automatically creates these folders to match what you've set up online.

NOTE: Not all kinds of email accounts permit the creation of your own filing folders, so you might not see anything but Inbox, Sent, and Trash.

The Message List—and Threading

If you tap an inbox's name, you wind up face to face with the list of incoming messages. At first, you see only the subject lines of your messages, plus, in light-gray type, the first few lines of their contents; that way, you can scan through new messages to see if there's anything important. You can flick upward to scroll this list. Blue dots indicate messages you haven't yet opened.

Each message bears a gray ⟩ at the right side. That means "Tap this message's row to read it in all its formatted glory."

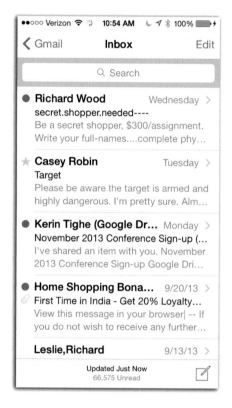
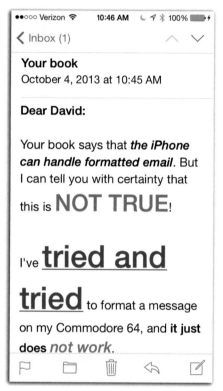

Here and there, though, you may spot a double arrow at the right side of the message list, like this: ⟩⟩ That means you're looking at some *threaded* messages. That's where several related messages—back-and-forths on the same subject—appear only once, in a single, consolidated Inbox entry. The idea is to reduce inbox clutter and to help you remember what people were talking about.

When you tap a threaded message, you first open an intermediate screen that lists the messages in the thread and tells you how many there are. Tap one of those to read, at last, the message itself.

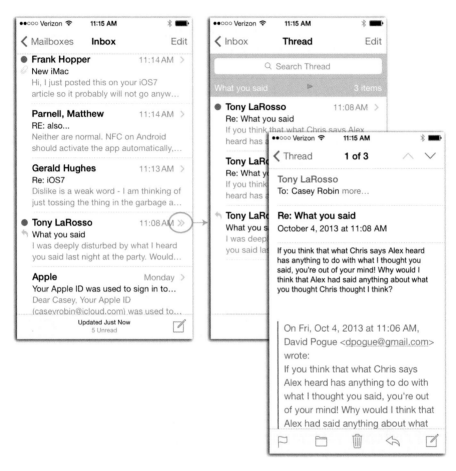

Of course, this also means that to return to the inbox, you have more back-tracking to do (swipe rightward twice).

In general, threading is a nice feature, even if, from time to time, it accidentally clumps in a message that has nothing to do with the others.

But if it bugs you, you can turn it off. Open Settings→Mail, Contacts, Calendars, scroll down, and turn off Organize By Thread.

VIPs and Flagged Messages

In the illustration on page 416, you might have noticed two "email accounts" that you didn't set up: VIP and Flagged. They're both intended to help you round up important messages from the thousands that flood you every day.

Each one magically rounds up messages from *all* of your account inboxes, so you don't have to go wading through lots of accounts to find the really important mail. (Note: That's *inboxes.* Messages in other mail folders don't wind up in these special inboxes, even if they're flagged or are from VIPs.)

VIPs

In the real world, VIPs are people who get backstage passes to concerts or special treatment at business functions (it stands for "very important person"). In iOS, it means "somebody whose mail is important enough that I want it brought to my attention immediately when it arrives."

So who should your VIPs be? That's up to you. Your spouse, your boss, and your doctor come to mind.

To designate someone as a VIP, proceed in either of these two ways:

- **On the accounts screen,** carefully tap the ⓘ next to the VIP item. Your master list of all VIPs appears (facing page, left). Tap Add VIP to choose a lucky new member from Contacts.

  This is also where you *delete* people from your VIP list when they've annoyed you. Swipe leftward across a name, and then tap Delete. Or tap Edit and then tap each ⊖ button; tap Delete to confirm.

- **In a message from the lucky individual,** tap his name in the From, To, or Cc/Bcc box. His Contact screen appears, complete with an Add to VIP button.

Once you've established who's important, lots of interesting things happen:

- The VIP inbox automatically collects messages from your VIPs.

- A gray star appears next to every VIP's name in every mail list.

- If you use iCloud, the same person is now a VIP on all your other iPhones and iPads (running iOS 6 or later) and Macs (running OS X Mountain Lion or later).

- Best of all, you can set things up so that when a new message from a VIP comes in, the iPhone lets you know. In **Settings→Notification Center→Mail→VIP**, specify how you want to be alerted: with a sound, a banner, an alert bubble, and so on.

TIP: In iOS 7, you can now hide the VIP inbox on the main Mailboxes screen—handy if you don't really use this feature. Tap **Edit**, and then tap the ✓ to turn it off. Tap **Done**.

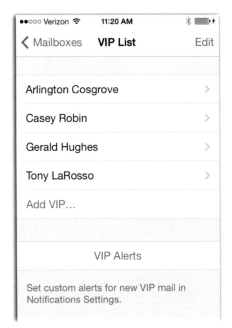

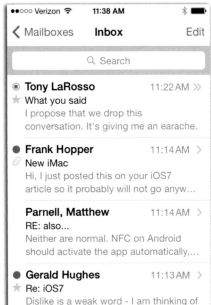

Flag It

Sometimes you receive email that prompts you to some sort of action, but you may not have the time (or the fortitude) to face the task at the moment. ("Hi there, it's me, your accountant. Would you mind rounding up your expenses for 1999 through 2013 and sending me a list by email?")

That's why Mail lets you *flag* a message, summoning a little flag icon or a little orange dot in a new column next to the message's name. (You can see the actual dot in the message below at right.) It can mean anything you like—it simply calls attention to certain messages.

To flag an open message, tap ⚑ at the bottom of the screen. When the confirmation sheet slides up (below, left), tap **Flag**.

You can also rapidly flag messages in a message list (the inbox, for example). Tap **Edit**, tap the little circles next to the messages you want to flag, tap **Mark**, and then tap **Flag**.

The dot or ⚑ icon appears in the body of the message, next to the message's name in your message list. (In the picture here at right, the top dot looks more like a bullseye; that's because it's flagged *and* unread.) The flat even appears on the corresponding message in your Mac or PC email program, thanks to the miracle of wireless syncing.

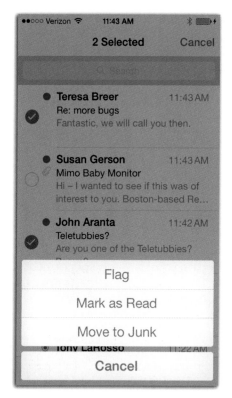
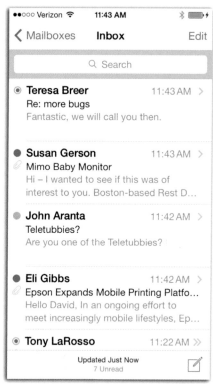

Finally, the Flagged mailbox appears in your list of accounts, making it easy to work with all flagged messages, from all accounts, in one place.

TIP: If you don't really use this feature, you can hide the Flagged folder. Tap **Edit**, and then tap the ● to turn it off. Tap **Done**.

What to Do with a Message

Once you've opened a message, you can respond to it, delete it, file it, and so on. Here's the drill.

 TIP: The following instructions show you how to process an *open* message (reply, forward, flag, delete, and so on). But you can also perform these tasks at the message *list,* before you've actually tapped a message to open it. Swipe leftward across a message's name; tap the weird little More button that appears. Up pops the master list of commands: Reply, Forward, Flag, Mark as Unread, Move, and so on.

Read It

The type size in email messages can be pretty small. Fortunately, you have some great iPhoney enlargement tricks at your disposal. For example:

- **Spread two fingers** to enlarge the entire email message.

- **Rotate the phone 90 degrees.** The text gets bigger.

- **Double-tap a narrow block of text** to make it fill the screen, if it doesn't already.

  Drag or flick your finger to scroll through or around the message.

- **Choose a larger type size for all messages**. See page 509 for details.

It's nice to note that links are "live" in email messages. Tap a phone number to call it, a Web address to open it, a YouTube link to watch the video, an email address to write to it, a time and date to add it to your calendar, and so on.

 TIP: If you're using a Gmail account—a great idea—then any message you send, reply to, delete, or file into a folder is reflected on the Web at Gmail.com. Whether deleting a message really deletes it (after 30 days) or adds it to Gmail's "archived" stash depends on the tweaky settings described at *http://tinyurl.com/yokd27*.

Reply to It

To answer a message, tap the **Reply/Forward** icon (◀) at the bottom of the screen; tap **Reply**. If the message was originally addressed to multiple recipients, then you can send your reply to everyone simultaneously by hitting **Reply All** instead.

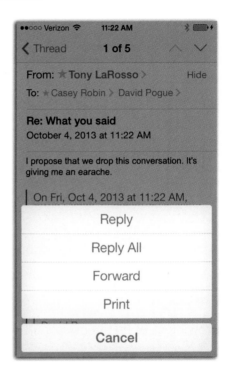

A new message window opens, already addressed. As a courtesy to your correspondents, Mail places the original message at the bottom of the window.

TIP: If you select some text before you tap, then the iPhone pastes only that selected bit into the new, outgoing message. In other words, you're quoting back only a portion—just the way it works on a full-sized computer.

At this point, you can add or delete recipients, edit the subject line or the original message, and so on. When you're finished, tap **Send**.

Use the Return key to create blank lines in the original message. (Use the loupe—page 54—to position the insertion point at the proper spot.)

Forward It

Instead of replying to the person who sent you a message, you may some-times want to pass the note on to a third person. To do so, tap ⤺. This time, tap **Forward**.

A new message opens, looking a lot like the one that appears when you reply. You may wish to precede the original message with a comment of your own, like, "Frank: I thought you'd be interested in this joke about your mom."

Finally, address and send it as you would any outgoing piece of mail.

Filing or Deleting One Message

Once you've opened a message that's worth keeping, you can file it into one of your mail account's folders ("mailboxes") by tapping the 🗂 at the bottom of the screen. Up pops the list of your folders; tap the one you want.

It's a snap to delete a message you no longer want, too. If it's open in front of you, simply tap the 🗑 or ⬚ button at the bottom of the screen. The message rapidly shrinks into the icon and disappears.

NOTE: If that one-touch Delete method makes you a little nervous, by the way, you can ask the iPhone to display a confirmation box before trashing the message forever. Visit **Settings→Mail, Contacts, Calendars→Ask Before Deleting**.

You can also delete a message from the message *list*—the inbox, for example. Just swipe your finger leftward across the message listing. (It doesn't have to be an especially broad swipe.) The red **Trash** button appears (bearing a number, if this is a threaded sequence of messages); tap it to confirm, or tap anywhere else if you change your mind.

TIP: Gmail doesn't want you to throw anything away. That's why swiping like this produces a button that says **Archive**, not **Delete**, and why the usual 🗑 button in a message looks like a filing box ⬚. If you prefer to delete a message for good, hold down the ⬚ until the **Delete** and **Archive** buttons appear. Or, to change the **Archive** button into a **Delete** button for good, tap **Settings→Mail, Contacts, Calendars→**[your Gmail account name]. Turn off **Archive Messages**.

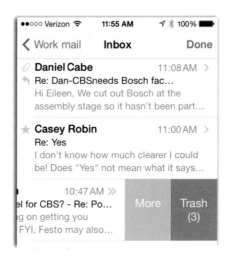

There's a long way to delete messages from the list, too, as described next. But for single messages, the finger-swipe method is *much* more fun.

Filing or Deleting Batches of Messages

You can also file or delete a bunch of messages at once. In the message list, tap **Edit**. A circle appears beside each message title. You can tap as many of these circles as you like, scrolling as necessary, adding a ✓ with each touch.

Finally, when you've selected all the messages in question, tap either **Trash (Archive)** or **Move**.

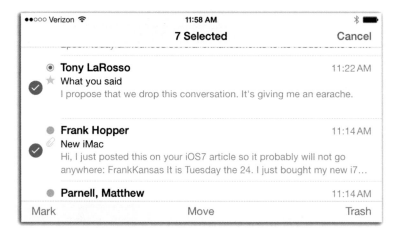

If you tap **Move**, you're shown the folder list so you can say where you want them moved. If you tap **Trash**, the messages disappear.

If you decide you've made a mistake, just shake the phone lightly—the iPhone's "Undo" gesture. Tap **Undo Move** to put the filed messages back where they just came from.

Add the Sender to Contacts

When you get a message from someone new who's worth adding to your iPhone's Contacts address book, tap that person's name (in blue, where it says "From"). You're offered buttons for **Create New Contact** and **Add to Existing Contact**. Use the second button to add an email address to an existing person's "card."

Open an Attachment

The Mail program downloads and displays the icons for *any* kind of attachment—but it can *open* only documents from Microsoft Office (Word, Excel, PowerPoint), those from Apple iWork (Pages, Keynote, Numbers), PDFs, text, RTFs, VCFs, graphics, .zip files, and un-copy-protected audio and video files.

Just scroll down, tap the attachment's icon, wait a moment for downloading, and then marvel as the document opens up, full screen. You can zoom in and out, flick, rotate the phone 90 degrees, and scroll just as though it were a Web page or a photo.

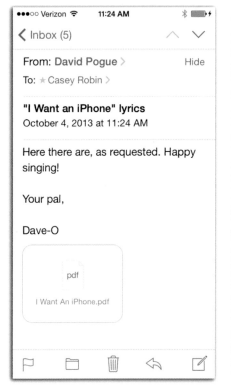

When you're finished admiring the attachment, swipe rightward to return to the original email message.

Snagging (or Sending) a Graphic

One of the great joys of iPhone mail is its ability to display graphics that the sender embedded right in the message. If you get sent a particularly good picture, just hold your finger still on it. You're offered the Save sheet, filled with options like Save (into your Photo app's Camera Roll), Copy, Print, and Assign to Contact (as a person's face photo). All the usual sending methods are represented here, too, so that you can fire off this photo via AirDrop, Messages, Mail, Twitter, and Facebook.

View the To/From Details

When your computer's screen measures only 4 inches diagonally, there's not a lot of extra space. So Apple designed Mail to conceal header details (To, From, and so on) that you might need only occasionally. For example, you usually don't actually see the word "From:"—you usually see only the sender's name, in blue. The To and Cc lines may show only first names, to save space. (The on/off switch for that feature is in Settings→Mail→Short Names.) And if there's a long list of addresses, you may see only "Michael (& 15 more)"—not the actual list of names.

You get last names, full lists, and full sender labels when you tap **More** following the header information.

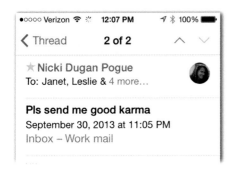 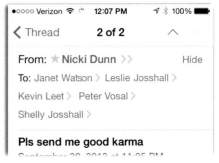

Tap **Hide** to collapse these details.

> **TIP:** When you tap a sender's name in blue, you open the corresponding info card in Contacts. It contains one-touch buttons for calling someone back, sending a text message, or placing a FaceTime audio or video call—which can be very handy if the email message you just received is urgent.

Mark as Unread

In the inbox, any message you haven't yet read is marked by a blue dot (●). Once you've opened the message, the blue dot goes away.

By tapping ⚑ and then **Mark as Unread**, you make that blue dot *reappear.* It's a great way to flag a message for later, to call it to your own attention. The blue dot can mean not so much "unread" as "un–dealt with."

Move On

Once you've had a good look at a message and processed it to your satisfaction, you can move on to the next (or previous) message in the list by tapping ∧ or ∨ in the upper-right corner.

Or you can swipe rightward to return to the inbox (or whatever mailbox you're in).

Searching

Praise be—there's a search box in Mail. The search box is hiding *above* the top of every mail list, like your inbox. To see it, scroll up, or just tap the status strip at the top of the screen.

Tap inside the search box to make the keyboard appear. As you type, Mail hides all but the matching messages; tap any one of the results to open it.

You'll quickly discover that search is finally fixed in iOS 7; it's been drastically improved:

- You no longer have to specify *which fields* to search (From, To, Subject, Body). You're searching everywhere.

- You no longer have to specify which *folder* to search (Inbox, Trash, and so on). You're searching everywhere.

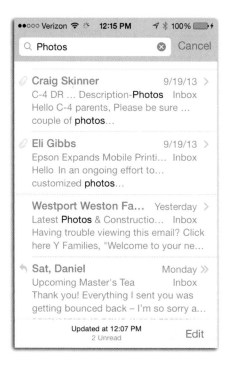

- The baffling "Continue on server" button is gone. Now search works exactly like you'd expect.

In iOS 7, the iPhone searches the From, To, Subject, and body fields simultaneously. Wait long enough, and the search continues with messages that are still out there on the Internet but are so old that they've scrolled off your phone.

TIP: If, after typing a few letters, you tap **Search**, the keyboard goes away and an **Edit** button appears. Tapping it lets you select a whole bunch of the search results—and then delete or file them simultaneously.

Writing Messages

To compose a new piece of outgoing mail, open the Mail app, and then tap ☑ in the lower-right corner. A blank new outgoing message appears, and the iPhone keyboard pops up.

TIP: Remember: You can turn the phone 90 degrees to get a widescreen keyboard for email. It's easier to type this way. Of course, dictating is much, *much* faster than typing.

Here's how you go about writing a message:

1. **In the To field, type the recipient's email address—or grab it from Contacts.** Often, you won't have to type much more than the first couple of letters of the name *or* email address. As you type, Mail displays all matching names and addresses so you can tap one instead of typing. (It thoughtfully derives these suggestions by analyzing both your Contacts *and* people you've recently exchanged email with.)

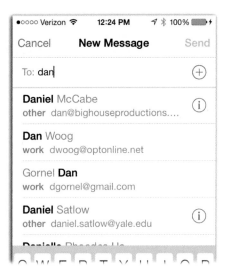

As you type into the To box, the iPhone displays a list of everyone whose name matches what you're typing. The ones bearing ⓘ buttons are the people you've recently corresponded with but who are not in your Contacts. Tap the ⓘ to open a screen where you can add them to Contacts—or *remove* them from the list of recent correspondents, so Mail's autocomplete suggestions will no longer include those lowlifes.

If you hold your finger down on the period (.) key, you get a pop-up palette of common email-address suffixes, like .com, .edu, .org, and so on.

Alternatively, tap the ⊕ button to open your Contacts list. Tap the name of the person you want.

You can add as many addressees as you like; just repeat the procedure.

There's no Group mail feature on the iPhone, which would let you send one message to a predefined set of friends. But at *http://groups.yahoo.com*, you can create free email groups. You can send a single email message to the group's address, and everyone in the group will get a copy. (You have to set up one of these groups in a Web browser—but lo and behold, your iPhone has one!)

Incidentally, if you've set up your iPhone to connect to a corporate Exchange server (Chapter 15), then you can look up anybody in the entire company directory at this point. Page 492 has the instructions.

2. **To send a copy to other recipients, enter the address(es) in the Cc or Bcc fields.** If you tap Cc/Bcc, From, the screen expands to reveal two new lines beneath the To line: Cc and Bcc.

Cc stands for *carbon copy.* Getting an email message where your name is in the Cc line implies: "I sent you a copy because I thought you'd want to know about this correspondence, but I'm not expecting you to reply."

Bcc stands for *blind carbon copy.* It's a copy that goes to a third party secretly—the primary addressee never knows who else you sent it to. For example, if you send your coworker a message that says, "Chris, it bothers me that you've been cheating the customers," you could Bcc your supervisor to clue her in without getting into trouble with Chris.

Each of these lines behaves exactly like the To line. You fill each one up with email addresses in the same way.

TIP: You can drag people's names around—from the To line to the Cc line, for example. Just hold your finger down briefly on the name before dragging it. (It puffs and darkens once it's ready for transit.)

3. **Change the email account you're using, if you like.** If you have more than one email account set up on your iPhone, you can tap **Cc/Bcc, From** to expand the form and then tap **From** to open up a spinning list of your accounts. Tap the one you want to use for sending this message.

4. **Type the topic of the message in the Subject field.** It's courteous to put some thought into the subject line. (Use "Change in plans for next week," for instance, instead of "Yo.") Leaving it blank only annoys your recipient. On the other hand, don't put the *entire* message into the subject line, either.

5. **Type your message in the message box.** All the usual iPhone keyboard and dictation tricks apply (Chapters 2 and 4). Don't forget that you can use Copy and Paste, within Mail or from other programs. Both text and graphics can appear in your message.

6. **Attach a photo or video,** if you like. Hold down your finger anywhere in the body of the message until the **Select** buttons appear. Tap the ▶ button to reveal the **Insert Photo or Video** button (bottom left).

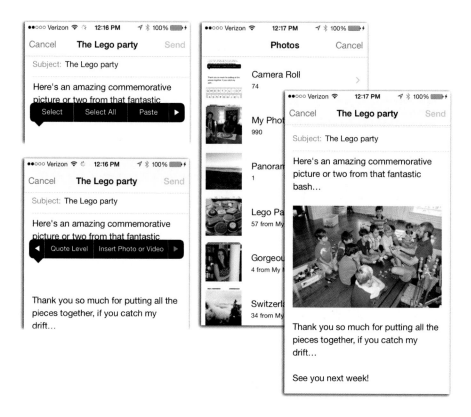

When you tap it, you're shown your iPhone's usual photo browser so that you can choose the photos and videos you want to attach (middle). Tap the collection you want; you're shown all the thumbnails inside. Tap the photo or video, and then tap **Choose**.

You return to your message in progress, with the photo or video neatly inserted (above, right). You can repeat this step to add additional photo or video attachments. When you tap **Send**, you're offered the opportunity to scale down the photo to a more reasonable email-able size.

7. **Format the text,** if you like. You can apply bold, italic, or underlining to mail text you've typed.

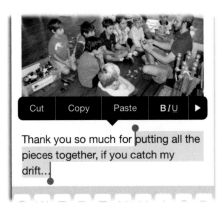 

The trick is to select the text first (page 65). When the button bar appears, tap the **B I U** button. Tap that to make the **Bold**, **Italics**, and **Underline** buttons appear on the button bar; tap away. Not terribly efficient, but it works.

8. **Tap Send (to send the message) or Cancel (to back out of it).** If you tap **Cancel**, the iPhone asks if you want to save the message. If you tap **Save Draft**, then the message lands in your Drafts folder.

Later, you can open the Drafts folder, tap the aborted message, finish it up, and send it.

> **TIP:** If you **hold down** the button for a moment, the iPhone presents a list of your saved drafts. Clever stuff—if you remember it!

Signatures

A *signature* is a bit of text that gets stamped at the bottom of your outgoing email messages. It can be your name, a postal address, or a pithy quote.

Unless you intervene, the iPhone stamps "Sent from my iPhone" at the bottom of every message. You may be just fine with that, or you may consider it the equivalent of gloating (or free advertising for Apple). In any case, you can change the signature if you want to.

From the Home screen, tap Settings→Mail, Contacts, Calendars→ Signature. You can make up one signature for All Accounts, or a different one for each account (tap Per Account). A Signature text area appears, complete with a keyboard, so you can compose the signature you want.

> **TIP:** You can use bold, italic, or underline formatting in your signature, too. Just follow the steps on the previous page for formatting a message: Select the text, tap the ▶ to bring the B I U button into view, and so on.

Surviving Email Overload

If you don't get much mail, you probably aren't lying awake at night trying to think of ways to manage so much information overload on your tiny phone.

If you do get a lot of mail, here are some tips.

Avoiding Spam

The key to keeping spam (junk mail) out of your inbox is to keep your email address out of spammers' hands in the first place. Use one address for actual communication. Use a different address in the public areas of the Internet, like chat room posting, online shopping, Web site and software registration, and newsgroup posting. Spammers use automated software robots that scour these pages, recording email addresses they find. Create a separate email account for person-to-person email—and *never* post that address on a Web page.

If it's too late, and you're getting a lot of spam on your phone, you have a couple of options. You could accept your fate and set up a new email account (like a free Gmail or Yahoo account), sacrificing your old one to the spammers.

You could install a spam blocker app on your phone, like SpamDrain ($15 a year) or SpamBlocker (free).

Or, if you're technically inclined, you could create a shadow Gmail account that downloads your mail, cleans it of spam, and then passes it on to your iPhone. You can find tutorials for this trick by searching in, of course, Google.

Condensing the Message List

Messages in your inbox are listed with the subject line in bold type *and* a couple of lines, in light-gray text, that preview the message itself.

You can control how many lines of the preview show up here, from None (you see more message titles on each screen without scrolling) to 5 Lines. Tap Settings→Mail, Contacts, Calendars→Preview.

Spotting Worthwhile Messages

The iPhone can display a little **To** or **Cc** logo on each message in your inbox. At a glance, it helps you identify which messages are actually intended for *you.* Messages without those logos are probably spam, newsletters, mailing lists, or other messages that weren't specifically addressed to you.

To turn on these little badges, visit Settings→Mail, Contacts, Calendars and turn on Show To/Cc Label.

Managing Accounts

If you have more than one email account, you can delete one or just temporarily deactivate one—for example, to accommodate your travel schedule.

Visit Settings→Mail, Contacts, Calendars. In the list of accounts, tap the one you want. At the top of the screen, you see the On/Off switch (at least for POP accounts); Off makes an account dormant. And at the bottom, you see the Delete Account button.

> **TIP:** If you have several accounts, which one does the iPhone use when you send mail from other apps—like when you email a photo from Photos or a link from Safari?
>
> It uses the *default* account, of course. You determine which one is the default account in Settings→Mail, Contacts, Calendars→Default Account.

13

Syncing with iTunes

Just in case you're one of the six people out there who've never heard of it, iTunes is Apple's multifunction, multimedia jukebox software. It's been loading music onto iPods since the turn of the 21st century.

Most people use iTunes to manipulate their digital movies, photos, and music, from converting songs off a CD into iPhone-ready music files to buying songs, audiobooks, and movies online.

But as an iPhone owner, you need iTunes even more urgently, because it's the most efficient way to get masses of music, videos, apps, email, addresses, appointments, ringtones, and other stuff *onto* the phone. It also backs up your iPhone automatically.

If you've never had a copy of iTunes on your computer, then fire up your Web browser and go to *www.apple.com/itunes/download*. Once the file lands on your computer, double-click the installer icon and follow the onscreen instructions to add iTunes to your life.

This chapter gives you a crash course in iTunes and tells you how to sync it with your iPhone.

TIP: Technically, iTunes is not *required.* It's perfectly possible to use all of an iPhone's features without even owning a computer. You can download all that stuff—music, movies, apps—right from the Internet, and you can back up your phone using iCloud (described in the next chapter).

Using iTunes, however, is still more efficient, and it's nice to know your stuff is backed up on a machine that's within your control. Besides: You can keep using your iPhone even while it's syncing—a very nice perk.

The Three Faces of iTunes

The first thing to understand is that iTunes is three apps in one. It's designed to be the viewer for all the music, videos, apps, and ebooks in three places: (1) on your computer, (2) on your phone, and (3) in Apple's online store.

The button at top right lets you choose either **Library** (what's on your computer) or **iTunes Store**. When your iPhone is connected, it has a button of its own right next to the **Library** button.

TIP   The **Library** button is also a pop-up menu. From it, you can jump directly to the lists of Movies, Music, TV Shows, and other categories on your computer. You can also view the lists of stuff you've bought, either on your iPhone or your computer.

The playback and volume controls, which work just as they do on the iPhone, are at the top-left corner of iTunes. At the upper-right corner is a search box that lets you pluck one track out of a haystack.

The following pages take you through the three worlds—computer, store, iPhone—one by one.

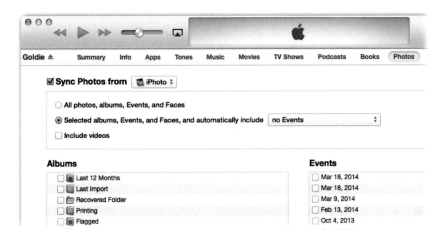

Library

The library is "all the music, videos, apps, and ebooks that you've down-loaded to your Mac or PC." To see it, click Library at the upper-right corner of iTunes. (If that button says iTunes Store instead, you're already *seeing* your library.)

At this point, you're supposed to drill down to the material you want to manage or play:

1. **Use the pop-up button at the top-left side of iTunes** to specify what *kind* of file you want to look at: Music, Movies, or whatever.

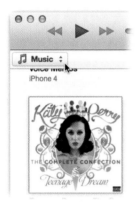

2. **Use the buttons across the top** to further isolate or sort what you're after. For example, if you chose Music in step 1, your options are Songs, Albums, Artists, Genres, Playlists, Radio, Internet, and Match. If you choose Movies, the options are Unwatched, Movies, Genres, Home Videos, and List. You get the idea.

    When you click one of these headings, the contents appear in the center part of the iTunes window. You may see wildly different things here, depending on what you clicked. For example, if you click Songs, you see a huge alphabetical list; if you click Albums, you see a square grid of album covers.

Three Ways to Fill Your Library

Once you have iTunes, the next step is to start filling it with music and video so you can get all that goodness onto your iPhone. iTunes gives you at least three options right off the bat.

- **Let iTunes find your files.** If you've had a computer for longer than a few days, you probably already have some songs in the popular MP3 format on your hard drive, perhaps from a file-sharing service or a free music Web site. If so, then the first time you open iTunes, it offers to search your PC or Mac for music and add it to its library. Click Yes; iTunes goes hunting around your hard drive.

> **TIP:** If you use Windows, you may have songs in the Windows Media Audio (WMA) format. Unfortunately, iTunes and the iPhone can't play WMA files. But when iTunes finds nonprotected WMA files, it offers to convert them automatically to a format that it *does* understand. That's a convenient assurance that your old music files will play on your new toy. (iTunes/iPhone can *not,* however, convert *copy-protected* WMA files like those sold by some music services.)

- **Visit the iTunes Store.** Another way to feed your iPhone is to shop at the iTunes Store, as described in the next section.

- **Import music from a CD.** iTunes can also convert tracks from audio CDs into iPhone-ready digital music files. Just start up iTunes and then stick a CD into your computer's CD drive. The program asks if you want to convert the songs to audio files for iTunes. (If it doesn't ask, click Import CD at the bottom of the window.)

  If you're connected to the Internet, the program automatically downloads song titles and artist information from the CD and begins to add the songs to the iTunes library.

  If you want time to think about which songs you want from each CD, then you can tell iTunes to download only the song *titles,* and then give you a few minutes to ponder your selections. To do that, choose iTunes→Preferences→General (Mac) or Edit→Preferences→General (Windows). Use the When you insert a CD pop-up menu to choose Show CD.

  From now on, if you don't want the entire album, you can exclude the dud songs by turning off their checkmarks. Then click Import CD.

> **TIP:** If you always want *all* the songs on that stack of CDs next to your computer, then change the iTunes CD import preferences to Import CD and Eject to save yourself some clicking. When you insert a CD, iTunes imports it and spits it out, ready for the next one.

In that same Preferences box, you can also click Import Settings to choose the *format* (file type) and *bit rate* (amount of audio data compressed into that format) for your imported tracks. The factory setting is the AAC format at 128 kilobits per second.

Most people think these settings make for fine-sounding music files, but you can change your settings to, for example, MP3, which is another format that lets you cram big music into a small space. Upping the bit rate from 128 to 256 kbps makes for richer-sounding music files—which also happen to take up more room because the files are bigger (and the iPhone's "hard drive" doesn't hold as much as your computer's). The choice is yours.

Once the importing is finished, each imported song bears a green checkmark, and you have some brand-new files in your iTunes library.

Playlists

A *playlist* is a list of songs you've decided should go together. It can be any group of songs arranged in any order, all according to your whims. For example, if you're having a party, you can make a playlist from the current Top 40 and dance music in your music library. Some people may question your taste if you, say, alternate tracks from *La Bohème* with Queen's *A Night at the Opera,* but hey—it's your playlist.

To create a playlist in iTunes, press ⌘-N (Mac) or Ctrl+N (Windows). Or choose File→New→Playlist.

TIP: You can also create playlists right on the phone; see page 192.

A freshly minted playlist starts out with the impersonal name "Playlist." Just type a better name: "Cardio Workout," "Shoe-Shopping Tunes," "Hits of the Highland Lute," or whatever you want to call it. But don't click Done yet.

Now you can add your songs or videos. The quickest way is to drag their names directly onto the playlist's icon. Use any of the buttons across the top—Songs, Albums, Artists, whatever—to find the songs; then drag their names into the empty Playlist column at the right side.

TIP: Instead of making an empty playlist and then dragging songs into it, you can work the other way. You can scroll through a big list of songs, selecting tracks as you go by ⌘-clicking (on the Mac) or Ctrl-clicking (in Windows)—and then, when you're finished, choose File→New→Playlist From Selection. All the songs you selected immediately appear on a brand-new playlist.

When you drag a song title onto a playlist, you're not making a copy of the song. In essence, you're creating an *alias* or *shortcut* of the original, which means you can have the same song on several different playlists.

iTunes even starts you out with some playlists of its own devising, like "Top 25 Most Played" and "Purchased" (a convenient place to find all your iTunes Store goodies listed in one place). To see all your playlists, make sure you're viewing your library, and your music; click Playlists at the top.

Editing and Deleting Playlists

A playlist is easy to change. Here's what you can do with just a little light mousework. Start by making sure you're viewing your library, and your music, and you've clicked Playlists at the top:

- **Change the order of songs in the playlist.** Drag song titles up or down within the playlist window to reorder them.

- **Add new songs to the playlist.** Click Add To (upper right), and then tiptoe through your iTunes library and drag more songs into a playlist.

- **Delete songs from the playlist.** If your playlist needs pruning, or that banjo tune just doesn't fit in with the brass-band tracks, you can ditch it quickly: Click the song in the playlist window and then hit Delete or Backspace to get rid of it. When iTunes asks you to confirm your decision, click Remove.

Deleting a song from a playlist doesn't delete it from your music library—it just removes the title from your *playlist.*

- **Delete the whole playlist.** To delete an entire playlist, click its name in the list of playlists (far left) and then press Delete (Backspace). Again, this zaps only the playlist itself, not all the songs you had in it. (Those are still in your computer's iTunes folder.)

iTunes Store

The iTunes software's second purpose is to be the face of Apple's online iTunes Store. (From your library, click iTunes Store at upper right).

Once you land on the store's main page and set up your iTunes account, you can buy and download songs, audiobooks, ebooks, apps, and videos. This material goes straight into your iTunes library, just a sync away from the iPhone.

Your iPhone, of course, can also get to the iTunes Store, wirelessly; just tap that purple iTunes icon on the Home screen. Any songs you buy on the phone get copied back to iTunes the next time you sync.

To navigate the iTunes Store, click the buttons across the top strip: Music, Movies, TV Shows, App Store, Books, Podcasts, and iTunes U.

Music

Ah, here it is, the store that made Apple a powerhouse in the music industry: the Music store. Here are millions of songs, individually downloadable, all without copy protection, for 79 cents, $1, or $1.29, depending on how popular they are.

There are all kinds of ways to slice, dice, and search this catalog:

- **Use the Music button.** At the top of the screen, that Music button is actually a pop-up menu. Use it to choose a category or genre, like Free on iTunes (free songs!), Recent Releases, Blues, Metal, and so on.

- **Search.** Use the search box (top right) to find a song by name, album name, band, composer, and so on.

- **Scroll down.** The various buttons on the front page of the Music Store represent music Apple thinks you might like: new releases, big hits, Genius recommendations (songs Apple thinks you'll like based on an analysis of what's already in your library), and so on.

- **Bestseller lists.** Down the right side of the window, you see lists of the top-selling songs and albums. A handy way to see what the rest of your fellow music lovers are buying, if you don't mind being a sheep.

Learning these tools for finding songs is handy, because the same tools are available for finding TV shows, movies, podcasts, audiobooks, and so on.

TV, Movies, and Movie Rentals

The iTunes store also offers an increasingly vast selection of downloadable TV episodes ($2 apiece, no ads) and movies (some you can buy for $10 to $20, others you buy *or* rent for $3 to $56).

Once you rent a movie, you have 30 days to start watching—and once you start, you have 24 hours to finish before it turns into a pumpkin (actually, it deletes itself from your computer and phone).

You can do your renting and buying in two ways. First, you can use the iTunes software on your Mac or PC and then sync it to the iPhone by following the steps later in this chapter.

Second, you can download videos straight to the phone when you're in a WiFi hotspot. (The difference: If you download a rental movie to your phone, you can't move it to any other gadget. If you download it to iTunes, you can move it from computer to phone to iPad, or whatever, although it can exist on only one machine at a time.)

Podcasts

Not everything in the iTunes Store costs money. In addition to free iPhone apps, there are plenty of free audio and video podcasts, suitable for your iPhone, in the **Podcasts** area of the store.

Podcasts are free audio (and video!) recordings put out by everyone from big TV networks to a guy in his barn with a microphone.

To explore podcasts, click the **Podcasts** tab at the top of the store's window.

Many podcasters produce regular installments of their shows, releasing new episodes onto the Internet when they're ready. You can have iTunes keep a look out for fresh editions of your favorite podcasts and automatically download them for you, where you can find them in the Podcasts area in the iTunes Source list. All you have to do is *subscribe* to the podcast, which takes a couple of clicks in the store.

If you want to try out a podcast, click the price button (**Free**) near its title to download just that one show. If you like it (or know that you're going to like it before you even download the first episode), then there's also a Subscribe button that signs you up to receive all future episodes.

You play a podcast just like any other file in iTunes: Double-click the file name in the iTunes window and use the playback controls in the upper-left corner. On the iPhone, podcasts show up in their own list—or in their own app, if you've download Apple's free Podcasts app.

App Store

See Chapter 8 for details on grabbing iPhone apps, using your computer as a loading dock.

Books

Some people like to curl up with—or listen to—a good book, and iTunes has plenty to offer, both as ebooks (which you read in the iBooks app) and as audiobooks (which you listen to as you work in the garden or drive). (To find the audiobooks, use the Books pop-up menu at the top of the screen.)

If iTunes doesn't offer the audiobook you're interested in, you can find a larger collection (over 50,000 of them) at Audible.com. This Web store sells all kinds of audiobooks, plus recorded periodicals like *The New York Times* and radio shows. To purchase Audible's wares, though, you need to go to the Web site and create an Audible account.

If you use Windows, then you can download from Audible.com a little program called Audible Download Manager, which catapults your Audible downloads into iTunes for you. On the Mac, Audible files land in iTunes automatically when you buy them.

iTunes U

Here, for your personal-growth pleasure, are hundreds of thousands of downloadable college courses, all of them free and many of them amazing. Watch the videos of the professors, follow along with the reading materials. You won't actually earn a college degree this way, but you **will** attain a degree of enlightenment.

Authorizing Computers

All movies and TV shows, and some old music files, are still copy-protected.

When you create an account in iTunes, you automatically **authorize** that computer to play copy-protected songs from the iTunes Store. Authorization is Apple's way of making sure you don't go playing those music tracks on more than five computers, which would greatly displease the movie studios.

You can copy those songs and videos onto a maximum of four other computers. To authorize each one to play music from your account, choose Store→Authorize Computer. (Don't worry; you have to do this just once per machine.)

When you've maxed out your limit and can't authorize any more computers, you may need to **deauthorize** one. On the computer you wish to demote, choose Store→Deauthorize Computer.

Syncing the iPhone

The third and final function of iTunes is to load up, and back up, your iPhone. You can connect it to your computer either wirelessly, over WiFi, or wirefully, with the white USB cable that came with it.

Once the phone is connected, click the iPhone button at the top-right corner of the iTunes screen. (That button doesn't appear when you're in the store. In that case, click Library first.) Now you can look over the iPhone's contents or sync it (read on).

> **NOTE:** If you have more than one iPhone, and they're all connected, this button is a pop-up menu. Choose the name of the one you want to manipulate.

Connecting the Phone with a Cable

Pretty simple: Plug one end of the white cable (supplied with your iPhone) to your computer's USB jack. Connect the other end to the phone. If the phone is turned on and awake, it's officially connected.

Connecting over WiFi

The familiar white USB cable is all well and good—but the phone is a wireless device, for Pete's sake. Why not sync it to your computer wirelessly?

The phone can be charging in its bedside alarm clock dock, happily and automatically syncing with your laptop somewhere else in the house. It transfers all the same stuff to and from your computer—apps, music, books, contacts, calendars, movies, photos, ringtones—but through the air instead of via your USB cable.

Your computer has to be turned on and running iTunes. The phone and the computer have to be on the same WiFi network.

To set up wireless sync, connect the phone using the white USB cable, one last time. Ironic, but true.

Now open iTunes and click the iPhone button at top right. On the Summary tab, scroll down; turn on Sync with this iPhone over Wi-Fi. Click Apply. You can now detach the phone.

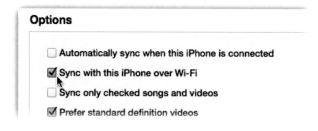

From now on, whenever the phone is on the WiFi network, it's automatically connected to your computer, wirelessly. You don't even have to think about it. (Well, OK—you have to think about leaving the computer turned on with iTunes open, which is something of a buzzkill.)

Just *connecting* it doesn't necessarily mean *syncing* it, though; that's a more data-intensive, battery-drainy process. Syncing happens in either of two ways:

- **Automatically.** If the phone is plugged into power (like a speaker dock, an alarm-clock dock, or a wall outlet), and it's on the same WiFi network, it syncs with the computer all by itself.

- **Manually.** You can also trigger a sync manually—and this time, the iPhone doesn't have to be plugged into power. To do that, open Settings→General→iTunes Wi-Fi Sync and tap Sync Now. (You can also trigger a WiFi sync from within iTunes—just click the Sync button. It says "Sync" only if, in fact, anything has changed since your last sync.)

All About Syncing

Transferring data between the iPhone and the computer is called *synchronization.* In general, syncing begins automatically when you connect the phone. The ↻ icon whirls in the top left corner of the screen, but you're welcome to keep using your iPhone while it syncs.

NOTE: Your photo-editing program (like iPhoto or Photoshop Elements) probably springs open every time you connect the iPhone, too. See page 468 if that bugs you.

Now, ordinarily, the iPhone-iTunes relationship is automatic and complete, according to this scheme:

- **Bidirectional copying (iPhone <-> computer).** Contacts, calendars, and Web bookmarks get copied in both directions. That is, after a sync, your computer and phone contain exactly the same information.

  So if you entered an appointment on the iPhone, it gets copied to your computer—and vice versa. If you edited the same contact or appointment on both machines at once while they were apart, then your computer displays the two conflicting records and asks you which one "wins."

- **One-way sync (computer→iPhone).** Music, apps, TV, movies, ringtones, and ebooks you bought on your computer; photos from your computer; and email account information. All of this gets copied in one direction: computer→phone.

- **One-way sync (iPhone→computer).** Photos and videos taken with the iPhone's camera; music, videos, apps, ringtones, and ebooks you bought right from the phone—it all gets copied the other way, from the phone to the computer.

- **A complete backup.** iTunes also takes it upon itself to back up *everything else* on your iPhone: settings, text messages, call history, and so on. Details on this backup business are covered at the end of this chapter.

> **TIP:** If you're in a hurry, you can skip the time-consuming backup portion of the sync. Just click the ✖ at the top of the iTunes window whenever it says "Backing up." iTunes gets the message and skips right ahead to the next phase of the sync—transferring contacts, calendars, music, and so on.

Manual Syncing

OK, but what if you don't *want* iTunes to fire up and start syncing every time you connect your iPhone? What if, for example, you want to change the assortment of music and video that's about to get copied to it? Or what if you just want to connect the USB cable to charge the phone, not to sync it?

In that case, you can stop the autosyncing in any of three ways:

- **Interrupt a sync in progress.** Click the ✖ button in the iTunes status window until the syncing stops.

- **Stop iTunes from syncing with the iPhone just this time.** As you plug in the iPhone's cable, hold down the Shift+Ctrl keys (Windows) or the ⌘-Option keys (Mac) until the iPhone pops up in the iTunes window. Now you can see what's on the iPhone and change what will be synced to it—but no syncing takes place until you command it.

- **Stop iTunes from auto-syncing with this iPhone.** Connect the iPhone. Click iPhone in the upper-right corner of iTunes. On the Summary tab, turn off Automatically sync when this iPhone is connected (shown in the previous illustration).

- **Stop iTunes from autosyncing any iPhone, ever.** In iTunes, choose Edit→Preferences (Windows) or iTunes→Preferences (Mac). Click the Devices tab and turn on Prevent iPods, iPhones, and iPads from syncing automatically. You can still trigger a sync on command when the iPhone is wired up—by clicking the Sync button.

Once you've made iTunes stop syncing automatically, you've disabled what many people consider the greatest feature of the iPhone: its magical self-updating with the stuff on your computer.

Still, you must have turned off autosyncing for a reason. And that reason might be that you want to control what gets copied onto it. Maybe you're in a hurry to leave for the airport, and you don't have time to sit there for an hour while six downloaded movies get copied to the phone. Maybe you have 50 gigabytes of music but only 16 gigs of iPhone storage.

In any case, here are the two ways you can sync manually:

- **Use the tabs in iTunes.** With the iPhone connected, you can specify exactly what you want copied to it—which songs, which TV shows, which apps, and so on—using the various tabs in iTunes, as described on the following pages. Once you've made your selections, click the Summary tab and then click Apply. (The Apply button says Sync instead if you haven't actually changed any settings.)

- **Drag files onto the iPhone icon.** Once your iPhone is connected to your computer, you can click its icon and then turn on **Manually manage music and videos** (on the Summary screen). Click Apply.

Now you can drag songs and videos directly onto the iPhone's icon to copy them there. Wilder yet, you can bypass iTunes *entirely* by dragging music and video files *from your computer's desktop* onto the iPhone's icon. That's handy when you've just inherited or downloaded a bunch of song files, converted a DVD to the iPhone's video format, or whatever.

Just two notes of warning here. First, unlike a true iPod, the iPhone accommodates dragged material from a *single* computer only. Second, if you ever turn off this option, all those manually dragged songs and videos will disappear from your iPhone at the next sync opportunity.

TIP: Also on the Summary tab, you'll find the baffling little option called Sync only checked songs and videos. This is a global override—a last-ditch "keep the embarrassing songs off my iPhone" option.

When this option is turned on, iTunes consults the tiny checkboxes next to every single song and video in your iTunes library. If you turn off a song's checkbox, it will not get synced to your iPhone, no matter what—even if you use the Music tab to sync All songs or playlists, or explicitly turn on a playlist that contains this song. If the song's or video's checkbox isn't checked in your Library list, then it will be left behind on your computer.

iTunes Tabs

Once your iPhone is connected to the computer, and you've clicked its name in the upper-right corner of iTunes, the top of the iTunes window reveals a horizontal row of word buttons: Summary, Info, Apps, Tones, Music, Movies, TV Shows, Podcasts, Books, Photos, and On This iPhone. For the most part, these represent the categories of stuff you can sync to your iPhone.

The following pages cover each of these tabs, in sequence, and detail how to sync each kind of iPhone-friendly material.

TIP: At the bottom of the screen, a colorful graph shows you the amount and types of files: Audio, Video, Photos, Apps, Books, Documents & Data, and Other (for your personal data). More importantly, it also shows you how much room you have left, so you won't get overzealous in trying to load the thing up.

Point to each color block without clicking to see how many of each item there are ("2031 photos") and how much space they take.

Summary Tab

This screen gives basic stats on your iPhone, like its serial number, capacity, and phone number. Buttons in the middle control how and where the iPhone gets backed up. Checkboxes at the bottom of the screen let you set up manual syncing, as described previously.

> **TIP:** If you click your phone's serial number, it changes to reveal the *unique device identifier* (UDID). That's Apple's behind-the-scenes ID for your exact product, used primarily by software companies (developers). You may, during times of beta testing a new app or troubleshooting an existing one, be asked to supply your phone's UDID. Once you've revealed it, you can right-click it (or, on the Mac, Control-click it) to get the Copy UDID command. Now your iPhone's UDID is on the Clipboard, ready to paste into an email message or text message.

Info Tab

On this tab, you're offered the chance to copy some distinctly non-entertainment data over to your iPhone: your computer's calendar, address book, email settings, and Web bookmarks. The PalmPilot-type stuff (Rolodex, datebook) is extremely useful to have with you, and the settings and bookmarks save you a lot of tedious setup on the iPhone.

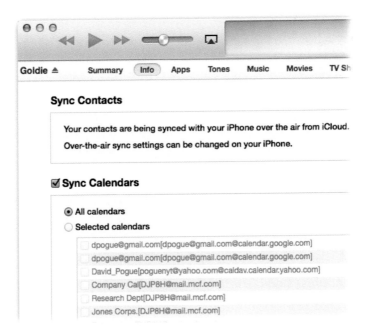

Syncing Contacts

If you've been adding to your address book for years in a program like Microsoft Outlook or OS X's Contacts, then you're just a sync away from porting all that accumulated data right over to your iPhone. Once there, phone numbers and email addresses show up as links, so you can reach out and tap someone.

Here's how to sync up your contacts with the iPhone. The steps depend on which program you keep them in.

- **Outlook.** Turn on Sync contacts with and, from the pop-up menu, choose Outlook. Finally, click Apply.

    Note that some of the more obscure fields Outlook lets you use, like Radio and Telex, won't show up on the iPhone. All the major data points do, however, including name, email address, and (most importantly) phone number.

- **Outlook Express.** Microsoft's free email app for Windows XP stores your contacts in a file called the Windows Address Book. To sync it with your iPhone, turn on Sync contacts from, choose Windows Address Book from the pop-up menu, and then click Apply.

- **Windows Live Mail.** Windows Live Mail, a free download for Windows 7 and 8 (and called Windows Mail in Vista), is essentially a renamed version of Outlook Express. You set it up to sync with the iPhone's Contacts program just as described—except in iTunes, choose Windows Contacts, rather than Windows Address Book, before clicking Apply.

- **Yahoo Address Book.** The Yahoo Address Book is the address book component of a free Yahoo Mail account. It's therefore an *online* address book, which has certain advantages—like the ability to be accessed from any computer on the Internet.

To sync with it, turn on **Sync contacts from** and then choose **Yahoo Address Book** from the pop-up menu. (On the Mac, just turn on **Yahoo Address Book**; no menu is needed.)

Since Yahoo is an *online* address book, you need an Internet connection and your Yahoo ID and password to sync it with the iPhone. Click **Configure**, and then type your Yahoo ID and password. When finished, click **OK**. Now click **Apply** to get syncing.

Because it's online, syncing your Yahoo address book has a couple of other quirks.

First, Yahoo Address Book, ever the thoughtful program, lets you remember both birthdays and anniversaries in two data fields. The iPhone, however, grabs only the birthday part, leaving you to remember the anniversary dates yourself. Just don't forget your own!

Furthermore, any custom labels you slap on phone entries on the iPhone side get synced into the **Other** field when they get to Yahoo. It seems Yahoo is just not as creative as you are when it comes to labeling things.

Finally, Yahoo Address Book doesn't delete contacts during a sync. So if you whack somebody on the iPhone, you still have to log into Yahoo and take 'em out there, too.

- **Google Contacts.** The addresses from your Gmail, Google Mail, and Google Apps accounts can sync up to the iPhone as well. Turn on **Sync contacts from** and then choose **Google Contacts** from the pop-up menu. (On the Mac, just turn on **Google Contacts**; no menu is needed.) Agree to the legal disclaimer about iTunes' snatching data.

Since Google Contacts are kept on the Web, you need an Internet connection and your Gmail/Google ID and password to sync your contacts with the iPhone. In the password box that pops up (click **Configure** on the Info screen if it doesn't), type your Gmail name and password. When finished, click **OK**. Now click **Apply** to get syncing.

Only one contact per email address gets synced, so if you have multiple contacts with the same address, someone will get left out of the syncing party. Google has a page of troubleshooting tips and info for other Contacts-related questions at *www.google.com/support/contactsync*.

- **OS X Contacts.** Apple products generally love one another, and the built-in contact keeper that comes with OS X is a breeze to sync up with your iPhone. Turn on Sync contacts from and then pick Address Book or Contacts from the pop-up menu.

  If you've gathered sets of people together as *groups* in your address book, you can also transfer *them* to the iPhone by turning on Selected groups and then checking the ones you want. When finished, click Apply to sync things up.

- **Entourage, Outlook for Mac.** Entourage and its Mac successor, Outlook, the email program in Microsoft Office for the Mac, also play nicely with the iPhone, as long as you introduce them properly first.

  In Entourage, choose Entourage→Preferences. Under General Preferences, choose Sync Services. Turn on Synchronize contacts with Address Book and .Mac.

  In Outlook, choose Outlook→Preferences. Click Sync Services. Turn on Contacts.

  Click OK, and then plug the iPhone into the Mac. Click the iPhone's icon in the iTunes Source list, and then click the Info tab. Turn on Sync contacts from and, from the pop-up menu, choose Address Book. Finally, click Apply to sync.

- **Other programs.** Even if you keep your contacts in a Jurassic-era program like Palm Desktop, you may still be able to get them into the iPhone/iTunes sync dance. If you can export your contacts as vCards (a contacts-exchange format with the extension .vcf), then you can import them into Windows' Address Book or the Mac's Contacts.

  Now you can sync to your heart's delight.

Syncing Your Calendar

With its snazzy-looking Calendar program tidily synced with your computer, the iPhone can keep you on schedule—and even remind you when you have to call a few people.

Out of the box, the iPhone's calendar works with Outlook 2003 and later for Windows, and with Calendar and Entourage/Outlook on the Mac.

Here again, setting up the sync depends on the calendar program you're using on your computer.

If you have Windows Vista or Windows 7/8, then you have a built-in calendar program—Windows Live Calendar—but no way to sync it with the iPhone. The reason, according to Apple, is that Microsoft has not made public the format of its calendar program.

- **Outlook Calendar (Windows).** In the Calendars area of the Info tab, turn on Sync calendars from Outlook.

  You can also choose how many days' worth of old events you want to have on your iPhone, since you probably rarely need to reference, say, your calendar from 2002. Turn on Do not sync events older than ___ days, and then specify the number of days' worth of old appointments you want to have on hand.

  Events you add on the iPhone get carried back to Outlook when you reconnect to the computer and sync up.

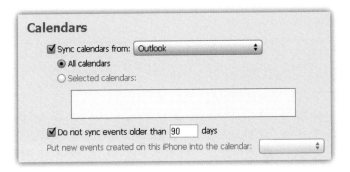

- **Calendar (Macintosh).** OS X comes with a nimble little datebook called Calendar (formerly iCal), which syncs right up with the iPhone. To use it, on the Info tab's Calendars area, turn on Sync Calendar (iCal) calendars.

  If you have several different *calendars* (color-coded categories) in Calendar—Work, Home, Book Club, and so on—then you can turn on Selected calendars and choose the ones you want to copy to the iPhone.

  Near the bottom of the calendar-sync preferences, there's a place to indicate how far back you want to sync old events.

  Once you get all your calendar preferences set up the way you like, click Apply to get your schedule in sync.

- **Entourage or Outlook (Mac).** Entourage can sync its calendar events with the iPhone, too. Start by opening Entourage, and then choose Entourage→Preferences. Under General Preferences, choose Sync Services, and then turn on Synchronize events and tasks with iCal and MobileMe . Click OK, and then plug the iPhone into the computer.

  Click the iPhone icon in the iTunes Source list, and then, on the Info tab, turn on Sync iCal calendars. Click the Apply button to sync.

Syncing Email Accounts

Teaching a new computer of *any* sort to get and send your email can be stressful; the job entails plugging in all sorts of user-hostile information bits called things like the SMTP Server Address and Uses SSL. Presumably, though, you've got your email working on your Mac or PC—wouldn't it be great if you didn't have to duplicate all that work on your iPhone?

That's exactly what iTunes can do for you. It can transfer the *account setup information* to the iPhone so it's ready to start hunting for messages immediately.

NOTE: No mail *messages* are transferred to or from the iPhone over the cable. For that sort of magic, you need iCloud or Exchange service (see Chapters 14 and 15).

It can do that—*if,* that is, your current email program is Mail or Entourage/Outlook (on the Mac) or Outlook or Outlook Express (in Windows).

On the iTunes Info tab, scroll down to Mail Accounts. The next step varies by operating system:

- **Windows.** Turn on Sync selected mail accounts from and, from the shortcut menu, choose Outlook or Outlook Express.

- **Macintosh.** Turn on Sync selected Mail accounts.

Finally, if your email program collects messages from multiple accounts, then turn on the checkboxes of the accounts you want to see on your iPhone. Click Apply to start syncing.

Syncing Bookmarks

Bookmarks—those helpful shortcuts that save you countless hours of mis-typing Web site addresses—are a reflection of your personality, because they tend to be sites that are important to *you.*

iTunes can transfer your bookmarks from Internet Explorer or Safari (Windows), or from Safari on a Mac. In iTunes, on the Info tab, scroll down to the section called Web Browser. Then:

- **In Windows,** turn on Sync bookmarks from and then choose either Safari or Internet Explorer from the pop-up menu. Click Apply to sync.

- **On the Mac,** turn on Sync Safari bookmarks and then click Apply.

And what if Firefox is your preferred browser? You can still get those favor-ites moved over to the iPhone, thanks to an ingenious free Firefox plug-in called Sync. It's available at *www.mozilla.com/en-US/firefox/sync/*, or you can just Google it.

The Sync add-on doesn't just copy your bookmarks to the phone—it cre-ates a live, two-way wireless sync between your computer and your phone. Bookmarks, yes, but also your History list and even your open tabs.

Actually, *most* other browsers can export their bookmarks. You can use that option to export your bookmarks file to your desktop and then use Safari's File→Import Bookmarks command to pull it from there.

Apps Tab

On this tab, you get a convenient duplicate of your iPhone's Home screens. You can drag app icons around, create folders, and otherwise organize your Home life much faster than you'd be able to do on the phone itself (because you have a mouse, a keyboard, and a big screen). See page 282 for details.

Tones Tab

Any ringtones that you've bought from the iTunes Store or made yourself (Chapter 5) appear here; you can specify which ones you want synced to the iPhone. (This tab was once called "Ringtones," but the iPhone can handle tones for all kinds of different events, like incoming text messages or mail, tweets, reminders, and so on.) You can choose either **All tones** or, if space on your phone is an issue, **Selected tones** (and then turn on the ones you want).

Be sure to sync over any ringtones you've assigned to your frequent callers so the iPhone can alert you with a personalized audio cue, like Pink's rendition of "Tell Me Something Good" when they call you up.

Music Tab

Turn on **Sync Music**. Now you need to decide *what* music to put on your phone.

- If you have a big iPhone and a small music library, you can opt to sync the **Entire music library** with one click.

- If you have a big music collection and a small iPhone, you'll have to take only *some* of it along for the iPhone ride. In that case, click **Selected playlists, artists, and genres**. In the lists below, turn on the checkboxes for the playlists, artists, and music genres you want to transfer. (These are cumulative. If there's no Electric Light Orchestra in any of your selected playlists, but you turn on ELO in the Artists list, you'll get all your ELO anyway.)

> **TIP:** Playlists make it fast and easy to sync whole batches of tunes over to your iPhone. But don't forget that you can add individual songs, too, even if they're not in any playlist. Just turn on **Manually manage music and videos**. Now you can drag individual songs and videos from your iTunes library onto the iPhone icon to install them there.

If you've got music videos or voice memos (recorded by the iPhone and now residing on your computer), you'll see that they get their own checkboxes.

Making It All Fit

Sooner or later, everybody has to confront the fact that an iPhone holds only 8, 16, 32, or 64 gigabytes of music and video. (Actually less, because the operating system itself eats up over a gigabyte.) That's enough for around 2,000, 4,000, 8,000, or 16,000 average-length songs—assuming you don't put any videos or photos on there.

Your multimedia stash may be bigger than that. If you just turn on **Sync All** checkboxes, you'll get an error message telling you that it won't all fit on the iPhone.

One way to solve the problem is to tiptoe through the tabs, turning off checkboxes and trying to sync until the "too much" error message goes away.

If you don't have quite so much time, turn on **Automatically fill free space with songs**. It makes iTunes use a little artificial Genius intelligence to load up your phone automatically, using your most played and most recent music as a guide. (It does not, in fact, fill the phone completely; it leaves a few hundred megabytes for safety—so you can download more stuff on the road, for example.)

Another helpful approach is to use the *smart playlist,* a music playlist that assembles itself based on criteria that you supply. For example:

1. **In iTunes, click Done. From the top-left pop-up menu, choose Music; then choose File→New Smart Playlist.** The Smart Playlist dialog box appears.

2. **Specify the category.** Use the pop-up menus to choose, for example, a musical genre, or songs you've played recently, or *haven't* played recently, or have rated highly.

3. **Turn on the "Limit to" checkbox, and set up the constraints.** For example, you could limit the amount of music in this playlist to 2 giga-bytes, chosen at random. That way, every time you sync, you'll get a fresh, random supply of songs on your iPhone, with enough room left for some videos.

4. **Click OK.** The new Smart Playlist appears in the list of playlists at left; you can rename it.

Click it to look it over, if you like. Then, on the Music tab, choose this playlist for syncing to the iPhone.

Movies and TV Shows Tabs

When it assumes the role of an iPod, one of the things the iPhone does best is play video on its gorgeous, glossy screen. TV shows and movies you've bought or rented from the iTunes Store look especially nice. (And if you started watching a rented movie on your computer, the iPhone begins playing it right from where you left off.)

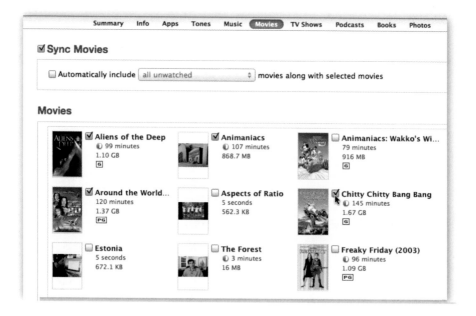

Syncing TV shows and movies works just like syncing music or podcasts. You can have iTunes copy all your stuff to the iPhone, but video fills up your storage awfully fast. That's why you can turn on the checkboxes of just the individual movies or shows (either seasons or episodes) you want—or, using the **Automatically include** pop-up menu, request only the most recent, or the most recent ones you haven't seen yet.

Remember that if you've rented a movie from the iTunes Store and started watching it, you have fewer than 24 hours left to finish before it vanishes from your phone.

Podcasts Tab

One of the great joys of iTunes is the way it gives you access, in the iTunes Store, to thousands of free amateur and professional **podcasts** (basically, downloadable radio or TV shows), including free college lectures and videos in the iTunes U category.

Here you can choose to sync all podcast episodes, selected shows, all unplayed episodes—or just a certain number of episodes per sync. Individual checkboxes let you choose *which* podcast series get to come along for the ride, so you can sync to suit your mood at the time.

Books Tab

Here are the thumbnails of your audiobooks and your ebooks—those you've bought from Apple, those you've downloaded from the Web, and those you've dragged right into iTunes from your desktop (PDF files, for example). You can ask iTunes to send them all to your phone—or only the ones whose checkboxes you turn on.

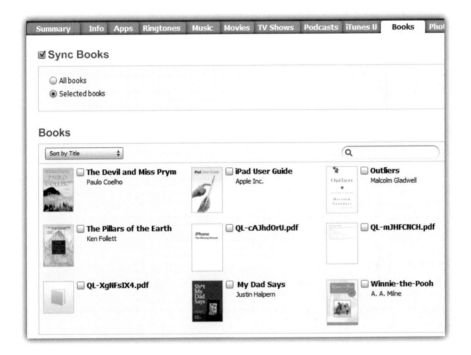

Photos Tab (Computer→iPhone)

Why corner people with your wallet to show them your kid's baby pictures, when you can whip out your iPhone and dazzle them with a finger-tapping slideshow?

iTunes can sync the photos from your hard drive onto the iPhone. If you use a compatible photo-management program, you can even select individual albums of images that you've already assembled on your computer.

Here are your photo-filling options for the iPhone:

- **Photoshop Elements 3.0 or later** for Windows.

- **Photoshop Album 2.0 or later** for Windows.

- **iPhoto 4.0.3 or later** on the Mac.

- **Aperture,** Apple's high-end program for photography pros.

- **Any folder of photos on your hard drive,** like My Pictures (in Windows), Pictures (on the Mac), or any folder you like.

The common JPEG files generated by just about every digital camera work fine for iPhone photos. The GIF and PNG files used by Web pages work, too.

When you're ready to sync your photos, click the Photos tab in iTunes. Turn on Sync photos from, and then indicate *where* you'd like to sync them from (Photoshop Elements, iPhoto, or whatever).

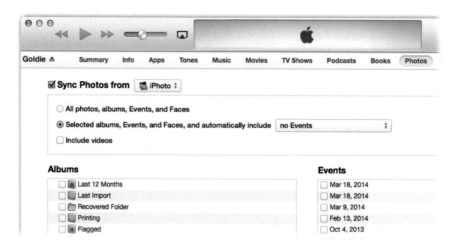

If you want only *some* of the albums from your photo-shoebox software, then click Selected albums, events, and faces. Turn on the checkboxes of the albums, events, and faces you want synced. (The "faces" option is available only if you're syncing from iPhoto or Aperture on the Mac, and only if you've used the Faces feature, which groups your photos according to who's in them.)

Once you make your selections and click Apply, the program computes for a very long time, "optimizing" copies of your photos to make them look great on the iPhone (for example, downsizing them from 10-megapixel overkill to something more appropriate for a 0.6-megapixel screen), and then ports them over.

After the sync is complete, you'll be able to wave your iPhone around, and people will *beg* to see your photos.

Syncing Photos and Videos (iPhone→Computer)

The previous section described copying photos in only one direction: from the computer to the iPhone. But here's one of those rare instances when you can actually *create* data on the iPhone so that you can later transfer it to the computer: photos and videos that you take with the iPhone's own camera. You can rest easy, knowing that they can be copied back to your computer for safekeeping with only one click.

Now, it's important to understand that *iTunes is not involved* in this process. It doesn't know anything about photos or videos coming *from* the iPhone; its job is just to copy pictures *to* the iPhone.

So what's handling the iPhone-to-computer transfer? Your operating system. It sees the iPhone as though it's a digital camera and suggests importing them just as it would from a camera's memory card.

Here's how it goes: Plug the iPhone into the computer with the USB cable. What you'll see is probably something like this:

- **On the Mac.** iPhoto opens. This free photo-organizing/editing software comes on every Mac. Shortly after it notices that the iPhone is on the premises, it goes into Import mode. Click Import All, or select some thumbnails from the iPhone and then click Import Selected.

  After the transfer, click Delete Photos if you'd like the iPhone's cameraphone memory cleared out after the transfer. (Both photos and videos get imported together.)

- **In Windows.** When you attach a camera (or an iPhone), a dialog box pops up that asks how you want its contents handled. It lists any photo-management program you might have installed (Picasa, Photoshop Elements, Photoshop Album, and so on), as well as

Windows' own camera-management software. (That would be the **Scanner and Camera Wizard** in Windows XP; **Using Windows** in Vista or Windows 7 or 8).

Click the program you want to handle importing the iPhone pictures and videos.

You'll probably also want to turn on **Always do this for this device**, so it'll happen automatically the next time.

Shutting Down the Importing Process

Then again, some iPhone owners would rather **not** see some lumbering photo-management program firing itself up every time they connect the phone. You, too, might wish there were a way to **stop** iPhoto or Windows from bugging you every time you connect the iPhone. That is easy enough to change—if you know where to look.

- **Windows XP.** With the iPhone connected, choose Start→My Computer. Right-click the iPhone's icon. From the shortcut menu, choose Properties. Click the Events tab; next, click Take no action. Click OK.

Windows Vista, Windows 7

Windows XP

- **Windows Vista, Windows 7 and 8.** When the AutoPlay dialog box appears, click Set AutoPlay defaults in Control Panel. (Or, if the AutoPlay dialog box is no longer on the screen, choose Start→Control Panel→AutoPlay.)

  Scroll all the way to the bottom until you see the iPhone icon. From the pop-up menu, choose Take no action. Click Save.

- **Macintosh.** Open iPhoto. Choose iPhoto→Preferences. Where it says Connecting camera opens, choose No application. Close the window.

From now on, no photo-importing message will appear when you plug in the iPhone. (You can always import its photos manually, of course.)

On This Phone

The final tab is called On This Phone. It's a tidy list of everything that is, in fact, on your phone, organized by type (Music, Movies, and so on). There's not really much you can *do* here—you can get more information about some items by pointing to them—but just seeing your multimedia empire arrayed before you can be very satisfying.

One iPhone, Multiple Computers

In general, Apple likes to keep things simple. Everything it ever says about the iPhone suggests that you can only sync *one* iPhone with *one* computer.

That's not really true, however. You can actually sync the same iPhone with *multiple* Macs or PCs.

And why would you want to do that? So you can fill it up with material from different places: music and video from a Mac at home; contacts, calendar, ebooks, and iPhone applications from your Windows PC at work; and maybe even the photos from your laptop.

iTunes derives these goodies from different sources to begin with—pictures from your photo program, addresses and appointments from your contacts and calendar programs, music and video from iTunes. So all you have to do is set up the tabs of each computer's copy of iTunes to sync *only* certain kinds of material.

On the Mac, for example, you'd turn on the Sync checkboxes for only the Music, Podcasts, and Video tabs. Sync away.

Next, take the iPhone to the office; on your PC, turn on the Sync checkboxes on only the Info, Books, and Apps tabs. Sync away once more. Then, on the laptop, turn off Sync on all tabs except Photos.

And off you go. Each time you connect the iPhone to one of the computers, it syncs that data according to the preferences set in that copy of iTunes.

One Computer, Multiple iPhones

It's fine to sync multiple iPhones with a single computer, too. iTunes cheerfully fills each one up, and backs each one up, as they come. In fact, if you open the Preferences box (in the iTunes menu on the Mac, the Edit menu on Windows), the Devices tab lists all the iPhones (and iPads and iPod Touches) that iTunes is tracking.

If you use Windows, however, here's a note of warning: You have to use the same sync settings for everyone's phones.

If, for example, you try to switch your Contacts syncing from Google to Outlook Express, an iTunes dialog box informs you that your changes will affect everyone else syncing iPods and iPhones on the PC. (If you really want every family member happy, have each person sign in with his own Windows user account and copy of iTunes.)

One-Way Emergency Sync

In general, the iPhone's ability to handle bidirectional syncs is a blessing. It means that whenever you modify the information on one of your beloved machines, you won't have to duplicate that effort on the other one.

It can also get hairy. Depending on what merging, fussing, and button-clicking you do, it's possible to make a mess of your iPhone's address book or calendar. You could fill it with duplicate entries, or the wrong entries, or entries from a computer that you didn't intend to merge in there.

Fortunately, as a last resort, iTunes offers a **forced one-way sync** option, which makes your computer's version of things the official one. Everything on the iPhone gets replaced by the computer's version, just this once. At least you'll know exactly where all that information came from.

To do an emergency one-way sync, connect the iPhone. Click its button in iTunes. On the Info tab, scroll all the way to the bottom, until you see the Advanced area. There it is: Replace information on this iPhone, complete with checkboxes for the five things that iTunes can completely replace on the phone: Contacts, Calendars, Bookmarks, Notes, and Mail Accounts. Click Apply to start minty fresh.

Backing Up the iPhone

You've spent all this time tweaking preferences, massaging settings, and getting everything just so on your expensive iPhone. Wouldn't it be great if you could **back up** all that work so that if something bad happens to the phone, you wouldn't have to start from scratch?

Fortunately, you can. Your iPhone can back up everything your computer doesn't already have a copy of: stuff you've downloaded to the phone (music, ebooks, apps, and so on), plus less-visible things, like your iPhone's mail and network settings, your call history, contact favorites, notes, text messages, and other personal preferences that are hard or impossible to recreate.

> **TIP:** If you turn on the new Encrypted iPhone Backup option, then your backup will include all your *passwords*: for WiFi hot spots, Web sites, email accounts, and so on. That can save you tons of time when you have to restore the phone from the backup. (The one downside: You'll be asked to make up a password *for the backup*. Don't forget it!)

You can create your backups in either of two places:

- **On your computer.** You get a backup every time the iPhone syncs with iTunes. The backup also happens before you install a new iPhone firmware version from Apple. iTunes also offers to do a backup before you use the Restore option described below.

- **On iCloud.** You can also back up your phone wirelessly and automatically—to iCloud, if you've signed up. That method has the advantage of being available even if your computer gets lost or burned to a crisp in a house fire. See the next chapter for details.

You make this choice on the Summary tab described above. (You also have the option of encrypting the *backup,* so that no NSA snoop can steal your laptop and root around in your backup files.)

Using That Backup

So the day has come when you really need to *use* that backup of your iPhone. Maybe it's become unstable, and it's crashing all over. Or maybe you just lost the dang thing, and you wish your replacement iPhone could have all your old info and settings on it. Here's how to save the day (and your data):

1. Connect the iPhone to the computer you normally use to sync with.

2. Click the iPhone button; click the Summary tab.

3. Take a deep breath and click Restore iPhone. A message announces that after iTunes wipes your iPhone clean and installs a fresh version of the iPhone firmware, you can restore your personal data.

It may also announce that you have to ***turn off Find My iPhone*** before you proceed. That's a security measure to stop a thief from erasing a stolen phone. He can't restore the phone without turning off Find My iPhone, and he can't turn off Find My iPhone without your iCloud password.

4. Take iTunes up on its offer to restore all your settings and stuff from the backup. If you see multiple backup files listed from other iPhones (or an iPod Touch), be sure to pick the backup file for ***your*** phone. Let the backup restore your phone settings and info. Then resync all your music, videos, and podcasts. Exhale.

TIP: For the truly paranoid, there's nothing like a ***backup*** of your backup. Yes, you can actually back up the iTunes backup file, maybe on a flash drive, for safekeeping. On a Mac, look in Home→Library→Application Support→MobileSync→Backup. For Windows Vista or Windows 7 or 8, visit C: drive→User→App Data (hidden folder)→Roaming→Apple Computer→MobileSync→ Backup.

If you get in a situation where you need to restore your iPhone through iTunes on a different computer (say if your old machine croaked), install iTunes on it and then slip this backup file into the same folder on the new computer. Then follow the steps on these pages to restore your data to the iPhone.

Deleting a Backup File

To save disk space, you can delete old backups (especially for i-gadgets you no longer own). Go to the iTunes preferences (Edit→Preferences in Windows or iTunes→Preferences on the Mac) and click the Devices tab.

Click the dated backup file you don't want and hit Delete Backup, as shown on the next page.

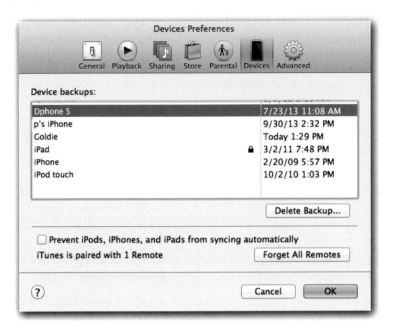

14

iCloud

Apple's free iCloud service may have opened for business in October 2011, but it's had a long history. It began life as something called iTools, resurfaced as a service called .Mac, popped up again as a $100-a-year entity called MobileMe, and has now become iCloud.

In each case, though, it all stems from Apple's brainstorm that, since it controls both ends of the connection between a Mac and the Apple Web site, it should be able to create some pretty clever Internet-based features.

This chapter concerns what iCloud can do for you, the iPhone owner.

> **NOTE:** To get a free iCloud account if you don't already have one, sign up at *www.icloud.com*. Then enter your iCloud email address and password in **Settings→iCloud**.

What iCloud Giveth

So what is iCloud? Mainly, it's these things:

- **A synchronizing service.** It keeps your calendar, address book, and documents updated and identical on all your gadgets: Mac, PC, iPhone, iPad, iPod Touch. That's a huge convenience—almost magical.

- **Find My iPhone.** Find My iPhone pinpoints the current location of your iPhone on a map. In other words, it's great for helping you find your phone if it's been stolen or lost.

  You can also make your lost gadget start making a loud pinging sound for a couple of minutes by remote control—even if it was set to Vibrate mode. That's brilliantly effective when your phone has slipped under the couch cushions.

- **An email account.** Handy, really: An iCloud account gives you a new email address. If you already have an email address, great! This new one can be a backup account, one you never enter on Web sites so that it never gets overrun with spam. Or vice versa: Let *this* be your junk account, the address you use for online forms. Either way, it's great to have a second account.

- **An online locker.** Anything you buy from Apple—music, TV shows, ebooks, and apps—is stored online, for easy access at any time. For example, whenever you buy a song or a TV show from the online iTunes Store, it appears automatically on your iPhone and computers. Your photos are stored online, too.

- **Back to My Mac.** This option to grab files from one of your other Macs across the Internet isn't new, but it survives in iCloud. It lets you access the contents of one Mac from another one across the Internet.

- **Automatic backup.** iCloud can back up your iPhone—automatically and wirelessly (over WiFi, not over cellular connections). It's a quick backup, since iCloud backs up only the changed data.

  If you ever want to set up a new i-gadget, or if you want to restore everything to an existing one, life is sweet. Once you're in a WiFi hotspot, all you have to do is re-enter your Apple ID and password in the setup assistant that appears when you turn the thing on. Magically, your gadget is refilled with everything that used to be on it.

  Well, *almost* everything. An iCloud backup stores everything you've bought from Apple (music, apps, books); photos and videos in your Camera Roll; settings, including the layout of your Home screen; text messages; and ringtones. Your mail, and anything that came from your computer (like music/ringtones/videos from iTunes and photos from iPhoto), have to be reloaded.

So there's the quick overview. The rest of the chapter covers each of these iCloud features in greater depth.

iCloud Sync

For many people, this may be the killer app for iCloud right here: The iCloud Web site, acting as the master control center, can keep multiple Macs, Windows PCs, and iPhones/iPads/iPod Touches synchronized. That offers both a huge convenience factor—all your stuff is always on all your gadgets—and a safety/backup factor, since you have duplicates everywhere.

It works by storing the master copies of your stuff—email, notes, contacts, calendars, Web bookmarks, and documents—on the Web. (Or "in the cloud," as the product managers would say.)

Whenever your Macs, PCs, or i-gadgets are online—over WiFi or cellular— they connect to the mother ship and update themselves. Edit an address on your iPhone, and shortly thereafter, you'll find the same change in Contacts (on your Mac) and Outlook (on your PC). Send an email reply from your PC at the office, and you'll find it in your Sent Mail folder on the Mac at home. Add a Web bookmark anywhere and find it everywhere else. Edit a spreadsheet in Numbers on your iPad and find the same numbers updated on your Mac.

Actually, there's even another place where you can work with your data: on the Web. Using your computer, you can log into *www.icloud.com* to find Web-based clones of Calendar, Contacts, and Mail.

To control the syncing, tap **Settings→iCloud** on your iPhone. Turn on the checkboxes of the stuff you want to be synchronized all the way around:

- **Mail.** "Mail" refers to your actual email messages, plus your account settings and preferences from OS X's Mail program.

- **Contacts, Calendars.** There's nothing as exasperating as realizing that the address book you're consulting on your home Mac is missing

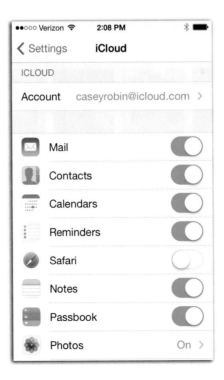

somebody you're *sure* you entered—on your phone. This option keeps all your address books and calendars synchronized. Delete a phone number on your computer at home, and you'll find it gone from your phone. Enter an appointment on your iPhone, and you'll find the calendar updated everywhere else.

- **Reminders.** This option refers to the to-do items you create in the phone's Reminders app; very shortly, those reminders will show up on your Mac (in Reminders, Calendar, or BusyCal) or PC (in Outlook). How great to make a reminder for yourself in one place and have it reminding you later in another one!

- **Safari.** If a Web site is important enough to merit bookmarking while you're using your phone, why shouldn't it also show up in the Bookmarks menu on your desktop PC at home, your Mac laptop, or your iPad? This option syncs your Safari Reading List, too.

- **Notes.** This option syncs the notes from your phone's Notes app into the Notes app on the Mac, the email program on your PC, your other i-gadgets, and, of course, the iCloud Web site.

- **Passbook.** If you've bought tickets for a movie, show, game, or plane flight, you sure as heck don't want to be stuck without it because you left the barcode on your other gadget.

- **Keychain.** New in iOS 7: The login information for your Web sites (names and passwords), and even your credit card information, can be stored right on your phone—and synced to your other iPhones, iPads, and Macs (running OS X Mavericks or later).

Now, you could argue that Web-site passwords and credit card numbers are more important than, say, your Reminders. For this category, you don't want to mess around with security.

Therefore, when you turn on the Keychain switch in Settings, you're asked to enter your iCloud password.

Then you get a choice of ways to confirm your realness—either by entering a code that Apple texts to you or by using another Apple device to set up this one. Once that's done, your passwords and credit cards are magically synced across your computers and mobile gadgets, saving you unending headaches.

- **Photos.** Here are two on/off switches. One is My Photo Stream, which keeps your last 1,000 photos synchronized among Mac, PC, phone, and other i-gadgets. The other is Photo Sharing, which lets you "publish" favorite pictures to a few lucky people's iPhones and iPads. (Or you can "subscribe" to theirs.)

- **Documents & Data.** Some programs are available for more than one machine—including Apple's own iWork suite (Numbers, Pages, Keynote). Those programs are available for Mac, iPhone/iPod Touch, and iPad.

  In that delicious situation, you can create or edit a document on *one* kind of machine, and marvel as iCloud automatically syncs it with all your *other* devices.

  When you fire up one of the iWork programs on the iPhone, the start-up screen offers two buttons: Later (don't connect to iCloud now) or Use iCloud (copy your work wirelessly to iCloud, so your other computers and gadgets can get at it).

  From now on, you don't have to do anything special; any document you create or edit appears automatically on your other iCloud-connected machines. If you have iWork for your Mac, your documents are auto-synced to iCloud *if* you've turned on the checkbox in System Preferences.

  On your Mac, same deal: When you save a document (from within a Documents-in-the-Cloud-compatible app), you're offered a choice of where to save it: On My Mac or iCloud.

To set up syncing, turn on the switches for the items you want synced. That's it. There is no step 2.

> **NOTE:** You may notice that there are no switches here for syncing stuff you buy from Apple, like books, movies, apps, and music. They're not so much *synced* as they are *stored* for you online. You can download them at any time to any of your machines.

Photo Stream, Photo Sharing

These iCloud features are described in glorious detail in Chapter 7—the photos chapter.

Find My iPhone

Did you leave your iPhone somewhere? Did it get stolen? Has that mischievous 5-year-old left it somewhere in the house again?

At that point, you're ready to avail yourself of one of Apple's finest creations: Find My iPhone.

The first step is to log into iCloud.com and click **Find My iPhone**. Immediately, the Web site updates to show you, on a map, the current location of your phone—and Macs, iPod Touches, and iPads. (If they're not online, or if they're turned all the way off, you won't see their current locations.)

If you own more than one, you may have to click **All Devices** and, from the list, choose the one you're looking for.

If just knowing where the thing *is* isn't enough to satisfy you, click the dot representing your phone, click the ⓘ next to its name, and marvel at the appearance of these three buttons (shown on the facing page):

- **Play Sound.** When you click this button, the phone starts dinging and vibrating loudly for 2 minutes, wherever it is, so you can figure out which jacket pocket you left it in. It beeps even if the ringer switch is off, and even if the phone is asleep. Once you find the phone, just wake it in the usual way to make the dinging stop.

- **Lost Mode.** When you lose your phone for real, proceed immediately to Lost Mode. Its first step: Prompting you to password protect it, if you haven't already. Without it, the sleazy crook can't get into your phone without erasing it. (If your phone is already password-protected, you don't see this step.)

  The passcode you dream up here works just as though you'd created one yourself on the phone. That is, it remains in place until you, with the phone in hand, manually turn it off in Settings→General→Passcode Lock.

Next, the Web site asks for a phone number where you can be reached, and (when you click **Next**) for a message you want displayed on the iPhone's Lock screen. If you actually left the thing in a taxi or on some restaurant table, you can use this feature to plead for its return.

When you click **Done**, your message appears on the phone's screen, wherever it is, no matter what app was running, and the phone locks itself.

Whoever finds it can't miss the message, can't miss the **Call** button that's right there on the Lock screen, and can't do anything without dismissing the message first.

If the finder of your phone really isn't such a nice person, at least you'll get an automatic email every time the phone moves from place to place, so you can track the thief's whereabouts. (Apple sends these messages to your @me.com or @icloud.com address.)

- **Erase iPhone.** This is the last-ditch security option, for when your immediate concern isn't so much the phone as all the private stuff that's on it. Click this button, confirm the dire warning box, enter your iCloud ID, and click **Erase**. By remote control, you've just erased everything from your phone, wherever it may be. (If it's ever returned, you can restore it from your backup.)

Once you've wiped the phone, you can no longer find it or send messages to it using Find My iPhone.

 TIP: There's an app for that. Download the Find My iPhone app from the App Store. It lets you do everything described above from another iPhone, in a tidy, simple control panel.

Activation Lock

Thousands of people have found their lost or stolen iPhones by using Find My iPhone. Yay!

Unfortunately, thousands more will never see their phones again. Until now, Find My iPhone has had a back door the size of Montana: the thief can simply turn it off. Or, if your phone was password-protected, the thief could just erase it and sell it on the black market, which was his goal all along. Suddenly, your phone is lost in the wilderness, and you have no way to track or recover it.

That's why, in iOS 7, Apple introduced the ingenious Activation Lock feature. It's very simple: Nobody can erase it, or even turn off Find My iPhone, without entering your iCloud password (your Apple ID).

So even if the bad guy has your phone and tries to sell it, the thing is useless. It's still registered to you, you can still track it, and it still displays your message and phone number on the Lock screen. Without your iCloud password, your iPhone is just a worthless brick. Suddenly, stealing iPhones is a much less attractive prospect.

Email

Apple offers an email address as part of each iCloud account. Of course, you already *have* an email account. So why bother? The first advantage is the simple address: *YourName@me.com* or *YourName@icloud.com.*

Second, you can read your me.com email from any computer anywhere in the world, via the iCloud Web site, or on your iPhone/iPod Touch/iPad.

To make things even sweeter, your me.com or icloud.com mail is completely synced. Delete a message on one gadget, and you'll find it in the Deleted Mail folder on another. Send a message from your iPhone, and you'll find it in the Sent Mail folder on your Mac. And so on.

Video, Music, Apps: Locker in the Sky

Apple, as if you hadn't noticed, has become a big seller of multimedia files. It has the biggest music store in the world. It has the biggest app store, for both i-gadgets and Macs. It sells an awful lot of TV shows and movies. Its ebook store, iBooks, is no Amazon.com, but it's chugging along.

Once you buy a song, movie, app, or book, you can download it again as often as you like—no charge. In fact, you can download it to your *other* Apple equipment, too—no charge. iCloud automates, or at least formalizes, that process. Once you buy something, it's added to a tidy list of items that you can download to all your *other* machines.

Here's how to grab them:

- **iPhone, iPad, iPod Touch.** *For apps:* Open the App Store icon. Tap Updates (App Store only). Tap Purchased. Tap Not On This iPhone.

  For music, movies, and TV shows: The iTunes Store app. Tap More, then Purchased; tap the category you want. Tap Not On This iPhone.

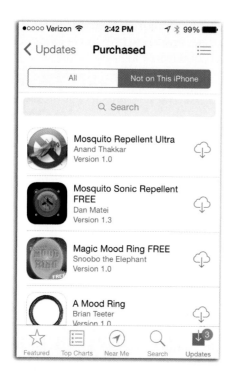
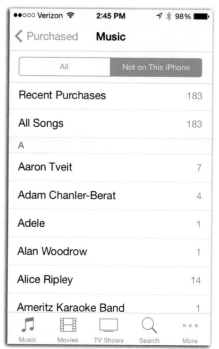

There they are: all the items you've ever bought, even on your *other* machines using the same Apple ID. To download anything listed here onto *this* machine, tap the ☁ button. Or tap an album name to see the list of songs on it so you can download just *some* of those songs.

You can save yourself all that tapping by opening Settings→Store and turning on Automatic Downloads (for music, apps, and books). From now on, whenever you're in WiFi, stuff you've bought on other Apple machines gets downloaded to this one *automatically,* in the background.

- **Mac or PC.** Open the Mac App Store program (for Mac apps) and click Purchases. Or open the iTunes app (for songs, TV shows, books, and movies). Click Store and then, under Quick Links, click Purchased. There are all your purchases, ready to open or re-download if necessary.

TIP: To make this automatic, open iTunes. Choose iTunes→Preferences→ Store. Under Automatic Downloads, turn on Music, Apps, and Books, as you see fit. Click OK. From now on, iTunes will auto-import anything you buy on any of your other machines.

Any bookmark you set in an iBook book is synced to your other gadgets, too. The idea, of course, is that you can read a few pages on your phone in the doctor's waiting room and then continue from the same page on your iPad on the train ride home.

iTunes Match

Anything you've ever bought from the iTunes music store is now available for playing on any Apple gadget you own. You get it.

A lot of people, however, have music in their collections that *didn't* come from the iTunes Store. Maybe they ripped some audio CDs into their computers. Maybe they acquired some music from, ahem, a friend.

What a sad situation! You've got some of your music available with you on your iPhone, and some that's stranded at home on your computer.

Enter iTunes Match. It's an Apple service that lets you store your *entire* collection, including songs that didn't come from Apple, online, for $25 a year.

The iTunes software analyzes the songs in your collection. If it finds a song that's also available in iTunes, then—bing!—that song becomes available for your playback pleasure, without your actually having to transfer your copy to Apple. Apple says, in effect: "Well, our copy of the song is just as good as yours, so you're welcome to listen to our copy on any of your machines."

Truth is, in fact, Apple's copy is probably *better* than your copy. You get to play back the song at iTunes' 256 Kbps quality, no matter how grungy your copy.

If there's a song or two in your collection *not* among Apple's 20 million tracks, then you can upload them to Apple.

The advantages of forking over the $25 a year are (a) you can listen to *all* your music from any computer/phone/tablet, (b) you get that audio-quality upgrade, (c) you can listen to iTunes Radio without interruptions from ads, and (d) using the song-matching system saves you huge amounts of uploading time. (The rival services from Google and Amazon require uploading your entire music collection, which can take days.)

The disadvantage: You're paying $25 a year.

To get started, make sure you have the latest version of iTunes on your computer. Click **Store**. Under Quick Links, click **iTunes Match** and sign up. Wait awhile as iTunes does its analyzing, matching, and uploading business.

Once that's done, any songs on the iPhone that are actually sitting online are marked by a ☁ icon in the Music app. And any song you buy on any machine shows up as available to play on any of them.

These songs behave exactly like songs that are stored physically on your phone. (In fact, they often are; if you tap a ☁ song to play it, the iPhone downloads and stores it so it won't have to bother the next time.)

> **TIP:** Listening to streaming iTunes Match music over a cellular connection eats up your monthly data limit fast! To protect yourself, turn off **Settings→iTunes & App Stores→Use Cellular Data**; now you can listen only over a WiFi connection.

If you plan to be offline for a while (like on a flight to Tokyo), you can hide the online songs by turning off **Settings→Music→Show All Music**.

The Price of Free

A free iCloud account gives you 5 gigabytes of online storage. That may not sound like much, especially when you consider how big some music, photo, and video files are.

Fortunately, anything you buy from Apple—like music, apps, books, and TV shows—doesn't count against that 5-gigabyte limit. Neither do the photos in your Photo Stream.

So what's left? Some things that don't take up much space, like settings, documents, and pictures you take with your iPhone, iPad, or iPod Touch—and some things that take up a lot of it, like email, commercial movies, and home videos you transferred to the phone from your computer. (Your iPhone backup might hog space, but you can pare that down in **Settings→iCloud→Storage & Backup→Manage Storage**. Tap an app's name and then tap **Edit**.)

You can, of course, expand your storage if you find 5 gigs constricting—for $2 a gigabyte a year. So you'll pay $20, $40, or $100 a year for an extra 10, 20, or 50 gigs. You can upgrade your storage online, on your computer, or right on the iPhone (in **Settings→iCloud→Storage & Backup**).

15

The Corporate iPhone

n its younger days, people thought of the iPhone as a *personal* device, meant for consumers and not for corporations. But somebody at Apple must have gotten sick of hearing, "Well, the iPhone is cool, but it's no BlackBerry." The iPhone now has the security and compatibility features your corporate technical overlords require. (And the BlackBerry—well...)

Even better, the iPhone can talk to Microsoft Exchange ActiveSync servers, staples of corporate computer departments that, among other things, keep smartphones wirelessly updated with the calendar, contacts, and email back at the office. (Yes, it sounds a lot like MobileMe or iCloud. Which is probably why Apple's MobileMe slogan was, "Exchange for the rest of us.")

The Perks

This chapter is intended for you, the iPhone owner—not for the highly paid, well-trained, exceedingly friendly IT (information technology) managers at your company.

Your first task is to convince them that your iPhone is now secure and compatible enough to welcome into the company's network. Here's some information you can use:

- **Microsoft Exchange ActiveSync.** Exchange ActiveSync is the technology that keeps smartphones wirelessly synced with the data on the mother ship's computers. The iPhone works with Exchange ActiveSync, so it can remain in wireless contact with your company's Exchange servers exactly like BlackBerry and Windows Mobile phones do.

  (*Exchange ActiveSync* is not to be confused with regular old *ActiveSync,* which is a much older technology that's designed to update smartphones and palmtops over a cable.)

Your email, address book, and calendar appointments are now sent wirelessly to your iPhone so it's always kept current—and they're sent in a way that those evil rival firms can't intercept. (It uses 128-bit encrypted SSL, if you must know.)

NOTE: That's the same encryption used by Outlook Web Access (OWA), which lets employees check their email, calendar, and contacts from any Web browser. In other words, if your IT administrators are willing to let you access your data using OWA, they should also be willing to let you access it with the iPhone.

- **Mass setup.** Using a free software program for Mac or Windows called the iPhone Configuration Utility, your company's network geeks can set up a bunch of iPhones all at once.

  This program generates iPhone *profiles* (.mobileconfig files): canned iPhone setups that determine all WiFi, network, password, email, and VPN settings.

  The IT manager can email this file to you or post it on a secure Web page; either way, you can just open that file on your iPhone, and presto—you're all configured and set up. And the IT manager never has to handle the phones individually.

  Said manager can now send you new custom apps wirelessly, without your having to sync up to iTunes.

- **Security.** In the event of the unthinkable—you lose your iPhone, or it gets stolen, and vital company secrets are now "in the wild," susceptible to discovery by your company's rivals—network administrators have a handy tool at their disposal. They can erase your entire iPhone by remote control, even though they have no idea where it is or who has it. (iCloud users can do this on a personal iPhone, too.)

  The iPhone can connect to wireless networks using the latest, super-secure connections (WPA Enterprise and WPA2 Enterprise), which are highly resistant to hacker attacks. And when you're using virtual private networking, as described at the end of this chapter, you can use a very secure VPN protocol called IPSec. That's what most companies use for secure, encrypted remote access to the corporate network. Juniper and Cisco VPN apps are available, too.

  Speaking of security: Not only does the iPhone let you create much tougher-to-crack passwords than the feeble four-digit passwords of time gone by, but these passwords now encrypt all email, email attachments, and the data of any apps that are written to take advantage of this feature.

- **iOS 7 improvements.** At the network-geek cocktail parties, all the buzz is about the steps Apple took in iOS 7 to make the iPhone even more corporate-friendly. New features like "Open in" management (IT geeks can control which apps are listed in your Share Sheets to open documents so that you can't open a secret file in a non-secure app); per-app VPN (an app can connect to a virtual private network automatically, and your own personal browsing doesn't travel over the VPN); MDM (mobile device management—means IT gurus can wirelessly set up certain apps and make other setup changes); enterprise SSO (single sign-on, which means that your name and password can be used across apps, without having to re-enter them over and over); third-party app data protection (your apps' data is encrypted until you unlock the phone). All of this makes the phone more secure and more controllable by your IT overlords.

- **Fewer tech-support calls.** Finally, don't forget to point out to the IT staff how rarely you'll need to call them for tech support. It's pretty clear that the iPhone is easier to figure out than, ahem, certain rival smartphones.

And what's in it for you? Complete synchronization of your email, address book, and calendar with what's on your PC at work. Send an email from your iPhone, find it in the Sent folder of Outlook at the office. And so on.

You can also accept invitations to meetings on your iPhone that are sent your way by coworkers; if you accept, they're added to your calendar automatically, just as on your PC. You can also search the company's master address book, right from your iPhone.

The biggest perk for you, though, is just getting permission to *use* an iPhone as your company-issued phone.

Setup

Once you've convinced the IT squad of the iPhone's work-worthiness, they can set up things on their end by consulting Apple's free, downloadable setup guide: the infamous *iPhone OS Enterprise Deployment Guide*. (It incorporates Apple's individual, smaller guides for setting up Microsoft Exchange, Cisco IPSec VPN, IMAP email, and Device Configuration profiles.)

This guide is filled with handy tips, like: "On the Front-End Server, verify that a server certificate is installed and enable SSL for the Exchange ActiveSync virtual directory (require basic SSL authentication)."

In any case, you (or they) can download the deployment guide from this site: *www.apple.com/support/iphone/business*.

At that point, they must grant you and your iPhone permission to access the company's Exchange server using Exchange ActiveSync. Fortunately, if you're already allowed to use Outlook Web Access, then you probably have permission to connect with your iPhone, too.

The steps for *you,* the lowly worker bee, to set up your iPhone for accessing your company's Exchange ActiveSync server are much simpler.

Your IT pros might send you a link that downloads a *profile*—a preconfigured file that auto-sets up all of your company's security and login information. It will create the Exchange account for you (and might turn off a few iPhone features, like the ability to switch off the passcode requirement).

If, on the other hand, you're supposed to set up your Exchange account yourself, tap **Settings→Mail, Contacts, Calendars→Add Account→ Exchange**. Fill in your work email address and password as they were provided to you by your company's IT person.

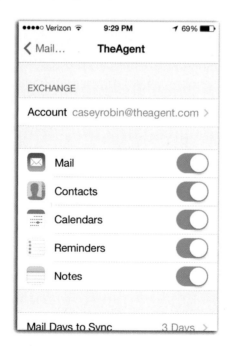

If the phone doesn't recognize your account immediately, you're offered a more detailed info screen; here the Username box is the only potentially tricky spot.

Sometimes, your user name is just the first part of your email address— so if your email address is *smithy@worldwidewidgets.com*, then your user name is simply **smithy.**

In other companies, though, you may also need to know your **Windows domain** and stick that in front of the user name, in the format **domain\ user name** (for example, **wwwidgets\smithy**). In some companies, this is exactly how you log into your PC at work or into Outlook Web Access. If you aren't sure, try your user name by itself first; if that doesn't work, then try **domain\user name.** And if **that** doesn't work, then you'll probably have to ask your IT people for the info.

> **TIP:** That's a **backslash,** folks—the regular slash won't work. So how do you find the backslash on the iPhone keyboard? First press the 123 key to find the "basic punctuation" keyboard; next, press the #+= key to get the "oddball punctuation" keyboard. There it is, on the second row: the \ key.

Incidentally, what's in the Description field doesn't matter. It can be whatever you want to call this particular email account ("Gol-Durned Work Stuff," for example).

When you're finished plugging in these details, tap Next at the top of the screen.

If your company is using Exchange 2007 or later, that should be all there is to it. You're now presented with the list of corporate information that the iPhone can sync itself with: Email, Contacts, and Calendars. This is your opportunity to turn **off** any of these things if you don't particularly care to have them sent to your iPhone. (You can always change your mind in Settings.)

However, if your company uses Exchange 2003 (or 2007/2010 with AutoDiscovery turned off—they'll know what that means), you're now asked to provide the **server** address. It's often the same address you'd use to get to the Web version of your Outlook account, like *owa.widgetsworld-wide.com*. But if in doubt, here again, your company techie should be able to assist. Only then do you get to the screen where you choose which kinds of data to sync.

And that's it. Your iPhone will shortly bloom with the familiar sight of your office email stash, calendar appointments, and contacts.

Life on the Corporate Network

Once your iPhone is set up, you should be in wireless corporate heaven:

- **Email.** Your corporate email account shows up among whatever other email accounts you've set up (Chapter 12); you can view it in the new unified inbox, if you like. In fact, you can now have *multiple* Exchange accounts on the same phone. And not only is your email "pushed" to the phone (it arrives as it's sent, without your having to explicitly *check* for messages), but it's also synced with what you see on your computer at work. If you send, receive, delete, flag, or file any messages on your iPhone, you'll find them sent, received, deleted, flagged, or filed on your computer at the office. And vice versa.

  All the iPhone email niceties described in Chapter 12 are available to your corporate mail: opening attachments, rotating and zooming into them, and so on. Your iPhone can even play back your office voicemail, presuming that your company has one of those unified messaging systems that send out WAV audio file versions of your messages via email.

  Oh—and when you're addressing an outgoing message, the iPhone's autocomplete feature consults *both* your built-in iPhone address book *and* the corporate directory (on the Exchange server) simultaneously.

- **Contacts.** In the address book, you gain a new superpower: You can search your company's master name directory right from the iPhone. That's great when you need to track down, say, the art director in your Singapore branch.

  To perform this search, tap Contacts on the Home screen. Tap the Groups button in the upper-left corner. On the Groups screen, your company's name appears; it may contain some group names of its own. But below these, a new entry appears that mere mortal iPhone owners never see. It might say something like Directory or Global Address Book. Tap it.

On the following screen, start typing the name of the person you're looking up; the resulting matches appear as you type. (Or type the whole name, and then tap Search.)

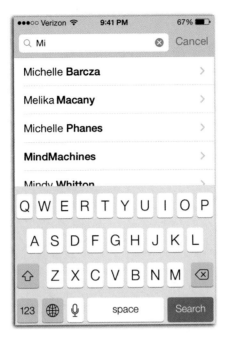

In the list of results, tap the name you want. That person's Info screen appears so you can tap to dial a number or compose a preaddressed email message. (You can't send a text message to someone in the corporate phone book, however.)

- **Calendar.** Your iPhone's calendar is wirelessly kept in sync with the master calendar back at the office. If you're on the road and your minions make changes to your schedule in Outlook, you'll know about it; you'll see the change on your iPhone's calendar.

There are some other changes to your calendar, too, as you'll find out in a moment.

> **TIP:** Don't forget that you can save battery power, syncing time, and mental clutter by limiting how much *old* calendar stuff gets synced to your iPhone. (How often do you really look back on your calendar to see what happened more than a month ago?) Page 525 has the details.

- **Notes.** If your company uses Exchange 2010 or later, your notes are now synced with Outlook on your Mac or PC, too.

Exchange + Your Stuff

The iPhone can display calendar and contact information from multiple sources at once—your Exchange calendar/address book and your own personal data, for example.

Here's how it works: Open your iPhone calendar. Tap the Calendars button at the top left. Now you're looking at all of the accounts your phone knows about; you might find separate headings for iCloud, Yahoo, Gmail, and so on, each with calendar categories listed under it. And one of them is your Exchange account (in this illustration, it's called TheAgent).

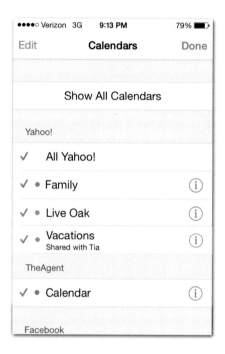

You can pull off a similar stunt in Contacts, Notes, and Reminders. Whenever you're looking at your list of contacts, for example, you can tap the Groups button (top left of the screen). Here, once again, you can tap All Contacts to see a combined address book—or you can look over only your iCloud contacts, your Exchange contacts, your personal contacts, and so on. Or tap [group name] to view only the people in your tennis circle, book club, or whatever (if you've created groups); or [your Exchange account name] to search only the company listings.

Invitations

If you've spent much time in the world of Microsoft Outlook (that is, corporate America), then you already know about *invitations.* These are electronic invitations that coworkers send you directly from Outlook. When you get one of these invitations by email, you can click Accept, Decline, or Maybe.

If you click Accept, then the meeting gets dropped onto the proper date in your Outlook calendar, and your name gets added to the list of attendees maintained by the person who invited you. If you click Maybe, then the meeting is flagged *that* way, on both your calendar and the sender's.

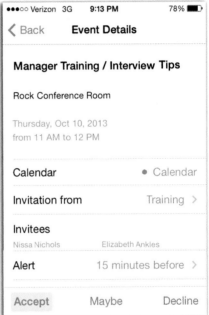

Exchange meeting invitations on the iPhone show up in *four places,* just to make sure you don't miss them:

- **In your face.** An incoming invitation pops up as a standard iPhone alert—a blue bubble, a top-of-screen banner, or whatever you've selected in Settings→Notifications→Calendar. Tap View to read what it's about, who else is coming, and where it's taking place.

  Here's also where you can tap Accept, Maybe, or Decline. ("Maybe" = Outlook's "Tentative.")

TIP: If you scroll down the Info screen, you'll see **Add Comments**. If you tap here and type a response, it will be automatically emailed to the meeting leader when you tap one of the response buttons (**Accept**, **Maybe**, **Decline**). Otherwise, the leader gets an empty email message, containing only your response to the invitation.

Tapping **Decline** deletes the invitation from every corner of your iPhone, although it will sit in your Mail program's Trash for a while in case you change your mind.

- **On your Home screen.** The Calendar icon on your Home screen sprouts a red, circled number, indicating how many invites you haven't yet looked at.

- **In email.** Invitations also appear as attachments to messages in your corporate email account, just as they would if you were using Outlook. Tap the name of the attachment to open the invitation Info window.

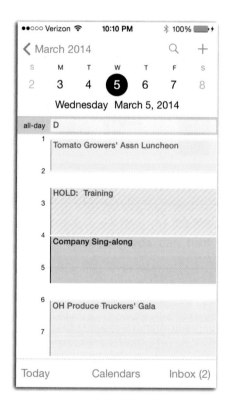

- **In Calendar.** When your iPhone is connected to your company's Exchange calendars, there's a twist: An Inbox button appears at the lower-right corner of your Calendar program.

  When an invite (or several) is waiting for you, a number in parentheses appears on this icon, letting you know you've got waiting invitations to attend to (and telling you how many). Tap the Inbox icon to see the Invitations list, which summarizes all invitations you've accepted, maybe'd, or not responded to yet.

> **TIP:** Invitations you haven't dealt with also show up on the Calendar's list view or day view with a dotted outline. That's the iPhone's clever visual way of showing you just how severely your workday will be ruined if you accept this meeting.

You can also *generate* invitations. When you're filling out the Info form for a new appointment, you get a field called Invitees. Tap there to enter the email addresses of the people you'd like to invite.

Your invitation will show up in whatever calendar programs they use, and they'll never know you didn't send it from some corporate copy of Microsoft Outlook.

A Word on Troubleshooting

If you're having trouble with your Exchange syncing and can't find any steps that work, then ask your Exchange administrators to make sure that ActiveSync's settings are correct on their end. You've heard the old saying that in 99 percent of computer troubleshooting, the problem lies between the keyboard and the chair? The other 1 percent of the time, it's between the *administrator's* keyboard and chair.

> **TIP:** You can access your company's SharePoint sites, too. That's a Microsoft document-collaboration feature that's also a common part of corporate online life.
>
> The iPhone's browser can access these sites; it can also open Word, Excel, PowerPoint, and PDF documents you find there. Handy indeed!

Virtual Private Networking (VPN)

The typical corporate network is guarded by a team of steely-eyed administrators for whom Job One is preventing access by unauthorized visitors. They perform this job primarily with the aid of a super-secure firewall that seals off the company's network from the Internet.

So how can you tap into the network from the road? Only one solution is both secure and cheap: the *virtual private network,* or VPN. Running a VPN lets you create a super-secure "tunnel" from your iPhone, across the Internet, and straight into your corporate network. All data passing through this tunnel is heavily encrypted. To the Internet eavesdropper, it looks like so much undecipherable gobbledygook.

VPN is, however, a corporate tool, run by corporate nerds. Your company's tech staff can tell you whether or not there's a VPN server set up for you to use.

If there is one, then you'll need to know what type of server it is. The iPhone can connect to VPN servers that speak *PPTP* (Point-to-Point Tunneling Protocol) and *L2TP/IPSec* (Layer 2 Tunneling Protocol over the IP Security Protocol), both relatives of the PPP language spoken by modems. Most corporate VPN servers work with at least one of these protocols.

The iPhone can also connect to Cisco servers, which are among the most popular systems in corporate America, and with a special app, Juniper's Junos Pulse servers, too.

To set up your VPN connection, visit Settings→General→VPN. Tap the On/Off switch to make the VPN configuration screen pop up. Tap L2TP, PPTP, or IPSec (that's the Cisco one), depending on which kind of server your company uses (ask the network administrator).

The most critical bits of information to fill in are these:

- **Server.** The Internet address of your VPN server (for example, *vpn. ferrets-r-us.com*).

- **Account; Password.** Here's your user account name and password, as supplied by the IT folks.

- **Secret.** If your office offers L2TP connections, then you'll need yet another password called a Shared Secret to ensure that the server you're connecting to is really the server you intend to connect to.

Once everything is in place, the iPhone can connect to the corporate network and fetch your corporate mail. You don't have to do anything special on your end; everything works just as described in this chapter.

NOTE: Some networks require that you type the currently displayed password on an *RSA SecurID card,* which your administrator will provide. This James Bondish, credit card–like thing displays a password that changes every few seconds, making it rather difficult for hackers to learn "the" password.

VPN on Demand

If you like to access your corporate email or internal Web site a few times a day, having to enter your name-and-password credentials over and over again can get old fast. Fortunately, iOS offers a huge time-saving assist with its introduction of *VPN on Demand.*

That is, you just open up Safari and tap the corporate bookmark; the iPhone creates the VPN channel automatically, behind the scenes, and connects.

There's nothing you have to do, or even anything you *can* do, to make this feature work; your company's network nerds have to turn this feature on at their end.

They'll create a **configuration profile** that you'll install on your iPhone. It includes the VPN server settings, an electronic security certificate, and a list of domains and URLs that will automatically turn on the iPhone's VPN feature.

From now on, whenever you open Safari and try to visit a Web page that's behind the company's firewall, the iPhone makes the VPN connection for you automatically. You're spared the hassle of entering a user name or password.

When your iPhone goes to sleep, it terminates the VPN connection, both for security purposes and to save battery power.

NOTE: Clearly, eliminating the VPN sign-in process also weakens the security the VPN was invented for in the first place. Therefore, you'd be well advised—and probably required by your IT guys—to use the iPhone's password feature, so some evil corporate spy (or teenage thug) can't just steal your iPhone and start snooping through the corporate servers.

16

Settings

The Settings app is like the Control Panel in Windows or System Preferences on the Mac. It's a tweaking center that affects every aspect of the iPhone: the screen, ringtones, email, Web connection, and so on. You scroll the Settings list as you would any iPhone list: by dragging your finger up or down the screen.

Most of the items on the Settings page are doorways to other screens, where you make the actual changes. When you're finished inspecting or changing the preference settings, you can return to the main Settings screen by tapping the Settings button in the upper-left corner—or by just pressing the Home button.

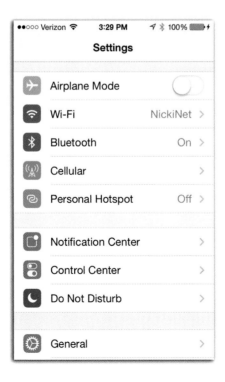

In this book, you can read about the iPhone's preference settings in the appropriate spots—wherever they're relevant. And the Control Center, of course, is designed to *eliminate* trips into Settings.

But so you'll have it all in one place, here's an item-by-item walkthrough of the Settings app and its new structure in iOS 7.

Two New Settings Tricks

The Settings app is many screens deep. You might "drill down" by tapping, for example, General, then Keyboard, then Shortcuts. It's a lot of tapping, a lot of navigation.

So in iOS 7, you have two kinds of shortcuts.

First, you can jump directly to a particular Settings screen—from within any app—using Siri (Chapter 4). You can say, for example, "Open Sound settings," "Open Brightness settings," "Open Notification settings," "Open WiFi settings," and so on. Siri promptly takes you to the corresponding screen—no tapping required.

Second, you can now *swipe to go back.* Once you've drilled down to, say, General→Keyboard→Shortcuts, you can "drill out" again by swiping across the screen to the right. (Begin swiping on the margin of the phone, outside the screen itself.)

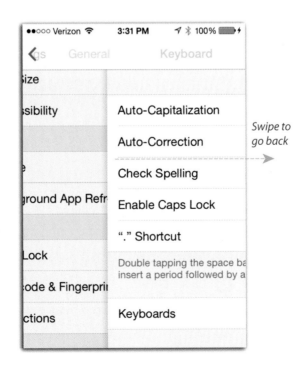

Airplane Mode

As you're probably aware, you're not allowed to make cellphone calls on U.S. airplanes. According to legend (if not science), a cellphone's radio can interfere with a plane's navigation equipment.

But the iPhone does a lot more than make calls. Are you supposed to deprive yourself of all the music, videos, movies, and email that you could be using in flight, just because cellphones are forbidden?

Nope. Just turn on Airplane mode by tapping the switch at the top of the Settings list (so the switch background turns green). The word Cellular dims there in Settings (you've turned off your cellular circuitry); but the WiFi and Bluetooth switches turn off instead—meaning that you're now welcome to switch them back on even while in Airplane Mode.

Now it's safe (and permitted) to use the iPhone in flight—at least after takeoff, when you hear the announcement about "approved electronics"— because the cellular features of the iPhone are turned off completely. You can't make calls, but you can do anything else in the iPhone's bag of non-wireless tricks.

 TIP: Turning Airplane mode on and off is faster if you use the Control Center (page 37). Same for WiFi, described next.

WiFi

WiFi—wireless Internet networking—is one of the iPhone's best features. This item in Settings opens the WiFi Networks screen, where you'll find three useful controls:

- **WiFi On/Off.** If you don't plan to use WiFi, then turning it off gets you a lot more life out of each battery charge. Tap anywhere on this On/Off slider to change its status.

 TIP: Turning on Airplane mode automatically turns off the WiFi antenna—but you can turn WiFi back on. That's handy when you're on a flight with WiFi on board.

- **Choose a Network.** Here's a list of all nearby WiFi networks that the iPhone can "see," complete with a signal-strength indicator and a padlock icon if a password is required. An Other item lets you access WiFi networks that are invisible and secret unless you know their names. See Chapter 10 for details on using WiFi with the iPhone.

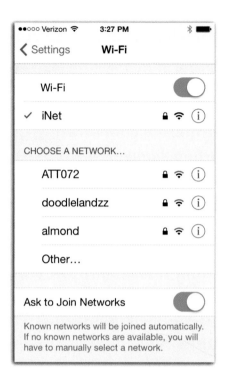

- **Ask to Join Networks.** If this option is On, then whenever you attempt to get online, the iPhone sniffs around to find a WiFi network. If it finds one you haven't used before, the iPhone invites you, with a small dialog box, to hop onto it.

  So why would you ever want to turn this feature off? To avoid getting bombarded with invitations to join WiFi networks, which can happen in heavily populated areas, and to save battery power. (The phone will still hop automatically onto hotspots it's joined in the past.)

Carrier

If you see this panel at all, then you're doubly lucky: First, you're enjoying a trip overseas; second, you have a choice of cellphone carriers who have roaming agreements with AT&T, Verizon, T-Mobile, or Sprint. Tap your favorite and prepare to pay some serious roaming fees.

Bluetooth

Here's the on/off switch for the iPhone's Bluetooth transmitter, which is required to communicate with a Bluetooth earpiece, keyboard, laptop (for tethering), or hands-free system in a car. When you turn the switch on, you're offered the chance to pair the iPhone with other Bluetooth equipment; the paired gadgets are listed here for ease of connecting and disconnecting.

> **TIP:** The Control Center (page 37) has a Bluetooth button. It's faster to use that than to visit Settings.

Cellular

These days, not many cellphone plans let you use the Internet as much as you want; most have monthly limits. For example, your $120 a month might include 4 gigabytes of Internet data use.

Most of the settings on this screen are meant to help you control how much Internet data your phone uses.

- **Cellular Data.** This is the on/off switch for Internet data. If you're traveling overseas, you might want to turn this off to avoid racking up insanely high roaming charges. Your smartphone becomes a dumb-phone, suitable for making calls but not for getting online. (You can still get online in a WiFi hotspot.)

- **Enable LTE.** Here you can turn off LTE. Every now and then, you'll be in some area where you can't connect to the Internet even though you seem to have an LTE signal; forcing your phone to the 4G or 3G network often gives you at least some connection. Turning LTE off does just that.

- **Roaming.** These controls, which appear only for CDMA carriers like Verizon and Sprint, give you power to prevent staggering international roaming fees. For example, you might set your phone to "off" for Data Roaming, but "on" for Voice Roaming. Turning off the last item, International CDMA, forces the phone to use only the more common GSM networks while roaming; sometimes you get better call and data quality that way, and you may save money (ask your carrier in advance).

- **Personal Hotspot.** Here's where you go the very first time you turn on Personal Hotspot (page 376). Once that's done, a new Personal Hotspot on/off switch appears on the main Settings screen, so you won't have to dig this deep in the future.

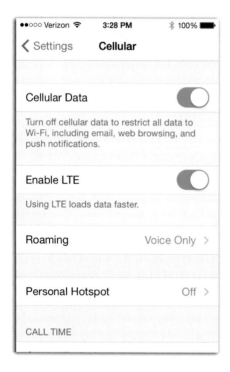 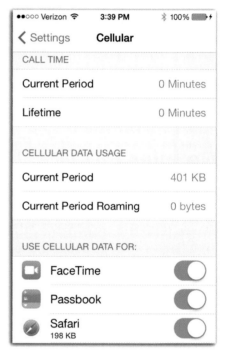

- **Call Time.** The statistics here break down how much time you've spent talking on the iPhone, both in the Current Period (that is, this billing month) and in the iPhone's entire Lifetime. That's right, folks: You now own a cellphone that keeps track of your minutes, to help you avoid exceeding the number you've signed up for (and therefore racking up 45-cent overage minutes).

- **Cellular Data Usage.** The phone also helps you track how much Internet data you've used this month, too, expressed as megabytes of data, including email messages and Web-page material. These are extremely important statistics, because your iPhone plan is probably capped at, for example, 2 gigabytes a month. If you exceed your monthly maximum, you're instantly charged $15 or $20 for another chunk of data. So keeping an eye on these statistics is a very good idea.

  (The Current Period means so far this month; Current Period Roaming means overseas or in places where your cell company doesn't have service.)

Now, your cellphone company is supposed to text you as you get closer and closer to your monthly limit—but in iOS 7, for the first time, you can now check your Internet spending at any time.

- **Use cellular data for:** This list offers individual on/off switches for every single Internet-using app on your phone. Each one is an item that could consume Internet data without your awareness. Now, at last, you can shut up the data hogs you really don't feel like spending megabytes on.

Personal Hotspot

Once you've turned this feature on (page 376) in Cellular, this command appears here, too—on the main Settings screen for your convenience.

Notification Center

This panel lists all the apps that think they have the right to nag for your attention. Flight-tracking programs alert you that there's an hour before takeoff. Social-networking programs ping you when someone's trying to reach you. Games let you know when it's your move. Instant-messaging apps ding to let you know that you have a new message. It can add up to a lot of interruption.

On this panel, you can tailor, to an almost ridiculous degree, how you want to be nagged. See Chapter 1 for a complete description.

Control Center

The glorious new Control Center is written up on page 37. There are two settings to change here. If you turn off Access on Lock Screen, then the Control Center isn't available on the phone's Lock screen. No passing prankster can change your phone's settings without your password.

And if you turn off Access Within Apps, you won't land in the Control Center by accident when you're playing some game that involves a lot of swiping.

Do Not Disturb

Ah, yes, here it is: one of iOS's most brilliant and useful features. See page 95.

General

The General pages offer a *huge,* motley assortment of settings governing the behavior of the virtual keyboard, the Bluetooth transmitter, the password-protection feature, and about 6 trillion other things.

- **About.** Tapping this item opens a page for the statistics nut. Here you can find out how many songs, videos, and photos your iPhone holds; how much storage your iPhone has; techie details like the iPhone's software and firmware versions, serial number, model, WiFi and Bluetooth addresses, and so on. (It's kind of cool to see how many applications you've installed.)

  At the very top, you can tap the phone's name to rename it.

- **Software Update.** When Apple releases a new software update for your iPhone, you can download it directly to the phone. You no longer need to connect to a Mac or a PC for that job.

  You'll know when an update is waiting for you, because you'll see a little number badge on the Settings icon, as well as on the word General in Settings. Tap it, and then tap Software Update, to see and install the update. (If no number badge is waiting, then tapping Software Update just shows you your current iOS version.)

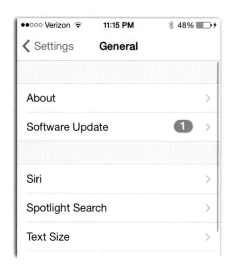

- **Siri.** If you have an iPhone 4s or later, you have this item. It offers the master on/off switch for Siri, the amazing voice-commanded virtual-assistant feature described in Chapter 4. (If you turn it off, then your iPhone offers the older, more limited Voice Control feature that controls only dialing and music playback.)

  Also on this panel: a choice of languages; a Voice Gender setting (male or female); an option to have Siri's responses read aloud only when you're on headset (so you don't disturb those around you); an option to choose your own Contacts card, so Siri knows, for example, where to go when you say, "Give me directions home"; and Raise to Speak, which triggers Siri whenever you hold the phone up to your head (thus saving you holding down the Home button).

- **Spotlight Search.** Here you can control which kinds of things Spotlight finds when it searches your phone. Tap to turn off the kinds of data you don't want it to search: Mail, Notes, Calendar, whatever.

TIP: You can also drag these categories into a new order, using the little ☰ as a handle. Why? Because that's the order that things will appear in the results list when you actually perform a search. If you mainly search your text messages, for example, then by all means drag Messages to the top of the list, so they'll appear first.

- **Text Size.** In iOS 7, Apple finally realized what anyone over 40 already knows: As you age, small type becomes harder to read. For the first time, there's now a universal text-size slider for every app on your phone—and this is it.

  Technically, what you're seeing is the front end for the new *Dynamic Type* feature. And even more technically, not all apps work with Dynamic Type (yet). But most of the built-in Apple apps do—Contacts, Mail, Maps, Messages, Notes, Phone, Reminders, and Safari Reader—and other software companies will follow suit.

TIP: If the largest type setting here still isn't big enough, you're not out of luck. Hiding in the Accessibility panel described next, there's an option called Larger Type. Tap it and then turn on Larger Dynamic Type to make the large end of the type-size scale twice as big. Now you can read the phone from the moon.

- **Accessibility.** These options are intended for people with visual, hearing, and motor impairments, but they might come in handy now and then for almost anyone. All of these features are described in Chapter 5.

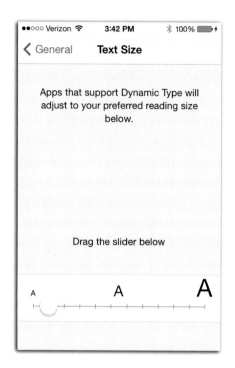
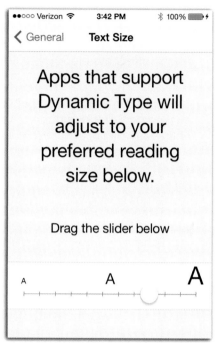

- **Usage.** This screen is proof that the iPhone is an obsessive-compulsive. You find out here that it knows everything about you, your apps, and your iPhone activity.

  For example, the Storage section lists every single app on your iPhone, along with how much of your storage it's eating up. (Biggest apps are at the top.) Better yet, you can tap an app to see how much it and its associated documents consume—and, for apps you've installed yourself, there's a Delete App button staring you in the face.

  The idea, of course, is that if you're running out of space on your iPhone, this display makes it incredibly easy to see what the space hogs are—and delete them.

  The next section, iCloud, also reports on storage—but in this case, it shows you how much storage you're using on your iCloud account. (Remember, you get 5 gigabytes free; after that, you have to pay.) If you tap Manage Storage, you get to see how much of that space is used up by which apps—Mail is usually one of the biggest offenders.

  The next item, Battery Percentage, appears on this screen for no apparent reason; still, it's nice. Turn it On to see your battery gauge with a numeric percentage readout (for example, "89%").

The **Usage** readout shows, in hours and minutes, how much time you've spent using all iPhone functions since the last time it was charged up (although it's not broken down by activity, alas). **Standby** is how much time the iPhone has spent in Sleep mode, awaiting calls.

- **Background App Refresh.** For years, Apple resisted giving the iPhone full multitasking. If all of your apps could happily churn away in the background, the argument went, they'd chew through your battery in an eye blink. So Apple permitted only a few lucky ones, like music playback and GPS, to run in the background.

  No more. In iOS 7, any app is allowed to keep running behind the scenes. You still run the risk of having your battery run down—but at least you can now specify exactly which apps are allowed to keep running. The list that appears here identifies apps that try to access the Internet to update themselves, even when they're not the app you're using.

  You can also turn off the master Background App Refresh switch here. Now the only apps that can run in the background are the standard limited suite (like music and GPS).

- **Auto-Lock.** As you may have noticed, the iPhone locks itself after a few minutes of inactivity on your part. In locked mode, the iPhone ignores screen taps. Without this mode, reaching into your pocket for a toothpick or a ticket stub could, at least theoretically, fire up some iPhone program or even dial a call from your pocket.

  On the **Auto-Lock** screen, you can change the interval of inactivity before the auto-lock occurs (1 minute, 2 minutes, and so on), or you can tap **Never**. In that case, the iPhone locks only when you click it to sleep.

- **Passcode Lock** or **Passcode & Fingerprint.** Here's where you set up a password for your phone, or (if you have an iPhone 5s) where you teach the phone to recognize your fingerprints. Full details appear at the end of Chapter 1.

- **Restrictions.** This means "parental controls." (Apple called it "Restrictions" instead so as not to turn off potential corporate customers. Can't you just hear it? " 'Parental controls?' This thing is for *consumers?!*") Complete details appear on page 549.

- **Date & Time.** At the top of this screen, you'll see an option to turn on **24-hour time**, also known as military time, in which you see "1700" instead of "5:00 PM." (You'll see this change everywhere times appear, including at the top edge of the screen.)

Set Automatically refers to the iPhone's built-in clock. If this item is turned on, then the iPhone finds out what time it is from an atomic clock out on the Internet. If not, then you have to set the clock yourself. (Turning this option off produces two more rows of controls: the Time Zone option becomes available, so you can specify your time zone, and a "number spinner" appears so you can set the clock.)

- **Keyboard.** Here you can turn off some of the very best features of the iPhone's virtual keyboard. (All of these shortcuts are described in Chapter 2.)

It's hard to imagine why you wouldn't want any of these tools working for you and saving you time and keystrokes, but here you go: Auto-Capitalization is where the iPhone thoughtfully capitalizes the first letter of every new sentence for you. Auto-Correction is where the iPhone suggests spelling corrections as you type. Check Spelling, of course, refers to the pop-up spelling suggestions. Enable Caps Lock is the on/off switch for the Caps Lock feature, in which a fast double-tap on the Shift key turns on Caps Lock. Finally, "." Shortcut turns on or off the "type two spaces to make a period" shortcut for the ends of sentences.

Below those options is International Keyboards. Tap it to view the 46 keyboard layouts and languages the iPhone offers for your typing pleasure. See page 62 for details on how you rotate among them.

NOTE: There are some crazy keyboard options in here. For example, you can add a new keyboard, like English UK, and then tap its name to change its layout independently for the software keyboard (onscreen); you can also specify the layout of a wireless Bluetooth keyboard that you've attached.

Finally, you get iOS's typing-shortcuts feature, which expands abbreviations that you set up (like "sys") to longer phrases (like "See you soon!"). See page 59.

- **International.** The iPhone: It's not just for Americans anymore. The Language screen lets you choose a language for the iPhone's menus and messages; Voice Control determines what language the iPhone listens for when you utter spoken commands. (You can choose one language for Siri, another language for voice dialing on non-Siri phones.) The Keyboards item here opens the same keyboard-choosing screen described above. Region Format controls how the iPhone displays dates, times, and numbers. (For example, in the U.S., Christmas is on 12/25; in Europe, it's 25/12.)

And **Calendar** lets you choose which kind of calendar system you want to use: Gregorian (that is, "normal"), Japanese, or Buddhist.

- **iTunes Wi-Fi Sync.** You can sync your iPhone with a computer wirelessly, as long as the phone is plugged in and in WiFi. Details on page 450.

- **VPN**. See Chapter 15 for details on Virtual Private Networking.

- **Profiles.** Here's where you choose a configuration profile that may have been distributed to you by your corporate overlords, as described in Chapter 15.

- **Reset.** On the Reset screen, you'll find six ways to erase your tracks. **Reset All Settings** takes all the iPhone's settings back to the way they were when it came from Apple. Your data, music, and videos remain in place, but the settings you've changed all go back to their factory settings.

  Erase All Content and Settings is the one you want when you sell your iPhone, or when you're captured by the enemy and want to make sure they will learn nothing from you or your iPhone.

> **NOTE:** This feature takes awhile to complete—and that's a good thing. The iPhone doesn't just delete your data; it also overwrites the newly erased memory with gibberish to make sure the bad guys can't see any of your deleted info, even with special hacking tools.

  Reset Network Settings makes the iPhone forget all the memorized WiFi networks it currently autorecognizes.

  Reset Keyboard Dictionary has to do with the iPhone's autocorrection feature, which kicks in whenever you're trying to input text. Ordinarily, every time you type something the iPhone doesn't recognize—some name or foreign word, for example—and you don't accept the iPhone's suggestion, it adds the word you typed to its dictionary so it doesn't bother you with a suggestion again the next time. If you think you've entered too many words that aren't legitimate terms, you can delete from its little brain all the new "words" you've taught it.

  Reset Home Screen Layout undoes any icon-moving you've done on the Home screen. It also consolidates all your Home screen icons, fitting them, 20 per page, onto as few screens as possible.

Finally, **Reset Location & Privacy** refers to the "OK to use location services?" warning that appears whenever an iPhone program, like Maps or Camera, tries to figure out where you are. This button makes the iPhone forget all your responses to those permission boxes. In other words, you'll be asked permission all over again the first time you use each of those programs.

Sounds

Here's a more traditional cellphone settings screen: the place where you choose a ringtone sound for incoming calls.

- **Vibrate on Ring, Vibrate on Silent.** Like any self-respecting cellphone, the iPhone has a Vibrate mode—a little shudder in your pocket that might get your attention when you can't hear the ringing. As you can see, there are two on/off controls for the vibration: one for when the phone is in Silent mode and one for when the ringer's on.

- **Ringer and Alerts.** The slider here controls the volume of the phone's ringing.

  Of course, it's usually faster to adjust the ring volume by pressing the up/down buttons on the left edge whenever you're not on a call or playing music or video. But if you find that your volume buttons are getting pressed accidentally in your pocket, you can also turn off Change with Buttons. Now you can adjust the volume *only* with this slider, here in Settings.

- **Sounds and Vibration Patterns.** The iPhone is, of course, a cellphone—and therefore, of course, it sometimes rings. The sound it makes when it rings is up to you; by tapping Ringtone, you can view the iPhone's list of 25 built-in ringtones, plus 27 "alert tones," plus any new ones you've added yourself.

  Tap a ring sound to hear it. After you've tapped one you like, confirm your choice by tapping Sounds to return to the Sounds screen.

NOTE: Of course, you can choose a different ringtone for each person in your phone book (page 86).

But why stop with a ringtone? The iPhone can make all kinds of other sounds to alert you: to the arrival of a new voicemail, text message, or email; to the successful sending of an outgoing email message, tweet, or Facebook post; to calendar or Reminders alarms; to the arrival of AirDrop files; and so on.

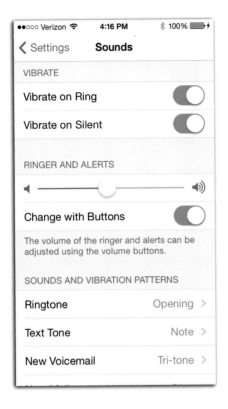

This is a big deal—not just because you can express your individuality through your choice of ringtones, text tones, reminder tones, and so on, but also because you can finally distinguish your iPhone's blips and bleeps from somebody else's in the same family or workplace.

For each of these events, tap the light-gray text that identifies the current sound for that event ("Tri-tone" or "Ding," for example). On the resulting screen, tap the different sound options to find one you like; then tap Sounds to return to the main Sounds screen.

On that Sounds screen, you can also turn on or off the Lock Sounds (the sounds you get when you tap the Sleep/Wake switch on the top of the phone) and the Keyboard Clicks that play when you type on the virtual keyboard.

Wallpapers & Brightness

Ordinarily, the iPhone controls its own screen brightness. An ambient-light sensor hidden behind the smoked glass at the top of the iPhone's face samples the room brightness each time you wake the phone and adjusts the screen automatically: brighter in bright rooms, dimmer in darker ones.

When you prefer more manual control, here's what you can do:

- **Brightness slider.** Drag the handle on this slider to control the screen brightness manually, keeping in mind that more brightness means shorter battery life.

  If Auto-Brightness is turned on, then the changes you make here are relative to the iPhone's self-chosen brightness. In other words, if you goose the brightness by 20 percent, then the screen will always be 20 percent brighter than the iPhone would have chosen for itself.

> **TIP:** The Control Center (page 37) gives you a much quicker road to the Brightness slider. This version in Settings is just for old-timers.

- **Auto-Brightness On/Off.** Tap anywhere on this switch to disable the ambient-light sensor completely. Now the brightness of the screen is under complete manual control.

Wallpaper can mean either the photo on the Unlock screen (what you see when you wake the iPhone up), or the background picture on your Home screen. On this panel, you can change the image used for either one. Page 248 has step-by-step instructions.

Privacy

By "privacy," Apple means "apps accessing your data."

A hullabaloo arose in the spring of 2011, when researchers discovered that the iPhone was keeping a record of your geographical movements.

The information wasn't being transmitted to Apple, the government, or the Warren Commission; it was just sitting there on your hard drive, accessible only with Unix commands. But even so, conspiracy theorists immediately went into hysterics. "Apple is tracking you," went the headlines.

Apple was quick to explain. No, it wasn't tracking you. It was collecting the locations of WiFi hotspots, as described on page 336. Even so, Apple quickly stopped backing up the location database to your computer, changed the duration of the storage to only a week's worth, and stopped collecting hotspot locations if you turned off Location Services.

But it's not just your location. Many an app works better, or claims to, when it has access to your address book, calendar, photos, and so on. Generally, when you run such an app for the first time, it explicitly asks you for permission to access each kind of data. But here, `on this iOS 7 panel, you have a central dashboard—and on/off switches—for each data type and the apps that want it.

Location Services

Suppose, for example, that you tap Location Services. At the top of the next screen, you'll find the master on/off switch for all Location Services. If you turn it off, then the iPhone can no longer determine where you are on a map, geotag your photos, find the closest ATM, tell your friends where you're hanging out, and so on.

Furthermore, this screen goes on to list every single app that uses your location information, and it lets you turn off this feature on a per-app basis. You might want to do that for privacy's sake—or you might want to do that to save battery power, since the location searches sap away a little juice every time.

The little ➹ icon indicates which apps have actually *used* your location data. If it's gray, that app has checked your location in the past 24 hours; if it's purple, it's locating you right now; if it's hollow, that app is using a geofence—it's waiting for you to enter or leave a certain location, like Home or Work. The Reminders app uses the geofencing feature, for example.

Even more controls await if you tap System Services. Here are the on/off switches for the iPhone's own features that use your location:

- **Cell Network Search** lets your phone tap into Apple's database of cellular frequencies by location, which speeds up connections.

- **Compass Calibration** lets the Compass app know where you are, so that it can accurately tell you which way's North.

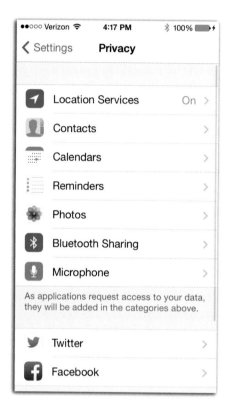

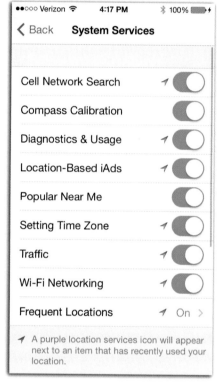

- **Diagnostics and Usage** sends location information back to Apple, along with diagnostic information so that, for example, Apple can see where calls are being dropped.

- **Location-Based iAds** refer to advertisements that Apple slaps at the bottom of certain apps. Or, rather, to the ones whose advertisers are near you, based on your current location. Turn this off, and the ads won't know where you are.

- **Popular Near Me,** a new iOS 7 feature, means "apps downloaded by people around here." If you turn this switch on, you'll see a new section in the App Store listing these apps.

- **Setting Time Zone.** Here's where you can prevent the iPhone from setting its own clock when you arrive in a new time zone. You'd be crazy to do that, but, hey—if you're really paranoid, Apple wants to give you every possible way to shut it down.

- **Traffic.** Turn this off if it bothers you that Apple is collecting anonymous speed/location data from your phone. (This data, collected from millions of iPhone owners, allows Maps to know where there are traffic tie-ups.)

- **WiFi Networking.** Your iPhone knows where it is using GPS circuitry, aided by references to Apple's massive database of known WiFi hotspots (see page 336). If you want to opt out of Apple's massive WiFi hotspot-detection network, then turn this off.

- **Frequent Locations.** You know the new Today view of the Notification Center (page 43)? It's smart enough to tell you, voluntarily, what the traffic will be like on your commute. And how does it know what your commute is? Because iOS 7 notices places you go a lot. (This information also provides a similar function to iOS in the Car—it thinks ahead about your commute.)

NOTE: About a dozen car companies have said that they'll introduce iOS in the Car in their 2014 models. Basically, it makes the iPhone screen image appear on the car's dashboard screen. You can now make phone calls, play your music, send and receive messages, get directions, and so on, using the car's dashboard screen instead of your phone.

Your frequent locations are stored only on your phone, in an encrypted form; they're not backed up on iTunes or iCloud or transmitted to anyone, not even Apple. But if you'd rather your phone stop noticing where you're going, you can turn that off here.

- **Status Bar Icon.** Your phone doesn't just let you determine which kinds of information Apple collects from it; it even shows you *when* that data is being collected. If this switch is on, the Location symbol (➤) appears on your menu bar, in real time, whenever your phone is transmitting any data (of the types listed above) to Apple.

Contacts, Calendars...

Below the Location Services heading, this panel lists a number of core iPhone data types that your apps might sometimes seek to access. A photo-sharing program might want to tap into your Contacts, for example, to make it easier to send pictures. A flight-tracking app might want to access your Calendar data.

Tap a category—Contacts, for example—to see a list of the apps that are merrily tapping into its data. And to see the on/off switch, which you can use to block that app's access.

Twitter, Facebook

Similarly, new apps you download may sometimes want access to your Facebook and Twitter accounts. Lots of apps, for example, harness your existing Facebook account for the purpose of logging in or finding friends to play games with. Tap Twitter or Facebook to see which apps are using your account information.

iCloud

Here's where you enter your iCloud name and password—and where you find the on/off switches for the various kinds of data synchronization that iCloud can perform for you. Chapter 14 tells all.

Mail, Contacts, Calendars

There's a lotta stuff going on in one place here. Breathe deeply; take it slow.

Accounts

Your email accounts are listed here; this is also where you set up new ones. See page 412 for details.

Fetch New Data

More than ever, the iPhone is a real-time window into the data stream of your life. Whatever changes are made to your calendar, address book, or email back on your computer at home (or at the office) can magically show up on your iPhone, seconds later, even though you're across the country.

That's the beauty of "push" email, contacts, and calendars. You get push email if you have a free Yahoo Mail account. You get all three if you've signed up for an iCloud account (Chapter 14), or if your company uses Microsoft Exchange (Chapter 15).

Having an iPhone that's updated with these critical life details in real time is amazingly useful, but there are several reasons why you might want to turn off the Push feature. You'll save battery power, save money when you're traveling abroad (where every "roaming" Internet use can run up your cellular bill), and avoid the constant "new mail" jingle when you're try-ing to concentrate (or sleep).

And what if you don't have a push email service, or if you turn it off? In that case, your iPhone can still do a pretty decent job of keeping you up to date. It can check your email every 15 minutes, every half-hour, every hour, or only on command (**Manually**). That's the decision you make in the **Fetch New Data** panel here. (Keep in mind that more frequent checking means shorter battery life.)

TIP: The iPhone always checks email each time you open the Mail program, regardless of your setting here. If you have a push service like iCloud or Exchange, it also checks for changes to your schedule or address book each time you open Calendar or Contacts—again, no matter what your setting here.

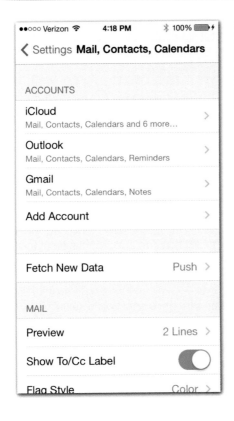
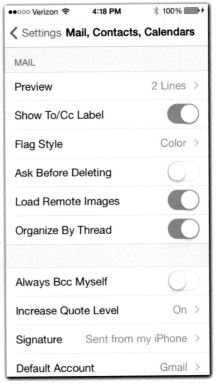

Mail

Here you set up your email account information, specify how often you want the iPhone to check for new messages, how you want your Mail app to look, and more.

- **Preview.** It's cool that the iPhone shows you the first few lines of text in every message. Here you can specify how many lines of text appear. More lines mean you can skim your inbound messages without having to open many of them; fewer lines mean more messages fit without scrolling.

- **Show To/Cc Label.** If you turn this option on, then a tiny, light-gray logo appears next to many of the messages in your inbox. The **To** logo indicates that this message was addressed directly to you; the **Cc** logo means you were merely "copied" on a message primarily intended for someone else.

  If there's no logo at all, then the message is in some other category. Maybe it came from a mailing list, or it's an email blast (a Bcc), or the message is from you, or it's a bounced message.

- **Flag Style.** In iOS 7's Mail app, you can flag messages to draw your own attention to them (page 420). You can use the old-style flag icon—or, for more information and visual spark, you can apply an orange dot. Here's where you choose.

- **Ask Before Deleting.** Ordinarily, you can delete an open message quickly and easily, just by tapping the 🗑 icon. But if you'd prefer to encounter an additional confirmation step before the message disappears, then turn this option on.

NOTE: The confirmation box appears only when you're deleting an open message—not when you delete one from the list of messages.

- **Load Remote Images.** Spammers, the vile undercrust of lowlife society, have a famous trick. When they send you email that includes a picture, they don't actually paste the picture into the message. Instead, they include a "bug"—a piece of code that instructs your email program to *fetch* the missing graphic from the Internet. Why? Because that gives the spammer the ability to track who has actually opened the junk mail, making their email addresses much more valuable for reselling to other spammers.

  That's a long explanation for a simple feature: If you turn this option off, then the iPhone does not fetch "bug" image files at all. You're not flagged as a sucker by the spammers. You'll see empty squares in the email where the images ought to be. (Graphics sent by normal people and legitimate companies are generally pasted right into the email, so they'll still show up just fine.)

- **Organize By Thread.** This is the on/off switch for the feature that clumps related back-and-forths into individual items in your Mail inbox.

- **Always Bcc Myself.** If this option is on, then you'll get a secret copy of any message you send. That's handy if you want your computer to have a record of replies you sent from your phone.

- **Increase Quote Level.** Each time you reply to a reply, it gets indented more, so you and your correspondents can easily distinguish one reply from the next.

	Display "Last, First"	Display "First, Last"
Sort order "First, Last"	O'Furniture, Patty Minella, Sal Peace, Warren	Patty O'Furniture Sal Minella Warren Peace
Sort order "Last, First"	Minella, Sal O'Furniture, Patty Peace, Warren	Sal Minella Patty O'Furniture Warren Peace

- **Signature.** A signature is a bit of text that gets stamped at the bottom of your outgoing email messages. Here's where you can change yours.

- **Default Account.** Your iPhone can manage an unlimited number of email accounts. Here, tap the account you want to be your *default*—the one that's used when you create a new message from another program, like a Safari link, or when you're on the All Inboxes screen of Mail.

Contacts

Contacts is a first-class citizen with an icon of its own on the Home screen, so it gets its own little set of options in Settings.

- **Sort Order, Display Order.** The question is: How do you want the names in your Contacts list sorted—by first name or by last name?

  Note that you can have them *sorted* one way but *displayed* another way. This table shows how a very short Contacts list would appear, using each of the four combinations of settings:

  As you can see, not all of these combinations make sense.

- **Short Name.** When this new iOS 7 switch is on, the Mail app may fit more email addressees' names into its narrow To box by shortening them. It may display "M. Mouse," for example, or "Mickey," or even "M.M."—whatever you select here.

  Prefer Nicknames is similar. It instructs Mail to display the *nicknames* for your friends (as determined in Contacts) instead of their real names.

- **My Info.** Tap here to tell the phone which card in Contacts represents *you.* Knowing who you are is useful to the phone in a number of places—for example, it's how Siri knows what you mean when you say, "Give me directions home."

- **Default Account.** Here again, the iPhone can manage multiple address books—from iCloud, Gmail, Yahoo, and so on. Here, tap the account you want new contacts to fall into, if you haven't specified one in advance.

- **Import SIM Contacts.** If you came to the iPhone from another, lesser GSM phone, then your phone book may be stored on its little SIM card instead of in the phone itself. In that case, you don't have to retype all those names and numbers to bring them into your iPhone. This button can do the job for you. (The results may not be pretty. For example, some phones store all address-book data in CAPITAL LETTERS.)

Calendars

Your iPhone's calendar can be updated by remote control, wirelessly, through the air, either by your company (via Exchange, Chapter 15) or by somebody at home using your computer (via iCloud, Chapter 14).

- **New Invitation Alerts.** Part of that wireless joy is receiving invitations to meetings, which coworkers can shoot to you from Outlook or even the iPhone—wirelessly, when you're thousands of miles apart. Very cool.

  Unless, that is, you're getting a lot of these invitations, and it's beginning to drive you a little nuts. In that case, turn New Invitation Alerts off.

- **Time Zone Support.** Now, here's a mind-teaser for you world travelers. If an important event is scheduled for 6:30 p.m. New York time, and you're in California, how should that event appear on your calendar? Should it appear as 3:30 p.m. (that is, your local time)? Or should it remain stuck at 6:30 (East Coast time)?

  It's not an idle question, because it also affects reminders and alarms.

Out of the box, **Time Zone Support** is turned on.

That is, everything stays on the calendar just the way you entered it, even as you travel from time zone to time zone.

If you turn Time Zone Support off, then the iPhone automatically translates all your appointments into the local time. If you scheduled a reminder to record a TV movie at 8:00 p.m. New York time, and you fly to California, then the reminder will pop up at 5:00 p.m. local time. The iPhone actually learns (from the local cell towers) what time zone it's in, changes its own clock automatically, and literally slides appointments around on your calendar. Handy—but dangerous if you forget what you've done.

NOTE: If Time Zone Support is turned on, you can still make it shift your appointments to the local time—by setting the time zone manually. You do that by tapping **Time Zone** on this screen. (Of course, this control's real purpose is for you to establish the "home" time zone, so the iPhone knows those calendar appointments' *real* times.)

- **Sync.** If you're like most people, you refer to your calendar more often to see what events are *coming up* than to see the ones you've already lived through. Ordinarily, therefore, the iPhone saves you some syncing time and storage space by updating only relatively recent events on your iPhone calendar. It doesn't bother with events that are older than 2 weeks, or 6 months, or whatever you choose here. (Or you can turn on **All Events** if you want your entire life, past and future, synced each time—storage and wait time be damned.)

- **Start Week On.** This new iOS 7 option specifies which day of the week appears at the *left edge of the screen* in the calendar's Day and Month views. For most people, that's Sunday, or maybe Monday—but for all iOS 7 cares, your week could start on a Thursday.

- **Default Calendar.** This option lets you answer the question: "When I add a new appointment to my calendar on the iPhone, which *calendar* (category) should it belong to?" You can choose Home, Work, Kids, or whatever category you use most often.

- **Shared Calendar Alerts.** It's great that you can share calendars with other people on other systems. But it's even greater that now your phone can alert you if somebody makes a change to an appointment you've shared.

Notes

As noted in Chapter 9, Notes can sync with various online services: iCloud, Gmail, Yahoo, and so on. Tap **Default Account** here to specify which one should receive new notes you create if you haven't specifically chosen one.

> **NOTE:** Before iOS 7 came along, this panel also gave you a choice of three fonts for Notes. That's gone now. Hope you like Helvetica Neue.

Reminders

Here are the preference settings for the Reminders app.

- **Sync.** This option answers the question: How far back do you want Reminders to go when it syncs its to-do lists with your computer, iCloud, and various other calendar programs?

- **Default List.** Suppose you've created multiple Reminder lists (Groceries, Movies to Rent, To Do, and so on). When you create a new item—for example, by telling Siri, "Remind me to fix the sink"—which list should it go onto? Here's where you specify.

Phone

These settings have to do with your address book, call management, and other phone-related preferences.

- **My Number.** Here's where you can see your iPhone's own phone number. You can even edit it, if necessary (just how it appears—you're not actually changing your phone number).

- **Contact Photos in Favorites.** New in iOS 7: Your Favorites list (that is, the Phone app's speed-dial list) can show a tiny photo of each person. If you'd rather see only names and numbers, then turn this option off.

- **Respond with Text.** This feature is described on page 95; here's where you can edit the three choices of canned "Can't talk right now" text messages.

- **Call Forwarding, Call Waiting** (AT&T and T-Mobile only). Here are the on/off switches for Call Forwarding and Call Waiting, which are described in Chapter 5.

- **Show My Caller ID** (AT&T and T-Mobile only). If you don't want your number to show up on the screen of the person you're calling, turn this off.

- **Blocked.** Another new iOS 7 goody: You can block certain people's calls, texts, and FaceTime video calls.

  This isn't a telemarketer-blocking feature; you can block only people who are already in your Contacts. It's really for blocking harassing ex-lovers, jerky siblings you're not speaking to, and collection agencies. Tap **Add New** to view your Contacts list, where you can tap to choose the blockee. (You can also see and edit this list in the Messages and FaceTime panels of Settings.)

- **TTY.** A TTY (teletype) machine lets people with hearing or speaking difficulties use a telephone—by typing back and forth, sometimes with the assistance of a human TTY operator who transcribes what the other person is saying. When you turn this iPhone option on, you can use the iPhone with a TTY machine, if you buy the little $20 iPhone TTY adapter from Apple.

- **Change Voicemail Password.** Yep, pretty much just what it says.

- **Dial Assist.** When this option is turned on, and when you're dialing from another country, the iPhone automatically adds the proper country codes when dialing U.S. numbers. Pretty handy, actually.

- **SIM PIN.** Your SIM card (on AT&T iPhones, or Sprint/Verizon phones when you travel overseas) stores all your account information. SIM cards are especially desirable abroad, because in most countries, you can pop yours into any old phone and have working service. If you're worried about yours getting stolen or lost, then turn this option on. You'll be asked to enter a passcode.

  Then, if some bad guy ever tries to put your SIM card into another phone, he'll be asked for the password. Without the password, the card (and the phone) won't make calls.

TIP: And if the evildoer guesses wrong three times, the words "PIN LOCKED" appear on the screen, and the SIM card is locked forever. You'll have to get another one from AT&T. So don't forget the password.

- **[Your carrier] Services.** This choice opens up a cheat sheet of handy numeric codes that, when dialed, play the voice of a robot providing useful information about your cellphone account. For example, *225# lets you know the latest status of your bill, *646# lets you know how many airtime minutes you've used so far this month, and so on.

> **TIP:** The button at the bottom of the screen opens up your account page on the Web, for further details on your cellphone billing and features.

Messages

These options govern text messages (SMS) and iMessages, both of which are described in Chapter 5:

- **iMessage.** This is the on/off switch for iMessages. If it's off, then your phone never sends or receives these handy, free messages—only regular text messages.

- **Send Read Receipts.** If this is on, then people who send you iMessages will know when you've seen them. They'll see a tiny gray text notification beneath the iMessage bubble that contains their message. If you're creeped out by them being able to know when you're ignoring them, then turn this item off.

- **Send as MMS.** If you try to send an iMessage to somebody when there's no Internet service, what happens? If this item is on, then the message goes to that person as a regular text message, using your cell carrier's network. If it's off, then the message won't go out at all.

- **Send & Receive.** Here you can enter additional email addresses that people can use to send your phone iMessages.

  This screen also offers a **Start new conversations from** item that lets you indicate what you want to appear on the other guy's phone when you send a text: your phone number or email address.

- **MMS Messaging.** This is the on/off switch for picture and video messages (as opposed to text-only ones).

- **Group Messaging, Show Subject Field, Character Count.** These options are described on page 158.

- **Blocked.** Here's another way to build up a list of people you don't want to hear from, as described on page 527. It's the exact same feature.

FaceTime

These options pertain to FaceTime, the video calling feature described in Chapter 3. Here, for example, is the on/off switch for the entire feature; a place to enter your Apple ID, so people can make FaceTime calls to you; and a place to enter email addresses and a phone number, which can also be used to reach you.

The Caller ID section lets you specify how you want to be identified when you place a call to somebody else: either as a phone number or an email address.

Finally, here yet again is the Blocked option—a third way to edit the list of people you don't want to hear from (page 527).

Maps

The Maps app has a few settings of its own:

- **Navigation Voice Volume.** As Siri gives you spoken navigational instructions, how loud do you want her to be? Or would you like her to shut up entirely?

- **Distances.** Measured in miles or kilometers, sir/madam?

- **Map Labels.** Would you like place names to appear in English—or in their native spellings?

- **Preferred Directions.** If you have a car, you probably want Maps to give you driving directions most of the time. If you're mostly on foot, you'll save a tap or two per location search by choosing Walking.

Compass

You wouldn't think that something as simple as the Compass app would need a Settings page, but here it is: an on/off switch called Use Truth North. (*True* north is the "top" point of the Earth's rotational axis. If you turn it off, then Compass uses *magnetic* north, the spot traditional compasses point to; it's about 11 degrees away from true north).

Safari

Here's everything you ever wanted to adjust in the Web browser but didn't know how to ask.

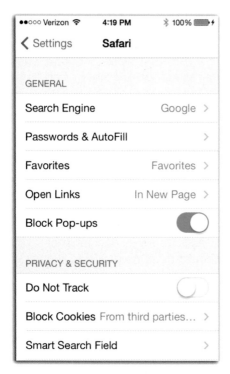 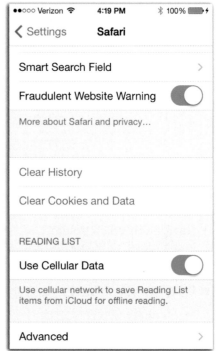

General

- **Search Engine.** Your choice here determines who does your searching from the search bar: Google, Bing, or Yahoo.

- **Passwords & AutoFill.** Safari's AutoFill feature saves you tedious typing by filling in your passwords, name, address, and phone numbers on Web forms automatically (just for the sites you want). In iOS 7, it can even store your credit card information, which makes buying things online *much* easier and quicker.

- **Favorites.** As described on page 404, your Favorites in Safari are just ordinary bookmarks in an extraordinary folder. Here, you can choose a *different* folder as the home of your Favorites.

- **Open Links.** When you tap a link with your finger, should the new page open in front of the current page—or behind it? Answer here.

- **Block Pop-ups.** In general, you want this turned on. You really don't want pop-up ad windows ruining your surfing session. Now and again, though, pop-up windows are actually useful. When you're buying concert tickets, for example, a pop-up window might show the location of the seats. In that situation, you can turn this option off.

Privacy & Security

- **Do Not Track.** If you turn this on, then Web sites agree not to secretly track your activity on the Web. The problem is, of course, that this program is voluntary—and the sleazy operators just ignore it.

- **Block Cookies.** These settings are like a paranoia gauge. If you click Always, you create an acrylic shield around your phone. No cookies can come in, and no cookie information can go out. You'll probably find the Web a very inconvenient place; you'll have to re-enter your information upon every visit, and some Web sites may not work properly at all.

   A less-drastic choice is From third parties and advertisers, which accepts cookies from sites you want to visit but blocks cookies deposited on your hard drive by sites you're not actually visiting—cookies that an especially evil banner ad gives you, for example.

   And Never, of course, means that you accept all cookies from all sites.

- **Smart Search Field.** As you type into Safari's search box, it tries to save you time in two ways. First, it sprouts a list of common search requests, based on what millions of other people have sought. This list changes with each letter you type. Second, Safari may autocomplete the address based on what you've typed so far, using suggestions from your History and bookmarks list. You can turn off both of these features here.

   (And why is this option listed under Privacy & Security? Because in order to show you its suggestions, Safari has to transmit what you're typing to Apple's and Google's servers for analysis.)

- **Fraudulent Website Warning.** *Phishing* is a scheme to separate you from your money. You get an email message that purports to be from your bank, or eBay, or PayPal. Apparently there's a problem with your account! So you click the provided link for the account-verification Web page—which is a fake. The bad guy's computers collect your name and password as you "log in." This Safari feature is supposed to display a big warning box when you attempt to visit one of these phony sites.

- **Clear History.** Like any Web browser, Safari keeps a list of Web sites you've visited recently to make it easier for you to revisit them: the History list. And like any browser, Safari therefore exposes your tracks to any suspicious spouse or crackpot colleague. If you're nervous about that prospect, then tap Clear History to erase your tracks.

- **Clear Cookies and Data.** This feature deletes all the cookies that Web sites have deposited on your "hard drive."

Reading List

- **Use Cellular Data.** The Reading List feature (page 395) is wonderful. But because it requires downloading entire Web pages to your phone—and then syncs them to all your other Apple gadgets—it uses a lot of data. If you fear going over your cellphone plan's monthly data allotment, then turn this off. You'll be allowed to save sites to your Reading List only when in a WiFi hotspot.

- **Advanced.** Safari recognizes HTML5, a Web technology that lets Web sites store data on your phone, for accessing even when you're not online (like your Gmail stash). In Website Data, you can see which Web apps have created these databases on your phone and delete them if necessary.

  JavaScript is a programming language whose bits of code frequently liven up Web pages. If you suspect some bit of code is choking Safari, however, you can turn off its ability to decode JavaScript here.

  The Web Inspector is for Web-site programmers. You connect your phone to a Mac with a USB cable; then, in Safari on the computer, you choose Debug→iPhone→[the name of the Web site currently on the iPhone's screen]. You'll be able to examine errors, warnings, tips, and logs for HTML, JavaScript, and CSS—great when you're designing and debugging Web pages or Web apps for the iPhone.

iTunes & App Store

If you've indulged in a few downloads (or a few hundred) from the App Store or iTunes music store, then you may well find some settings of use here. For example, if you tap your Apple ID at the top of the panel, you get these buttons:

- **View Apple ID.** This takes you to the Web, where you can look over your Apple Account information, including credit card details.

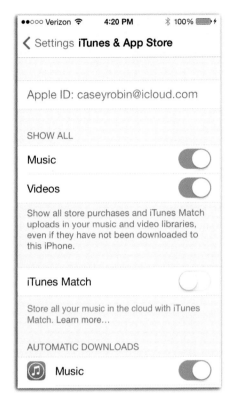
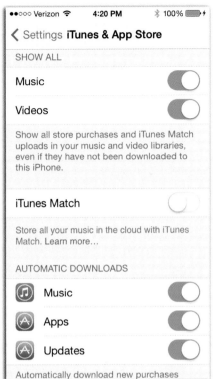

- **Sign Out.** Tap when, for example, a friend wants to use her own iTunes account to buy something on your iPhone. As a gift, maybe.

- **iForgot.** If you've forgotten your Apple ID password, tap here. You'll be offered a couple of different ways of establishing your identity—and you'll be given the chance to make up a new password.

Show All

This option is handy if you own more than one Apple gadget. It means that, in your lists of Music and Videos, you'll see the names of songs and movies you've bought using your *other* Apple phones, tablets, and computers—even though they're not on this iPhone yet. Seeing them listed makes it easy to download them to your phone, no extra charge.

In related news, the iTunes Match option gives your iPhone access to your entire music collection online—if you've signed up for Apple's iTunes Match service ($25 a year; see page 485).

Automatic Downloads

If you have an iCloud account (and you probably should), then a very convenient option is available to you: automatic downloads of music, apps, and ebooks you've bought on other iOS gadgets. For example, if you buy a new album on your iPad, turning on Music here means that your iPhone will download the same album automatically next time it's in a WiFi hotspot.

In iOS 7, in fact, there's a new option here: Updates. It means that if you accept an updated version of an app on one of your other Apple gadgets, it will be auto-updated on this phone, too.

Those downloads are, however, big. They can eat up your cellphone's monthly data allotment right quick and send you deep into Surcharge Land. That's why the iPhone does that automatic downloading only when you're in a WiFi hotspot—unless you turn on Use Cellular Data. Hope you know what you're doing.

Music

On this panel, you can adjust a bunch of iPod playback features. Most of them—Shake to Shuffle, Sound Check, EQ, Volume Limit, Lyrics & Podcast Info, and Group By Album Artist—are described on page 206.

Then come the Show All Music and iTunes Match options. They're identical to the Show All/Music and iTunes Match options already described.

Finally, there's Home Sharing. Conveniently enough, you can access your iTunes music collection, upstairs on your computer, right from your iPhone, over your home WiFi network. Or at least you can if both machines are signed into the same Apple ID. Here's where you enter the Apple ID that matches your iTunes setup.

Videos

Here's what you can adjust for the Videos app:

- **Start Playing.** When you play a video you've seen before, you can have it begin either from Where Left Off or From Beginning.

- **Show All Videos.** Here's another way to access the Show All/Videos option described above.

- **Home Sharing.** You can also access your iTunes video collection, as described a few paragraphs ago. Same deal here.

Photos & Camera

Here's a motley collection of photo-related settings:

- **My Photo Stream, Photo Sharing.** These are the master on/off switches for Photo Streams, which are among iCloud's marquee features (page 250).

- **Summarize Photos.** In the Photos app, the Years and Collections screens generally display one tiny thumbnail for every single photo. This feature is designed to make those displays more manageable by displaying fewer, but representative, thumbnails. (You won't see any difference unless you have a pretty huge collection of photos.)

- **Play Each Slide For.** How long do you want each photo to remain on the screen? You can choose 2, 3, 5, 10, or 20 seconds. (Hint: 2 is plenty, 3 at most. Anything more than that will bore your audience silly.)

- **Repeat, Shuffle.** These options work just as they do for music. Repeat makes the slideshow loop endlessly; Shuffle plays the slides in random order.

- **Grid** turns the "Rule of Thirds" grid on or off (the tic-tac-toe lines) on the camera's viewfinder screen.

- **Keep Normal Photo.** See the tip on page 224.

iBooks

Why, it's every setting imaginable that pertains to the iBooks ebook reading app. They're described on page 332.

Game Center

You can read about the Game Center on page 321. This page of preferences offers options like these:

Game Invites

More security stuff. Do you want your phone to permit invitations from other people to play games? How about people in the same room or building, inviting you to play over WiFi or Bluetooth? Here are the on/off switches for Allow Invites and Nearby Players.

Game Center Profile

Here's your Game Center player name. Tap it to edit your nickname, make your Game Center listing invisible to strangers (**Public Profile**), or associate a new email address with your account.

Friend Recommendations

Playing games isn't much fun without friends to play against, so Game Center is happy to suggest fellow Game Center participants from your Contacts list or your Facebook account. Unless you turn off these switches.

Twitter, Facebook, Flickr, Vimeo

These pages let you enter your name and password just once, in this one place, for each of these popular Web services—so that the iPhone, and other apps, can freely access those accounts without having to bother you.

Each of these panels also offers an **Install** button, making it quick and easy to download the official Twitter, Facebook, Flickr, and Vimeo apps.

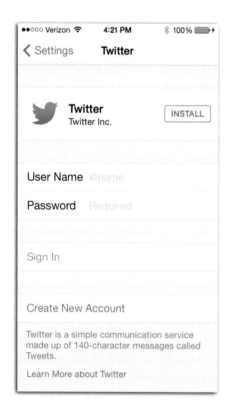
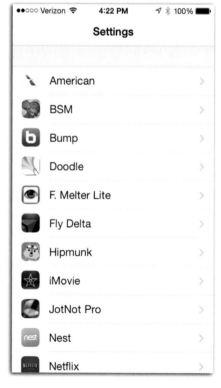

The Twitter and Facebook options offer some additional choices:

Twitter. The Update Contacts button adds your friends' Twitter account names to their cards in Contacts, saving you that tedious data entry.

• **Facebook.** You get some extra-juicy preference options here. Tapping Settings lets you tell the phone how to alert you when new Facebook posts arrive: with vibration or a sound, for example. You can also limit Facebook video recordings to standard definition, to avoid massive data charges.

The Allow These Apps items let you control which built-in apps can access your Facebook account; for example, turn off Calendar if you don't want to see your friends' Facebook birthdays on your calendar.

Finally, Update All Contacts is the powerful button that adds photos and Facebook account names to the corresponding friends' cards in your Contacts app, as described on page 85.

App Preferences

At the bottom of the Settings app screen, you see a list of apps that have installed setting screens of their own. For example, here's where you can edit your screen name and password for the AIM chat program, change how many days' worth of news you want the NY Times Reader to display, and so on. Each one offers a motley assortment of changeable preference options.

It can get to be a very long list.

Appendixes

A

Signup & Setup

You gotta admit it: Opening up a new iPhone brings a certain excitement. There's a prospect of possibility, of new beginnings. Even if you intend to protect your iPhone with a case, there are those first few minutes when it's shiny, spotless, free of fingerprints or nicks—a gorgeous thing.

This chapter is all about getting started, whether that means buying and setting up a new iPhone, or upgrading an iPhone 4s or iPhone 5 to the new iOS 7 software that's described in this book.

Buying a New iPhone

Each year's new iPhone model is faster, has a better camera and screen, and comes packed with more features than the previous one. Still, "new iPhone" doesn't have to mean the iPhone 5s ($200 with a two-year contract) and 5c ($100). You can still get an iPhone 4s for free (with contract).

In any case, once you've chosen the model you want, you also have to choose which cellphone company you want to provide its service: AT&T, Verizon, T-Mobile, or Sprint. Each has something to offer.

Verizon has the best cellular coverage—the fewest dropped calls—and by far the most 4G LTE (high-speed Internet) areas. Most Sprint plans include unlimited Internet use, which is a rare perk these days. T-Mobile's plans cost the least, but the coverage area is the smallest. AT&T's high-speed Internet networks are faster than anyone else's.

Research the coverage where you live and work. (Each company's Web site shows a map of its coverage.)

You can buy your iPhone from a phone store (Verizon, Sprint, T-Mobile, AT&T), an Apple store, or from the Apple Web site. You can buy the phone either with or without a 2-year contract. Yes, that surprises many people—

but most people still opt for the contract, because the 16-gigabyte phone's initial price is $200 that way. Without the contract, it costs $600 or more.

With a contract, the phone is locked to the cellphone company you're choosing; it works *only* with that company's network. For example, a locked AT&T phone won't work with Verizon, Sprint, T-Mobile, or any other carrier, and you can't insert the SIM card from a non-AT&T phone and expect it to work. (The exception: When you travel overseas with a Sprint or Verizon iPhone 4s or later, you can insert a different country's SIM card into it for use while you're there.)

Hackers have succeeded in unlocking the iPhone so it can be used on other cell companies' networks; their primary motivation for doing so was to be able to use it in countries where the iPhone hasn't been available. But now that the iPhone is sold legitimately in 90 countries (and counting), there may be less reason to go that questionable route.

All right then: Here you are in the phone store, or sitting down to do some ordering online. Here are some of the decisions you'll have to make:

- **Transferring your old number.** You can bring your old cellphone or home phone number to your new iPhone. Your friends can keep dialing your old number—but your iPhone will ring instead of the old phone.

  It usually takes under an hour for a cellphone-number transfer to take place, but it may take several hours. During that time, you can make calls on the iPhone, but you can't receive them.

NOTE: Transferring a land-line number can take several *days.*

- **Select your monthly calling plans.** Signing up for cellphone service involves more red tape than a government contract. In essence, you have to choose *three* plans: one for voice calls (required), one for Internet service (required), and one for text messages (optional).

  AT&T's plans are typical. There's a $40 monthly plan, which offers 450 weekday calling minutes. But there's a 900-minute plan for $60 and an unlimited calling plan for $70.

  The AT&T plans offer *rollover minutes.* That is, if you don't use up all your minutes this month, the unused ones are automatically added to your allotment for next month, and so on.

  Next, you have to choose an Internet data plan for your iPhone's email, Web, iCloud, and app-downloading pleasure. AT&T and Verizon offer *capped* data plans, in which you pay a monthly fee (for example,

$30) for a certain amount of Internet uploading and downloading (for example, 2 gigabytes). If you opt for the Personal Hotspot feature (page 376), you usually pay about $20 more.

Of course, who has any idea what 2 gigabytes of data is? How much of that do you eat up with email alone? How much is one YouTube video?

As you approach your monthly limit, you'll get warnings by text message. You can also check the Web site or dial a code on your phone. Yes, it's a pain to have to worry about data limits, but at least monitoring them is fairly easy. If you use more than your allotted amount, you're automatically billed a surcharge—for example, $10 for each additional gigabyte.

All four cell companies offer unlimited free calls to other phones from the same company. All but the cheapest plans offer unlimited calls on nights and weekends.

AT&T's voice and Internet plans don't include any text messages. For those, you'll have to pay $20 for unlimited messages. Of course, you can always pay à la carte, too: 20 cents for each message sent or received.

NOTE: If the people you'll be texting also have Apple gadgets, don't spend a lot on a texting plan. Remember that all messages you send to other iOS machines automatically turn into iMessages, which are unlimited and free. See page 154.

Verizon requires new customers to sign up for what amounts to a family plan. You pay $40 a month per phone, plus a bucket of data to be shared by all of them ($60 a month for 2 GB, for example); you get unlimited calling and texting.

Sprint offers unlimited text messages and Internet use for $110—a huge relief to most people. Its voice plans cost more than its rivals', but the total monthly bill is usually lower as a result.

T-Mobile's unlimited-everything plan costs $70 a month, which is the least expensive such plan; just make sure there's T-Mobile coverage where you plan to use the phone.

All iPhone plans require a two-year commitment and an "activation fee" (ha!).

As you budget for your plan, keep in mind that, as with any cellphone, you'll also be paying taxes as high as 22 percent, depending on your state. Ouch.

Setting Up a New Phone

In the olden days, you couldn't use a new iPhone at all without hooking it up to a computer. That first date with iTunes was mandatory to set up the basic iPhone settings. Now, though, the setup process takes place entirely on the phone's screen.

You don't need a computer to back up your phone, because iCloud backs it up. You don't need a computer to store your music and video collections, because the App Store remembers what you've bought and lets you redownload it at any time. You don't need a computer to download and install iPhone software updates, because they come straight to the phone now. You don't even need a computer to edit photos or to create mail folders, because all that's on the phone, too.

The first time you turn on a brand-new iPhone—or an older one that you've erased completely—the setup wizard appears. Swipe your finger where it says **slide to set up**. Now you're asked some important questions:

- **Language; Country.** You won't get very far setting up your phone if you can't understand the instructions. So the very first step here is to tell it what language you speak. When you tap a language, you're next asked to tell the phone where in the world you live. (It proposes the country where you bought the phone. Clever, eh?)

- **Wi-Fi Networks.** Here's where you're shown a list of wireless networks nearby and given the chance to join one. Tap the name of the WiFi network you want, enter the password if required, and tap **Join**.

  Or, if there's no WiFi you can (or want to) hop onto right now, tap **Choose Cellular Connection**.

- **Location Services.** The iPhone knows where you are. That's how it can pinpoint you on a map, tag the photos you take with their geographical locations, find you a nearby Mexican restaurant, and so on.

  Some people are creeped out by the phone's knowing where they are, worrying that Apple, by extension, also knows where you are (it doesn't). So here's your chance to turn off all the iPhone's location features. Tap either Enable Location Services or Disable Location Services.

- **Set Up Your iPhone.** If you've owned an iPhone before—either an older model, or this same phone after you've erased it—you don't have to load it up with all your apps and settings by hand. This screen

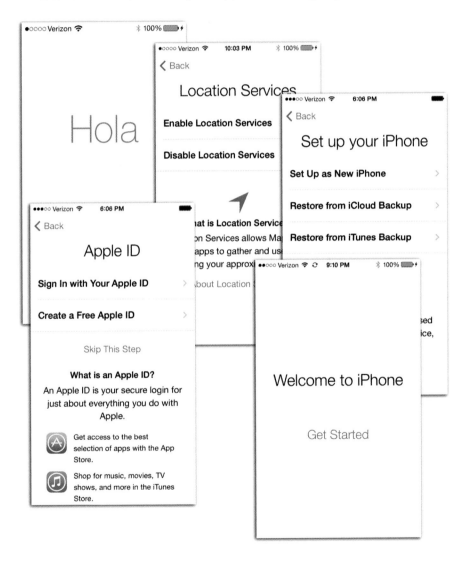

is offering to reload all your stuff from your most recent backup. (See Chapter 13 for details on iPhone backups.)

Tap **Restore from iCloud Backup** (if your backup was on iCloud) or **Restore from iTunes Backup** (if your backup was on your computer, in iTunes).

And if you've never owned an iPhone before, you can choose **Set Up as New iPhone** to start fresh.

- **Apple ID.** A million features require an Apple ID—just about any transaction you make with Apple online. Buying anything from Apple, from a song to a laptop. Signing up for an iCloud account (Chapter 14). Playing games against other people online. Making an Apple Store appointment at the Genius Bar.

  If you already have one (and if you've ever bought anything from Apple or iTunes or the App Store, you do), tap **Sign In with Your Apple ID** and enter it here. If you don't have one, tap Create a Free Apple ID. You'll be asked to provide your name, birthday, email address (or you can create a new iCloud email address), a password of your choice, a security question (you'll have to answer it correctly if you ever forget your password), and if you'd like the honor of receiving junk email from Apple.

  On the screen full of legalese, tap **Agree**, then **Agree**. You must agree with everything Apple's lawyers say, or you can't play

  (You can tap **Skip This Step** if you don't want an Apple ID, at least for now. You can get one later in Settings.)

- **Use iCloud.** You get this screen, and the next two, only if you did sign in with your Apple ID .

  Since you've had a glance at Chapter 14, you already know how useful Apple's free iCloud service can be. Here's where you indicate whether or not you want to use iCloud at all.

- **Find My iPhone.** If you did opt into iCloud, you're also asked if you'd like to tap **Use Find My iPhone**. If you do, you'll be able to locate your lost iPhone on a map, using any Web browser. You'll also be able to command it to start pinging loudly, so you can find where you left it in the house. It's a pretty great feature.

  If you turn Find My iPhone on, you're also asked to make up a four-digit password so that the bad guys can't get around you just by turning Find My iPhone *off.*

- **Set up Siri.** If you have an iPhone 4s or later, here's your chance to turn off Siri, the single greatest new phone feature in 15 years. So why would you ever want to turn it off? Because it works by sending your voice utterances to Apple's computers for processing, and that thought alarms the privacy-obsessed.

- **Diagnostics.** Behind the scenes, your iPhone sends records back to Apple, including your location and what you're doing on your iPhone. By analyzing this data en masse, Apple can figure out where the dead spots in the cellular network are, how to fix bugs, and so on. The information is anonymous—that is, it's not associated with you in particular. But if the very idea seems invasive to you, here's your chance to prevent this data from being sent.

- **Welcome to iPhone.** Your phone is set up. Tap Get Started to jump to the Home screen.

Upgrading an Older iPhone to iOS 7

If you bought an iPhone 5c or 5s, great! The iOS 7 software comes on it preinstalled.

But you can also upgrade an iPhone 4, iPhone 4s, or iPhone 5 to this new software—in any of three ways:

- **Upgrade it wirelessly.** *Upgrading* means installing iOS 7 on top of whatever is already on your iPhone. All the data and settings on the phone are preserved.

  This is the easiest way to upgrade. You've probably already seen the little red number on your Settings app icon, and on the word "General" inside it; they're trying to tell you that iOS 7 is ready to download. Tap Settings→General→Software Update to see the iOS 7 logo; tap Download and Install to begin the process. (You have to be in a WiFi network, and it's wise to have your iPhone plugged in to power.)

- **Upgrade it from iTunes.** If you wish, you can also perform the upgrade using the iTunes program on your computer. This method takes less time, but, of course, it requires sitting at your computer.

  To begin, make sure you have the latest version of iTunes (choose iTunes→Check for Updates).

  Connect your iPhone and click its name in the upper-right (see Chapter 13 for details). On the Summary screen, click Update, and then click Download and Update.

- **Restore it.** This is a more dramatic step, which you should choose only if you've been having problems with your phone or if, for some other reason, would like to start completely fresh. This step backs up the phone, erases it completely, installs iOS 7, and then copies your stuff back onto the phone.

  Connect the phone to your computer, open iTunes, and then click Restore.

The updating or restoring process takes awhile. You'll see the iPhone restart. When it's all over, the PC-free setup process described on the previous pages begins automatically.

NOTE: Not all features work on all phones. For example, even with iOS 7, an iPhone 4s doesn't get AirDrop or filters in the Camera app; the iPhone 4 also doesn't get Siri and panorama photos.

The iPhone 4 may also be very slow with iOS 7—you've been warned—and there's no way to go back to iOS 6.

If you find your iPhone 4 crawling, especially when you type, consider turning off Background App Refresh in Settings→General. And leave some space free; a full phone is a slow phone (page 557).

If your iPhone 4 is *still* zipping along like an anesthetized slug, there's always the Nuclear Option: erase it completely and load it up again. Many people report happier tidings after that extreme procedure.

Software Updates

As you're probably aware, phone software like the iPhone's is a perpetual work in progress. Apple constantly fixes bugs, adds features, and makes tweaks to extend battery life and improve other services.

Updating Directly on the Phone

One day you'll be minding your own business, and you'll see a red numbered badge appear on the Settings app's icon on the phone. Open Settings→General→Software Update to read about the new update and install it. Note, though, that unless it's plugged into a power source, your phone won't install an iOS update unless its battery is at least half full.

Install Updates from Your Computer

Maybe you're not that adventurous and you'd prefer to install your software update the old-fashioned way. No problem: Connect the iPhone to iTunes, wirelessly or not (Chapter 13). Then click the iPhone's icon in iTunes; on the Summary pane, tap Check for Update.

548 Appendix A

Restrictions and Parental Controls

If you're issuing an iPhone to a child, or someone who acts like one, you'll be gratified to discover that iOS 7 offers a good deal of protection. That's protection of your offspring's delicate sensibilities (it can block pornography and dirty words) and protection of your bank account (it can block purchases of music, movies, and apps without your permission).

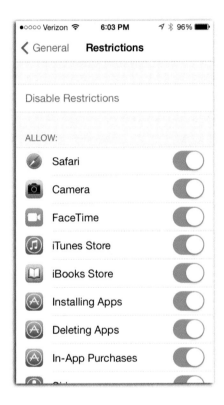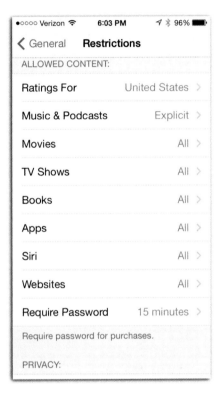

To set this up, visit Settings→General→Restrictions. When you tap Enable Restrictions, you're asked to make up a four-digit password (not the same as the regular iPhone passcode) that permits only you, the all-knowing parent, to make changes to these settings. (Or you, the corporate IT administrator who's doling out iPhones to the white-collar drones.)

Once you've changed the settings described below, the only way to change them again (when your kid turns 18, for example) is to return to the Restrictions page and correctly enter the password. That's also the only way to turn off the entire Restrictions feature (tap Disable Restrictions and correctly enter the password). To turn it back on, you have to make up a password all over again.

Once Restrictions is turned on, you can put up data blockades in a number of different categories.

Allow

For starters, you can turn off access to iPhone features that locked-down corporations might not want their employees—or parents might not want their children—to use, because they're considered either security holes, time drains, or places to spend your money: Safari (can't use the Web at all), the Camera, FaceTime, iTunes and the iBookstore, the ability to go Installing Apps or Deleting Apps, Siri, or AirDrop.

Many of these restrictions work by *removing icons altogether* from the iPhone's Home screen: Safari, iTunes, Camera, and Installing Apps (that is, the App Store), for example. When the switch says Off, the corresponding icon has been taken off the Home screen and can't be found even by Spotlight searches.

Allowed Content

Here you can spare your children's sensitive eyes and ears by blocking inappropriate material.

Ratings are a big deal; they determine the effectiveness of the parental controls described below. Since every country has its own rating schemes (for movies, TV shows, games, raunchy song lyrics, and so on), you use the Ratings For control to tell the iPhone which country's rating system you want to use.

Once that's done, you can use the Music & Podcasts, Movies, TV Shows, Books, and Apps controls to specify what your kid is allowed to watch, play, and listen to. For example, you can tap Movies and then tap PG-13; any movies rated "higher," like R or NC-17, won't play on the iPhone now. (And if your sneaky offspring try to buy these naughty songs, movies, or TV shows wirelessly from the iTunes Store, they'll discover that the Buy button is dimmed and unavailable.)

For some categories, like Music & Podcasts and Siri, you can turn off Explicit to prevent the iPhone from playing iTunes Store songs that contain naughty language, or speaking them.

Websites lets you shield impressionable young eyes from pornography online. It offers three settings:

- **All Websites.** No protection at all.

- **Limit Adult Content.** Apple will apply its own judgment in blocking dirty Web sites, using a blocked-site list that it has compiled.

  That doesn't mean you can't override Apple's wisdom, however. The Always Allow and Never Allow controls let you add the addresses of Web sites that you think should be OK (or should not be OK).

- **Specific Websites Only.** This is a "whitelist" feature. It means that the entire Web is blocked except for the few sites listed here: safe bets like Disney, PBS Kids, Smithsonian Institution, and so on. You can add your own sites to this list, but the point is clear: This is the Web with training wheels.

In-App Purchases permits you to buy new material (game levels, book chapters, and so on) from within an app that you've already bought. In other words, even if you've shut down access to your offspring's ability to install new apps, as described above, this loophole remains. You can specify how soon after buying something online the iPhone requires your password again for the next purchase (15 minutes, for example).

Privacy

These on/off switches permit or prohibit the unauthorized user from making changes to the phone's privacy settings, which are described on page 517.

Allow Changes

These items (Accounts, Find My Friends, Cellular Data Use, Background App Refresh, Volume Limit) are safeguards against your offspring fiddling with limits you've set.

Game Center

The controls here let you stop your kid from playing multiplayer games (against strangers online, in other words) or adding game-playing friends to the center.

Cases & Accessories

Like the iPods that came before it, the iPhone has inspired a torrent of accessories that seems to intensify with every passing month. Stylish cases, speakers, docks, cables—the list goes on.

Just be sure you're buying something that fits your phone. For example, the Lightning connector (where the charging cable connects) on the iPhone 5, 5c, and 5s doesn't fit any of the charging accessories that came before it—at least not without the help of Apple's $30 adapter (or the $40 adapter that has an 8-inch cable "tail").

Slowly, accessory companies are introducing Lightning-compatible versions of their gear. But for now, buyer beware—or buyer stock up on $30 adapters.

So what might you add to your iPhone?

- **Cases.** It should be called the iPhone Paradox: People buy the thinnest, sleekest, shiniest, most gorgeous smartphone in existence—and then bury it in a thick carrying case. There's just something so wrong about that.

  On the other hand, this thing is made of a layer of breakable glass; the instinct to protect it is perfectly understandable.

  Hundreds of cases are available. If you're worried about droppage, choose a silicone rubber case; it does a better job of protecting your phone than hard plastic cases. You can also get cases with built-in battery backups, credit-card slots, and even speakers.

- **Everything else.** Speaker docks. Bluetooth speakers. Headphones and earbuds, wired and cordless. Credit-card readers. Car cigarette-lighter adapters. Alarm clocks. Video-out cables. Stylish styluses. Touchscreen-compatible gloves. Tripods. Panorama stands. Kickstands. Car mounts. Activity monitors. Lenses. You Google it, you'll find it. The iPhone is, without a doubt, the most accessorized phone in the world.

B

Troubleshooting & Maintenance

The iPhone is a computer, and you know what that means: Things can go wrong. This particular computer, though, is not quite like a Mac or a PC. It runs a spin-off of the OS X operating system, but that doesn't mean you can apply the same troubleshooting techniques.

Therefore, let this appendix be your guide when things go wrong.

First Rule: Install the Updates

There's an old saying: "Never buy version 1.0 of anything." In the iPhone's case, the saying could be: "Never buy version 7.0 of anything."

The very first version (or major revision) of anything has bugs, glitches, and things the programmers didn't have time to finish the way they would have liked. The iPhone is no exception.

The beauty of this phone, though, is that Apple can send it fixes, patches, and even new features through software updates. One day you'll connect the phone to your computer for charging or syncing, and—bam!—there'll be a note from iTunes, or your Settings app, that new iPhone software is available.

So the first rule of trouble-free iPhoning is to accept these updates when they're offered. With each new software blob, Apple removes another few dozen tiny glitches.

And sure enough: Within the first two weeks of iOS 7's existence, software updates 7.0.1 and 7.0.2 came down the pike, offering security fixes, bug fixes, and many other subtle improvements. More will come.

Seven Ways to Reset the Phone

The iPhone runs actual programs, and as actual programs do, they actually crash. Sometimes, the program you're working in simply vanishes and you find yourself back at the Home screen. Just reopen the program and get on with your life.

If the program you're in just doesn't seem to be working right—it's frozen or acting weird, for example—then one of these seven resetting techniques usually clears things right up.

NOTE: Proceed down this list in order! Start with the easy ones.

- **Exit the app.** On an iPhone, you're never aware that you're launching and exiting programs. They're always just *there,* like TV channels, when you switch to them. There's no Quit command. But if a program starts acting glitchy, you can make it quit, so that you can reopen it afresh.

  To do that, double-press the Home button to bring up the app switcher. Find the "card" that represents your balky app, and then flick it upward to make it quit. Try reopening it to see if the problem has gone away.

- **Force quit the app.** If the phone is so frozen that you can't even bring up the app switcher, you'll have to *force* quit the stuck app. Hold down the Sleep switch until the slide to power off message appears. Then hold down the Home button for 10 seconds, or until the frozen program quits. The next time you open the troublesome program from the Home screen, it should be back in business.

- **Turn the phone off and on again.** If it seems something more serious has gone wrong, then hold down the Sleep switch for a few seconds. When the screen says slide to power off, confirm by swiping. The iPhone shuts off completely.

  Turn it back on by pressing the Sleep switch for a second or two.

- **Force restart the phone.** If you haven't been able to force quit the program, and you can't shut the phone off either, you might have to force a restart. To do that, hold both the Home button and the Sleep switch for 10 seconds. Keep holding, even if the screen goes black or you see the "power off" slider. Don't release until you see the Apple logo appear, meaning that the phone is restarting.

- **Reset the phone's settings.** Relax. This procedure doesn't erase any of your data—only the phone's settings. From the Home screen, tap Settings→General→Reset→Reset All Settings.

- **Erase the whole phone.** From the Home screen, tap **Settings→ General→Reset→Erase All Content and Settings**. Now, *this* option zaps all your stuff—*all* of it. Music, videos, email, settings, apps, all gone, and all overwritten with random 1's and 0's to make sure it's completely unrecoverable. Clearly, you're getting into last resorts here. Of course, you can sync with iTunes to copy all that stuff back onto your iPhone.

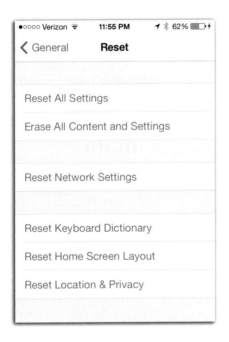

- **Restore the phone.** If none of these steps seem to solve the phone's glitchiness, it might be time for the Nuclear Option: erasing it completely, resetting both hardware and software back to a factory-fresh condition.

TIP: If you're able to sync the phone with iTunes *first,* do it! That way, you'll have a backup of all those intangible iPhone data bits: text messages, call logs, Recents list, and so on. iTunes will put it all back onto the phone the first time you sync after the restore.

To restore the phone, connect it to your computer, as described in Chapter 13. In iTunes, click the iPhone icon and then, on the Summary tab, click **Restore**.

The first order of business: iTunes offers to make a backup of your iPhone (all of its phone settings, text messages, and so on) before proceeding. Accepting this invitation is an excellent idea. Click **Back Up**.

TIP: If you've opted to back up your phone onto iCloud, you can also restore it from Apple's online backups. (You can restore this way only if your iPhone is completely wiped empty. If it's not, manually erase it using iTunes first.)

During the setup screens described on page 544, tap **Restore from iCloud Backup**. You're shown a list of the three most recent backups; tap the one you want. The phone goes right to work downloading your settings and account information. Then it restarts and begins to download your apps; if you're in a hurry for one particular app, tap its icon to make iCloud prioritize it. At any time, you can check the restore process's status in **Settings→iCloud→Storage and Backup**.

When that's all over, you can get to work downloading your music (if you're an iTunes Match subscriber).

What Else to Try

If the phone is still glitchy, try to remember what changes you made to it recently. Did you install some new App Store program, add a new video, mess around with your calendar?

It's worth fishing through iTunes, turning off checkboxes, hunting for the recently changed items, and resyncing, in hopes of figuring out what's causing the flakiness.

iPhone Doesn't Turn On

Usually, the problem is that the battery's dead. Just plugging it into the USB cord or USB charger doesn't bring it to life immediately, either; a completely dead iPhone doesn't wake up until it's been charging for about 10 minutes. It pops on automatically when it has enough juice to do so.

If you don't think that's the trouble, then try the resetting tactics on the previous pages.

The Force Restore

If your phone gets stuck starting up at the Apple logo, or it just stays black, then something more serious may have happened. Phones, like the best of us, sometimes get confused.

The solution is the drastic, but effective, force restore process (known to techies as the Default Firmware Update mode).

Open iTunes on your computer. Connect the iPhone with its white USB cable.

Now hold down the Sleep switch and Home button simultaneously for 10 seconds—then release **only** the Sleep switch.

Keep the Home button pressed until iTunes tells you that an iPhone in Recovery mode has been detected; click OK. (If you see anything but blackness on your iPhone's screen—an Apple logo, for example—then the process didn't work. If the problem has not, in fact, gone away, then you should start again.)

Now, iTunes tells you again that you're in Recovery mode, and offers only one button: **Restore iPhone**. Click that, and then confirm by clicking **Restore & Update**. The process of reinstalling the latest, fresh copy of iOS 7 begins.

Once everything's running fine, you can restore all your apps and settings from the latest backup as described at the end of Chapter 13.

Battery Life Is Terrible

If your battery seems to drain faster after you've installed iOS 7, maybe it's because you're **using** the phone constantly, checking out the cool new features. If you set it aside for a while, does the battery gauge seem to drop as fast? If not, maybe it's just draining because you're using it nonstop.

The next step is to consult the battery-saving tips on page 32.

Finally, investigate how many battery-hungry apps are running all the time in the background: Pandora, GPS navigation apps, voice or video apps like Skype. Quit them.

Out of Space

It happens all the time. You couldn't imagine filling up 32 or 64 gigabytes of storage, so you saved some money by buying an iPhone with less. And now you can't even take a video or a photo, because your phone reports that it's full. You're frozen out until you have the time and expertise to delete some less important stuff.

The biggest space hogs on your phone are video files, photo files, apps, and music files. Heck, just deleting one downloaded movie or TV show could solve your storage crunch instantly.

Fortunately, iOS 7 makes it very easy to see what's eating up your space—and to delete the fattest ones to make the most room with the least effort. The key is to visit Settings→General→Usage→Manage Storage.

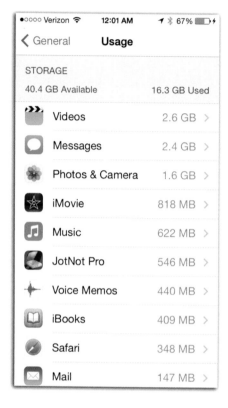
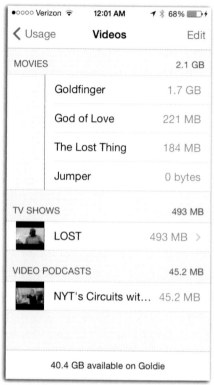

The list before you shows what's using up your space, biggest first; by tapping the > button, you can see the details and, in most cases, make some deletions on the spot.

Delete Photos and Recorded Videos

Unfortunately, this display shows how much space your Camera videos and photos take up, but it doesn't let you delete them. To purge your photos, the quickest method is to hook up to iTunes, import the photos, and take advantage of the option to delete the freshly imported photos from the phone (page 467).

Turning off your Photo Stream can give you back an instant gigabyte, too (page 250).

Delete "Other" Items

You know the colored graph of what's on your phone that shows up in iTunes (page 454)? Often, the biggest item here is the mysterious Other category. What is that stuff? It's caches (Internet data stored on the phone to make repeated visits faster), backups, partial downloads, and data from iOS 7's built-in apps—all your text messages and email, for example. Here's how you clean them out:

- **Delete the Web browser cache.** The phone saves Web pages into its own memory, so that they'll appear faster the next time you try to visit them. If you've had your iPhone awhile, those cache files can really add up. Open Settings→Safari; tap Clear History and Clear Cookies and Data. You may get a speed boost as a side effect.

- **Delete text messages.** In the Messages app, you can delete individual texts or entire conversations (page 559); because they frequently include photo, audio, or video files, you can reclaim a lot of space.

- **Delete email attachments**. Files downloaded with your email take up a lot of space, too. The solution is to delete the email account (Settings→Mail, Contacts, Calendar→[Account Name]; scroll down and tap Delete Account)—and then add it again.

  In the process, you'll vaporize all the attachment files and message caches that you've ever downloaded and opened on your phone. When you add the account back again, those files will still be online, ready to download—but only when you need them. (This trick works for most account types—just not for POP3 accounts.)

- **Delete voice memos, music files, and ebooks.** Audio files and iBooks eat up a lot of space, too. Consider purging the recordings, books, and songs you can do without (from within the Voice Memos, iBooks, and Music apps).

Phone and Internet Problems

How can the phone part of the iPhone go wrong? Let us count the ways.

- **Can't make calls.** First off, do you have enough cellular signal to make a call? Check your signal-strength dots. Even if you have one or two, flakiness is par for the course, although one bar in a 3G, 4G, or LTE area is much better than one bar in a slower area. Try going outside, standing near a window, or moving to a major city (kidding).

Also, make sure Airplane mode isn't turned on. Try calling somebody else to make sure the problem isn't with the number you're dialing.

If nothing else works, try the resetting techniques described at the beginning of this chapter.

- **Can't receive calls.** If calls seem to go directly to voicemail and the phone never even rings, check to make sure Do Not Disturb isn't turned on (page 95).

- **Can't get on the Internet.** If you're not in a WiFi hotspot (there's no ●●○○○ at the top of the screen) and you don't have cell service (no **E**, **O**, **3G**, **4G**, or **LTE** logo at the top of the screen), well, then, you're in a "No Service" area, or the phone thinks you are. (In the latter case, try turning the phone off and then on again.)

- **Can't send text messages.** Make sure, of course, that you've signed up for a texting plan. Make sure you haven't turned on Show Subject Field (page 157) and forgotten to fill out the body of the message.

Email Problems

Getting your email settings right the first time isn't easy. There are all kinds of tweaky codes and addresses that you have to enter—if they weren't properly synced over from your computer, that is.

If email isn't working, here are some steps to try:

- Sometimes, there's nothing for it but to call your Internet provider (or whoever's supplying the email account) and ask for help. Often, the settings you use at home won't work when you're using a mobile gadget like the iPhone. Open Settings→Mail, Contacts, Calendars and tap your email account's name to view the Settings screen.

- If you're getting a "user not recognized" error, you may have typed your password wrong. (It's easy to do, since the iPhone converts each character you type into a • symbol about a second after you type it.) Delete the password in Settings and re-enter it.

- If you're having trouble connecting to your company's Exchange server, see the end of Chapter 15.

- Oh—and it probably goes without saying, but remember that you can't get email if you can't get online, and you can't get online unless you have a WiFi or cellular signal.

Can't Send Email

It's your settings. It's got to be your settings in Settings→Mail, Contacts, Calendars. Double-check every one of those geeky boxes (SMTP server, authentication method, and so on) with your Internet provider on the phone.

Warranty and Repair

The iPhone comes with a one-year warranty and 90 days of phone tech support. If you buy an AppleCare+ contract ($100), you're covered for a second year.

> **TIP:** AT&T, Sprint, T-Mobile, or Verizon tech support is free for both years of your contract. They handle questions about your iPhone's phone features.

If, during the coverage period, anything goes wrong that's not your fault, Apple will fix it free. (In fact, AppleCare+ even covers damage if it *is* your fault, for $50 each time—even if you drop the phone or get it wet. Maximum: twice.)

You can either take the phone to an Apple Store, which is often the fastest route, or call 800-APL-CARE (800-275-2273) to arrange shipping back to Apple. In general, you'll get the fixed phone back in three business days.

> **NOTE:** *Sync the phone before it goes in for repair.* The repair process generally erases the phone completely—Apple very often simply hands you a new (or refurbished) iPhone instead of your original. In fact, if you're worried that someone at Apple might snoop around, you might want to back up and then erase the phone *first.* (Use the Restore option—page 472.)
>
> Also, don't forget to remove your SIM card (page 22) before you send in your broken AT&T or T-Mobile iPhone—and to put it back in when you get the phone. Don't leave it in the loaner phone. AT&T or T-Mobile can get you a new card if you lose your original, but it's a hassle.

Out-of-Warranty Repairs

Once the year or two has gone by, or if you damage your iPhone in a way that's not covered by the warranty (backing your car over it comes to mind), Apple charges $200 to repair an iPhone (it usually just replaces it).

The Battery Replacement Program

Why did Apple seal the battery inside the iPhone, anyway? Everyone knows lithium-ion batteries don't last forever. After 300 or 400 charges, the iPhone battery begins to hold less charge (perhaps 80 percent of the original). After a certain point, the phone will need a new battery. How come you can't change it yourself, as on any normal cellphone?

Apple's reply: A user-replaceable battery takes up a lot more space inside the phone. It requires a plastic compartment that shields the guts of the phone from you and your fingers; it requires a removable door; and it needs springs or clips to hold the battery in place.

In any case, you can't change the battery yourself. If the phone is out of warranty, you must send it to Apple (or take it to an Apple Store) for an $85 battery-replacement job. (As an eco-bonus, Apple properly disposes of the old batteries, which consumers might not do on their own.)

Where to Go from Here

At this point, the iPhone is such a phenomenon that there's no shortage of resources for getting more help, news, and tips. Here are a few examples:

- **Apple's official iPhone User Guide.** Yes, there is an actual downloadable PDF user's manual. *http://support.apple.com/manuals/*

- **Apple's official iPhone help Web site.** Online tips, tricks, and tutorials; troubleshooting topics; downloadable PDF help documents; and, above all, an enormous, seething treasure trove of discussion boards. *www.apple.com/support/iphone/*

- **Apple's service site.** All the dates, prices, and expectations for getting your iPhone repaired. Includes details on getting a temporary replacement unit. *www.apple.com/support/iphone/service/faq/*

- **iMore blog.** News, tips, tricks, all in a blog format. *www.imore.com/*

- **iLounge.** Another great blog-format site. Available in an iPhone format so you can read it right on the device. *www.iLounge.com/*

- **MacRumors/iPhone.** Blog-format news; accessory blurbs; help discussions; iPhone wallpaper. *www.macrumors.com/iphone/*

- **iPhone Atlas.** Discussion, news, apps, how-tos. *www.iphoneatlas.com*

Index